Visual Programming

Visual Programming

Nan C. Shu

IBM Los Angeles Scientific Center

VAN NOSTRAND REINHOLD COMPANY

New York

Library of Congress Catalog Card Number: 87-31596
ISBN: 0-442-28014-9

Printed in the United States of America

Van Nostrand Reinhold Company Inc.
115 Fifth Avenue
New York, New York 10003

Van Nostrand Reinhold Company Limited
Molly Millars Lane
Wokingham, Berkshire RG11 2PY, England

Van Nostrand Reinhold
480 La Trobe Street
Melbourne, Victoria 3000, Australia

Macmillan of Canada
Division of Canada Publishing Corporation
164 Commander Boulevard
Agincourt, Ontario M1S 3C7, Canada

16 15 14 13 12 11 10 9 8 7 6 5 4 3 2 1

Library of Congress Cataloging-in-Publication Data

Shu, Nan C.
Visual programming / Nan C. Shu.
p. cm.
ISBN 0-442-28014-9 :
1. Visual programming (Computer science) I. Title.
QA76.65.S55 1988
004.6'6—dc19

Preface

The challenge of this decade is to bring computer capabilities, simply and usefully, to people without special training in programming. *Visual Programming* represents a conceptually revolutionary approach to meet this challenge.

Visual programming has gained momentum in recent years primarily because the falling cost of graphics-related hardware and software has made it feasible to use pictures as a means of communicating with computers and to use computer graphics as a medium to teach programming. However, even though work on visual-oriented computing is now mushrooming, there is no consensus on what visual programming is, let alone on a way to assess it.

The purpose of this book is manyfold: to shed light on the state of the art on this new frontier; to establish common understanding; to assimilate what we have; and to lay a foundation upon which various aspects of visual programming can be focused and examined.

The book is aimed at people who are interested in learning something about visual programming. Potential users may find it useful to know what visual programming is. Researchers and software developers in this wide area may find it useful to relate their own work to other efforts. People whose expertise is not in this field may want to satisfy their curiosity regarding the state of the art.

It would be helpful if the reader has a reasonable appreciation of the capabilities of a computer system. But this prerequisite is not particularly demanding, because it is not necessary to understand all the details in order to grasp the thrust of this book. What is important is the basic ideas conveyed. I hope that the book will prove suitable for anyone who wishes to broaden his general knowledge of the field.

This book is both a tutorial and a survey. Because it is a tutorial, I have decided not to include commercial products in the marketplace unless the principles underlying the commercial product have been reported in the literature. For my purpose, it is more important to put together the multiplicity of ideas that have shaped the current state of the art, and to discuss the reported efforts that have gone into making visual programming an exciting and promising field.

Since this book is also a survey, I have tried to be as thorough as possible. However, a book is like a theatrical play. Within the constraints of time, space, and interest, it is not possible to give every player an equally important role. Among the criteria that I have used in selecting materials to be included in this book, the two most important ones are the clarity of underlying concepts and the relevance to the topics of discussion. No doubt some reports or topics that should have been covered may have been overlooked. I hope, however, that the coverage is sufficiently broad and representative to be useful both to those who are curious about visual programming and those who have worked in some aspects of this many-faceted field.

Writing a book is a major undertaking. I am grateful to IBM for allowing much of the work to be done using company time. This book would not have been possible without the support of management, John Kepler, Arvid Schmalz, Jim Jordan, and Dick Bergstresser. However, I am responsible for the contents of the book. The views expressed are my own and in no way reflect the opinions of IBM.

Peter Woon deserves special thanks for his careful reading of the manuscript and his valuable suggestions. The LASC administrative staff prepared numerous figures within a short period of time. My thanks go to Carol Cumming for her coordination of a cooperative effort and to Connie Lee for her resourcefulness and her juggling of many "hats."

I would also like to thank Laszlo Belady for getting me involved with the IEEE Computer Society Workshop on Visual Languages in 1984. The heterogeneity of the topics discussed in that first workshop has inspired me to untangle the threads. Although unknown to him and to me at the time, that was the catalyst for writing this book.

Contents

Chapter 1

Introduction

It is software that gives form and purpose to a programmable machine much as a sculptor shapes clay.

Alan Kay [1]

THE DUAL BRAIN

The human brain is divided into two halves, or hemispheres, separated by the "corpus callosum" (a bundle of interconnecting nerve tissues). For the control of movement and analysis of sensation, the assignment of duties to the two hemispheres follows a simple pattern: each side of the brain is responsible mainly for the opposite side of the body. "The distribution of the more specialized functions is quite different," however, "and it is profoundly asymmetrical."[2] Linguistic ability is dependent primarily on the left hemisphere, while the perception of melodies and nonverbal visual patterns is largely a function of the right hemisphere.

To some degree, the two hemispheres also "think" and "operate" differently. It is generally believed that, for most people, the left hemisphere of the brain thinks analytically and logically. The right hemisphere, on the other hand, thinks in a more intuitive and artistic sense. The left hemisphere is thought of as a sequential information processor, highly developed for verbal expressions (spoken or written). The right hemisphere, on the other hand, seemingly is capable of parallel processing. An image is captured as a whole. For example, when you look at a face, you immediately recognize an individual (Figure 1-1).

Programming has always been thought of as an activity which draws upon our ability to think analytically, logically, and verbally. Visual programming represents a recent attempt to exploit our nonverbal capabilities. Various reasons have been cited for the interest in visual programming. Many of them pertain to the better use of the right half of the brain, which is needlessly at rest and underutilized for the purpose of computing. But, in addition to the aesthetic reasons, there is also a pragmatic motivation for the development of visual programming, which we shall now elaborate.

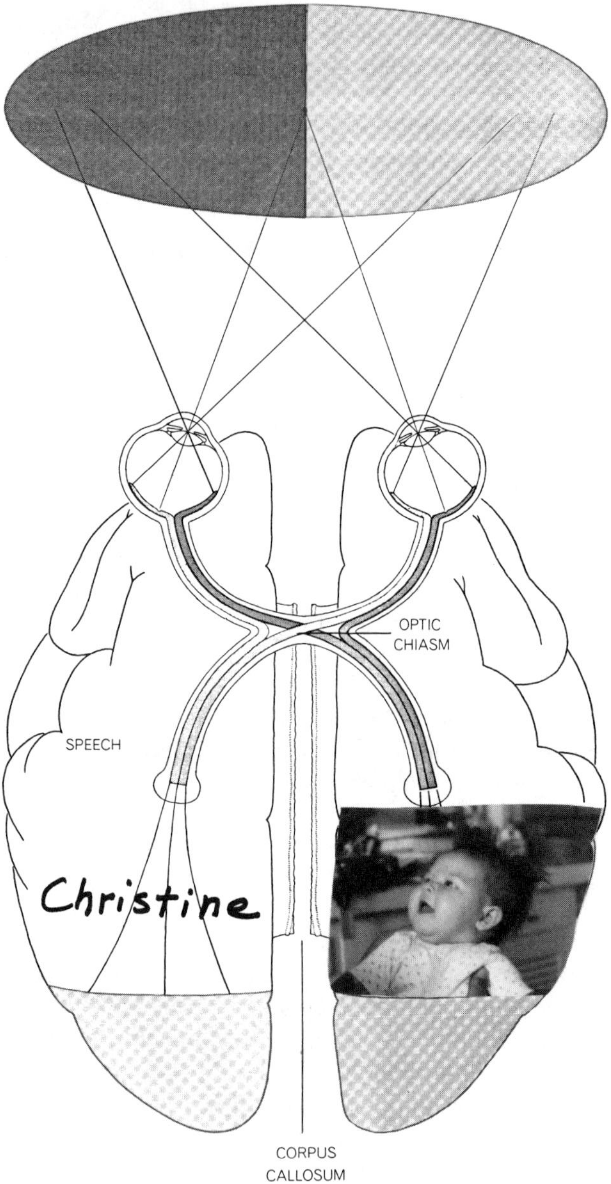

Figure 1-1. The dual brain.
(Based on "The Split Brain in Man" by M.S. Gazzaniga. Copyright © 1967, by Scientific American, Inc. All rights reserved.)

THE CHANGING USER POPULATION

The "application backlog" has become a serious problem in recent years, and the situation is likely to become worse unless better methods of developing applications are found.

Two approaches to reducing the backlog are apparent. One is to increase the productivity of the people who can program, and the other is to increase the number of such people.

In the 1970s, efforts were directed in earnest to increasing the productivity of professional programmers. During this period, useful methodologies and tools for all phases of the software development life cycle were developed, and software engineering was established as a discipline.

Recently, the decreasing cost of computing, coupled with the widespread use of personal computers, has acted as a catalyst for more applications. Now the applications logjam remains just as bad as before, but the nature of applications has changed. Routine processing is well understood and has been successfully computerized; users now turn to spontaneous demands for information to assist them in their daily work. We can no longer hope to train enough professional programmers to fulfill these insatiable demands. By necessity, end-user computing is becoming a major trend. Figure 1-2 illustrates how end-user computing, compared to operational computing, is expected to grow in the coming years.[3]

THE NEED FOR A NEW STYLE OF PROGRAMMING

It will be extremely difficult to achieve this phenomenal rate of growth unless the style of computing evolves to such a state that a large portion of the user population can use a computer without thinking deliberately about it—in a manner akin to driving a car.

Most of us can rent an automobile and drive away within a few minutes even if we are not familiar with that particular model of car. All we have to do is to locate the primary controls, make sure that there is gasoline, and turn on the ignition. If we had to have the training of an auto mechanic before we could use a car, or if we had to put on our goggles and crank the shaft every time we wanted to drive, there would not be as many automobiles on the roads as we have today. Thanks to the engineers who made it possible, we no longer have to be concerned with how an automobile works. Instead, our energy can be spent deciding how to get from one place to another. It is the engineers' responsibility to build the automobiles to our satisfaction. We, the ordinary people, simply use them as a means of transportation.

This, unfortunately, is not the case when using a computer. Joel Birnbaum

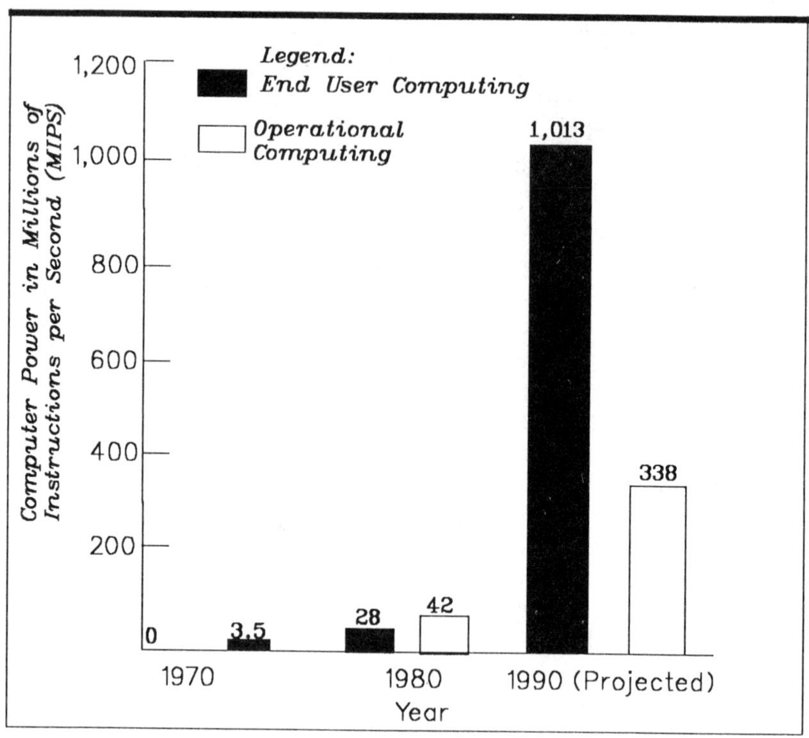

Figure 1-2. Growth of computing.
(Reprinted with permission from the *Journal of Information Systems Management*, Vol. 3, No. 1. © Auerbach Publishers Inc.)

(vice president and research director of Hewlett-Packard Laboratories in Palo Alto, California) has pointed out that "There are now more computers than people in the United States, and microprocessors are being produced at a rate that probably exceeds one million per day."[4] Obviously, the majority of potential computer users are noncomputer professionals whose aspirations are not to become computer scientists or programmers, but to use computers as tools to get their work done. Yet, most of our software today is still designed as if users are professional programmers.

There are historical reasons for this lack of emphasis on human convenience until recently. The computer scientists, for the last three decades, have concentrated on machine efficiency. Computing costs were high and human costs were relatively low. In the early years of computing, it was justifiable that efficiency took precedence over ease of programming. Somewhat less justifiable is the fantasy that people will get used to the machines. In a way, programmers themselves have fostered this fantasy. Programmers were trained to make do with whatever was handed to them. Without questions and without complaints, they learned how to get around difficult situations and took pride in their ability to handle complexities.

One certainty is that the future will not resemble the past. With the dramatic decline in computing costs, the industry has finally realized that it is the user base that must be expanded and the human resource that must be optimized. The challenge is to bring computer capabilities—usefully and simply—to people without special computer training.

To meet this challenge, facilities for end users have flourished. Indeed, icons, pointing devices, and menus have eased the pain of learning and remembering commands; word processors have become indispensable for document preparation; and query facilities, application generators, and spreadsheet programs serve as invaluable tools for simple inquiries and special-purpose applications. However, the usefulness of each tool is limited to a particular predesigned category of applications. Consequently, they are applicable only to a portion of the end users' interests.

To investigate the nature of end-user computing, Rockart and Flannery of the Sloan School of Management[5] have interviewed 200 end users and 50 members of information systems staff who have the responsibility for supporting end-user computing in seven major organizations. They found that, when classified by primary purpose of end-user applications, 9% of the use was for operational processing, 14% for report generation, 21% for inquiry and simple analysis, 6% for miscellaneous uses, and the remaining 50% for support of complex analytical assistance. In other words, about 50-56% of the end-user applications surveyed were *not in the predesigned categories.*

For their survey, Rockart and Flannery[5] randomly selected a subset of users designated by the company as "heavy and/or frequent users of time sharing." They belonged to the most involved user population at the time of the survey. Looking toward the future and taking the "wish lists" of the entire potential user population into consideration, it would not be surprising if the percentage of applications which do not belong to the predesigned categories exceeded 50-56%. Furthermore, even for the applications belonging to the predesigned categories, packages written for a mass audience seldom give every user all the capabilities that he or she needs. Those who wish to use the computer for doing something beyond the capabilities of canned programs discover that they will have to *program.*

Learning to program, unfortunately, is a time-consuming and often frustrating endeavor. Moreover, even after the skill is learned, writing and testing a program is still a time-consuming and labor-intensive chore. Many people avoid it simply because they cannot afford the time and effort required. For the few who do, it is often doubtful whether their time is well spent in programming. Programming has the tendency to lead to what has been termed "analysis paralysis." "The means become the ends as you forget what you wanted to get out of the computer and become wrapped up in the process of getting it out."[6]

It is not surprising then, that Rockart and Flannery[5] found that two-thirds of the applications used by the end users were developed by support personnel, data processing programmers, and consultants. In other words, even with the bias in the selection of "major users of the computing resource" for the survey, users still depend heavily on progammers as middlemen to develop their applications.

Clearly, increasing the number of people who can program would reduce the dependence on programmers, and consequently induce a win-win situation. End users know their applications best. By developing their own applications, they can avoid the time and effort involved in communicating their desires to the middlemen and get the results in a timely fashion. Computer professionals, on the other hand, know computing technology best. When relieved of their role as middlemen, they can devote their energy to producing software that is appealing to users on the outside, even though it may be very complex internally.

WHY "VISUAL PROGRAMMING"?

The attempt to ease programming, of course, is not new. For years, people have been trying to design or improve programming languages for ease of use. However, language design has been evolutionary rather than revolutionary. Only in the last few years has it become apparent that a radical departure from traditional programming is necessary if programming is to be made more accessible to a large population.

When we look at the progress made over the last thirty years, we observe that the programming languages have evolved from low level, to high level, to very high level, and now to ultra high level. These four levels correspond roughly to the four "generations" of programming languages. Figure 1-3 shows one way of viewing this progression.[1] Note that this classification is by no means universally agreed upon. Nor are there commonly accepted definitions of "level" and/or "generation." Nevertheless, one characteristic stands out without much dispute: as the level goes up, fewer details are required from the user.

Another observation is that, with few exceptions, the tradition of linear representations persists from generation to generation. Instructions are given to the computer in a statement-by-statement manner. The structure of the programming languages remains one-dimensional and textual.

In contrast, visual programming represents a conceptually revolutionary

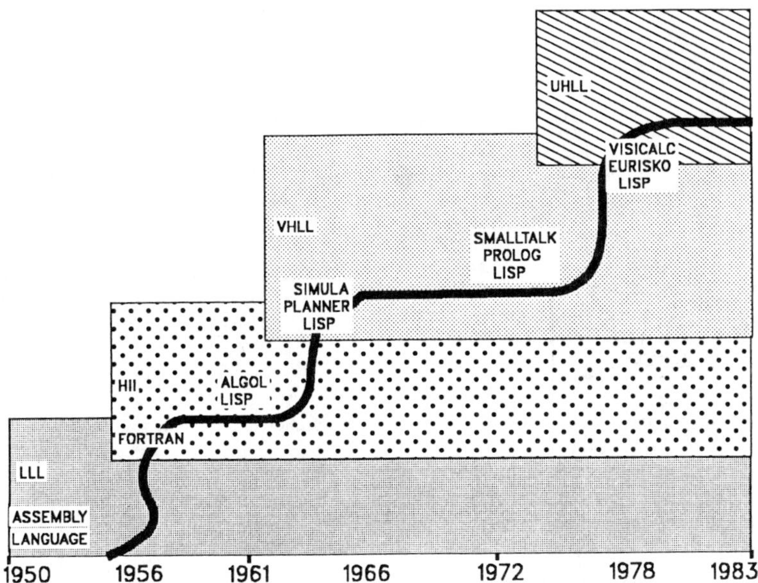

SOFTWARE GENRES succeed one another at sporadic intervals, as is shown here through the example of some programming languages. Languages are categorized rather arbitrarily by level, although the levels overlap. There are low-level languages (LLL), high-level languages (HLL), very-high-level languages (VHLL) and ultrahigh-level languages (UHLL). In the evolution of programming languages a genre is established (horizontal black lines), then after a few years an improvement is made (curved black lines). In time the improved language is seen to be not merely a "better old thing" but an "almost" new thing", and it leads to the next stable genre. The language LISP has changed repeatedly, each time become a new genre.

Figure 1-3. Software genres.
(Based on "Computer Software" by Alan Kay. Copyright © 1984, by Scientific American, Inc. All rights reserved.)

departure from this tradition. Graphical representations and pictures have come into play in the programming process. This form of programming is stimulated by the following premises:

1. Pictures are more powerful than words as a means of communication. They can convey more meaning in a more concise unit of expression. For example, see Figure 1-4.
2. Pictures aid understanding and remembering. For example, see Figure 1-5.

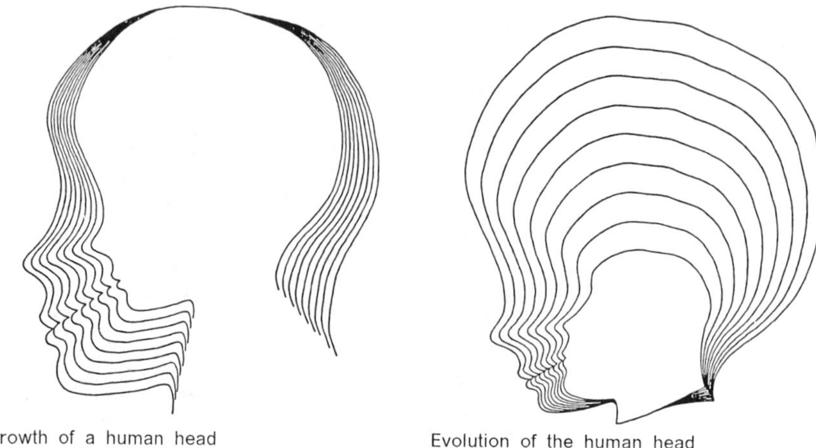

Figure 1-4. Growth vs. evolution of the human head.
From "The Perception of Human Growth" by J.T. Todd et al. Copyright © 1980, by Scientific American, Inc. All rights reserved.)

Figure 1-5. Automating a mess yields an automated mess.
(Reprinted with permission of Gary Viskupic.)

3. Pictures may provide an incentive for learning to program. For example, see Figure 1-6.
4. Pictures do not have language barriers. When properly designed, they are understood by people regardless of what language they speak. For example, see Figure 1-7.

Visual programming has gained momentum in recent years primarily because the falling cost of graphics-related hardware and software has made it feasible to use pictures as a means of communicating with the computers. However, even though visual-related works are now mushrooming in the literature, there is no consensus on what visual programming is, let alone on a way to assess it.

This lack of common understanding is not surprising since the field is very young, and the examples of visual programming have come into existence from varied backgrounds. Nevertheless, common and coherent understanding is important not only in making progress but also in making the progress known to the potential user community.

The purpose of this book is manyfold: to shed light on the state of the art on this new frontier; to establish common understanding among researchers, system developers, and potential users; to assimilate what we have developed; and to lay a foundation upon which various aspects of visual programming can be focused and examined.

Let us start with the question: what do we mean by "Visual Programming"?

WHAT IS VISUAL PROGRAMMING?

Since visual programming is an emerging field in its formative years, almost everyone has a different idea of what it is. We use the term "Visual Programming" to mean *the use of meaningful graphic representations in the process of programming.*

Programming can be defined as specifying a method for doing something the computer can do in terms the computer can interpret. There are many aspects of programming: the languages and environment used for the specifications; the specifications themselves; the determination of whether the computer has executed a specification as expected; the display of data involved in the execution of the specification; etc. Visual programming can be applied to all aspects of programming. An important question to ask is: are there any meaningful (not merely decorative) graphical objects involved in an aspect of programming?

One may argue whether the use of overlapping or tiled windows is visual programming. The answer merits more than a simple "yes" or "no." Having multiple windows is useful in many situations. It allows the user to view several objects or to control a number of separate activities more easily.

SCIENTIFIC
AMERICAN

COMPUTER SOFTWARE

$2.50

September 1984

Figure 1-6. Associating programming with fun.
(From Cover of Sept. 1984 *Scientific American*, Copyright © 1984, by Scientific American, Inc. All rights reserved.)

THE COVER

The illustration on the cover symbolizes the theme of this issue of SCIENTIFIC AMERICAN: computer software. The illustration is itself software: it is a program in a pictorial language called Mandala, under development by Jaron Z. Lanier and his colleagues at VPL Research in Palo Alto, Calif. Instructions are given to the computer by arranging icons, or small graphic symbols, on a display screen and setting them in motion. At the top a kangaroo hops from a triple-clef icon, which activates a program for playing three-part canons; to an icon that allows musical data to be viewed in traditional music notation and then to an ice cube, where the sequence of hops is "frozen" so that it can be referred to by a single symbol. An icon can represent a hierarchy of programming structures. The triple clef "expands" into the loop shown below it; the loop is executed once, launching (at intervals of four measures) the three birds that perform the canon. The sequence of instructions embodied in each bird is shown to the right of the loop. If a bird flying along the score is at a note, it sounds the note; otherwise, if it is at the end of the score, it returns to the beginning. The canon itself was composed by Lanier with the aid of the illustrated Mandala program.

Figure 1-6. *(continued)*

Figure 1-7. Informative signs.

Nevertheless, windows do not necessarily contain graphical objects pertaining to programming, and programming is not necessarily dependent on having multiple windows. Thus, by our definition, the *mere use* of windows is neither sufficient nor necessary in determining whether a programming aspect is visual or not. In other words, the style of interaction employing windows and convenient pointing devices is unquestionably valuable, regardless of whether any graphical objects are involved or not. But to be considered visual programming, some meaningful graphical representations must be used in the programming process.

When we examine the recent work reported in the literature, we see visual programming progressing in two major directions. In one direction, graphical techniques and pointing devices are used to provide visual environments for program construction and execution; for information retrieval and presentation; and for software design and understanding. In another direction, languages are designed to handle visual (image) information; to support visual interaction; and to actually program with visual expressions. These trends are catalogued in Table 1-1.

To understand the distinctions among the different categories of visual programming, we draw upon the research works reported in the literature. Because of the large amount of literature in this area, we cannot, of course, include every paper on the subject. In general, many systems can be cited for each category, but only a few from each category are chosen as the focal points. In some cases, they are chosen because of their high visibility or historical interest. But, more importantly, they are chosen because they serve as good examples that illustrate the concepts we wish to convey.

One should also bear in mind that some of the systems may have features that cover one or more categories. The use of system X as an example of

Table 1-1 Visual Programming

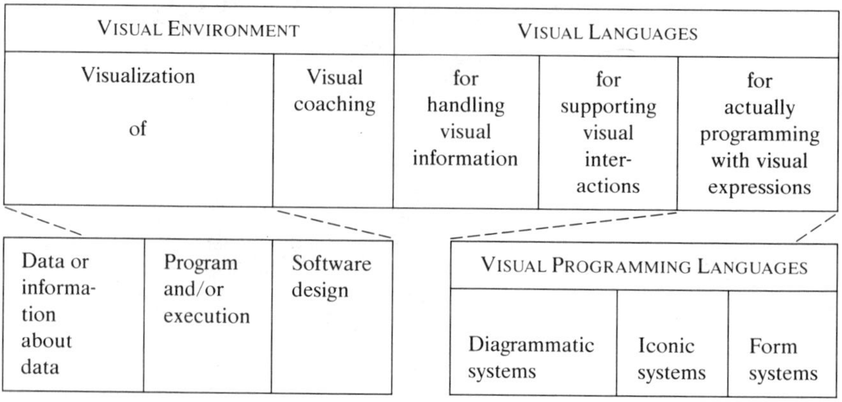

VISUAL ENVIRONMENT		VISUAL LANGUAGES		
Visualization of	Visual coaching	for handling visual information	for supporting visual inter-actions	for actually programming with visual expressions

Data or information about data	Program and/or execution	Software design

VISUAL PROGRAMMING LANGUAGES		
Diagrammatic systems	Iconic systems	Form systems

category A does not necessarily mean that system X can only be classified into category A. The purpose of the classification is to sharpen our understanding by focusing on the functional distinctions. In the following chapters, these different aspects of visual programming are examined. To give a bird's-eye view, we first present a brief synopsis of the coming chapters.

VISUALIZATION OF DATA OR INFORMATION ABOUT DATA

Chapter 2 concentrates on a category of work in the visual environment area which deals with visualization of data or information about data. Typically, the information or data is stored internally in traditional databases, but expressed in graphical form and presented to the user in a spatial framework. Users can traverse the graphical surface or zoom into it to obtain greater detail with a joystick or a pointing device. This approach permits many types of questions to be answered without the need for a keyboard. In essence, these systems are devoted primarily to using "direct manipulation" as a means of information retrieval, using a graphical view of a database for visualization of the information retrieved.

VISUALIZATION OF A PROGRAM AND/OR EXECUTION

Another category in the visual environment area provides graphical support for the visualization of programs and their run time states and results. The programs themselves are written in traditional programming languages. The objective is to use the high-resolution graphical displays to make the task of program development and testing easier. Activities in this area span a wide spectrum, ranging from "pretty-printing" the source code to watching the execution of a program in multiple displays or in animated forms. This area is covered in Chapter 3.

VISUALIZATION OF SOFTWARE DESIGN

Graphical techniques are expected to have a very high payoff in a software environment that supports the whole software life cycle. The success of using graphical techniques for the visualization of "programming in the small" has led to efforts in the visualization of "programming in the large." The goal is to provide a software development environment in which the requirements, specifications, design decisions, and system structures are all captured in graphical form for people who design, use, or maintain a software system or who want to find out about the system. Chapter 4 discusses the representative works in this area.

VISUAL COACHING

A number of systems have explored graphical programming with the intention of narrowing the gap between the mental process and the programming process of solving a problem. In the environment provided by these systems, a user does not need to mentally visualize the effects of his instructions while constructing a program. The effects take place on the screen before his eyes. The programming process relies almost completely on interactive graphics. The style of interaction, in general, "mimics the informal way we explain programs, by showing pictures of the data and defining the computation on them by pointing sequences *similar to handwaving*."[7] Language syntax in the traditional sense is absent from the user's point of view. We therefore use the term "Visual Coaching" to characterize this category. Many of the recent "programming by example" and "demonstrational" systems belong to this group. Chapter 5 describes this type.

Before we go on, note that the first three categories differ from each other because they focus on visualization of three distinct classes of objects. The fourth category (visual coaching) goes beyond visualization by using visual signaling as a means of programming. Thus, on a close look, these four represent four distinct categories of visual programming.

Looking from a higher level, however, it is clear that all four have the following characteristics in common: (1) they all provide a *visual environment* which captures the spirit of a completely new way for humans to interact with the computer, and (2) none provides anything new in terms of an approach to the *language* aspects of the programming process. In other words, the emphasis is on interaction, not language.

This second characteristic marks the sharp distinction between the two major areas of visual programming: visual environment and visual languages.

Depending on their objectives, visual languages can be further classified into three categories: languages for handling visual information; for supporting visual interaction; and for programming with visual representations.

LANGUAGES FOR HANDLING VISUAL INFORMATION

Languages in this category are mainly designed for the processing of visual or image information. They are motivated by the need to have easy-to-use languages for the manipulation and querying of pictorial data. Typically, the languages allow direct reference to pictures. However, even though the information being handled by the languages does involve pictures, the languages themselves are textual. In Chapter 6, representative systems are used to illustrate this category of visual languages.

LANGUAGES FOR SUPPORTING VISUAL INTERACTION

Advances in hardware technology have paved the way for the use of icons or graphical objects as a means of communication with computers. However, without software, icons and pictures could not come to life in the programming world. Thus, it is natural that languages were designed to define, create, and manipulate pictorial symbols. Languages in this category, in general, support visual representations and visual interactions, but the languages themselves are textual, not visual. They form the focus of Chapter 7.

VISUAL PROGRAMMING LANGUAGES: A FRAMEWORK

Still another category of visual languages concentrates on allowing users to actually *program with visual expressions*. They can be more aptly called the "Visual Programming Languages." In Chapter 8, visual programming language is defined and a framework for analysis (based on the language level, the scope of applicability, and the extent of visual expressions) is elaborated. This framework is used in the next three chapters, where three different classes of visual programming languages are discussed.

CHARTS AND DIAGRAMS

Based on the principles of design, most of the visual programming languages reported in the literature fall into three broad categories. At one extreme, *flow charts and diagrams that are already in use on paper* are either incorporated into programming constructs, as extensions to conventional programming languages, or made into machine-interpretable units to be used in conjunction with conventional programming languages. They are discussed in Chapter 9.

ICONIC OR PICTORIAL LANGUAGES

At the other extreme, icons or graphical symbols are *deliberately designed* to play the central role in programming. In recent years, we have seen a flurry of iconic or pictorial systems reported in the literature. The roles of icons and pictures are no longer restricted to representations of desktop objects and "commands" to manipulate these objects. Attempts have been made to teach and/or to carry out programming concepts by pictorial representations. They are the focus of attention in Chapter 10.

TABLE OR FORM-BASED LANGUAGES

Between the two extremes (i.e., charts/diagrams and iconic systems) lie the visual programming languages of the third kind. In this category, graphical representations are designed as an integral part of a language. However, unlike the icons in the pictorial systems, these graphical representations are not the "superstars" of the language. Yet, unlike the diagrammatic systems, these languages are not attempts to make "paper-and-pencil tools" executable.

Many of the table and form-based languages belong to this category. They are examined in Chapter 11.

FUTURE PROSPECTS

In spite of the current surge of interest, visual programming is by no means universally appreciated. Views on visual programming are often very subjective and intuitive. In Chapter 12, the last chapter, we emphasize the need to take a systematic and disciplined approach in assessing where we are and where we would like to go. Visual programming has advantages and limitations. With the speed at which computing technology is progressing, we are better guided for the future if our understanding of visual programming is sharpened and deepened.

REFERENCES

1. Kay, A., "Computer Software," *Scientific American,* Vol. 251, No. 3, pp. 53-59 (Sept. 1984).
2. Geschwind, N., "Specializations of the Human Brain," *Scientific American*, pp. 180-199 (Sept. 1979).

2a. Gazzaniga, M. S., "The Split Brain in Man," *Scientific American,* pp. 24-29 (Aug. 1967).

3. Leitheiser, R. L., and Wetherbe, J. C., "Approaches to End-User Computing: Service May Spell Success," *Journal of Information Systems Management,* pp. 9-14 (Winter 1986).
4. Birnbaum, J. S., "Toward the Domestication of Microelectronics," *Communications of the ACM,* Vol. 28, No. 11, pp. 1225-1235 (Nov. 1985).
5. Rockart, J. F., and Flannery, L. S., "The Management of End User Computing," *Communications of the ACM,* Vol. 26, No. 10, pp. 776-784 (Oct. 1983).
6. Brown, G. D., and Sefton, D. H., "The Micro vs. the Applications Logjam," *Datamation,* Vol. 30, No. 1, pp. 96-104 (Jan. 1984).

6a. Todd, J. T., Mark, L. S., Shaw, R. E., and Pittenger, J. B., "The Perception of Human Growth," *Scientific American,* Vol. 242, No. 2, pp. 132-144 (Feb. 1980).

7. Raeder, G., "Programming in Pictures," Ph.D. thesis, Department of Computer Science, University of Southern California (Nov. 1984).

Chapter 2

Visualization of Data and Information about Data

When a person uses an interactive graphics system to do real work, he wants the system to virtually disappear from his consciousness so that only his work and its ramifications have a claim on his energy.

James Foley[1]

Ivan Sutherland, a well-known pioneer whose "interest for some years has been the programming of computers to draw pictures on the face of a cathode ray tube," has said, "I think of a computer display as a window on Alice's Wonderland in which a programmer can depict either objects that obey well-known natural laws or purely imaginary objects that follow laws he has written into his program. Through computer displays I have landed an airplane on the deck of a moving carrier, observed a nuclear particle hit a potential well, flown in a rocket at nearly the speed of light and watched a computer reveal its innermost workings."[2]

That was 1970—at a time when the seemingly magical power of computer graphics was available to only a few members of the elite group. Graphic displays were used only in areas where written language is far from adequate and in areas where insight into complex natural or mathematical phenomena can best be gained through visual forms. The costs for computer graphics were high. Applications of interactive computer graphics were limited because few could justify and afford the costs.

The drastic decline in computing costs and the dramatic improvement in display technology have changed that situation. Now, less than two decades later, the privilege of exploring the "Wonderland" through visual means is becoming increasingly available to all kinds of users. And the potential application areas of interactive computer graphics are now becoming bounded only by imagination.

Indeed, interactive computer graphics is well on its way to becoming a pervasive means of delivering information. Visualization of data and information about data (such as data structures or schema) is a manifestation of this recent trend. In the rest of this chapter, examples are used to illustrate this point.

VISUALIZATION OF DATA

Spatial Data Management System (SDMS)

"Spatial data management" is the technique of accessing data through their graphical representations. It is motivated by the needs of a growing community of people who want to access information in a database management system but are not trained in the use of such systems.

In contrast to conventional database management systems, in which users access data by asking questions in a formal query language, spatial data management systems present the information graphically in a spatial framework, which enables the users to find the information they need without having to specify it precisely or know exactly where in the database it is stored.

The spatial data management concept was first proposed by Fields and Negroponte,[3] and later explored by Donelson in an experimental system [4] at the Massachusetts Institute of Technology. A prototype spatial data management system built at the Computer Corporation of America (CCA) which interfaces to a conventional database management system was reported by Herot.[5] In the rest of this section, we use SDMS to refer to the specific system implemented at CCA, not the spatial data management systems in the generic sense.

A user "retrieves" data from SDMS by examining a graphical data space upon which pictorial representations of the data are arranged. The graphical data space is accessed through a set of color raster-scan displays. One of the display screens presents a "world view"—a high-level global view of the data available to the database user. A highlighted rectangle indicates the user's position on the world view. A magnified view of the highlighted portion is displayed simultaneously on the main screen. The position of the highlighted rectangle in the world view, and thus the portion of the magnified portion shown on the main display, are controlled by the joystick.

The simultaneous presentation of a world view and a detailed view ensures that the user is always aware of his current location in the database. It also helps in finding a region of interest in a database.

Data presented to the user on the main display can come from

1. Images stored as bit arrays on a digital disk.
2. A conventional database.
3. An optical videodisk.

Tools are provided which allow the user or the database administrator to establish connections between data from these sources and their associated graphical representations.

As an example, consider the retrieval of information from a database of ships. This database originated as a conventional database managed by the INGRES database management system.[6] Tuples of the SHIP relation in the database are shown in Figure 2-1.

The graphical representation of a tuple is an icon provided by the database administrator. In this example, all icons are ship-shaped. The exact shape of each icon is determined by the type of the ship (e.g., carrier, destroyer, submarine). The color of each icon indicates the ship's readiness, and the size of each icon is a function of the beam of its associated ship.

The procedure by which the administrator produced the graphical representation is described in Chapter 7. For the example here, suffice it to say that the graphical views of the SHIP database have already been defined. The user can now proceed to browse. Figure 2-2 shows the SDMS workstation where the graphical views are shown to the user. Figure 2-3 shows the world-view map, which is presented on the leftmost of the three screens. It is an all-encompassing view of the data laid out on the graphical data space. The map has been divided into two rows, one for each of the two countries having ships in the database. Each column represents one class of ship. Within each column, each ship is represented by an icon.

Figure 2-4 shows the main data display which appears on the center screen. The display corresponds to the highlighted portion of the worldview, but it is in a magnified state. The icons have a more detailed shape, and beneath each shape are text strings which give the ship's radio call signal, name, and commanding officer. These information items are taken from the underlying database.

The user can traverse the data surface with the joystick. In this example, to retrieve information on a specific ship named *Daniels,* he pulls the joystick until Daniels is in the center of the screen and then releases the joystick. Now, to zoom in on the selected ship, he twists the joystick clockwise. The outline of the ship becomes more detailed, and the space under the ship is filled with more information from the database, as shown in Figure 2-5.

At this point, the user has a choice of actions. He can move laterally across the data surface and examine similarly detailed views of adjacent ships. He can twist the joystick counterclockwise to return to the less detailed views. Or he can, if the database administrator has provided for it, once again twist the joystick clockwise for views with more details.

In this manner, the user can traverse the graphical data space and zoom in or out for more or fewer details. This approach encourages browsing by direct manipulation, requires less prior knowledge of the contents and

uic	nam	type	nat	ircs	beam	ready
N00001	CONSTELLATION	CV	US	NABC	130	1
N00002	KENNEDY JF	CV	US	NABD	130	1
N00003	KITTY HAWK	CV	US	NABE	130	2
N00004	AMERICA	CV	US	NABF	130	5
N00005	SARATOGA	CV	US	NABG	130	1
N00006	INDEPENDENCE	CV	US	NABH	130	1
N00007	LOS ANGELES	SSN	US	NABI	33	1
N00008	BATON ROUGE	SSN	US	NABJ	33	1
N00009	PHILADELPHIA	SSN	US	NABK	33	1
N00010	STURGEON	SSN	US	NABL	32	1
N00011	WHALE	SSN	US	NABM	32	1
N00012	TAUTOG	SSN	US	NABN	32	1
N00013	GRAYLING	SSN	US	NABO	32	1
N00014	POGY	SSN	US	NABP	32	1
N00015	ASPRO	SSN	US	NABQ	32	1
N00016	SUNFISH	SSN	US	NABR	32	1
N00017	CALIFORNIA	CGN	US	NABS	61	1
N00018	SOUTH CAROLINA	CGN	US	NABT	61	1
N00019	DANIELS J	CG	US	NABU	55	1
N00020	WAINWRIGHT	CG	US	NABV	55	1
N00021	JOUETT	CG	US	NABW	55	1
N00022	HORNE	CG	US	NABX	55	1
N00023	STERETT	CG	US	NABY	55	3
N00024	STANDLEY WH	CG	US	NABZ	55	1
N00025	FOX	CG	US	NACA	55	1
N00026	BIDDLE	CG	US	NACB	55	1
N00027	LEAHY	CG	US	NACC	55	4
N00028	YARNELL HE	CG	US	NACD	55	1
N00029	WORDEN	CG	US	NACE	55	1
N00030	DALE	CG	US	NACF	55	1
N00031	TURNER RK	CG	US	NACG	55	1
N00032	GRIDLEY	CG	US	NACH	55	1
N00033	ENGLAND	CG	US	NACI	55	1
N00034	HALSEY	CG	US	NACJ	55	1
N00035	REEVES	CG	US	NACK	55	3
N00036	ADAMS CF	DDG	US	NACL	47	3
N00037	KING J	DDG	US	NACM	47	1
N00038	LAWRENCE	DDG	US	NACN	47	1
N00039	RICKETT CV	DDG	US	NACO	47	1
N00040	BARNEY	DDG	US	NACP	47	1
N00041	WILSON HB	DDG	US	NACQ	47	1
N00042	MCCORMICK L	DDG	US	NACR	47	1
N00043	TOWERS	DDG	US	NACS	47	1
N00044	SELLERS	DDG	US	NACT	47	1
N00045	ROBISON	DDG	US	NACU	47	1

Figure 2-1. SHIP database.
(Herot[5]. Copyright © 1980 Association for Computing Machinery, Inc., reprinted by permission.)

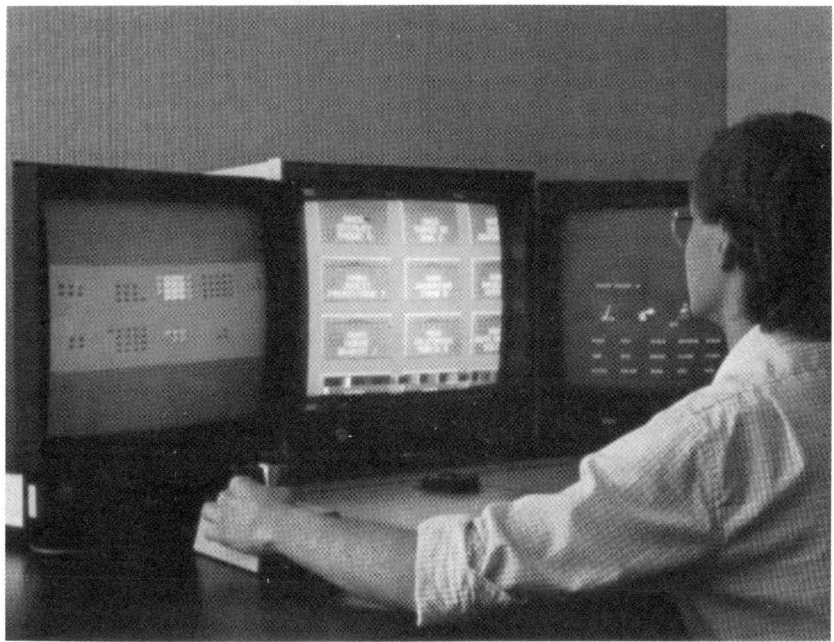

Figure 2-2. SDMS workstation.
(Herot[5]. Copyright © 1980 Association for Computing Machinery, Inc., reprinted by permission.)

structure of the database, and permits many questions to be answered without the need for a keyboard or a formal query language. "User response to the prototype has been quite encouraging, although a significant effort is required to build a complete set of data surfaces for realistic evaluation."[7]

The View System

According to Friedell, Barnett, and Kramlich (members of the CCA team for the SDMS project), "Prototype spatial data management systems have been built that successfully exploit computer graphics as a database access medium. However, this success is limited to a small number of applications using relatively small databases. These limitations are due principally to the large investment required to generate and store graphics environments. The costs of graphically presenting a large database are extremely high. Maintaining several different graphic representations of a single database—each tailored to a different task—is also impractical".[8]

Research on techniques to overcome these limitations led to the development of the View System, an extended SDMS, at the CCA.[8,9] In contrast to the earlier spatial data management systems, which present predefined

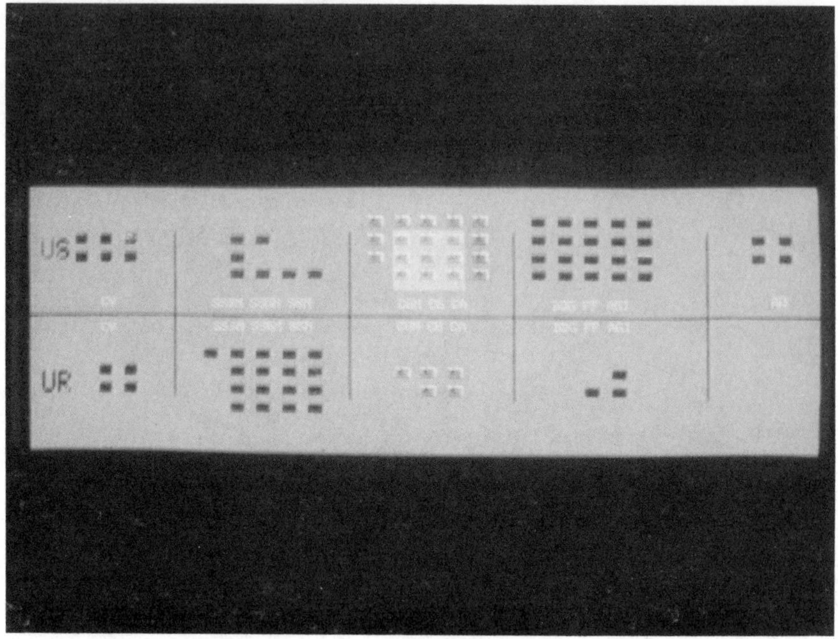

Figure 2-3. World-view map.
(Herot[5]. Copyright © 1980 Association for Computing Machinery, Inc., reprinted by permission.)

graphical data spaces, the View System defines and generates its graphics environment *dynamically*, in response to the user's viewing task, database queries, and motion through space.

The information used to create the graphical data space, i.e., information about the database, user context, and graphical presentation, is contained in an internal knowledge base.

The View System is composed of two major subsystems: the Answer Space Generator and the View Generator. The Answer Space Generator interacts with the user through a graphical query interface to produce a description of each query's answer space. The term "Answer Space" refers to the data that the system selects to respond to the user's query. In addition, an Answer Space Description also includes knowledge about the user's viewing preferences, task goals, and other information gathered throughout the query session. The View Generator then uses this description and the data resulting from the query to create the graphical data space.

Since the graphical data space is generated in real time, the View System is able to select from the knowledge base representational graphics and layout conventions that are preferred by the user for his task. Furthermore, while

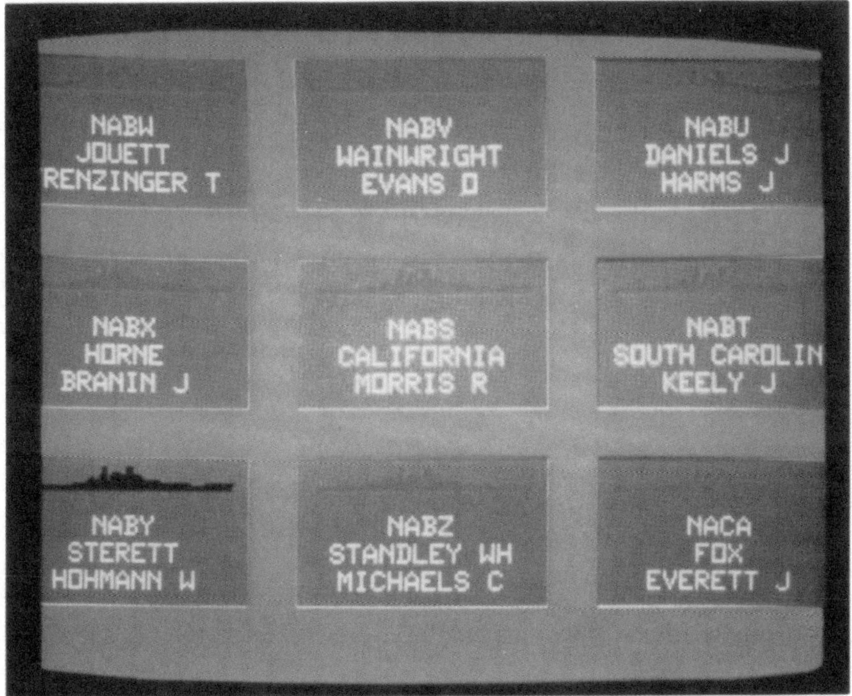

Figure 2-4. Magnified view of data surface.
(Herot[5]. Copyright © 1980 Association for Computing Machinery, Inc., reprinted with permission.)

the entire graphical data space is always logically defined, only a small portion is physically instantiated at any time. This approach gives the View System the capacity to present large databases graphically in a way that is tailored to the user's identity and task.

VGQF (Video Graphic Query Facility)

At Sperry Univac, Nancy McDonald developed a system with a multimedia interface to databases.[10] The purpose of this project is to provide a query/browsing facility for an inventory database using videodisk technology and interactive computer graphics.

McDonald's motivation is similar to that of SDMS. "In dealing with the typical database query language, one notices such annoying features as: (1). An investment in training must be incurred to ask even the simplest query. (2). Few languages make use of actual data characteristics (e.g. location in the database, appearance, value examples, etc.) (3). It is often difficult to

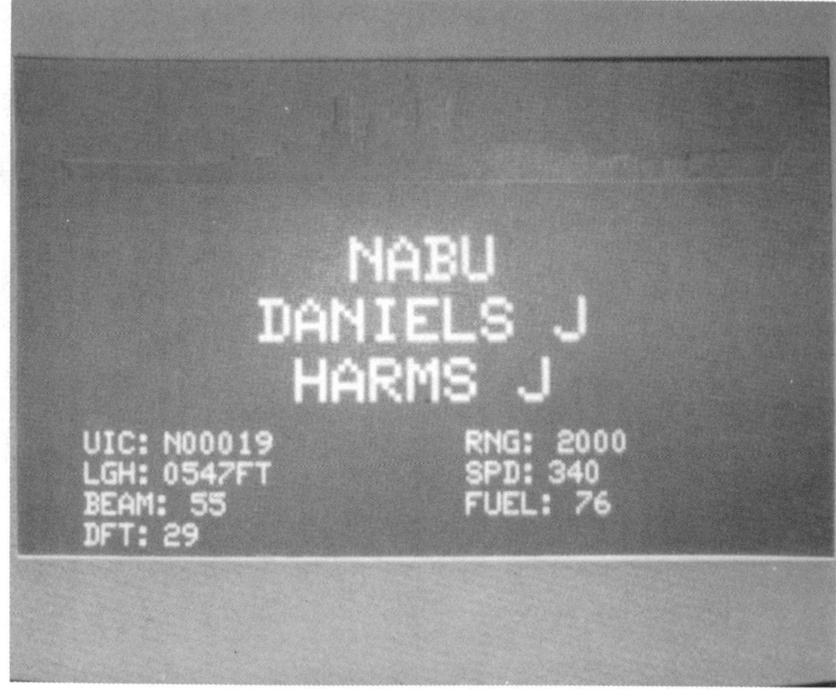

Figure 2-5. Zoomed-in view of data surface.
(Herot[5]. Copyright © 1980 Association for Computing Machinery, Inc., reprinted by permission.)

peruse the data. This tends to be more complex when the query can not be formulated precisely."[10]

The major features of this system include menu-select initiation, graphic feedback, and joystick and touch panel interactions. As with SDMS, the user station of VGQF has three display screens. The user may request various views of data to be presented in a coordinated mode for increased information. The user may also ask for simultaneous views of data in an uncoordinated manner, to augment his own associative powers for recognizing the object of interest.

Specific queries are graphically formulated. An interesting feature is that the user has the choice of formats to personalize the expression of the query. Figure 2-6 shows four of the several possible formats for user selection. After one is selected, the system guides the user through query construction, using any accompanying information.

The actual database entails a relational model of the typical data, along with additional spatial, video, and associative information in relational format. The video interactions are designed to be very simple; touching the

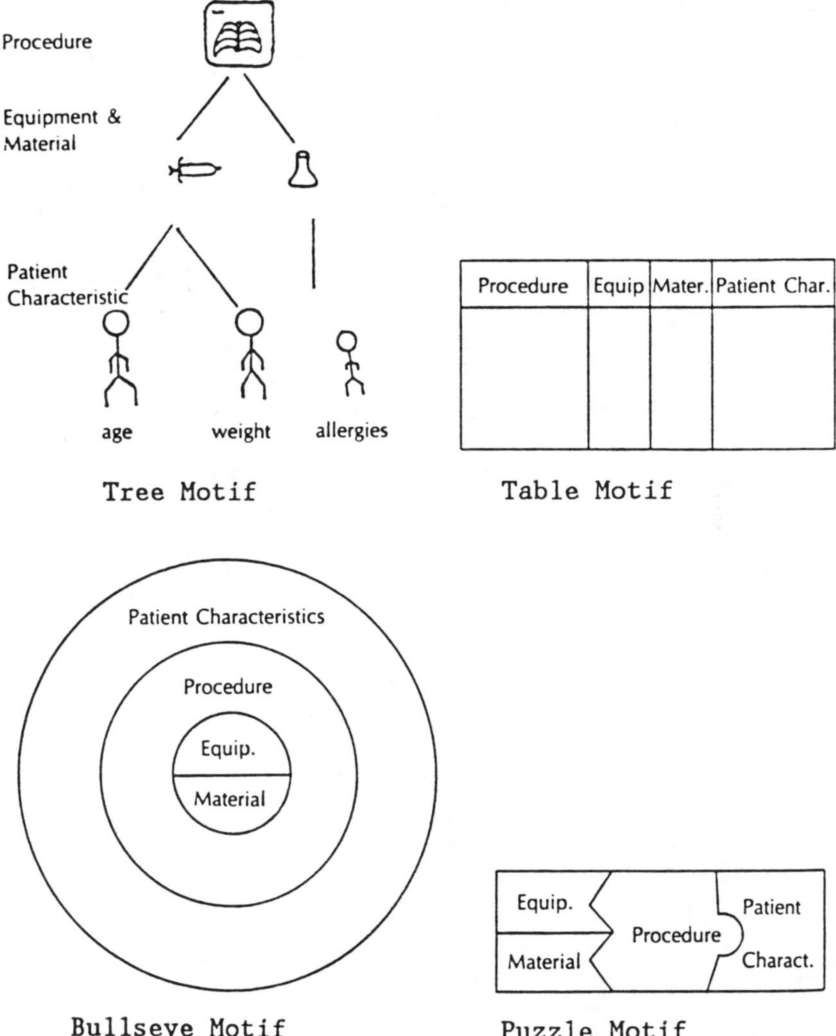

Figure 2-6. Four query motifs in VGQF.
(McDonald[10]. Reprinted with permission of Ablex Publishing Corp.)

video screen at the point where an item is displayed will stop the video sequence and select the item touched.

In several early experiences with using the system in a laboratory setting, McDonald reports that "system limitations in graphics caused an awkward design for user requests in video browsing."[10] Nevertheless, there is great promise in the use of various media additions to the human-machine interface.

VISUALIZATION OF DATA STRUCTURES

The systems that we discussed above represent a group of work intended for a person who is an infrequent or novice user with little or no programming expertise. Typically, users employ the system with a specific goal in mind. They need to find some information about an item for which no name is known. They are not skilled in the formal query languages provided by data management systems, and they have no idea of and no interest in how the data are structured and stored. For this group of users, the data-browsing facilities provided by the systems rely heavily on direct manipulation. *Visualization of data* plays a key role.

A second group of work is aimed at an entirely different user for a different purpose. The user is a programmer who has to deal with the intricacies of programming. The purpose is to provide a programming environment that enhances understanding. The emphasis is on visualization of data structures. Since data structures play a prominent role in programming, and since graphical representations found in every good textbook on data structures are known to be extremely useful, it is natural that the *visualization of data structures* is pursued. INCENSE and KAESTLE discussed below, represent two of these efforts.

INCENSE (a System for Displaying Data Structures)

At the Xerox Palo Alto Research Center, Brad Myers has developed a system, called INCENSE, for displaying data structures.[11] The project was motivated by the observation that many programming languages allow the programmer to define and use different data types, yet few programming systems allow similar flexibility when displaying these data structures in debugging, monitoring, and documenting programs.

Written in and for the Pascal-like language *Mesa,*[12] INCENSE allows the programmer to design and use pictorial representations for the display of data structures. Since a programmer may not want to define display forms for all (or possibly any) of the types used in his program, an extensive set of default forms is provided.

If desired, new forms of display can be created and associated with data structures. All input from the user is supplied by using the "mouse" to draw rectangles and to select or move displays. These user-defined forms can eliminate unnecessary details or more graphically depict the abstraction that the data structure is implementing. See Figure 2-7 for an example.

If a more radical change in a display form is desired, the user writes a program in Mesa defining the picture and associates it with a specific variable, a type, or a basic type.

The basic types of Mesa include STRINGs, INTEGERs, CARDINALs

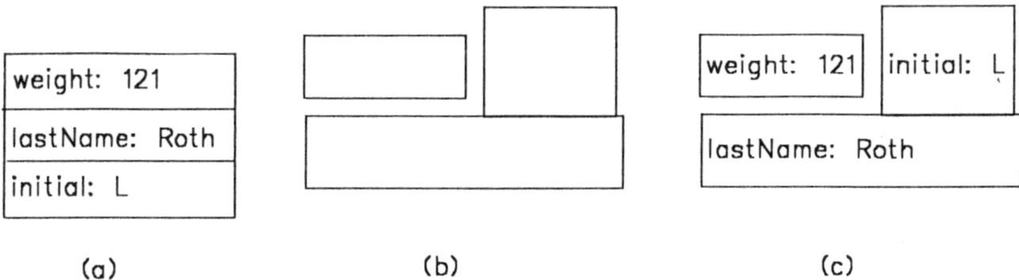

Figure 2-7. (a) Normal display for record; (b) form defined by user; (c) resulting display.

(positive INTEGERs), BOOLEANs, CHARACTERs, REALs, PROCEDUREs, UNSPECIFIEDS, WORDs, and Enumerated Types (lists of names, e.g., Mon, Tues, Wed, Thurs, Fri).

INCENSE can generate pictures for any data type during the execution of a Mesa program. The user need only specify at debug time the string name of a variable to get a pictorial display.

A typical programmer's notepad is often filled with pictorial sketches of data structures. A guiding principle of INCENSE is to automatically create displays that would be similar to those the programmer might have drawn on paper. Some examples of the displays are shown in Figure 2-8.

KAESTLE (a Graphic Editor for Lisp Data Structures)

The examples in Figure 2-8 show that a programmer's understanding of a problem can be enhanced by the pictorial representations of data structures. In his introduction to INCENSE, Myers stated, "Strongly typed languages, such as Pascal and Mesa, allow the programmer to define new types using the basic types supplied by the language. These new types can then be used to declare variables. Other languages, such as CLU[13] and Smalltalk,[14] have the definition of types and their operations as the central programming paradigm. A data display system like Incense would be a great asset to programmers using a language of either type."[11]

But, regardless of the underlying language type, a programmer's understanding of a problem can be enhanced through visualization of data structures is a well-recognized fact. For example, Lisp can be understood more readily when the pictures of data structures are drawn. "First, understanding list representation clears away some of the fog. Second, understanding list representation enables understanding certain functions that can surgically alter existing lists, such as NCONC, RPLACA, RPLACD, and DELETE."[15]

Aiming at exploiting the computer to provide visual information traditionally bound to paper and pencil, researchers at the University of Colorado and the University of Stuttgart, West Germany, launched a joint project. The group's

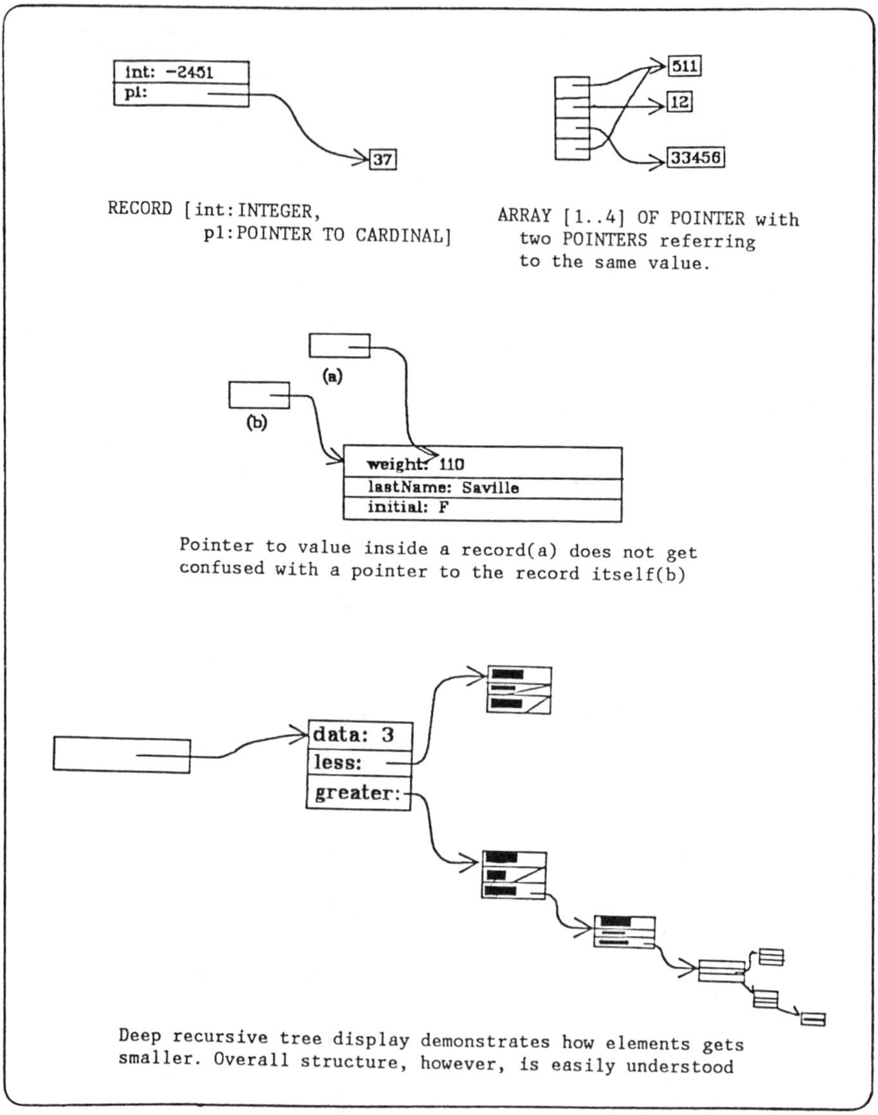

Figure 2-8. Examples of INCENSE displays.

long-range goal is to provide a "software oscilloscope" to the programmer, making the invisible visible.[16,17]

Among the collection of visualization tools developed by the Colorado/Stuttgart group is KAESTLE, a graphical editor for Lisp data structures.[18] With KAESTLE, the graphical representation of a list structure is generated

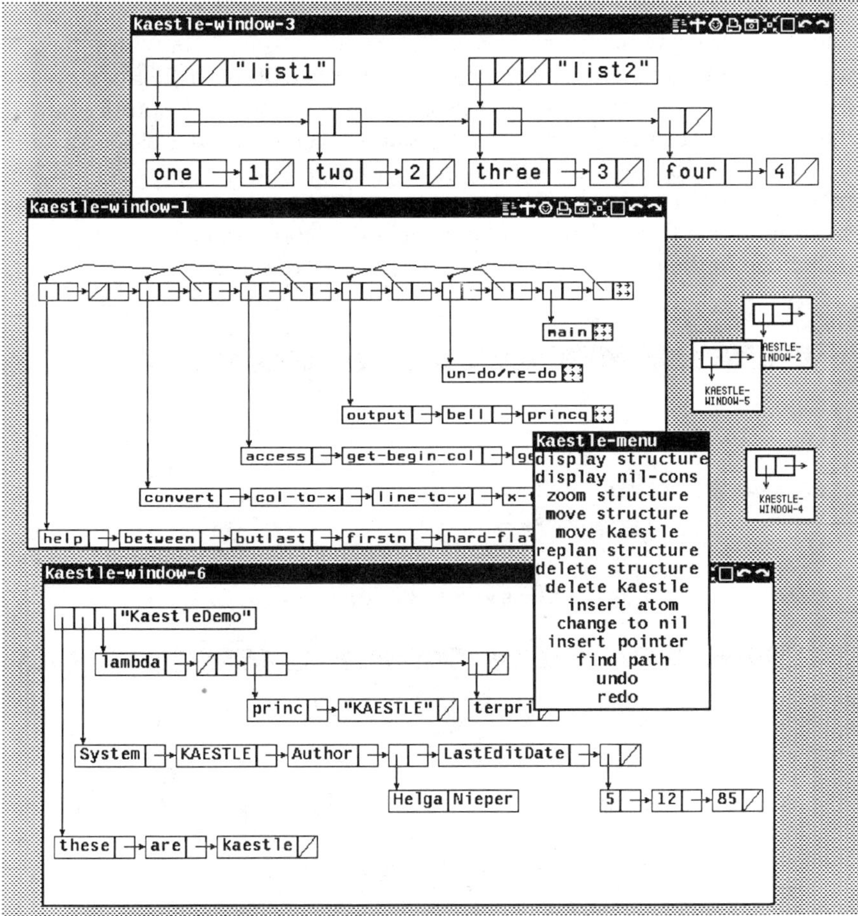

Figure 2-9. KAESTLE running in a window system.
(Boecker et al.[17]. Copyright © 1986 Association for Computing Machinery, Inc., reprinted by permission. Original art courtesy of H. Nieper.)

automatically and can be edited directly with a pointing device. KAESTLE is integrated in a window system. Multiple KAESTLE windows can be used at the same time. The user interface is menu based (see Figure 2-9).

The more experienced Lisp programmer can use KAESTLE to display and explore data structures which are difficult to represent symbolically, for example, circular and reentrant structures as seen in "kaestle-window-1" in Figure 2-9.

For the Lisp beginner, KAESTLE is a valuable tool for the understanding of certain aspects of the language which are difficult to explain otherwise.

For example, the difference between the nondestructive function *append* and the destructive function *nconc* is illustrated in Figure 2-10. With *append,* a copy is made of the first list, using spare memory cells from the free storage list, and then the second list is attached to the copy. *nconc,* on the other hand, puts two lists together by making a surgical change in the last cell in the first list, altering the value of any atom whose value is represented by a pointer into that first list. In the normal textual representation as seen in the window labeled "top level" (where the Lisp interpreter is running), no difference in the results of these two functions is revealed.

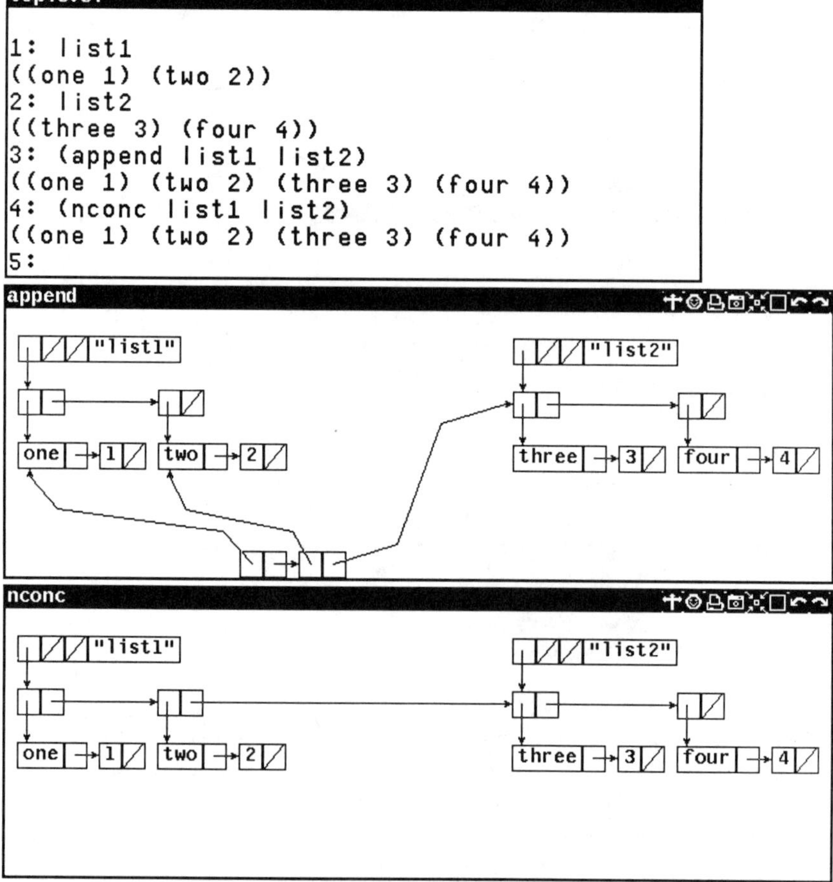

Figure 2-10. The Difference between *append* and *nconc.*
(Boecker et al.[17] Copyright © 1986 Association for Computing Machinery, Inc., Reprinted by permission. Original art courtesy of H. Nieper.)

Visualization of Database Schemas

From the visualization of data instances and data structures, it is natural that the next step is the visualization of database schemas.

In the past two decades, impressive progress has been made in providing users with fast, easy access to large volumes of actual data. Considerable less progress, however, has been made in the area of providing users with convenient access to database schemas. Most of the advances that have been made in the latter area are based on semantic database models. There are two reasons for this.

First, historically, semantic database models were originally introduced to facilitate the design of database schemas (e.g., Chen,[19] Hammer and McLeod[20]). At that time, the traditional database models (relational, hierarchical, and network) were gaining wide acceptance as efficient data management tools. The data structures used in these models are relatively close to those used for the physical representation of data in the computer. Conceptually, they are record oriented. Data are viewed ultimately as collections of records with printable or pointer field values. The structural component of the record-oriented models, however, is not sufficient to model accurately the different types of data relationships which arise frequently in database applications. Consequently, integrity constraints such as functional and inclusion dependencies must be used in conjunction with the structuring of a database. In other words, the semantics of a database are not readily apparent from the schema. They must be separately specified by the database designer and consciously applied by the user.

The limited expressiveness of the structural component of the record-oriented models has motivated the desire "to provide constructs for representing in a structural manner kinds of information which the relational model can represent only through constraints."[21] Semantic models were developed to provide a higher level of abstraction, allowing database designers and users to think of data in ways which correlate more directly with the way data arise in the world. Even without a full-fledged database management system based on semantic database models, a schema could first be designed in a high-level semantic model and then translated into hierarchical, network, or relational models for ultimate implementation.

Second, since a semantic model is more structured than a record-oriented model, a visual representation of a semantic schema is more expressive and thus conveys more information quickly. In fact, since semantic models are often explained with graphs drawn on paper, such a model is an obvious choice for capitalizing on the ability of graphic displays for exploring the semantic relationships in the schemas.

The field of semantic models is continuing to evolve. Hull and King, in their excellent 1986 review,[21] presented the fundamental concepts for semantic database modeling, surveyed the prominent and representative semantic models, and discussed various sorts of research activities which have involved or developed from the semantic database modeling. Providing graphical representations of semantic models in interactive database interfaces is an application derived from these activities. Based on various semantic database models, several experimental graphics-based interfaces have been proposed or prototyped as visual tools for schema browsing and/or definition. For example, *GUIDE* (a Graphical User Interface for Database Exploration)[22] is based on the ER (Entity-Relationship) model;[19] *DDEW* (the Database Design and Evaluation Workbench)[23] is based on the ER model extended to provide subtyping; *SKI* (the Semantics-Knowledgeable Interface)[24] and *ISIS* (Interface for a Semantic Information System)[25] support models that are functionally very similar to subsets of the Semantic Data Model (SDM)[20]; *SNAP* (a graphics-based schema manager)[26] supports the relatively complex IFO model (a formal semantic database model).[27]

All of the five above-mentioned systems present the schemas with graph structures. GUIDE and DDEW use ER diagrams. In GUIDE, the schema is statically structured and is not altered by the user. Schema definition is not supported. In DDEW, database schemas are represented as diagrams, which may be altered by the user with the aid of an editor. In SKI, the system controls the visual structure of the schema for the user. In SNAP and ISIS, the user identifies an object of interest by positioning the cursor over the object and pressing a mouse button. The system displays a pop-up menu with the applicable options for the selected object, and the user picks the desired option. In the case of SNAP, the selectable objects include schema nodes and edges, and the various windows and window borders. In ISIS, the selectable objects include various views of the schemas and the data contents.

ISIS is an experimental system, but it has the advantage of being a part of a larger effort at Brown University devoted to building a programming environment that explores visualization. Other components of Brown University's effort in building visual environments include BALSA (Brown and Sedgewick[28]), PECAN (Reiss[29]), and GARDEN system (Reiss[30]). In the following section, we describe ISIS in more detail to illuminate the fundamental concepts underlying the semantic model approach to the visualization of database schemas.

ISIS (Interface for a Semantic Information System)

Underlying Concepts. ISIS[25] supports a graphical interface to a modified subset of the Semantic Data Model (SDM).[20] Users create and manipulate *entities* when using an SDM database. An entity corresponds to an object in the application environment.

The most central concept in the SDM is that of a *class*. A class is a collection of homogeneous entities, all of the same type. Entities have associated *attributes*. An attribute is defined to have a *name* and a *value class*. A value class is some class in the SDM database from which the values of the attribute are drawn.

Classes can be related to each other via *interclass connections*. The two most common interclass connections are *subclass connections* and *grouping connections*.

A subclass connection represents a relationship between some class S and a class T that is constrained to contain a subset of the elements of S. T is said to be a subclass of S, and S is said to be a superclass of T. A class that has no superclasses is a *baseclass*. There are four predefined baseclasses: the Integers, the Reals, the Booleans (YES/NO), and the Strings.

A grouping connection is one that relates a class S to a grouping class T, where T contains sets of entities from S as members. In ISIS a grouping is allowed only on common values of an attribute.

Navigation is possible using the maps formed by attributes in the schema.

Members of a class are said to *inherit* the attributes from all of their superclasses. That is to say, if T is a subclass of S, all members of T will automatically be defined to have all those attributes that are defined on S, as well as the attributes of all the superclasses of S. In order to make the construction of the initial experimental version more tractable, ISIS limits the inheritance of a subclass to single-parent inheritance.

Graphical Representations. *Classes* have three parts: (1) a class name section (for baseclasses this is in reverse video); (2) a fill pattern unique to the class, which is provided automatically by the system; and (3) an attribute section containing a number of attributes. *Attribute,* in the class attribute section, contains the name and fill pattern of the value class. If an attribute is multivalued, this fill pattern is shown with a white border to signify that the attribute value is a set. *Groupings* are represented in the same way as classes, but they have no attribute sections, and their characteristic fill patterns have a white border to signify that their members are sets. *Maps* are represented by a stack of classes. These are the classes linked by the map attribute.

Various Views. ISIS operates at two levels: the *schema level* and the *data level*. Figure 2-11 illustrates how one moves among these levels during a database session. The data level provides views of the data. The schema level provides views of the schema. These views are the inheritance forest, the semantic network, and the predicate worksheet.

In the *inheritance forest view,* ISIS shows tree structures representing interclass connections (i.e., the superclass/subclass and the grouping

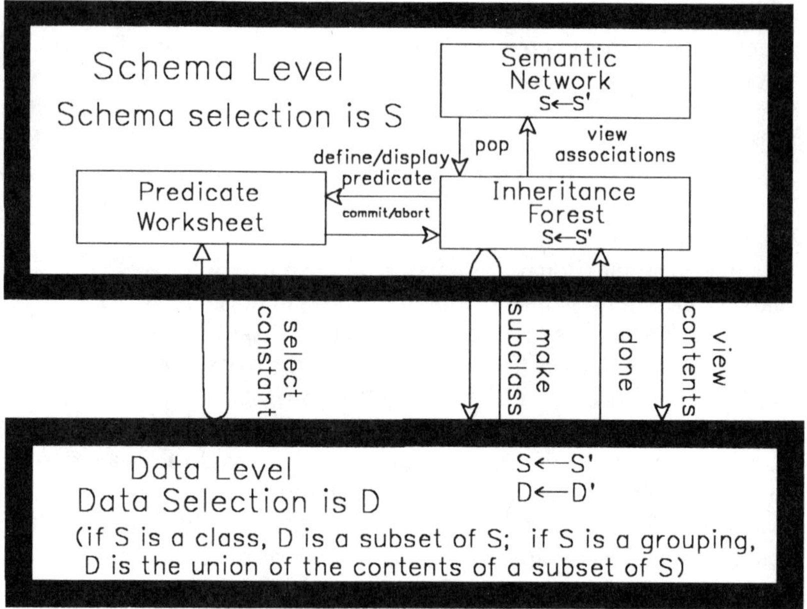

Figure 2-11. Moving between schema and data.

relationships). Each node in this view corresponds to a class and is shown with a system-created fill pattern. Nodes also contain the names of the attributes defined on the associated class, along with the fill pattern of the value class of each attribute.

An inheritance forest view of a sample schema is shown in Figure 2-12.

The database *Instrumental_music* has baseclasses *musicians, music-group, instrument,* and *families* (shown left to right in reverse video). A closer look reveals that the baseclass *musicians* has three attributes: *stage_name* (providing names for the entities); *plays* (a multivalued attribute with the value class *instruments,* indicating the set of instruments that each musician plays); and *union* (which maps into the YES/NO class, indicating whether or not the given musician belongs to the musicians' union).

The groupings *by_instrument* and *work_status* group the *musicians* according to the instruments they play and according to whether or not they are union members.

The subclass *play_strings* has an attribute, *in_group,* which maps into the *YES/NO* class and indicates whether or not the string player is the value of the *members* attribute of some entity in the class *music_group*. The *play_strings* subclass also has an associated grouping, *by_in_group,* which groups musicians on the basis of the attribute in_group. The subclass *soloists* is user defined (i.e., formed by hand-picking entities from the parent class).

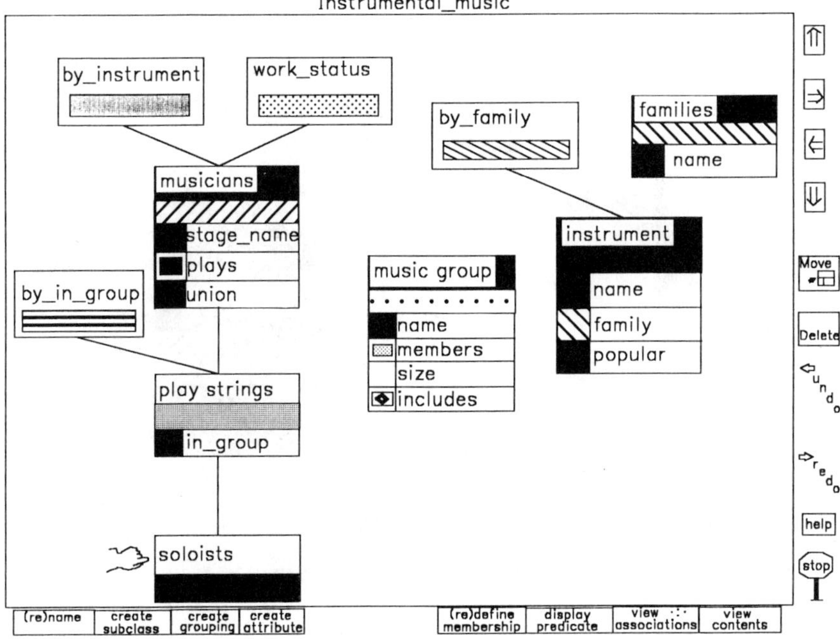

Figure 2-12. The inheritance forest view (with soloist as the schema selection.)

The baseclass *music_group* has four attributes: *name* (name of the *music_group*); *members* (a multivalued attribute which maps into the class *musicians* and represents the members of the given music group); *size* (which has the value class *INTEGER* and is the number of members in the group); and *includes* (which maps into the class *families* and contains the families of instruments that are played by the music group).

The baseclass *instrument* has three attributes: *name* (name of the given instrument); *family* (which maps into the class *families* and is the family of the instrument); and *popular* (an attribute mapping into the *YES/NO* class). The grouping *by_family* partitions the instruments into sets according to their *family* attribute.

The baseclass *families* contains types of instruments (e.g., brass) and has the attribute *name*.

From the inheritance forest view, one may move to the semantic network view by picking the *view associations* button (shown beneath the inheritance forest view in Figure 2-12).

The *semantic network view* is an alternative view at the schema level. It shows an entity class, all the attributes defined on it, and all the classes which map to it. An example is shown in Figure 2-13. The semantic network view

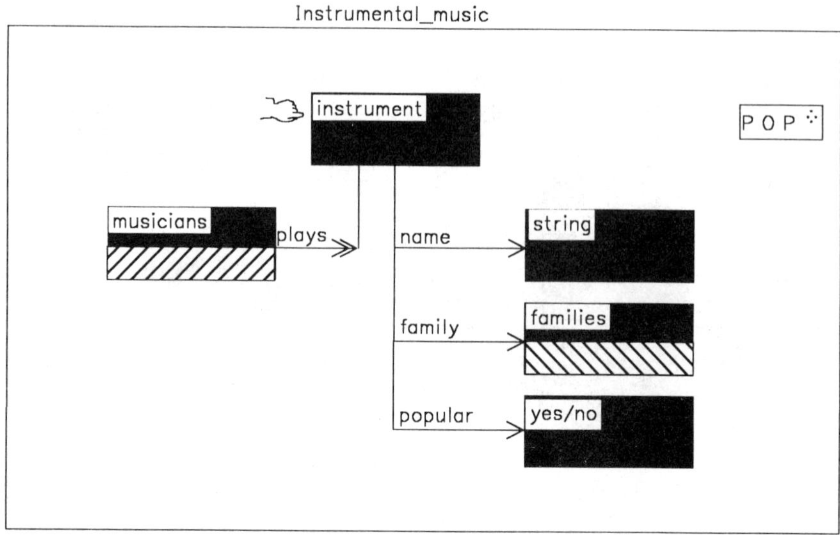

Figure 2-13. The semantic network view (with instrument as the schema selection).

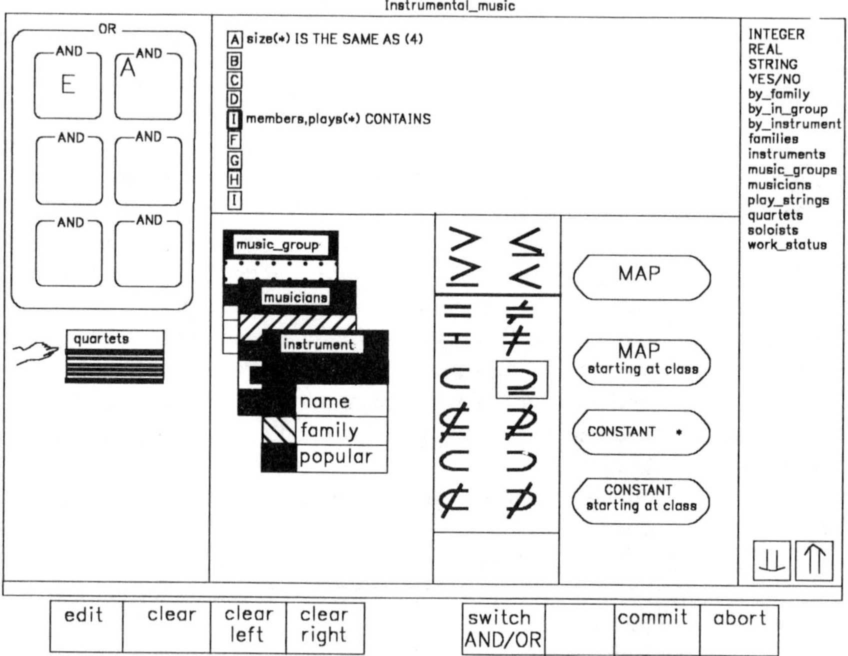

Figure 2-14. Constructing a predicate to define the membership of the quartets class.

may be used for navigation in the schema. At any point, one may *pop* back to the inheritance forest view with the new schema selection.

The *predicate worksheet* is used to define the membership of a class. An example is shown in Figure 2-14. This mechanism is useful when a user decides to formulate a query and store the result as a user-defined subclass. One moves from the inheritance forest view to the predicate worksheet by picking the *(re)define membership* or the *display predicate* button, and from the predicate worksheet back to the inheritance forest view by using *commit* or *abort*.

Buttons are also provided for moving between the inheritance forest view and the data contents. Figure 2-15 shows the result of selecting *oboe* from the *instruments* class at the data level.

In summary, ISIS allows users to construct schemas, to become familiar with the organization of a database by browsing through the database at both the schema and data levels, and to formulate queries that can be stored as part of the schema and reused at some later time. It exemplifies the research efforts that focus on visualization of database schemas to support database programming.

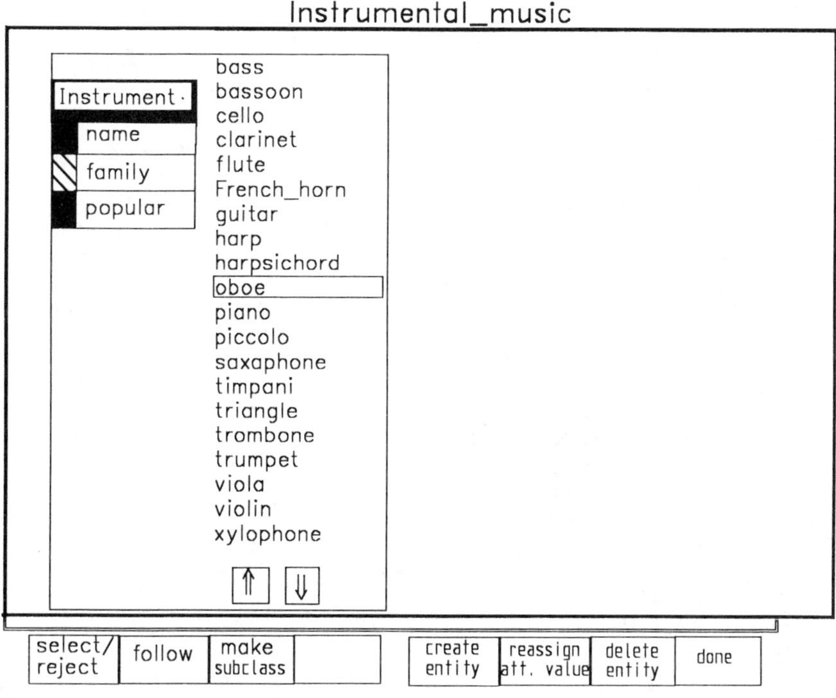

Figure 2-15. Selecting the entity oboe from the instrument class at the data level.

REFERENCES

1. Foley, J. D., Wallace, V. L., and Chan, P., "The Human Factors of Computer Graphics Interaction Techniques," *IEEE Computer Graphics and Applications,* Vol. 4, No. 11 (Nov. 1984), pp. 13-48.
2. Sutherland, I. E., "Computer Displays," *Scientific American* (June 1970), pp. 57-81.
3. Fields, C., and Negroponte, N., "Using New Clues to Find Data," *Proceedings of the Conference on Very Large Databases* (Oct. 1977)
4. Donelson, W. C., "Spatial Management of Information," *Proceedings of ACM SIGGRAPH '78* (Aug. 1978), pp. 203-209.
5. Herot, C. F., "Spatial Management of Data,"*ACM Transactions on Database Systems,* Vol. 5, No. 4 (Dec. 1980), pp. 493-514.
6. Held, G. D., Stonebraker, M. R., and Wong, E., "INGRES—A Relational Database System," *Proceedings of AFIPS,* Vol. 44 (1975), pp. 409-416.
7. Herot, C. F., "Graphical User Interfaces," in *Human Factors and Interactive Computer Systems,* edited by Y. Vissiliou, Ablex Publishing Corp. (1984), pp. 83-103.
8. Friedell, M., Barnett, J., and Kramlich, D., "Context-Sensitive Graphic Presentation of Information," *ACM Computer Graphics,* Vol. 16, No. 3 (July 1982), pp. 181-188.
9. Friedell, M., "Automatic Synthesis of Graphical Object Descriptions," *ACM Computer Graphics,* Vol. 18, No. 3 (July 1984), pp. 53-62.
10. McDonald, N. H., "A Multi Media Approach to the User Interface," in *Human Factors and Interactive Computer Systems,* edited by Y. Vissiliou, Ablex Publishing Corp. (1984), pp. 105-116.
11. Myers, B. A., "INCENSE: A System for Displaying Data Structures," *ACM Computer Graphics,* Vol. 17, No. 3 (July 1983), pp. 115-125.
12. Mitchell, J., et al., "Mesa Language Manual, Version 5.0," Xerox PARC CSL-79-3 (1979).
13. Liskov, B., Snyder, A., Atkinson, R., and Schaffert, C., "Abstract Mechanisms in CLU," *Communications of the ACM,* Vol. 20, No. 8 (Aug. 1977), pp. 564-576.
14. Shoch, J. F., "An Overview of the Programming Language Smalltalk-72," *ACM Sigplan Notices,* Vol. 14, No. 9 (Sept. 1979), pp. 64-73.
15. Winston, P. H., and Horn, B. K. P., *LISP,* Addison-Wesley Publishing Company, Inc. (1981).
16. Boecker, H.-D., and Nieper, H., "Making the Invisible Visible: Tools for Exploratory Programming," *Proceedings of the First Pan Pacific Computer Conference,* The Australian Computer Society, Melbourne, Australia (Sept. 1985).
17. Boecker, H.-D., Fischer, G., and Nieper, H., "The Enhancement of Understanding through Visual Representations," *Proceedings of the CHI'86 Conference, Human Factors in Computing Systems* (Aug. 1986), pp. 44-50.
18. Nieper, H., "KAESTLE: Ein graphischer Editor fuer LISP-Datenstrukturen," Studienarbeit Nr. 347, Institut fuer Informatik, Universitaet Stuttgart (1983).
19. Chen, P., "The Entity-Relationship Model—Toward a Unified View of Data," *ACM Transactions on Database Systems,* Vol. 1, No. 1 ((Mar. 1976), pp. 9-36.
20. Hammer, M., and McLeod, D., "Database Description with SDM: A Semantic Database Model," *ACM Transactions on Database Systems,* Vol. 6, No. 3 (Sept. 1981), pp. 351-386.
21. Hull, R., and King, R., "Semantic Database Modeling: Survey, Applications, and Research Issues," University of Southern California, Computer Science Department Technical Report TR-86-201 (1986).
22. Wong, H. K. T., and Kuo, I., "GUIDE: A Graphical User Interface for Database Exploration," *Proceedings of the Conference on Very Large Databases* (1982), pp. 22-32.
23. Reiner, D., Brodie, M., Brown, G., Friedell, M., Kramlich, D., Lehman, J., and Rosenthal, A., "The Database Design and Evaluation Workbench (DDEW) Project at CCA," *Bulletin*

of IEEE Technical Committee on Database Engineering, Vol. 7, No. 4 (Dec. 1984), pp. 10-15.

24. King, R., and Melville, S., "The Semantics-Knowledgeable Interface," *Proceedings of the Conference on Very Large Databases* (1984), pp. 30-37.
25. Goldman, K. J., Goldman, S. A., Kanellakis, P. C., and Zdonik, S. B., "ISIS: Interface for a Semantic Information System," *Proceedings of ACM SIGMOD International Conference on the Management of Data* (May 1985), pp. 328-342.
26. Bryce, D., and Hull, R., "SNAP: A Graphics-Based Schema Manager," *Proceedings of the Second IEEE International Conference on Data Engineering* (Feb. 1986), pp. 151-164.
27. Abiteboul, S., and Hull, R., "IFO: A Formal Semantic Database Model," Technical Report TR-84-304. University of Southern California, Computer Science Department
28. Brown, M. H., and Sedgewick, R., "A System for Algorithm Animation," *ACM Computer Graphics,* Vol. 18, No. 3 (July 1984), pp. 177-186.
29. Reiss, S. P., "PECAN: Program Development Systems that Support Multiple Views," *IEEE Transactions on Software Engineering,* Vol. SE-11, No. 3 (Mar. 1985), pp. 276-285.
30. Reiss, S. P., "Working in the Garden Environment for Conceptual Programming," *IEEE Software,* Vol. 6, No. 6 (Nov. 1987), pp. 16-27.

Chapter 3

Visualization of Programs and Execution

Developing technical skill is not merely a matter of learning a long list of facts. Rather, developing technical skill is an effort to learn the underlying structure of the knowledge domain.

Curtis et al.[1]

Elliot Soloway, in urging for a revised curriculum for introductory computer programming courses, reported the following observation:

> Textbooks used in introductory programming courses typically focus on the syntax and semantics of constructs in a language. New research with novice programmers, however, suggests that language constructs do not pose major stumbling blocks for novices learning to program. Rather, the real problems novices have lie in "putting the pieces together," composing and coordinating components of a program.[2]

Taking this view, "learning to program amounts to learning how to construct mechanisms and how to construct explanations." Continuing with this line of reasoning, one may generalize that "the products of the programming process are really mechanisms and explanations."[2]

The mechanism is for the computer. The instructions in a program dictate how a problem can be solved. The explanation is for the human audience. Any person who writes, tests, debugs, changes, or maintains a program needs to understand why the program solves the given problem.

Visualization of programs and execution help to manifest these artifacts. The goal is to provide programmers or users in general with an understanding of what the programs do, how they work, why they work, and what are the effects. This is beneficial not only to beginners just learning to program, but also to professionals dealing with various aspects of programming tasks: designing, debugging, testing, and modification.

Activities in this area span a wide spectrum, ranging from pretty-printing the source code to watching the execution of a program in animated forms.

In the following, we discuss a few representative systems to show the diversity in the approaches.

PRETTY-PRINTING

From its beginning, "pretty-printing" has meant the enhanced presentation of program source code. The primary motivation is to bring out the program structure in a vivid form so that the program is made more readable, more understandable, and less error prone.

At a time when the graphics tools were rather limited, the work on pretty-printing concentrated on various levels of program identation, well-placed commenting, blank-line insertion, and methods of extending the programming languages to include formatting conventions.[3-8]

More recently, prompted by the advances in the high-resolution bit map displays, laser printers, and computer-driven photosetters, Baecker and Marcus[9] have focused on the enhanced presentation beyond the conventional scope of pretty-printing. Their approach is to employ graphical design principles in conjunction with advanced display facilities to produce far richer representations of program source text than were previously possible on a line printer. This is done by using multiple fonts, variable point sizes, variable character widths, proportionate character spacing, nonalphanumeric symbols, gray scale tints, rules, and arbitrary spatial location of elements on a page.[9]

For their work, Baecker and Marcus have developed the *SEE visual compiler* for the programming language *C*. Driving a laser printer equipped with an appropriate set of fonts, the SEE processor takes a C program as input and produces a greatly enhanced presentation of the same program as an output. As an example, Figure 3-1 shows the listing of the second page of a desk calculator program. Figure 3-2 shows the first three pages of the same C program as output by the SEE processor.

Enhanced program presentation is not without its difficulties. As pointed out by Baecker and Marcus, "Visual compilers need to be highly parameterized since optimum program appearance is a highly individualistic and contentious issue. Visual compilation is also expensive, although wasted programmer time is more expensive. Finally, we cannot yet prove with hard empirical evidence that these methods of display make programs more readable, comprehensible, and maintainable."[9] Nevertheless, Figures 3-1 and 3-2 provide evidence that a very dull listing of the program text could be made a lot more vivid and interesting.

VISUALIZATION THROUGH DIAGRAMS

Flow charts and diagrams have, for a long time, provided a static means of showing the flow of control through a program. However, until the recent

```
/*                         Stack Management Module                          */

#define MAXVAL 100          /* maximum depth of val stack */

int sp = 0;                 /* stack pointer */
double val[MAXVAL];         /* value stack */

double push(f)              /* push f onto value stack */
double f;
{
        if (sp < MAXVAL)
                return (val[sp++] = f);
        else {
             printf("error: stack full\n");
             clear();
             return(0);
        }
}

double pop()                /* pop top value from stack */
{
        if (sp > 0)
                return(val[--sp]);
        else {
             printf("error: stack empty\n");
             clear();
             return(0);
        }
}

clear()                     /* clear stack */
{
        sp = 0;
}


/*                              Input Module                                */

getop(s, lim)               /* get next operator or operand */
char s[];                   /* operator buffer */
int lim;                    /* size of input buffer */
{
        int i, c;

        /* skip blanks, tabs and newlines */

        while ((c = getch()) == ' ' || c == '\t' || c == '\n')
                ;

        /* return if not a number */

        if (c != '.' && (c < '0' || c > '9'))
                return(c);
        s[0] = c;

        /* get rest of number */

        for (i = 1; (c = getchar()) >= '0' && c <= '9'; i++)
                if (i < lim)
                        s[i] = c;
```

Figure 3-1. Listing of a C program.
(Baecker and Marcus[9]. Copyright © 1986 Association for Computing Machinery, Inc., reprinted by permission.)

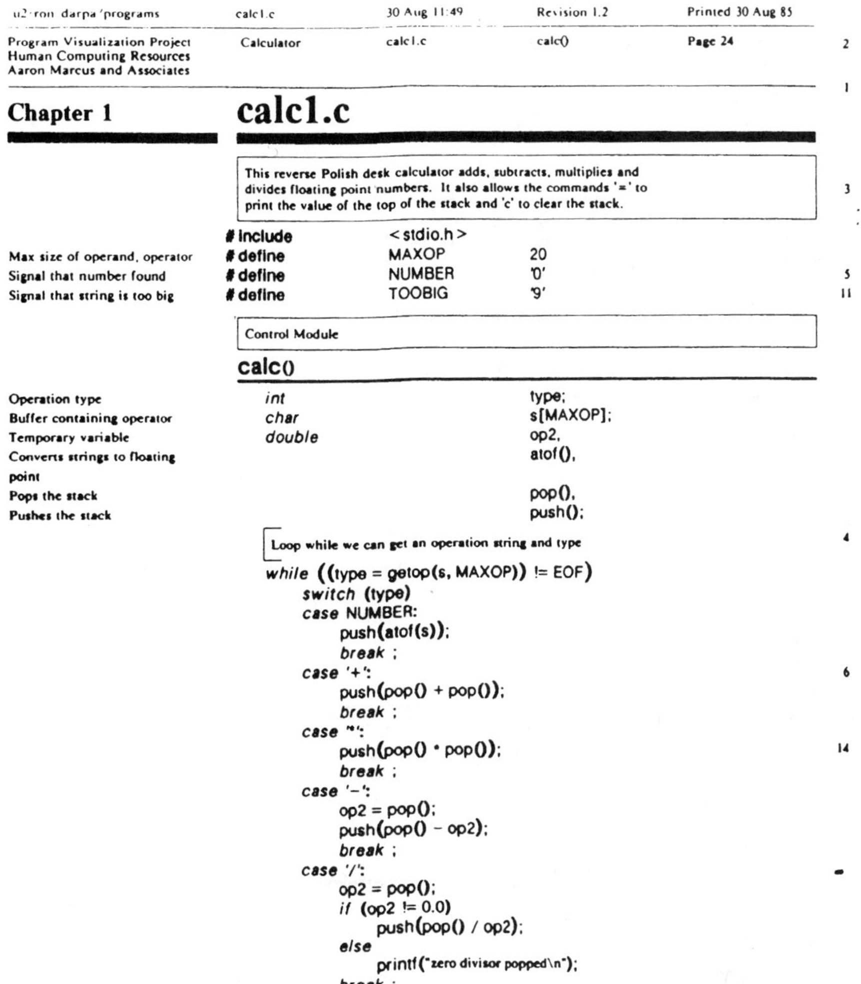

u2:ron darpa/programs | calc1.c | 30 Aug 11:49 | Revision 1.2 | Printed 30 Aug 85

Program Visualization Project | Calculator | calc1.c | calc() | Page 24 2
Human Computing Resources
Aaron Marcus and Associates

1

Chapter 1 **calc1.c**

This reverse Polish desk calculator adds, subtracts, multiplies and divides floating point numbers. It also allows the commands '=' to print the value of the top of the stack and 'c' to clear the stack. 3

```
                                  #include  <stdio.h>
Max size of operand, operator     #define   MAXOP     20
Signal that number found          #define   NUMBER    '0'      5
Signal that string is too big     #define   TOOBIG    '9'      11
```

Control Module

calc()

```
Operation type                    int       type;
Buffer containing operator        char      s[MAXOP];
Temporary variable                double    op2,
Converts strings to floating                atof(),
point
Pops the stack                              pop(),
Pushes the stack                            push();
```

Loop while we can get an operation string and type 4

```
while ((type = getop(s, MAXOP)) != EOF)
    switch (type)
    case NUMBER:
        push(atof(s));
        break ;
    case '+':                                           6
        push(pop() + pop());
        break ;
    case '*':
        push(pop() * pop());                            14
        break ;
    case '-':
        op2 = pop();
        push(pop() - op2);
        break ;
    case '/':
        op2 = pop();
        if (op2 != 0.0)
            push(pop() / op2);
        else
            printf("zero divisor popped\n");
        break ;
```

Figure 3-2. Output produced by SEE.
(Baecker and Marcus[9]. Copyright © 1986 Association for Computing Machinery, Inc., reprinted by permission.)

dramatic decline in computing costs, the high costs of graphic terminals and the large data storage needed to hold the graphic representation of a program kept flow charts and diagrams mainly on paper.

The advantages of showing programs in diagrammatic forms are nevertheless well recognized. Thus, as the costs of computation and memory plummeted, the efforts to display programs in graphical forms picked up momentum. Two of these attempts are briefly discussed in the following.

```
u2 ron/darpa/programs          calc1.c       30 Aug 11:49   Revision 1.2   Printed 30 Aug 85
---------------------------------------------------------------------------------------------
Program Visualization Project  Calculator    calc1.c        calc()         Page 25
Human Computing Resources
Aaron Marcus and Associates
---------------------------------------------------------------------------------------------
                          case '=':
                               printf("\t%f\n", push(pop()));
                               break ;
                          case 'c':
                               clear();
                               break ;
                          case TOOBIG:
                               printf("%.20s ... is too long\n", s);
                               break ;
                          default :
                               printf("unknown command %c\n", type);
                               break ;

                   | Stack Management Module |

Maximum depth of val stack  #define    MAXVAL        100                 12
Stack pointer               int                      sp = 0;             13
Value stack                 double                   val[MAXVAL];

                            double                                       22
Push f onto value stack     push(f)
                            ____________________________________________
                              double                 f;
                              ______________________________________
                              if (sp < MAXVAL)                            9
                         ☞          return (val[sp++] = f);
                              else
                                    printf("error: stack full\n");       10
                                    clear();
                         ☞          return (0);

                            double
Pop top value from stack    pop()
                            ____________________________________________
                              if (sp > 0)
                         ☞          return (val[--sp]);                  23
                              else
                                    printf("error: stack empty\n");
                                    clear();
                         ☞          return (0);

Clear stack                 clear()
                            ____________________________________________
                              sp = 0;
```

Figure 3-2. *(continued)*

A Visual Syntax Editor for Lisp

To make Lisp programs more readable, Levien[10] has implemented a "Visual Syntax Editor." "Visual Syntax is an editor for Lisp that displays programs as pictures with all data paths marked with arrows. . . . With Visual Syntax, you can scan through the entire library of Lisp functions and see intuitively how the functions work."[10]

As an example, Figure 3-3 shows a diagram displayed by the Visual Syntax Editor when the user types (edv '(* (+ 2 3) 4)). Note that the arrow takes the value on the left to the function on the right. Functions are in boxes, values are not. Also, to see the diagrammatic representation of the expression, the apostrophe before the expression is important. Without it, Lisp will evaluate

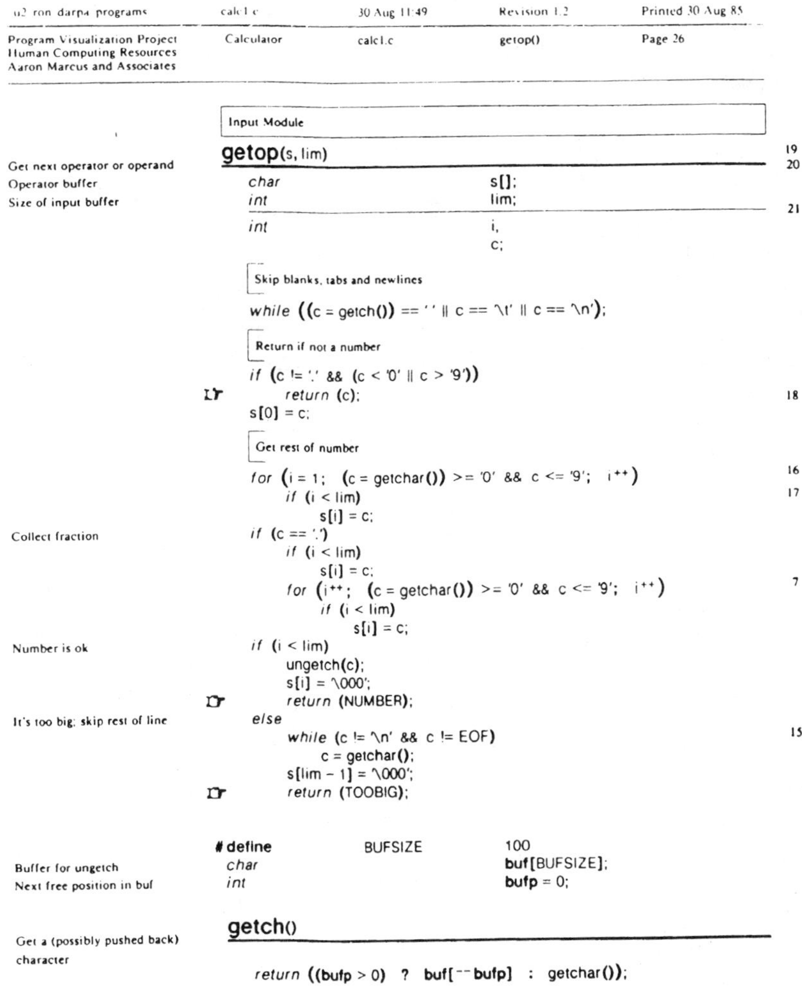

u2 ron darpa programs	calc1.c	30 Aug 11:49	Revision 1.2	Printed 30 Aug 85
Program Visualization Project Human Computing Resources Aaron Marcus and Associates	Calculator	calc1.c	getop()	Page 26

```
Input Module

getop(s, lim)                                                        19
                                   Get next operator or operand      20
    char        s[];               Operator buffer
    int         lim;               Size of input buffer              21
    int         i,
                c;

    Skip blanks, tabs and newlines
    while ((c = getch()) == ' ' || c == '\t' || c == '\n');

    Return if not a number
    if (c != '.' && (c < '0' || c > '9'))
        return (c);                                                  18
    s[0] = c;

    Get rest of number
    for (i = 1;  (c = getchar()) >= '0' && c <= '9';  i++)           16
        if (i < lim)                                                 17
            s[i] = c;
    if (c == '.')                  Collect fraction
        if (i < lim)
            s[i] = c;
        for (i++;  (c = getchar()) >= '0' && c <= '9';  i++)          7
            if (i < lim)
                s[i] = c;
    if (i < lim)                   Number is ok
        ungetch(c);
        s[i] = '\000';
        return (NUMBER);
    else                           It's too big; skip rest of line
        while (c != '\n' && c != EOF)                                15
            c = getchar();
        s[lim - 1] = '\000';
        return (TOOBIG);

#define     BUFSIZE     100
char        buf[BUFSIZE];          Buffer for ungetch
int         bufp = 0;              Next free position in buf

getch()                            Get a (possibly pushed back) character
    return ((bufp > 0)  ?  buf[--bufp]  :  getchar());
```

Figure 3-2. *(continued)*

the expression and the Visual Syntax Editor will display the result of evaluation, in this case, 20.

Similarly, Figure 3-4 shows the diagrammatic forms for the *CAR* and the *CDR* of the list (John is a good boy). For those who are not familiar with Lisp, *CAR* is a function that, upon evaluation, returns the first element of the given list, and *CDR* is a function that returns a list containing all but the first element.

Figure 3-5 shows a more complicated Lisp program as displayed in Visual Syntax. This program defines a Fibonacci function (called FIB) which

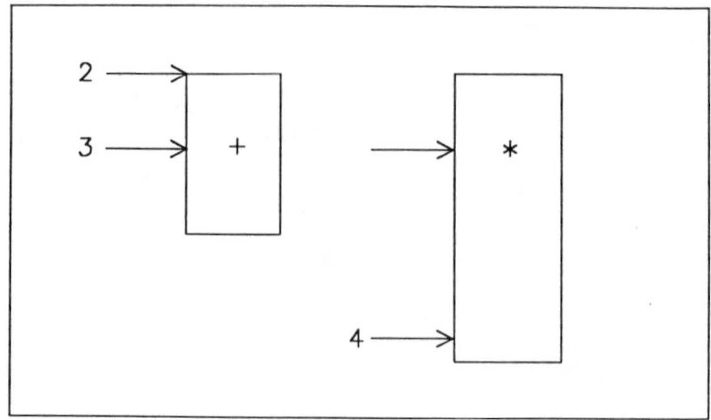

Figure 3-3. (* (+ 2 3) 4) displayed in Visual Syntax.

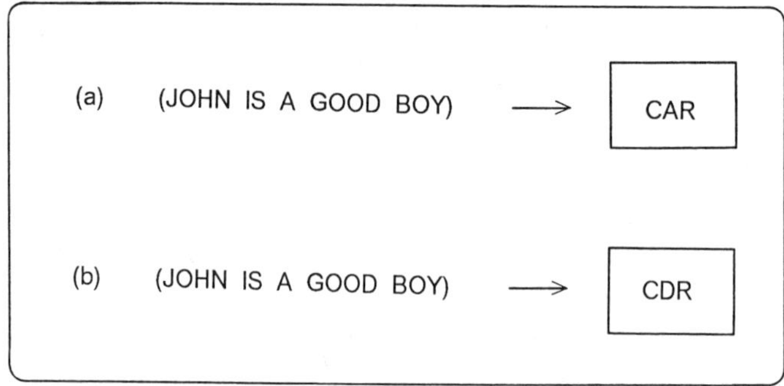

Figure 3-4. CAR and CDR of the list (John is a good boy) displayed in diagrammatic form.

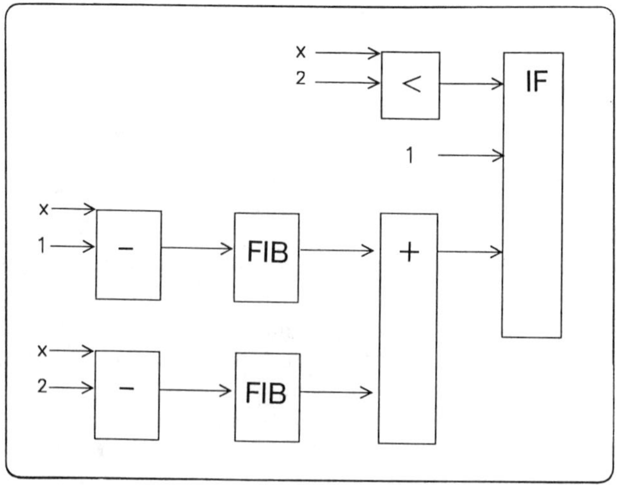

Figure 3-5. FIB function displayed in a diagram.

returns a value from the Fibonacci sequence for a given argument. In the Fibonacci sequence (0:*n*), the first two elements are 1 and the rest of the elements are the sum of the previous two elements (i.e., 1, 1, 2, 3, 5, 8, 13, . . .).The Fibonacci function of *x* is simply the *x*th value (counting from 0) in the sequence. For example, when 4 is given as an argument, FIB returns the value of 5.

The Lisp program which defines the Fibonacci function is (defun FIB(x) (if (< × 2) 1 (+ (FIB (− × 1)) (FIB (− × 2))))). As displayed in Visual Syntax, the function has one argument, *x*. The IF function tests the Boolean value of the first argument and returns either the value of the second or the third argument, depending on whether the value of the first argument is true or false. Therefore, in the FIB function, if (< × 2) is true, the result is 1; otherwise the result is (+ (FIB (− × 1)) (FIB (− × 2))).

In addition to the display of Lisp programs in diagrammatic forms, the Visual Syntax Editor allows the user to create, modify and edit the displayed diagrams, or to view the programs in the conventional Lisp notations with all the parentheses. Input to the editor is entirely through the keyboard. The process of creating and modifying the diagrams is not simple. The system is better used for simply viewing the Lisp programs in diagrams displayed by the Visual Syntax.

A Graphically Interacting Program Monitor for Pascal

Using *Pascal* as the host language, Clark and Robinson [11] have implemented a program monitor that can derive graphical representations (in Nassi-Shneiderman chart form[12]) from the control structures of Pascal programs.

The system comprises a preprocessing analysis stage, followed by a compilation. The monitor process is activated by a call inserted at the beginning of the revised program. Diagrams representing the Pascal program being monitored are drawn at runtime, and the current locus of control is marked to indicate the progress of control through the program.

Control over the amount of detail shown on the screen is exercised by considering each statement as existing within a context. The context is determined by the surrounding statements. For example, an assignment statement might exist in the simple context of a program or the complex context of a conditional statement.

Four levels of context can be defined by the user:

0. No internal detail of a block.
1. Structure only.
2. Structure plus control statements (e.g., iterative control).
3. All statements.

At runtime, the statement context is compared with the user-selected context to determine if the statement detail should be added to the diagram being shown.

According to Clark and Robinson, "The initial system, implemented at Brunel University (at Middlesex, UK), has been demonstrated to a number of potential users, from differing computer backgrounds. They have all found the diagrams easy to comprehend, and have been quick to relate the use of the system to their own environment.[11]

MULTIPLE VIEWS OF A PROGRAM AND ITS EXECUTION STATES

One of the most important impetuses for visualization of programs and their execution is to assist in the programming process itself. In the previous two sections, we have seen that pretty-printing can enhance the readability of a program and that diagrammatic representations can further improve program comprehension.

However, design, analysis, implementation, and maintenance of a program involve mental activities based not only on the appearance of a program but also on the observations of how a program works, why it works, how the components are put together, what effects they have on each other, and so on.

In other words, to assist in the programming process, a tool that provides multiple views of a program and its execution states would be more effective than a tool that focuses only on the program text. Some of the insights that one might derive from multiple views cannot be obtained from analysis of a single view.

Many interactive programming environments support multiple views. In fact, multiple-window systems, pervasive in the interactive environment, are designed precisely with multiple views in mind. However, as we mentioned earlier, not all window systems deal with the programming process and, even when they are used for programming, they do not necessarily contain graphical expressions. For example, many of the multiple-window systems are developed for document preparation and office automation, not for programming in the usual sense.

In other words, windowing and visual programming are orthogonal concepts. One may deal with visual programming without multiple windows or having multiple windows without using them for visual programming. When they overlap, the combined effect of having multiple windows and visual representations is indeed rewarding. But, for the purpose of this book, we can simply think of windows as allocated spaces on the screen in which related (or unrelated) objects and events can be effectively viewed, controlled, and coordinated. The actual mechanism of window management is beyond the scope of this book. What is important for us is the basic concepts that they carry.

For the visualization of multiple views of a program and its execution states, many recent efforts have been reported in the literature—for example, the Interlisp[13] and the Cedar[14] environments of Xerox, Magpie[15] of Tektronix, Inc., the PECAN[16] and GARDEN[17] systems of Brown University, CMU Tutor[18] of Carnegie-Mellon University, and VIPS, a visual debugger[19] of NTT, Japan, to name only a few. We discuss two examples in the following sections. The first one is suited for the "exploratory programming" style, while the second is geared to the "structured programming" approach.

Multiple Views in an Exploratory Programming Environment: The Xerox Interlisp System

Several interactive programming environments have been developed at the Xerox Palo Alto Research Center. Among them are the Smalltalk system,[20] the Interlisp environment,[13] the Mesa,[21] and the more recent Cedar[14,22] environment. They all support multiple views in an interactive programming environment. Although they differ from each other in one or more respects, to describe them all would be redundant, given the basic ideas that we wish to convey. Therefore, only one will be focused on.

As Teitelman stated, albeit in a different context, "There is no good objective way to evaluate a programming environment, no way of certifying that it 'works.' There are no solutions, only choices."[22] The Interlisp environment is chosen as the focus of this section mainly because, among the four environments just mentioned, Interlisp provides the sharpest contrast with PECAN, the system to be presented in the next section.

The contrast lies fundamentally in the style of programming and the type of the user community.

Interlisp is a programming environment developed for Lisp programmers. It has been used to develop and implement a wide variety of applications, including but not limited to solving artificial intelligence problems. Many of the Lisp applications have one characteristic in common: it is extremely difficult to give complete specifications because the user (often a researcher or a small team playing the roles of both the designer and the implementor) does not know and cannot anticipate what is required. For these problems, programming meant experimenting with various solutions and seeing how they work. A program invariably has to be restructured many times before it becomes reasonably proficient.

Beau Sheil calls this style of programming "*exploratory programming,* the conscious intertwining of system design and implementation."[23] Interlisp evolved in response to the need for a programming environment that facilitates this exploratory style. It allows the design to emerge from experimentation with the program, so that the design and the program evolve together.

The user community of Interlisp "tends to view change as an integral and desirable part of the program development cycle. . . . The Lisp programmer

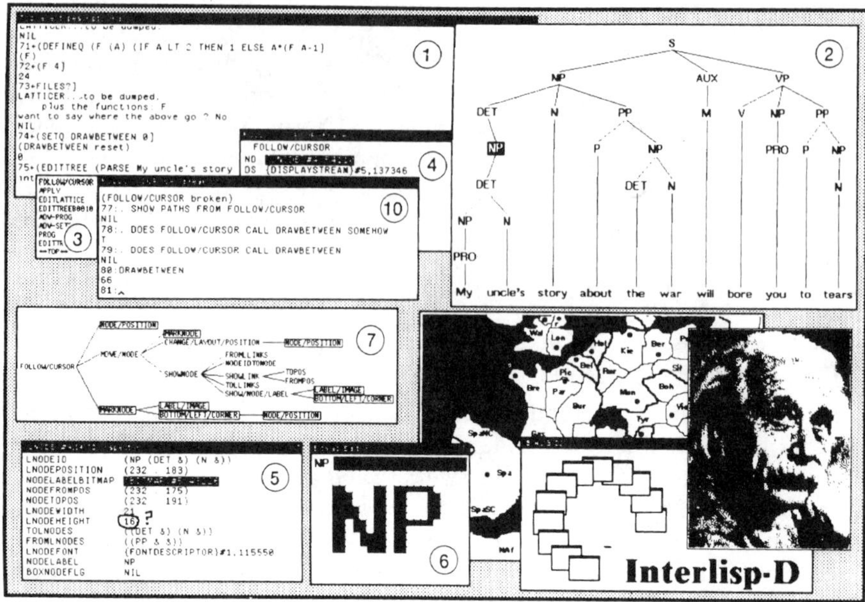

These two screen images show some of the exploratory programming tools provided in the Xerox Interlisp-D programming environment. The screen is divided into a series of rectangular areas or windows, each of which provides a view onto some data or process, and which can be reshaped and repositioned at will by the user. When they overlap, the occluded portion of the lower window is automatically saved, so that it can be restored when the overlapping window is removed. Since the display is bit-mapped, each window can contain an arbitrary mixture of text, lines, curves, and pictures composed of half-tones or solids. The image of Einstein, for instance, was produced by scanning a photograph and storing it digitally.

In the typescript window (labeled 1), the user has defined a program F (factorial) and has then immediately run it, giving an input of 4 and getting a result of 24. Next, in the same window, he queries the state of his files, finding that one file (LATTICER) has already been changed and one function (F) has been defined but not associated with any file yet. The user sets the value of DRAWBETWEEN to 0 in command 74, and the system notes that this is a change and adds DRAWBETWEEN to the set of "changed objects" that might need to be saved.

Then, the user runs the program EDITTREE, giving it a parse tree for the sentence "My uncle's story about the war will bore you to tears." This opens up the big window (2) on the right in which the sentence diagram is drawn. Using the mouse, the user starts to move the NP node on the left (which is inverted to show that it is being moved).

While the move is taking place, the user interrupts the tree editor, which suspends the computation and causes three "break" windows to appear on top of the lower edge of the typescript. The smallest window (3) shows the dynamic state of the computation, which has been broken inside a subprogram called FOLLOW/CURSOR. The "FOLLOW/CURSOR Frame" window (4) to the right shows the value of the local variables bound by FOLLOW/CURSOR. One of them has been selected (and so appears inverted) and in response, its value has been shown in more detail in the window (5) at the lower left of the screen. The user has marked one of the component values as suspicious by circling it using the mouse. In addition, he has asked to examine the contents of the BITMAP component, which has opened up a bitmap edit window (6) to the right. This shows an enlarged copy of the actual

Figure 3-6. Example of an Interlisp session (Part 1).
(Reprinted from *DATAMATION Magazine*, Feb. 1983 issue, © by Cahners Publishing Company.)

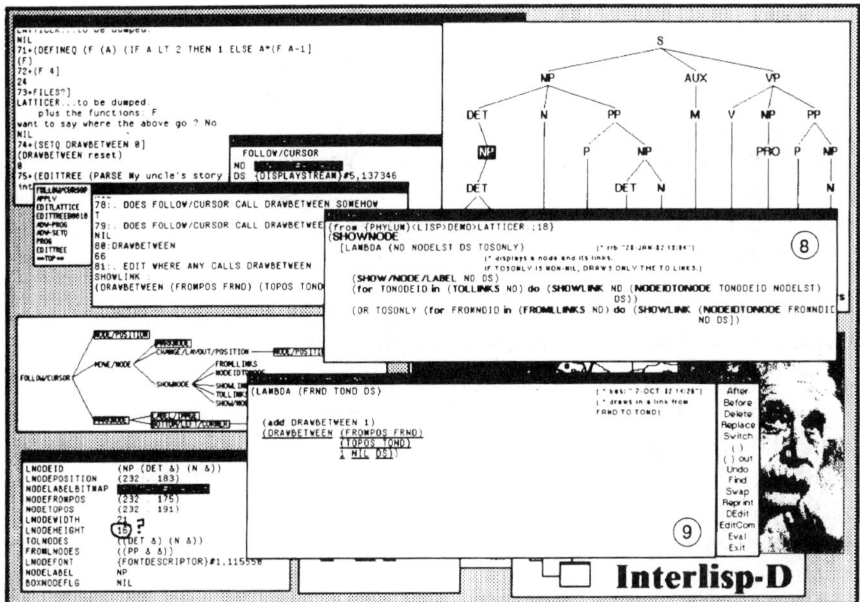

NP image that is being moved by the tree editor. Then, inside the largest of the three break windows (10) the user has asked some questions about the FOLLOW/CURSOR subprogram that was running when he interrupted, and queried the value of DRAWBETWEEN (now 66). The SHOW PATHS command brought up the horizontal tree diagram on the left (7), which shows which subprograms call each other, starting at FOLLOW/CURSOR.

Each node in the call tree produced by the SHOW PATHS command is an active element that will respond to the user's selecting it with the mouse. In the second image, the user has selected the SHOWNODE subprogram, which has caused its source code to be retrieved from the file (‹LISP›DEMO›LATTICER) on remote file server (PHYLUM) where it was stored, and displayed in the "Browser printout window" (8) which has been opened at middle right. User functions and extended Lisp forms (like *for* and *do*) are highlighted by system-generated font changes.

By selecting nodes in the SHOW PATHS window, the user could also have edited the code or obtained a summary description of any of its subprograms.

Instead, the user has asked (in the break typescript window (10)) to edit wherever anybody calls the DRAWBETWEEN system primitive (which draws lines between two specified points). This request causes the system to consult its dynamically maintained database of information about user programs, wherein it finds that the subprogram SHOWLINK calls DRAWBETWEEN. It therefore loads the code for SHOWLINK into an edit window (9) that appears under the "Browser printout window." The system then automatically finds and underlines the first (and only) call on DRAWBETWEEN. Note that on the previous line DRAWBETWEEN is used as a variable (the same variable the user set and interrogated earlier). The system, however, knows that this is not a subprogram call, so it has been skipped over. If the user were to make any change to this subprogram in the editor, not only would the change take effect immediately, but SHOWLINK would be marked as needing to be updated in its file and the information about it in the subprogram database would be updated. This, in turn, would cause the SHOW PATHS window to be repainted, as its display might no longer be valid.

Figure 3-6. Example of an Interlisp session (Part 2).
(Reprinted from *DATAMATION Magazine*, Feb. 1983 issue, © by Cahners Publishing Company.)

simply starts using his program, and analyzes and fixes problems as they come up. While pursuing the first problem he encounters, the Lisp user will often encounter a second, which leads to a third, and so on. When this happens, the Lisp user frequently, to use a programming metaphor, pushes the original problem onto his stack, and pursues the new one."[22] As illustrated in the two screen images of Figure 3-6,[23] the facilities of the Interlisp system support this paradigm.

Multiple Views in a Structured Programming Environment: The PECAN Program Development System

PECAN, a family of program development systems that support multiple views, is being developed at Brown University.[16,24] PECAN is designed for algebraic programming languages. The current version is based on Pascal, with the goal of supporting student programming. The long-term goal is to study environments that make full use of the computing power and graphics available on the new generation of personal machines. It is envisioned that these environments will be used by both experienced and novice programmers.

By selecting an algebraic language as the programming language supported, PECAN is inherently geared to the structured programming approach. In contrast to users of the exploratory style of programming—where the problems being solved, much less the algorithms being used, are not well understood—users in the PECAN environment have generally well-defined problems to tackle.

Furthermore, reflecting the bulk of existing programming practice, the PECAN environment is predicated on the assumption that the users have been taught first to design and then to implement. Unlike the Interlisp programmers, who need to *"debug the program into existence by experimenting with various solutions and seeing how they work,"*[22] Pascal programmers generally have algorithms already thought out before they start to program. Of course, the algorithms may have flaws, and unless the problem is trivial, design and implementation of the program are seldom perfect on the first shot. Nevertheless, to a Pascal programmer, debugging is not experimentation. It is, instead, a process to iron out the wrinkles and to ensure that the solution implemented indeed *produces the expected results.*

PECAN contains many of the best features of other similar systems. These include structured templates for building the program, immediate feedback of semantic and syntactic errors while the user is editing, an undo facility whereby the user can undo and redo any action back to the beginning of his session, and most of all, support for multiple concurrent views.

In PECAN, the program is represented internally as an abstract syntax tree. The user does not see this tree directly, but instead sees views or concrete representations of the syntax tree and its associated internal forms supported by PECAN. Reiss calls these forms "semantic views." They include the symbol table, data type definitions, expression trees, and control flow graphs.

Figure 3-7 shows several views of an example program. One such view is a "syntax-directed editor." This view displays the syntax tree in pretty-printed program text with multiple fonts (shown in the upper right window of Figure 3-7). Below it are views of the flow graph and the current data type. Below the data type display is a transcript window where the system shows the user all of its commands. On the left, the expression display shows the expression tree that is the current focus of editing operations; and the symbol table view displays the scopes and symbols that are defined for a particular syntax tree.

PECAN supports various views of program execution. These views are of three different types: control, program, and data. Figure 3-8 shows an example.

The execution control view (shown in the upper left window in Figure 3-8) contains messages that indicate the current execution state of the program. It also displays the program input and output, using different fonts. The control view provides debugging facilities that include the ability to reverse program execution, to step through the program one step at a time, either

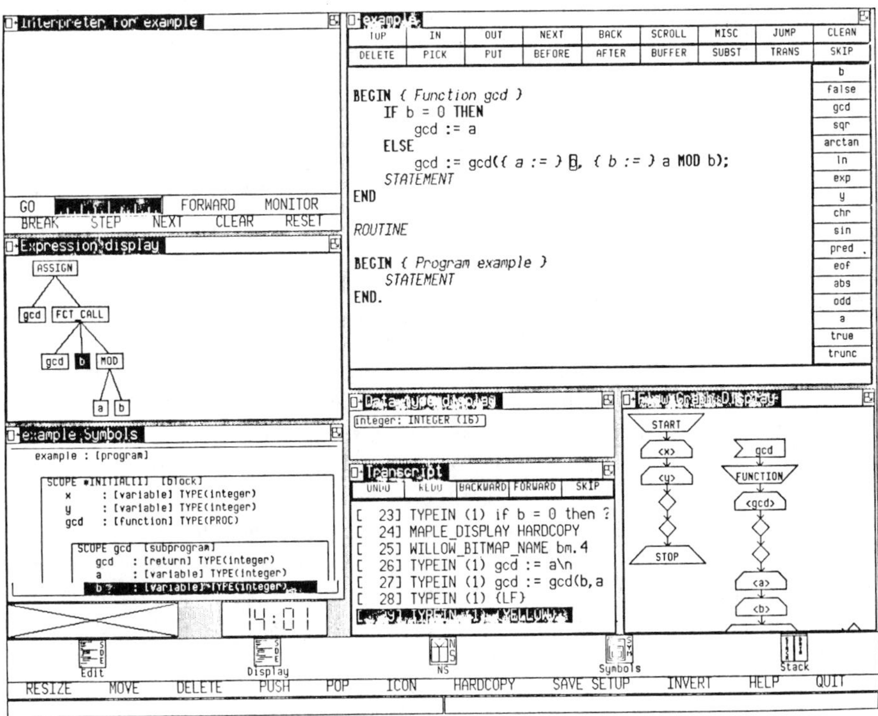

Figure 3-7. PECAN display showing program and semantic views. (Reiss[24].)

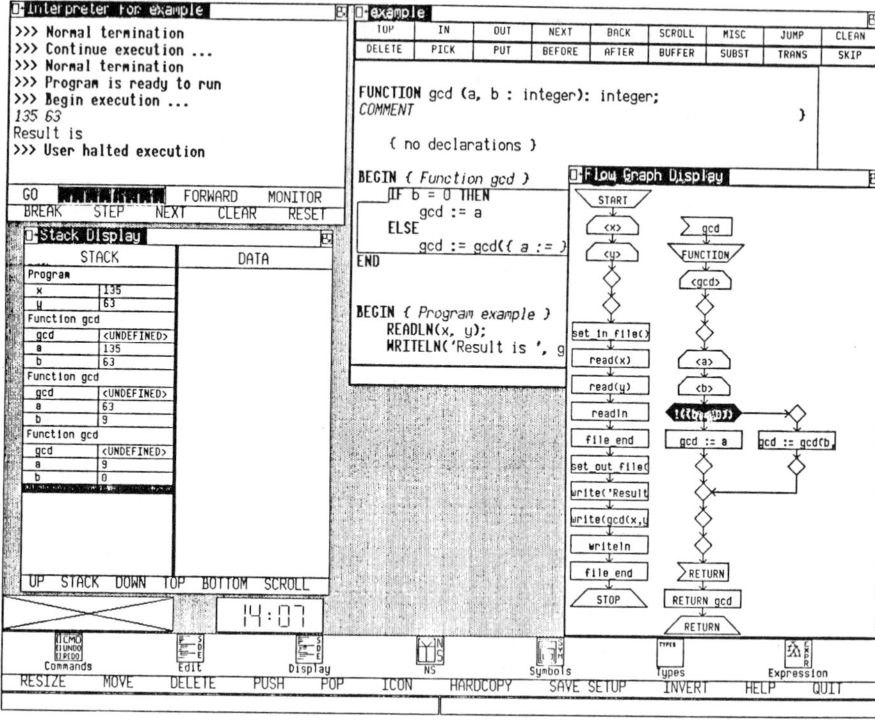

Figure 3-8. PECAN Display showing execution.
(Reiss[24].)

forward or backward, and to insert break points by pointing at the place to stop and then hit the BREAK button. It also provides a speed control so that the user can slow down the program execution.

Program feedback is provided by the syntax-directed editor and the flow graph view, both of which highlight each statement as it is executed. The stack display is the only current data view, although more views are planned. It shows the current state of the execution stack, including each current stack frame, the variables in that frame, and their values.

In short, PECAN is designed to provide the user with multiple displays that concurrently show different aspects of the program and its execution states in well-known programming terms. Having access to all this information can give the programmers a good feel for what is going on, and the system is indeed a powerful debugging tool.

UNDERSTANDING THROUGH ALGORITHM ANIMATION

"The adage 'a picture is worth a thousand words' describes the possibilities of a static page. An extention of this old saying captures the expressive power of a dynamic screen: a picture, proper use of timing, and animation allow you to keep the screen (and sometimes the user's mind) uncluttered with verbage."[25]

In this section, we concentrate on systems that use animation as an effective means of visualization to increase the understanding of a program.

In a way, the distinction between the work that we discussed in the previous section and the work that we are about to describe is not fundamentally sharp. After all, once the facility to observe a program in execution is in place, animation seems merely a matter of the control of timing. Yet, it is useful to distinguish these two categories because they instigate different levels of understanding for subtly different purposes.

As we indicated earlier, the Interlisp and PECAN systems represent a group of efforts which have in common a primary objective of providing an environment conducive to program development and debugging. At the same time, a new trend has emerged from the educators' desire to use the computer as an effective communication medium to teach computing. Controlled by the elements of time, dynamic graphical displays can be used to express many things compactly, vividly, and in a form more rapidly understandable. It is natural that animation has been adopted by many as a new communication medium.

Using animation as a communication medium per se, of course, is not new. In the entertainment field, Walt Disney developed a new art form some fifty years ago based on animation. His animated movies told us stories that are both enchanting and memorable. In the scientific and engineering fields, also, animation has a long history of being invaluable in presenting the results of simulation (a flight simulator for pilot training is everybody's favorite example). What is relatively new is the application of animation to the study of programming itself.

At the moment, the major efforts in this area are aiming at two different groups of people who can benefit most from program animation. One group consists of children taking their first step in programming. The other consists of the computer science students and researchers who need a deeper understanding of the algorithm's inner workings. Hughes and Moshell's *Visible Pascal,*[26] Brown and Sedgewick's *BALSA,*[27,28] and London and Duisberg's "animation system"[29] are representative of these efforts. In the following, we discuss Visible Pascal and BALSA in more detail.

Visible Pascal

From 1979 to 1982, Hughes and Moshell[26] led a team of computer scientists and high school teachers in a project to design a microcomputer-based high school computer science curriculum called the *Computer Power* curriculum.[30] To take advantage of interactivity and graphics capabilities, it was decided to use graphics as the primary program output medium.

During the development of Computer Power, a Pascal interpreter named *INTERPAS* was designed and implemented. INTERPAS served as the starting point for a series of field trials and revisions, culminating in 1985 with the production of a greatly enhanced interpreter called *PASPAL*. PASPAL is the nucleus of Visible Pascal, an integrated set of tools for learning about programming.

The Visible Pascal system provides a full screen text editor, a library of graphics animation routines, and an interpretive run-time environment for a subset of Pascal. Essentially the language subset includes all the program and control structures of Pascal and sufficient data structures to support the control of Turtlegraphics* and animation of two-dimensional figures. Omitted from the language are real numbers, dynamic records, most user-defined types, and pointers. Disk file input/output is supported only for arrays of integers, via special procedures.

In Visible Pascal, Turtlegraphics is used for line drawings. Two-dimensional figures and background scenes can be created using an accessory program called *ARTIST*. Twenty-four predrawn figures are supplied with PASPAL (see Figure 3-9).

From a user's perspective, the animation commands are carried out by procedures added to Pascal. Figure 3-10 demonstrates some of the animation primitives implemented in PASPAL. This program reads in two solid figure descriptions from the disk, a biplane, and a willow tree. The procedure *Star* uses Turtlegraphics commands to draw a five-sided star in the upper right corner. A ground scene is created by painting a region green, writing the text 'PASPAL Demo Program' in the region, and painting a copy of the tree on top of it. A series of statements is then used to create a picture of the plane followed by a streamer, and this picture is snipped out to make a new actor called "banner."

Once the setup has been completed, the main program uses the *printgraph* procedure to copy the screen image onto a printer. This snapshot is shown in Figure 3-11. Finally, the fly, spin, and reverse commands are used to make the plane turn around and upside down, fly across the screen, turn back around and right side up, fly back to the left, and finally turn around, fly off the screen, and disappear.

Visible Pascal divides the screen into an output window (displaying text

*Turtlegraphics is based on ideas developed as part of the *LOGO* [31] project. The LOGO system first consisted of a specialized keyboard and a computer-controlled turtle—a robot with wheels and a pen. Using the keyboard, children can program the robot by giving commands. These commands include directions which will move and turn the turtle, pick up and put down the pen, etc. With a sequence of commands, a child can make the turtle do the line drawings. PASPAL's Turtlegraphics provides the user with the same capability, except that the turtle is not a robot. It is an invisible screen object that draws colored lines as it moves around.

Figure 3-9. Set of predrawn PASPAL solid figures.
(Hughes and Moshell[26]. Reprinted with permission from the National Computer Graphics Association and the authors. Original art courtesy of C.E. Hughes.)

and graphics) and a program viewing window which displays a dynamic trace of source statements as the program is executed. Furthermore, the user can run the program rapidly or slowly, or use the immediate mode to try out individual statements.

As demonstrated in this example, Visible Pascal is designed to provide enjoyable, nonthreatening environments in which the users are introduced to programming. It is not intended to serve experienced programmers.

BALSA

At about the same time that Hughes and Moshell started the project for a microcomputer-based high school computer science curriculum, Robert Sedgewick and his colleagues in the Computer Science Department of Brown University embarked on a study of the applications of workstation

```
program NCGA1986;
const    BANNER = 1;
         PLANE  = 2;
         TREE   = 3;

procedure Star;
begin
    (* use recursion to draw a 5-sided star *)
    move( 15 );
    turn( -144 );
    if turtleanglw <> 0 then Star;
end; (* Star *)

procedure Setup;
const    PLANENAME = 'biplane';
         TREENAME  = 'tree';
begin
    (* bring in the actors *)
    getfigure( PLANE, PLANENAME );
    getfigure( TREE,  TREENAME  );

    (* make a star in the sky *)
    pencolor( NONE );
    moveto( 180, 120 );
    pencolor( BLUE );
    Star;

    (* create the ground *)
    fillbox( GREEN, 0, 279, 0, 30 );
    wtext( 70, 8, 'PASPAL Demo Program' );
    position( TREE, 140, 25 );
    paint( TREE );

    (* combine the plane and a banner to make a new actor *)
    position( PLANE, 50, 80 );
    fillbox( ORANGE, 98, 160, 83, 94 );
    wtext( 105, 85, 'NCGA''86' );
    paint( PLANE );
    makefigure( BANNER, 49, 160, 80, 100 );
    turnon( BANNER );
    fillbox( BLACK, 49, 160, 80, 100 );
end; (* Setup *)

begin (* NCGA1986 *)
    Setup;
    (* take a snapshot of the screen for Figure 4 *)
    printgraph( 1 );

    (* do some acrobatics *)
    spin( BANNER );
    fly( BANNER, 200, 0 );
    spin( BANNER );
    fly( BANNER, -250, 0 );
    reverse( BANNER );
    fly( BANNER, 280, 60 );
    turnoff( BANNER );
end. (* NCGA1986 *)
```

Figure 3-10. Example of a Visible Pascal program.
(Hughes and Moshell[26]. Reprinted with permission from the National Computer Graphics Association and the authors. Original art courtesy of C.E. Hughes.)

technology to education and research. In 1983 an electronic classroom, equipped with 55 high-performance workstations connected in a high-speed network, was installed.

Many of the introductory courses in the computer science curriculum, as well as some courses in mathematics, are now taught in this specially

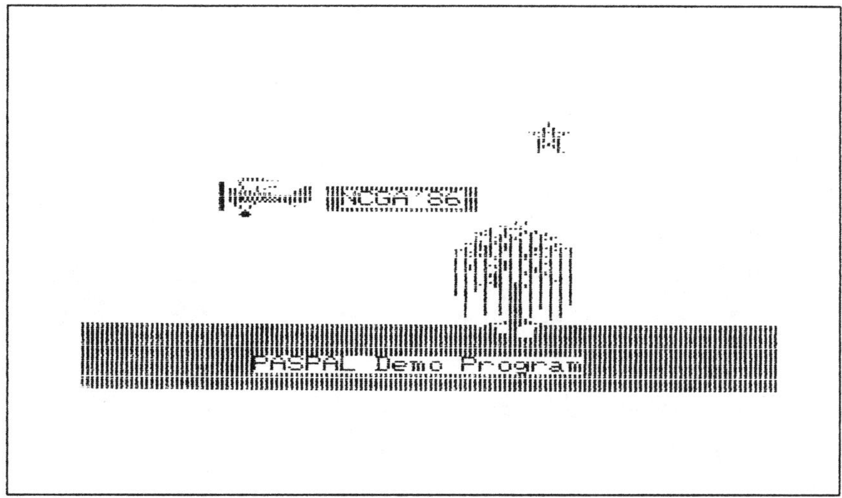

Figure 3-11. Snapshot of a scene.
(Hughes and Moshell[26]. Reprinted with permission from the National Computer Graphics Association and the authors. Original art courtesy of C.E. Hughes.)

constructed auditorium. Instead of using a blackboard, an instructor can now introduce a new topic by talking his way through an animated sequence of images viewed by all students and then letting each of them work independently on the same material.

The aim is to offer students an opportunity to "see" the abstract concepts before delving into the details of programming and to combine the classroom lectures with the laboratory experiment. The primary support environment, *BALSA* (the Brown Algorithm Simulator and Animator), enables users to control the speed of an animated sequence, to decide which views of the subject to look at, and to specify the input data to be processed.

The BALSA system has been used by hundreds of students and dozens of researchers since 1983. Extensive experience has been gained in actually using the system to animate scores of algorithms. The animated algorithms include mathematical algorithms (such as Euclid's GCD algorithm, ¾ Recursion, Random Numbers, Curve Fitting), sorting algorithms (such as Insertion Sort, Quick Sort, Radix Sort, Priority Queues, Merge Sort, External Sort), and searching algorithms (such as Sequential Search, Balanced Trees, Hashing, Radix Searching). An iconic table of contents for these animations (in left-to-right order) is shown in Figure 3-12.[27]

The iconic table of contents can be thought of as an index to a "dynamic book." Selecting an icon with a mouse causes a 10- to 15-minute dynamic

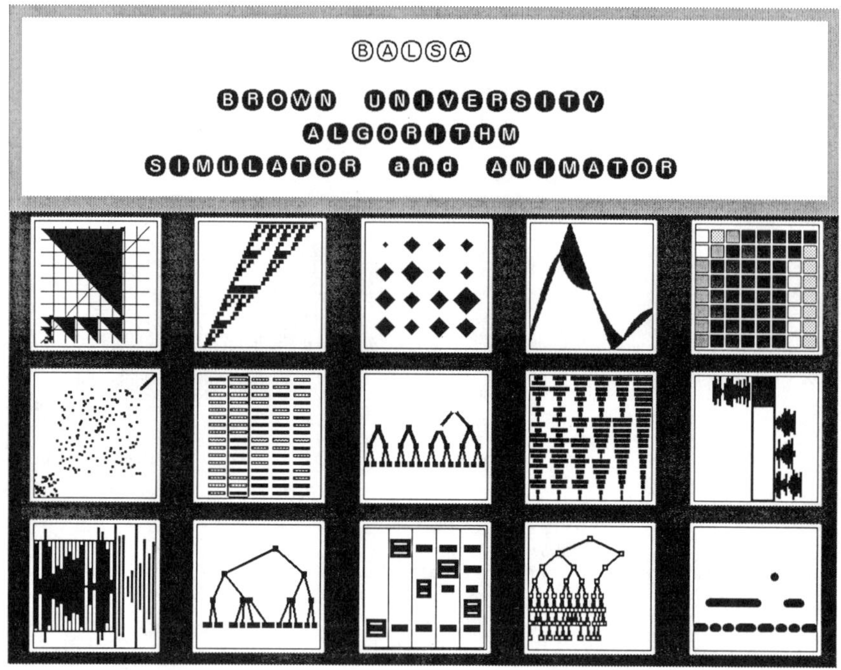

Figure 3-12. An iconic table of contents for some BALSA animations. (Brown and Sedgwick[27]. Copyright © 1984 Association for Computing Machinery, Inc., reprinted with permission. Original art courtesy of M. Brown.)

simulation of the selected topic to be run, with pauses at key images, after which the "reader" can interact with the algorithms and images.

In essence, the BALSA environment is tailored for the use of algorithm animation while also emphasizing quality user interface and performance. This special-purpose software environment supports four kinds of activities. The *algorithm designer* provides the programs that are to be animated, identifies key "interesting events" in the programs, and contributes to the design of graphical representations of the structures. The *animator* implements *views* that comprise the graphical representation. These views dynamically change in response to interesting events. The *scriptwriter* produce scripts containing specific material for presentation to users. The *user* makes use of these scripts or directly interacts with the dynamic graphical representations of the algorithms.[28]

The *interesting events* play a key role in the animation of an algorithm. Typically, the animator and algorithm designer agree on a general plan for various visualizations of the algorithms, mainly for the purpose of identifying the interesting events in the algorithm which should lead to changes in the image being displayed. Then the algorithm designer adds interesting

```
now := 0

for k:= 1 to V do
    begin  val [k] := unseen;  dad[k] := 0;   end;

pqconstruct;

repeat

   k := pqremove;

   if val[k] = unseen then

      begin

        IE ( IEaddfringe, dad[k], k, val[k] );
        val[k] := 0;
        now := now + 1;

      end

   IE (IEaddtree, dad[k], k, val[k]);

   t := adj[k];

   while t <> z do

      begin

        if val[t↑.v] = unseen  then  now := now + 1;
        if onpq (t↑.v) and (val[t↑.v] > now) then

           begin

             IE (IEaddfringe, k, t↑.v, now);
             pqchange (t↑.v, now);
             dad[t↑.v] := k;

           end;

        t := t↑.next

      end

until pqempty;
```

Figure 3-13. A fragment of an algorithm after augmented with interesting event markers (shown in italics).

event (IE) signals to the algorithm (see figure 3-13 for an example) and the animator writes the software which maintains the image (changing it in response to interesting events). The IE signals are implemented as procedure calls to the BALSA IE manager; the parameters are the name of the interesting event followed by algorithm-specific entities.

The primary function of the *scriptwriter* is to assemble algorithms and views into a coherent dynamic entity to tell a story. Some features are provided to allow different things to happen on playback. The one most commonly used is the *future freeze,* which is a no-op during interaction but a "pause" (wait for the user to press a button) during playback. Typically, the scriptwriter will create scenes or sequences of scenes consisting of several algorithms and views, and then create a script to run the algorithms on a variety of inputs, with future freezes inserted at particularly interesting points.

As it turned out, the animated sequences are not only valuable for students who wish to understand the properties of particular programs, they are also invaluable to researchers in the design and analysis of algorithms. A particularly useful property of BALSA is its capability of running multiple algorithms simultaneously and its facility for supporting multiple views of the same data. These points are illustrated in the following.

First, the ability to execute multiple algorithms in parallel on the same data has proven to be a very effective means of comparing and contrasting different methods. Figure 3-14[28] shows a comparison of two shortest path algorithms on a graph representing the Paris Metro. The nodes in the graph are dis-

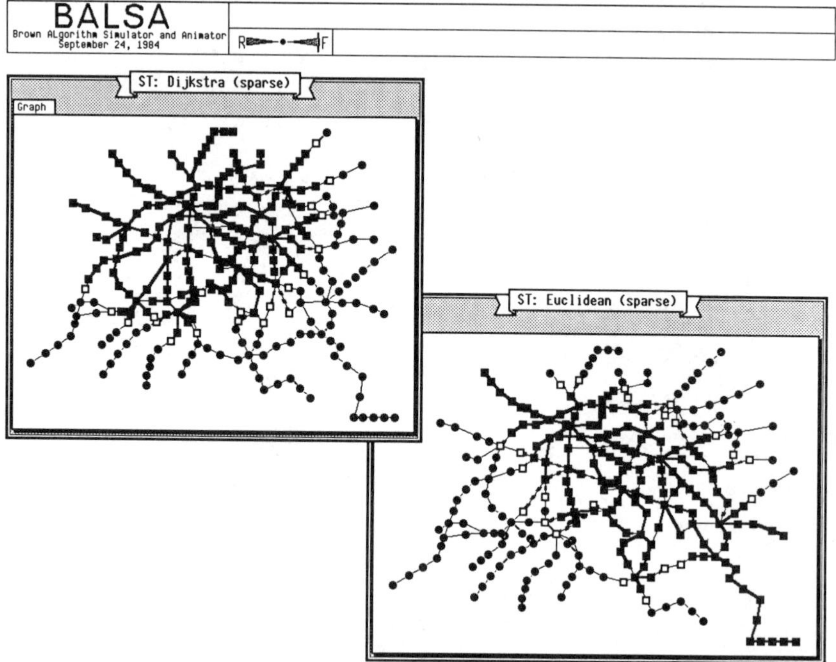

Figure 3-14. Comparison of two graph algorithms.
(Brown and Sedgwick[28]. Copyright © 1985 IEEE. Original art courtesy of M. Brown.)

played as dark circles in their initial "unvisited" state; as dark squares after they have been visited; and as light squares if they are ready to be visited. The edges also change from thin to dashed to thick to indicate the traversal.

The algorithm at the upper left side of Figure 3-14 is the classical Dijkstra's algorithm, while the one at the lower right is based on a heuristic method.[32] The classical algorithm must, in essence, perform a breadth-first traversal of the entire graph. The heuristic (looking at the distance from the start to the current spot in the tree plus the Euclidean distance to the target vertex) does not need to examine all of the nodes. The image is taken just after the heuristic algorithm has been completed; Dijkstra's algorithm still has a long way to go.

This type of "algorithm race" usually makes a lasting impression on students. At the same time, the contrasting dynamic properties of the algorithms often make it easier to understand the particular properties.

Furthermore, the ability to support multiple views of the same data provides a thread to reveal some properties which may not be obvious otherwise.

As an example, the image in Figure 3-15 compares two linear congruential

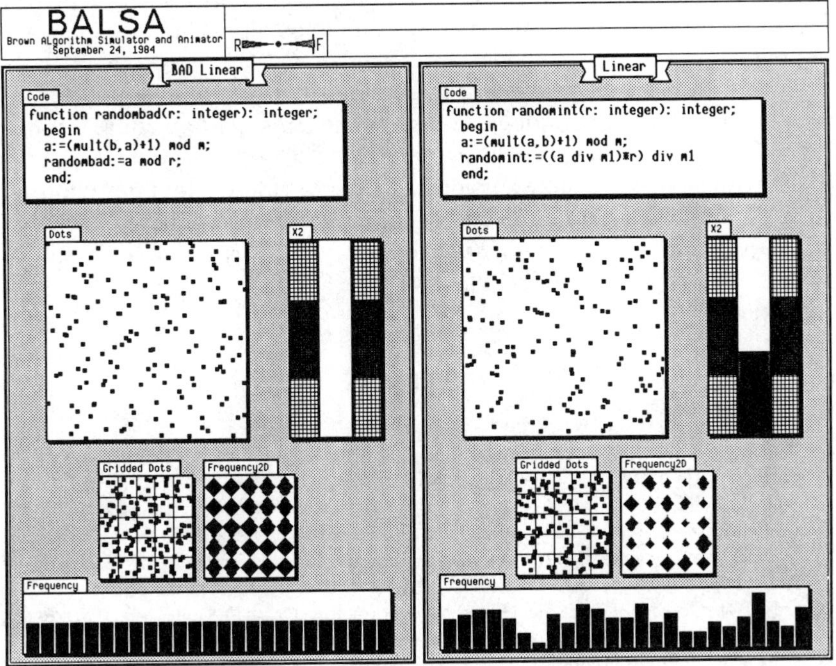

Figure 3-15. Random number example.
(Brown and Sedgwick[28]. Copyright © 1985 IEEE. Original art courtesy of M. Brown.)

methods for random number generation. The implementation code is displayed at the top. The algorithm on the left uses the least significant bits, whereas the algorithm on the right uses the most significant bits. The Dots view uses the numbers generated to plot points in Cartesian space. Note that the points produced by both random number generators appear equally random and well distributed in the Dots view. Below the Dots view is the Gridded Dots with grid markers partitioning the square. The distribution of points within each partition is shown both two-dimensionally (as diamonds) and as a more conventional histogram in row-major order (the bottom view). The rightmost view (labeled X2) is the χ^2 (chi-square) test to measure how random the numbers are, with the center dark region indicating the "passing" zone. The algorithm on the left produces numbers that are distributed too perfectly, an indication of nonrandomness.

Much work has begun at Brown University to learn how the techniques can be generalized, both to other subjects in science and engineering and to fields that have no tradition of graphically representing their objects and processes.

Andries van Dam, one of the chief instigators of the electronic classroom at Brown, said in his plenary address at Compcon Spring 87 (February 1987) that his hope is that the electronic classroom built at Brown University will be converted in the next two or three years to an all-color, real-time workstation laboratory.

"I want to be able to take an engineering structure, subject it to forces, watch what the structure does, and show the stress patterns in real time," he said. Getting it will require something like a "Crayette"—van Dam's term for a stripped-down, simple version of the Cray supercomputer. According to van Dam, "Well before the end of the century, you will have Cray-XMP, with a CT-6 image generator attached, on your desk. And you'll still be saying, 'Where are the MIPS, where are the FLOPS I really need to get my job done?' "

REFERENCES

1. Curtis, B., Soloway, E. M., Brooks, R. E., Black, J. B., Ehrlich, K., and Ramsey, H. R., "Software Psychology: The Need for an Interdisciplinary Program," *Proceedings of the IEEE,* Vol. 74, No. 8 (Aug. 1986), pp. 1092-1106.
2. Soloway, E. M., "Learning to Program = Learning to Construct Mechanisms and Explanations," *Communications of the ACM,* Vol. 29, No. 9 (Sept. 1986), pp. 850-858.
3. Hueras, J., and Ledgard, H., "An Automatic Formatting Program for Pascal," *ACM SIGPLAN Notices,* Vol. 12, No. 7 (July 1977), pp. 82-84.
4. Gustafson, G. G., "Some Practical Experiences Formatting Pascal Programs," *ACM SIGPLAN Notices,* Vol. 14, No. 9 (Sept. 1979), pp. 42-49.
5. Oppen, D. D., "Prettyprinting," *ACM Transactions on Programming Languages and Systems,* Vol. 2, No. 4 (Oct. 1980), p. 465-483.

6. Rose, G. A., and Welsh, J., "Formatted Programming Languages," *Software—Practice and Experience,* Vol. 11, No. 7 (July 1981), pp. 651-669.
7. Rubin, L., "Syntax-Directed Pretty Printing—A First Step Towards a Syntax-Directed Editor," *IEEE Transactions on Software Engineering,* Vol. 9, No. 2 (Feb. 1983), pp. 119-127.
8. Miara, R. J., Musselman, J. A., Navarro, J. A., and Schneiderman, B., "Program Indentation and Comprehensibility," *Communications of the ACM,* Vol. 26, No. 11 (Nov. 1983), pp. 861-867.
9. Baecker, R., and Marcus, A., "Design Principles for the Enhanced Presentation of Computer Program Source Text," *Proceedings of CHI '86, Human Factors in Computing Systems* (Apr. 1986), pp. 51-58.
10. Levien, R., "Visual Programming," *Byte,* Vol. 11, No. 2 (Feb. 1986), pp. 135-144.
11. Clark, B. E. J., and Robinson, S. K., "A Graphically Interacting Program Monitor," *The Computer Journal,* Vol. 26, No. 3 (June 1983), pp. 235-238.
12. Nassi, I., and Schneiderman, B., "Flowchart Techniques for Structured Programming," *ACM SIGPLAN Notices,* Vol. 8, No. 8 (Aug. 1973), pp. 12-26.
13. Teitelman, W., and Masinter, L., "The Interlisp Programming Environment," *IEEE Computer,* Vol. 14, No. 4 (Apr. 1981), pp. 25-34.
14. Teitelman, W., "A Tour Through Cedar," *IEEE Transactions on Software Engineering,* Vol. SE-11, No. 3 (Mar. 1985), pp. 285-302.
15. Delisle, N. M., Menicosy, D. E., and Schwartz, M. D., "Viewing a Programming Environment as a Single Tool," *Proceedings of ACM Sigsoft/Sigplan Software Engineering Symposium on Practical Software Development Environment* (May 1984), pp. 49-56.
16. Reiss, S. P., "PECAN: Program Development Systems That Support Multiple Views," *IEEE Transactions on Software Engineering,* Vol. 11, No. 3 (March 1985), pp. 276-285.
17. Reiss, S. P., Golin, E. J., and Rubin, R. V., "Prototyping Visual Languages with the GARDEN System," *Proceedings of the IEEE Computer Society Workshop on Visual Languages* (June 1986), pp. 81-90.
18. Sherwood, B. A., and Sherwood, J. N., "CMU Tutor: An Integrated Programming Environment for Advanced-Function Workstations," *Proceedings of the IBM Academic Information Systems University AEP Conference* (Apr. 1986), Vol. IV, pp. 29-37.
19. Isoda, S., Shimomura, T., and Ono, Y., "VIPS: A Visual Debugger," *IEEE Software,* Vol. 4, No. 3 (May 1987), pp. 8-19.
20. Goldberg, A., *Smaltalk-80: The Interactive Programming Environment,* Addison-Wesley (1983).
21. Mitchell, J. G., Maybury, W., and Sweet, R., "Mesa Language Manual," Version 5.0, Xerox Palo Alto Research Report CSL-79-3 (Apr. 1979).
22. Teitelman, W., "The Cedar Programming Environment: A Midterm Report and Examination," Xerox Palo Alto Research Center Report CSL-83-11 (June 1984).
23. Sheil, B., "Power Tools for Programmers," *Datamation* (Feb. 1983), pp. 131-144.
24. Reiss, S. P., "Graphical Program Development with PECAN Program Development Systems," *ACM SIGPLAN Notices,* Vol. 19, No. 5 (May 1984), pp. 30-41.
25. Nievergelt, J., "A Pragmatic Introduction to Courseware Design," *IEEE Computer,* Vol. 13, No. 9 (Sept. 1980), pp. 7-21.
26. Hughes, C. D., and Moshell, J. M., "Visible Pascal: A Graphics-Based Learning Environment," *Proceedings of Computer Graphics 86, National Computer Graphics Association* (May 1986), pp. 401-411.
27. Brown, M. H., and Sedgewick, R., "A System for Algorithm Animation," *ACM Computer Graphics,* Vol. 18, No. 3 (July 1984), pp. 177-186.
28. Brown, M. H., and Sedgewick, R., "Techniques for Algorithm Animation," *IEEE Software,* Vol. 2, No. 1 (Jan. 1985), pp. 28-39.

29. London, R. L., and Duisberg, R. A., "Animating Programs Using Smalltalk," *IEEE Computer,* Vol. 18, No. 8 (Aug. 1985), pp. 61-71.
30. Hughes, C. D., and Moshell, J. M., "Computer Power: A Coordinated Series of High School Curricula," *AEDS Convention Proceedings,* Orlando, Florida (1982), pp. 349-354.
31. Papert, S., *Mindstorms: Children, Computers, and Powerful Ideas,* Basic Books, Inc. (1980).
32. Vitter, J. S., "US&R: A New Framework for Redoing," *IEEE Software,* Vol. 1, No. 4 (Oct. 1984), pp. 39-52.

Chapter 4

Visualization of Software Design

Designing a computer system is very different from designing an algorithm: the external interface—that is, the requirement—is less precisely defined, more complex, and more subject to change; the system has much more internal structure—hence, many internal interfaces; and the measure of success is much less clear.

Butler Lampson[1]

An understanding of specifications, design decisions, system structures, dependencies among data and components, etc., are crucial throughout the software life cycle, and become increasingly difficult to grasp as the software increases in size and complexity. This observation, together with the success of using graphical techniques for the visualization of "programming in the small," has stimulated the efforts at visualization of "programming in the large." The primary goal is to provide a visual environment that supports the whole software life cycle for large, complex software systems.

The efforts in this area, however, are still in the developing stages. To illustrate the directions in which they are heading, we delve into two projects: the Program Visualization system of the Computer Corporation of America and the PegaSys system of SRI International. These two systems are singled out because they represent two contrasting approaches. The contrast reflects two often competing concerns: providing an effective environment for the programming of large systems and maintaining mathematical rigor. The first approach is more intuitive. Essentially, the users are provided with a set of graphical tools for creating views of their own choosing. The second approach, by contrast, is more rigorous. Formalism is introduced into graphical representations. The intent is to provide a mechanism so that the consistency between a formal diagram and a program can be proved or disproved by the system.

THE PROGRAM VISUALIZATION (PV) SYSTEM OF CCA

Since 1981, the Computer Corporation of America (CCA) has embarked on a project to design and implement a Program Visualization (PV) system.

"The aim is to support builders and maintainers of large (10**6 lines of code), complex systems.... The tool is targeted primarily for use with programs written in Ada."[2] One result of a six-month study conducted to provide a conceptual framework for Program Visualization produced a list of ten categories of illustrations that, together, can be of use throughout the software life cycle. The ten categories are:

1. System requirements diagrams
2. Program function diagrams
3. Program structure diagrams
4. Communication protocol diagrams
5. Composed and typeset program text
6. Program comments and commentaries
7. Diagrams of flow of control
8. Diagrams of structured data
9. Diagrams of persistent data
10. Diagrams of the program in the host environment.

"The number and variety of these categories suggests that fuller exploration of graphics can profoundly influence software production, just as text editing facilities have changed the way that papers are written," said Herot et al.[2]

Of these categories, some have already been well explored, and the PV project was able to draw on the existing work directly. Others present new challenges. In 1985, a prototype PV system was reported by Brown et al.[3] Instead of Ada, the prototype supports programming in C and itself is implemented in C.

The PV prototype supports a representative set of graphical capabilities that can be used during program execution to track changes in such common data structures as numeric variables, arrays, linked lists, and trees. To a certain extent, some of these capabilities overlap functionally with those discussed in the previous two chapters. We will not discuss them in this chapter except to point out that the multilevel viewing technique used in the SDMS (cf. Chapter 2) permeates the PV prototype. For example, Figure 4-1 depicts a mockup of an animation of a binary tree. The upper window shows the whole data structure; the highlighted rectangle is reproduced in detail in the lower window.

In this chapter, we highlight only the PV capabilities that are not the focal points of the systems discussed previously. They include the graphical display of system architecture and the tools for creating visualizations.

Graphical Displays of System Architecture

Figure 4-2 shows a diagram constructed on the PV prototype. The diagram shows one module of a distributed database system implemented at Com-

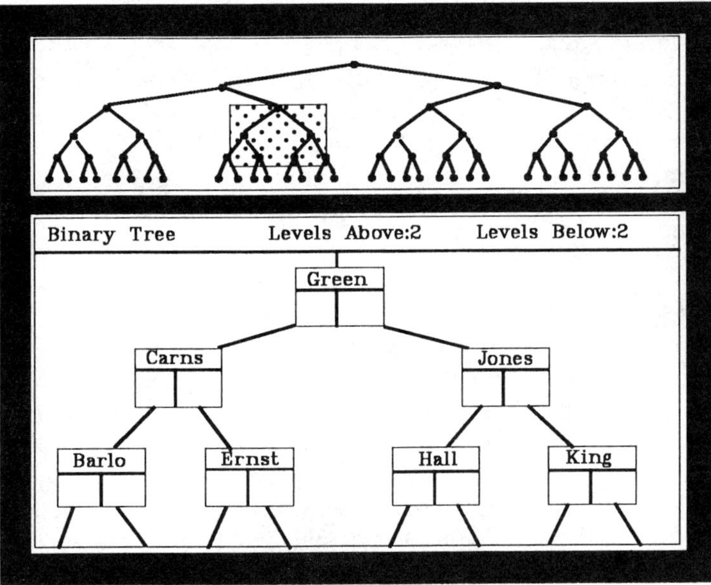

Figure 4-1. Mock-up of an animation of a binary tree.

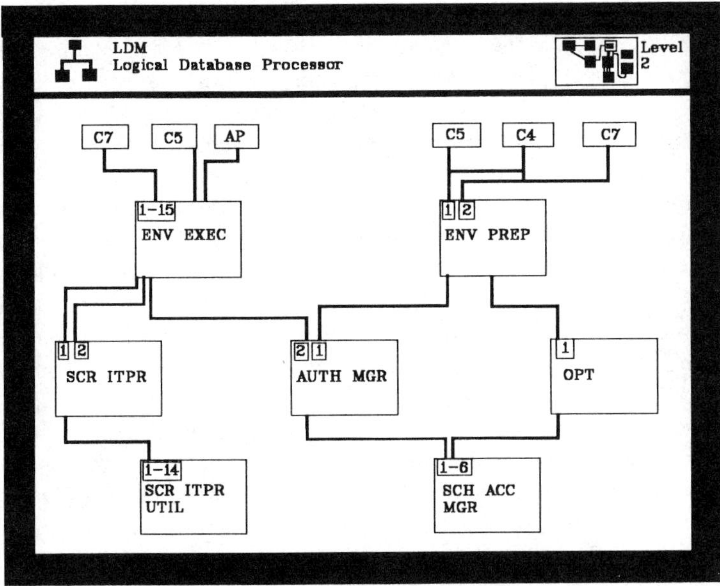

Figure 4-2. Example of an architecture diagram.

puter Corporation of America. The notation is adapted from in-house conventions developed to define system architecture. The diagram belongs to a set of diagrams that are linked hierarchically. The user can select the *zoom-in* command, point to a box of interest, and see the module the box represents at its next level of detail. A miniaturized view of this more detailed visualization is displayed in the upper right corner. If the user has zoomed more than one level down in the hierarchy, bars accumulate to the left of the miniaturization to indicate the current depth.

Tools for Creating Views

The PV prototype is not targeted to support any one software development methodology. Rather, it provides basic visualization tools that can be used for a programmer's chosen methodology. Three levels of support are implemented for the creation of visualizations: load-and-go visualization tools, support for the assembly of graphical objects, and "drawing" capabilities.

Load-and-go visualization tools are used to create program depictions with little or no help from the user. A code highlighter, for example, is a load-and-go tool that was built for the PV prototype.

Assembly can be viewed as an extension of the use of subroutine libraries. The main method of PV library access is by means of multilevel navigational aid (navaid). The library navaid, like other navaids proposed for the PV system, is a standard PV diagram. Figure 4-3 shows a sample library navaid constructed for the prototype that shows the library organization as a tree. Components stored in the library can be viewed and copied. Related components of different types can be grouped into clusters. For example, a code template and the templates for its associated graphical and textual documentation might make up a cluster. (Templates are objects with slots that the user can fill in with text or, in some cases, graphics).

Automatic access to components stored in the library is made possible via clusters. To access these components, the user first creates two editing windows (one for the graphics and the other for the code), selects one component from a cluster, and copies it to one of the windows. He then points to the component in the editing window and selects the *autoaccess* command. The system searches the library, finds the desired component, and propagates any slot fillers to the new component. It then displays the component in a temporary window. If the user is satisfied with the selection, he pushes a button that causes the component to be inserted into the second editing window. In this manner, a user can access data declaration templates from graphical components or access default graphical components by pointing to the declaration text.

For *drawing,* the PV prototype supports three underlying models: (1) The structural model includes polygonal and circular objects, connectors of

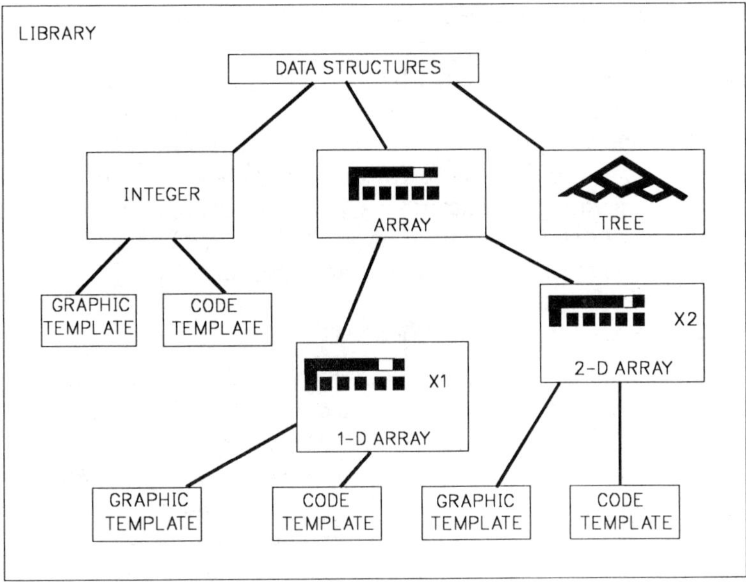

Figure 4-3. Example of a library navaid giving access to code and graphical components.

different widths, and slots. It has built-in capabilities for maintaining the integrity and the part-whole relationships of objects, with the result that a complex object can be referenced by one or two points. (2) The vector model includes lines, filled regions, and circles. It is used for detailed drawing of specific visual or symbolic characteristics of an object. (3) The text model includes a choice of text fonts and options for affixing textual labels and comments to an object.

To understand the difference between the structural and vector models, consider four lines drawn to form a square. If a user working within the vector model points to a place inside the square and close to one of the lines, the system interprets the reference as being to that closest line. A move command would result in one line being moved away from the other three. Pointing to the same place (or to anywhere within the square) while working within the structural model and issuing the move command would result in the object's being moved as a whole (all four lines and the space they enclose).

The PV prototype supports several manipulation operations for editing objects: copy, move, resize, delete, and recolor.

To specify dynamic graphics, the user selects the desired type of animation and then supplies the system with information that enables it to establish correspondences between the code and the static graphical components of the dynamic visualization. The process of establishing these correspondences is called *binding*.

Bindings are not implemented by inserting graphic statements into the source code. Instead, bindings constitute an independent mapping between code and graphics. Furthermore, binding may occur either before or after compilation of the code. These features are believed to be particularly important for creating visualizations of large software systems and allow programmers to create quick "throwaway" displays that help them to inspect facets of a program that have already started to run.

THE PEGASYS OF SRI INTERNATIONAL

PegaSys (Programming Environment for the Graphical Analysis of SYStems)[4] is an experimental system that supports extensive use of graphical representations as formal, machine-processable documentation. As with the PV system, the main purpose of PegaSys is to provide a visual environment for the development and explanation of large program designs (as opposed to detailed algorithms and data structures in a program). However, unlike the PV system, where tools are provided for the user to create visualizations for his chosen methodology, PegaSys strives for a practical balance between incorporating formalism into the programming environment and reducing complexity in the programming of large systems.

The value of knowing with mathematical certainty that a program has a desired property is often offset and consequently discouraged by its complexity. The complexity can be attributed to two factors[5]:

1. Formal specifications can be difficult to write and to understand, especially for large programs.
2. Proofs of consistency quite often cannot be mechanized and are too tedious and cumbersome to carry out by hand.

The complexity depends on the property to be dealt with. Work in the programming environment area generally eludes formalisms other than those of a syntactic nature (e.g., syntax-directed editors) and focuses on user friendliness at the expense of rigor. Program verification systems, on the other hand, tend to focus on mathematical rigor at the expense of productivity and friendliness.

The PegaSys system deals with a class of properties that lies in the middle ground—somewhere between the syntactic class dealt with by programming environments and the very general class dealt with by program verification systems. In particular, PegaSys supports the specification and analysis of data and control dependencies among the components of large programs.

PegaSys supports a formal description of dependencies in two ways. First, formal specifications in PegaSys are pictures called *formal dependency diagrams (FDDs)*, which are much more perspicuous than equivalent logical expressions. Formal properties of a program are described by standard graphical operations on icons rather than by sentences written in a formal logic. Second, PegaSys has the ability to represent and reason about different kinds of pictures within a single logical framework. The consistency between a formal dependency diagram and a program is proved or disproved without user assistance. Consequently, PegaSys gives the illusion that logical expressions do not exist.

Graphical Formalism

A program design is described in PegaSys by a hierarchy of interrelated pictures. Icons in a formal dependency diagram denote predefined or user-defined concepts about dependencies in programs. The predefined primitives denote objects (such as subprograms, modules, processes, and data structures), data dependencies (involving the declaration, manipulation, and sharing of data objects), and control dependencies (dealing with asynchronous and synchronous activities). A PegaSys user can define new concepts in terms of the primitives.

Figure 4-4 shows an example of a formal dependency diagram. The

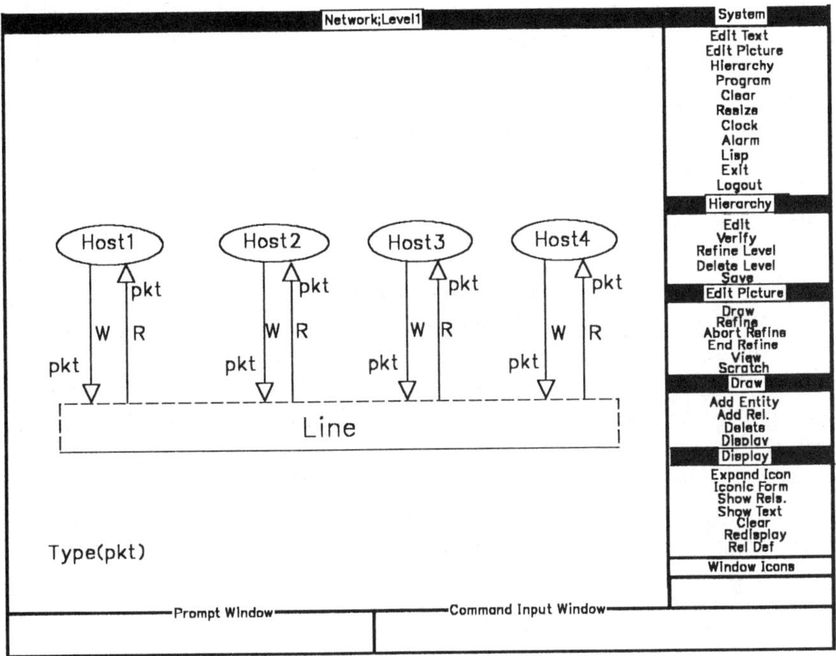

Figure 4-4. Formal dependency diagram for a network.

diagram contains several icons: four ellipses, a rectangle, several arrows, and several character strings. These icons denote several concepts about an example network. Each of the four hosts in the network is modeled as a *process* (indicated by an *ellipse*); the communication line by a *module* (indicated by a *dashed rectangle*); and a *packet of data* by a *type* (indicated by a *label on arcs*). *Dependencies* among hosts, packets, and the line are described by the *write* relation (denoted by the letter *W* on arrows) and the *read* relation (denoted by *R*).

At first approximation, the picture in Figure 4-4 says that the broadcast network consists of four hosts that communicate by means of a line. More precisely, processes named Host1, . . . Host4 write values of type pkt into a module called Line and read values of the same type from the Line module.

Form Calculus. A crucial aspect of PegaSys is its treatment of a picture as both a graphical and a logical structure. Icons in a picture correspond to predicates in the underlying logical representation of the structure. There is a one-to-one mapping between computationally meaningful icons and their associated predicates.

The logic in which pictures are represented is called the *form calculus.* A syntactically correct picture is said to describe the *form of a program* and is represented by a well-formed formula of the form calculus.

A simple example of a form, corresponding to the picture in Figure 4-4, is a conjunction of the predicates

process (Host1), process (Host2), process (Host3),
process (Host4), module (Line), type (pkt),
Write (Host1,Line,pkt), Read (Host1,Line,pkt)

with similar Write and Read predicates involving Host2, Host3, and Host4.

Logical constraints on graphical manipulations. Both syntactic and semantic constraints are placed on graphical manipulations. An example of syntactic constraints concerns the construction of pictures. While pictures are constructed by means of standard graphical operations, PegaSys uses the grammar of the form calculus to guide the construction of pictures in much the same way that a structure-oriented editor uses the grammar of a programming language to guide the construction of programs. Pictures may contain only concepts that are primitive or defined in the form calculus. The type constraints on predicates are used to prevent a nonsensical composition of concepts. For example, if a predicate has been defined to take two processes as its arguments, PegaSys ensures that both arguments are provided and both are processes.

Semantic constraints are used to restrict picture refinements and to analyze the relationship between a picture hierarchy and the program it is intended to describe. In both cases, it is necessary to prove logical formulas in the form calculus.

Multiple Levels of Description

Dependencies in a program are described by a hierarchy of FDDs, which can be constructed in a manner that greatly reduces the complexity of the specification.

In general, complexity can be managed by multiple levels of description. Each level in a picture hierarchy is a description of a program at a particular level of detail. A level is formed by a sequence of refinements to the immediately preceding level in the hierarchy. A *refinement adds detail* to an existing concept and is not allowed to delete concepts from a picture.

As an example, Figure 4-5 shows a picture of Network at level 2 after the refinement of Line. *Solid-lined rectangles* in Figure 4-5 denote *subprograms* that are intended to specify the interface to the Line; *Out_Pkt* is a variable modified by these subprograms. The *access* and *mod* relations in Figure 4-5 require *Out_Pkt* to be a variable belonging to the *Physical_Line* module.

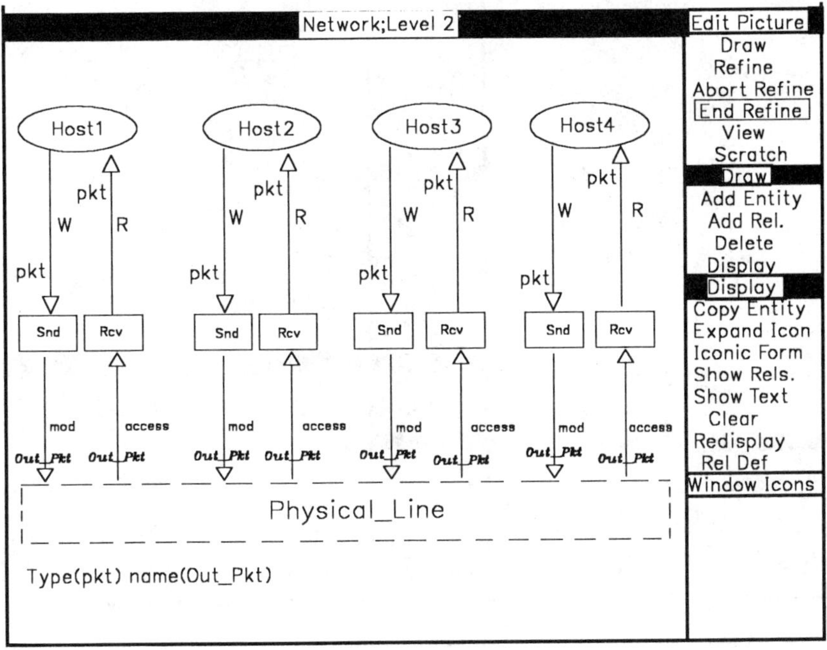

Figure 4-5. Picture of Network at level 2 after refinement of Line.

PegaSys checks that the relationships at level 1 are preserved at this level and that the entire picture at level 2 satisfies the type constraints imposed by the form calculus.

Multiple Views of the Same Picture

A *view* in PegaSys is a single grouping of logically related icons from a picture. In general, multiple views of the same picture are used to manage complexity or to emphasize particular aspects of a picture.

For example, Figure 4-6(a), i.e., the upper-left window, shows the first level in the design hierarchy for a host. This picture is not particularly perspicuous because it mixes several important properties of the host. These properties may be separated by means of three views, shown clockwise in windows (b) through (d) in Figure 4-6. The view in Figure 4-6(b) describes the establishment of a communication link (i.e., a channel) between hosts. If the channel is successfully opened, the variable OK has the value true and chan contains the name of the open channel. Otherwise, OK has the value false. The view in Figure 4-6(c) describes the transmission of an actual message. The third

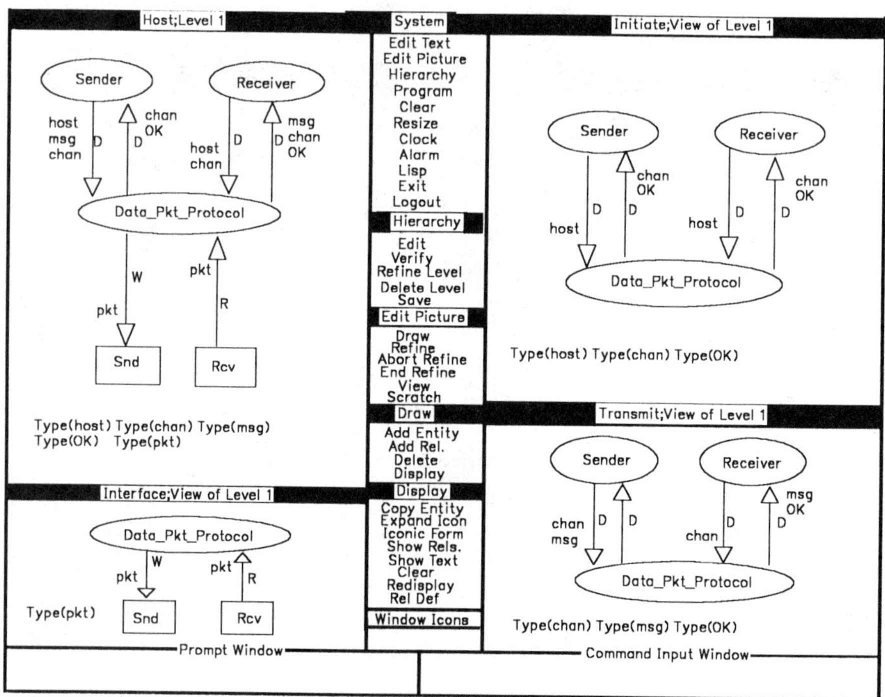

Figure 4-6. Multiple views at level 1 of protocol hierarchy for a host.

view, shown in Figure 4-6(d), describes the interface between a host and an external network. It says that a host reads and writes packets by means of subprograms Rcv and Snd.

The Verification Process

Programs are written interactively using the structure-oriented editor. The verification process (i.e., determination of whether a program meets its pictorial documentation) does not require human intervention except to establish the *correspondences* between entities in a picture and program constructs.

Each correspondence is specified by two structured selections, one from a picture and one from a program. This is illustrated in Figure 4-7, where the user has selected an entity called Send_Host_Pkt (indicated by the bold rectangle) and an Ada program unit called SEND_HOST_PACKET (text at the upper right). Issuing the *Associate* menu command (see the cursor) causes PegaSys to record the specified association.

PegaSys requires that each atomic entity (i.e., one that is not refined) be associated with exactly one program construct. After the associations are

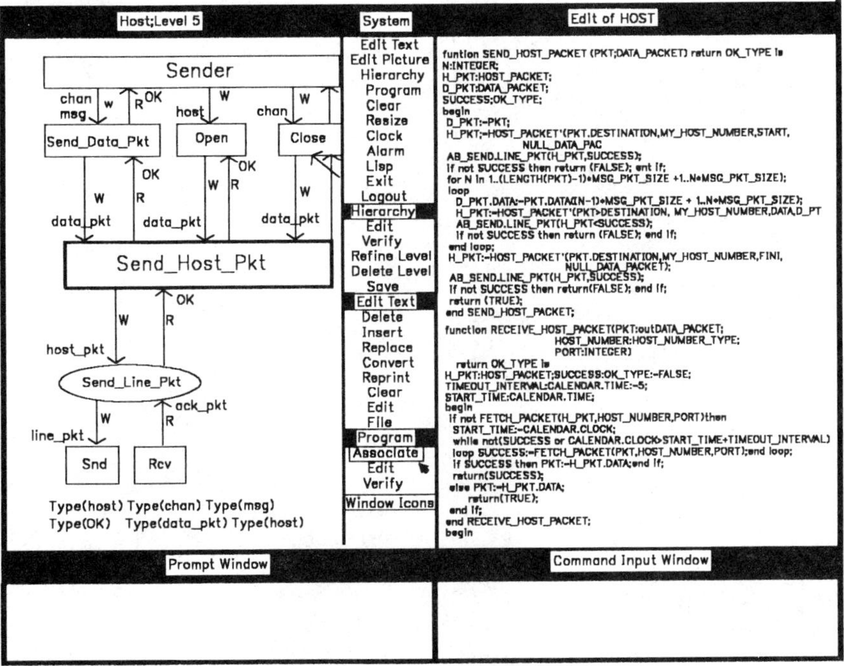

Figure 4-7. Associating entities in pictures with program text.

made, PegaSys can attempt to prove that the program and the hierarchy are logically consistent. In other words, PegaSys proves that the lowest level in a hierarchy is logically consistent with the program it is intended to describe.

Perhaps the contrasts between the Program Visualization system and the PegaSys system can be best summarized by the expectations of the two groups. As mentioned earlier, developers of the Program Visualization system said, "We expect interactive graphics to have a profound impact on software development—an impact analogous to the effect of word processors on production of text."[3] In contrast, the designers of PegaSys reached the following conclusion: "While the precision and descriptive capability of pictures has legitimately been questioned in the past, PegaSys seems to suggest that it is possible to profitably combine both graphics and logic for a rich domain. . . . It is our expectation that such uses of graphics will lead to the utilization of formal documentation and analysis techniques by a wide, possibly mathematically unsophisticated audience."[4]

REFERENCES

1. Lampson, B. W., "Hints for Computer System Design," *IEEE Software*, Vol. 1, No. 1 (Jan. 1984), pp. 11-28.
2. Herot, C. F., Brown, G. P., Carling, R. T., Friedell, M., Kramlich, D. A., and Baecker, R. M., "An Integrated Environment for Program Visualization," in *Automated Tools for Information Systems Design*, H. J. Schneider and A. I. Wasserman, editors, North-Holland Publishing Company (1982), pp. 237-259.
3. Brown, G. P., Carling, R. T., Herot, C. F., Kramlich, D. A., and Souza, P., "Program Visualization: Graphical Support for Software Development," *IEEE Computer*, Vol. 18, No. 8 (Aug. 1985), pp. 27-35.
4. Moriconi, M., and Hare, D. F., "Visualizing Program Designs Through PegaSys," *IEEE Computer*, Vol. 18, No. 8 (Aug. 1985), pp. 72-85.
5. Moriconi, M., "PegaSys and the Role of Logic in Programming Environments," *Preprints of the Proceedings of the International Workshop on Advanced Programming Environments* (June 1986), pp. 55-62.

Chapter 5

Visual Coaching

In its most ideal case, the programmer acts like the teacher and just gives examples to the computer and the computer, like an intelligent pupil, intuits the abstraction that covers all the examples.

Brad Myers[1]

CONTRASTS WITH VISUALIZATION AND VISUAL LANGUAGES

In the previous three chapters, we have described systems designed to provide a visual environment for the visualization of data, of programs and their execution states, of system structures, or a combination of them. Their main purpose is to provide visual aids to conventional programming. In these systems, programs are specified in conventional textual manner, and data are stored in the conventional database. "Visualization" means the use of graphics and pictures to illuminate some aspects of a program or to make data "come to life."

To put it simply, from the user's point of view, visualization systems can be characterized as *"Show me what I have"* (in terms of program/data/system design) or *"Show me what is going on"* (in terms of run-time execution).

In contrast, "visual coaching" has a different objective, which can be characterized as *"Do what I show you"* or *"Do according to my signal."* Like the visualization systems, visual coaching systems operate in highly visual environments. However, a system that falls into the category of visual coaching goes beyond visualization and actually attempts to produce a program based on what has been shown.

Because the central goal of visual coaching is to construct programs, some people do not make the distinction between visual coaching and visual programming languages (see Chang[2], for example). However, in order to sharpen our understanding, it is important to note the distinctions.

In visual programming languages (whether they have icons or other graphical representations such as charts, diagrams, or forms), programs are constructed from the language components in the traditional sense. The language primitives (e.g., icons, lines, boxes, arrows) have well-defined *syntax* and *semantics*. The "sentences" expressed in these languages (e.g., icons connected with flow paths, nodes connected by arrows, structured charts, stylized forms) can be *"parsed"* and *"interpreted"*.

Visual coaching, on the other hand, embarks on a program construction *technique, independent of languages.* Typically, a user shows the computer how to perform the desired computation by actually demonstrating with some sample data, and the system applies the demonstrated behavior for application with other data. Program construction relies almost completely on interactions. The style of interaction "mimics the informal way we explain programs, by showing pictures of the data and defining the computation on them by pointing sequences similar to handwaving."[3] Language syntax, in the traditional sense, is made obscure from the user's point of view.

Thus, even though both the visual coaching and the visual programming language systems have a common end (i.e., to produce a program), the means used to reach the end are quite different. While the visual programming languages are used to instruct the computer to *"Do as I tell you,"* visual coaching takes the *"Do as I show you"* approach.

PROGRAMMING BY EXAMPLE/DEMONSTRATION: BACKGROUND

Almost all visual coaching systems are *inspired* by the programming by examples or programming by demonstration approach. Therefore, a brief overview of the concepts is useful.

Most people are much better at dealing with specific, concrete objects than with abstract ideas. Examples and demonstrations are concrete and specific. When cleverly chosen and properly used, they help people understand the abstract concepts. Programming by example or demonstration attempts to extend these ideas to programming.

From the user's point of view, the fundamental idea underlying programming by example or demonstration is really quite simple. In essence, the user writes a program (i.e., makes a *specification*) by giving examples to the computer of what he wants the program to do. The system records, and hopefully also generalizes, what has been shown.

The specification might consist of examples of the desired output for each given input, or examples of how the program might process the input, or a combination of both. In the following, examples from Barr and Feigenbaum[4] are used to illustrate these two different types of examples.

Examples of Input/Output Pairs

In this specification method, the user gives examples of typical inputs to the program desired, along with the corresponding output expected. Consider describing a program that concatenates two lists. It might be straightforward to use an example:

CONCAT [(A B C), (D E)] = (A B C D E).

Given certain commonsense assumptions, this sample input/output pair should suffice to specify what the desired program is to do. In slightly more complicated cases, where the commonsense assumptions are not sufficient, more examples must be given. For instance, the example above could be misinterpreted as a program that always give (A B C D E):

CONCAT [x, y] = (A B C D E).

In such a case, giving an additional example,

CONCAT [(L M), (N O P)] = (L M N O P),

would probably clear up the confusion.

In certain cases, generalizations of specific examples are more useful. For instance, the generic example

REVERSE [(x1 x2 x3 . . . xn)] = (xn . . . x3 x2 x1)

describes a list-reversal function. Here, the x1, x2, . . . xn are variables and the list (x1 x2 . . . xn) corresponds to any list of arbitrary length—a generic list.

Examples of Program Traces

Traces of the desired program's operation on sample data allow more imperative specifications than do sample input/output pairs alone. For instance, a program trace could be used to express a sorting program as follows:

```
SORT [( 3 1 4 2 )] −> ( )
        ( 1 4 2 )  −> ( 3 )
          ( 4 2 )  −> ( 1 3 )
            ( 2 )  −> ( 1 3 4 )
              ( )  −> ( 1 2 3 4 ).
```

Another example of traces, illustrating the Euclidean algorithm to compute the greatest common divisor, might be:

```
GCD (12, 18) ->
    ( 6, 12) ->
    ( 0,  6) ->
          6
```

More formally, Barr and Feigenbaum state, "A programming domain can be thought of as consisting of a set of abstract objects, a set of possible representations (called data structures) for these abstract objects, a basic set of operators to transform these representations, and a class of questions or predicates that can be evaluated on these data structures. . . . For a given program operating on some data objects in the domain, a trace is a sequence of changes of these data structures and control flow decisions that have caused these changes during execution of the program."[4]

Traces are usually expressed in terms of operations applied to data objects, results of tests as to whether predicates (constraints) hold at certain points during program execution, state snapshots of data values, or functional compositions of these types of information. Like generic examples of input/output pairs, generic traces can also be used for program specification.

Traces are classified as *complete* if they carry all information about operators applied, data structures changed, control decisions taken, and so forth. Otherwise, they are *incomplete.* Depending on how much imperative and descriptive information is presented, there could be a whole spectrum of traces for a given program.

THE EMERGENCE OF VISUAL COACHING

Because of the natural appeal of using examples to explain concepts, specification by example has long enjoyed the attention of researchers in the automatic programming community. Specification by examples can indeed be natural and easy for the user to formulate. However, from the system standpoint, program synthesis from examples involves considerable difficulties.

First of all, examples must be chosen so as to specify *unambiguously* the desired program. In general, generic examples are less ambiguous than non-generic examples. Traces are less ambiguous than input/output pairs, and traces also allow some imperative specification of the flow of control. However, to specify a trace, the user must have some idea of how the desired program is to operate.

Furthermore, specification by examples is rarely *complete,* since a few examples will not fully describe the behavior of the desired program in all cases. The system must be able to work with partial or fragmented information and determine whether the user's specification is consistent and whether the system's "model" of what the user wants is indeed the *right program.*

In addition, when the process is attempted in the most general case, the system must enumerate the set of all possible programs. The cost of enumeration could be very high, even with the current technology of artificial intelligence.

These difficulties can be circumvented by restricting the problem domain or area of intended application. When the scope of the problem area is relatively small and precise, the chances of success are greater. When the system is not required to "infer" the general case, the task is an order of magnitude easier.

The difficulties can be further reduced by providing an interactive graphics environment. Graphics help to make the examples concrete. Interaction helps the user to communicate with the system with greater ease, which, in turn, could lead to an increase in both the clarity and the amount of information that a user conveys to the system. Moreover, an interactive graphics environment encourages cooperation between the user and the system and allows program construction to be accomplished in a more dynamic manner.

A new style of programming, which we call "visual coaching," represents various attempts to couple the power of examples with the benefits of working in an interactive visual environment. To make the task tractable, most of the visual coaching systems limit the applications to a relatively small and precise problem domain, and few attempt to do inductive inferencing.

While it is hard to categorize the approaches of these systems, there are now enough systems so that we can identify some common issues. Roughly speaking, they can be divided into two groups.

For the first group, the crucial issue is the development of a *generalized program,* that is, one that can account for more than the examples given in the specification. Even though graphical interactions are used in the process of specification, the center of the focus is the system's ability to do *inductive inferencing* of what the user wants on the basis of program specifications that only partially describe the program's behavior. For this reason, systems in this group can be better characterized as researches into automatic programming technology as a subfield of artificial intelligence (see Biermann[5,6] for tutorials).

In contrast, systems of the second group focus on *graphical interaction as a means of programming.* They generally limit their applications to a relatively small and precise domain, and do not attempt to do inductive inferencing. In the current state of the art, most visual coaching systems belong to the second group.

In the remainder of this chapter, we first briefly mention some of the research work that falls into the category of visual coaching and then describe two systems (*AutoProgrammer*[7] and *Programming by Rehearsal*[8]) in somewhat greater length as representative examples of the two groups.

One of the earliest works that can be classified as visual coaching is David Smith's *Pygmalion*[9]. Smith devoted nearly half of his dissertation to an in-depth discussion of a psychological model of creative thought, forming the basis for the Pygmalion design principles. He concluded that (1) visual communication with a computer is a productive metaphor for assisting the thinking and learning processes of human beings; and (2) emphasis of a programming environment should be placed on "doing" rather than "telling", since many people find it easier to demonstrate what they want done than to describe it. A prototype of Pygmalion was implemented on the Xerox Alto. As a demonstrational system, all programming is done by examples. With the aid of a mouse, the user demonstrates the steps of a computation using sample data values. The user's manipulations are recorded and stored. Pygmalion then replays the exact sequence to perform the desired computation on other data.

Gael Curry's *Programming by Abstract Demonstration (PAD)*[10] is an extension of Pygmalion. It allowed user demonstration to be carried out on potentially unbounded ranges of values, (e.g., integer) which Curry calls "abstract data". The user can look at what a program does by executing it abstractly, without supplying real data.

Pygmalion served also as the initial impetus for the work of Daniel Halbert[11]. Halbert implemented a system, which he calls "Programming by Example", on *SmallStar,* a prototype version of the Xerox's Star system[12]. Like Star, SmallStar is basically a Direct Manipulation System[13] based on the desktop metaphor of an office. Interaction with the system involves selecting an object with the mouse and pressing a command key that affects the selected object. Designed for the users to execute and reexecute their office procedures, Halbert's system provides a mechanism to record the sequential user actions. Branching or iteration (i.e., a control structure that alters program flow) is specified by program editing. The system does not have the capability for inductive inferencing. The following example gives the flavor of the system.

Suppose the user wanted to write a short program to copy the document called Meetings-Today, save the copy in the folder called Meetings, and then print Meetings-Today. He would do the following sequence of keystrokes and mouse-button clicks:

Start recording
press *Point* over Meetings-Today
COPY
press *Point* over Meetings
press *Point* over Meetings-Today

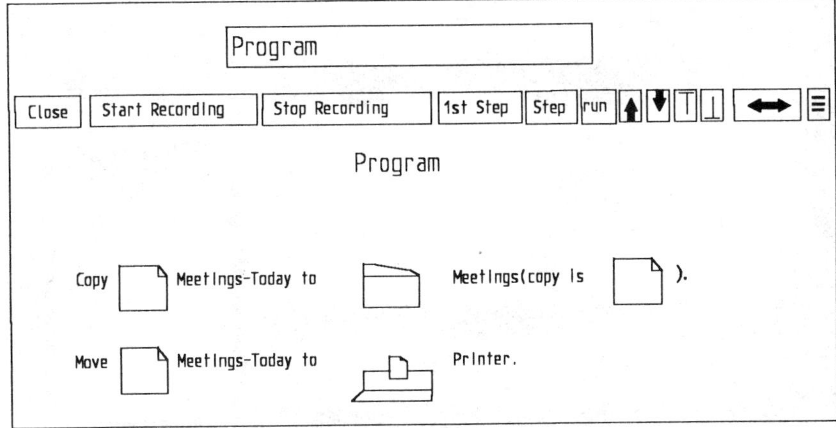

Figure 5-1. A sample Small Star program.

MOVE
press *Point* over Printer
Stop Recording

The program produced is shown in Figure 5-1.

At Brown University, *ThinkPad,* a graphical system for programming by demonstration,[14] has been developed by Rubin, Golin, and Reiss. In using ThinkPad, the user first designs data structures by selecting appropriate graphical representations and specifying constraints on them. Functions on these structures are then defined by editing the representations.

In defining a data structure, a *Data Editor* provides support for the graphical layout of fields in a data structure. A *Constraints Editor* provides support for the definition of constraints. Constraints are used (1) to provide and enforce strong typing, (2) to denote the internal and graphical hierarchy of the data structure, and (3) to express dependencies and relationships among the fields of a data structure. Type constraints on the data are made through the use of predicate formats commonly available in Prolog. Relationships in the data structure are also mapped directly into a set of Prolog assertions.

Figure 5-2 shows the definition of a "node" data structure, representing a binary tree data abstraction. The ThinkPad screen is shown. The icons along the bottom are used to invoke the components of the system. The Data Editor is displayed. It contains three windows. The *Data Window* displays the graphical layout. The *Type Window* displays the types of the structures in the Data Window. The *Prolog View* is a display of the Prolog code generated for the data structure being defined.

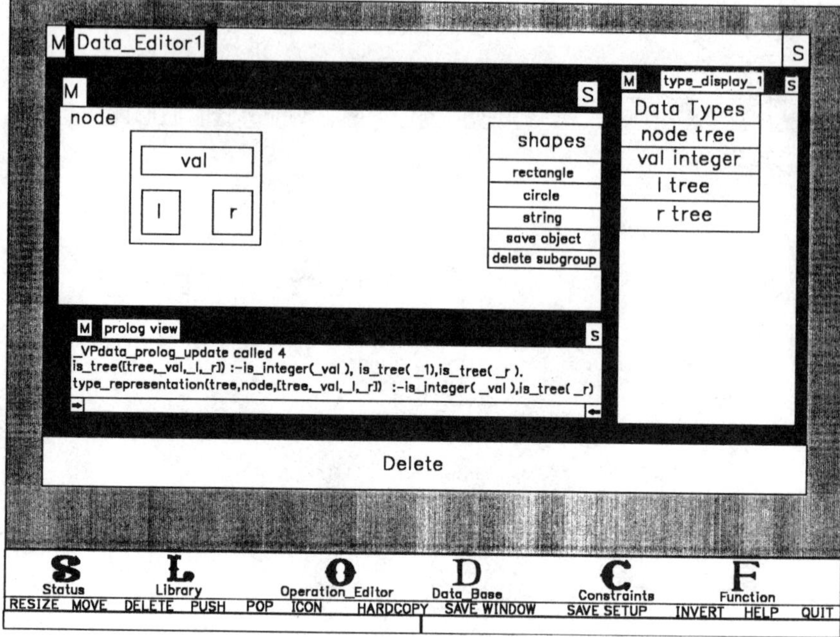

Figure 5-2. Definition of the "node" data structure.

Once a data structure is defined, operations (e.g., insertion into a binary tree) can be defined with the support of an *Operations Editor*. Figure 5-3 shows a view of the Operations Editor. Editing generally consists of pointing to the objects of interest and selecting the desired expression from the menu and/or depressing the appropriate buttons provided by the editor (e.g., COPY, REPLACE). This makes editing in ThinkPad the operational equivalent of programming.

Georg Raeder's *PiP* (Programming in Pictures)[3] also uses graphical editing as the equivalent of programming. PiP, however, differs from ThinkPad in at least two respects: (1) ThinkPad makes heavy use of constraints throughout the implementation and in its underlying models. PiP, on the other hand, is based on Backus' Functional Programming model.[15] (2) In ThinkPad, the user "draws" a data structure by selecting a graphical representation from "a menu of shapes."[14] In PiP, rather than supplying predefined formats for data, the user is provided with a facility to draw data types in free format.

PiP consists of four integrated editors:

1. A *Picture Editor* allows the user to create bitmap drawings.
2. A *Type Editor* provides a template that the user can fill with various data components.

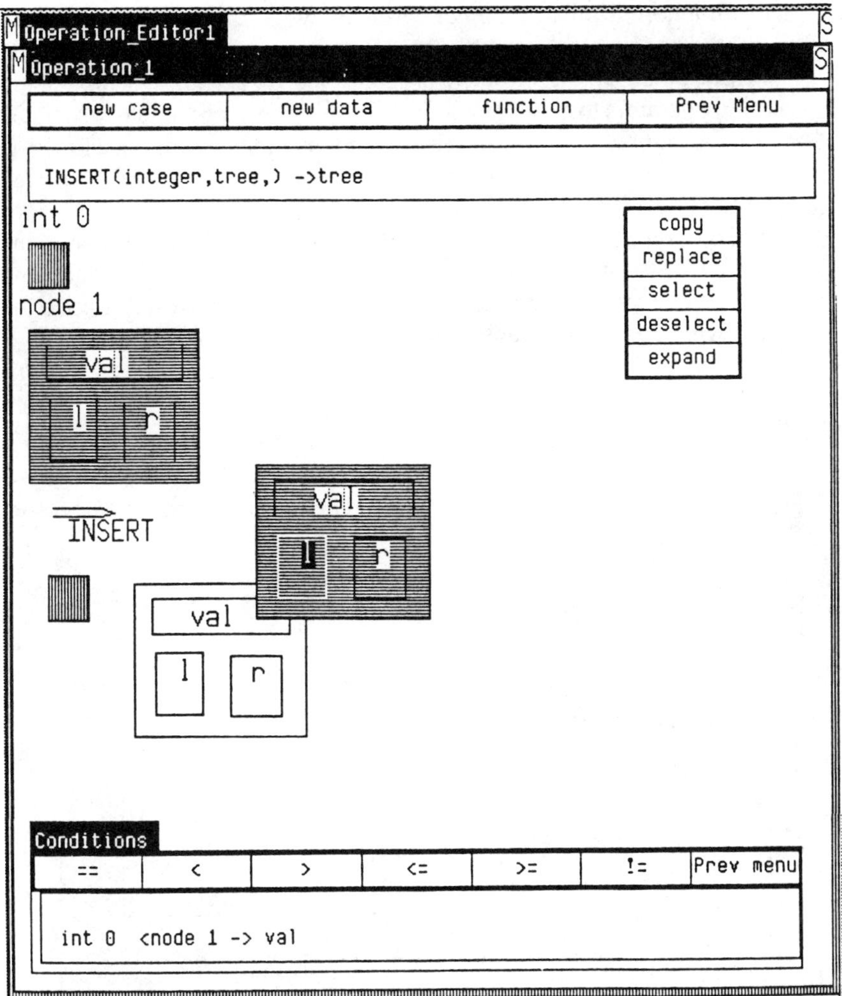

Demonstrating the operation. The result was generated by copying *node 1* from the argument. The function button was then depressed to invoke the INSERT function. The first argument was copied from *int 0,* and the *l field* was selected as the second argument. The *l field* was then expanded.

Figure 5-3. Demonstrating the Operation.
(Rubin et al.[14]. © 1985 IEEE.)

3. A *Function Editor at object level* allows a simple function to be created. At this level, the display represents an example of input and output data. An algorithm is programmed by pointing at inputs and using operators to combine them. The resulting expression is associated with output by pointing, and the system responds by adding a function graph to the display (Figure 5-4). The program can be executed immediately.
4. A *Function Editor at function level* provides the means for combining simple functions into compound functions and allows conditionals and loops to be included. Figure 5-5 shows a program corresponsing to the following Pascal fragment:

```
GetData;
while NotDone do
  begin Density; GetData end;
```

The four editors can be entered and exited at the touch of a mouse button,

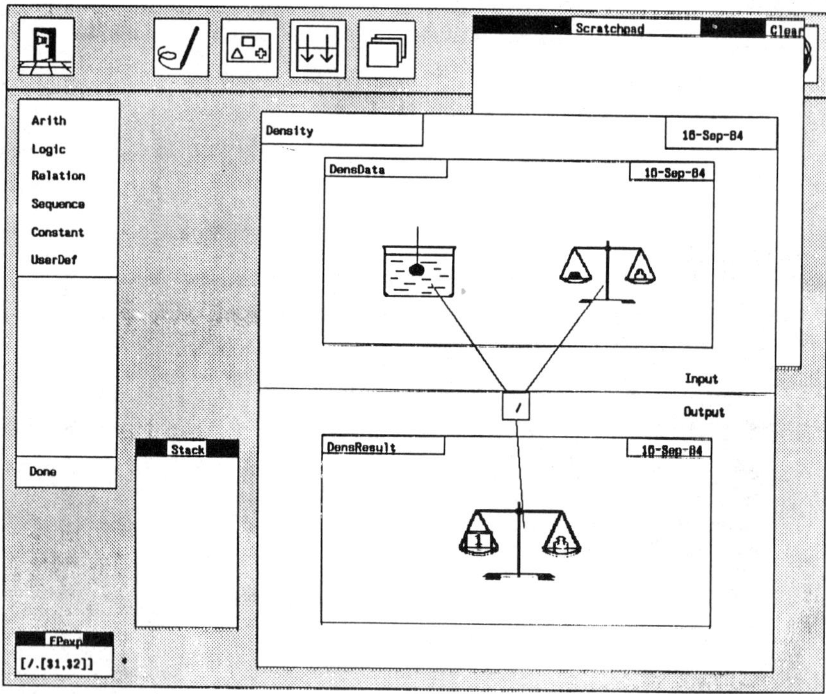

Figure 5-4. Displaying a function at the object level. (Raeder[3]. Original art courtesy of G. Raeder.)

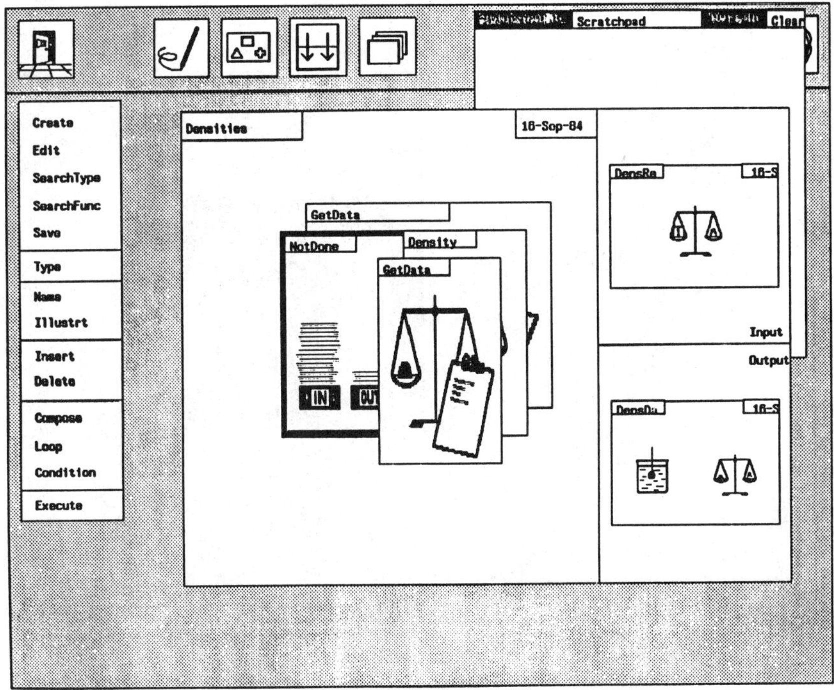

Figure 5-5. Composing a function at the function level. (Raeder[3]. Original art courtesy of G. Raeder.)

and the state of each editor is preserved between entries. A global scratch pad is used to transfer entities between the editors.

A user interface management system called *Peridot*[16,17] is currently under development by Myers and Buxton at the University of Toronto. Peridot is an acronym for "Programming by Example for Real-time Interface Design Obviating Typing." Peridot restricts the form of user interface to *graphical, direct manipulation interfaces* and aims at creating code for these user interfaces while the designer *demonstrates* how the interface should look and work.

The general strategy is to allow the designer to *draw* the screen display that the end user will see and to perform actions that the end user might do (such as moving a mouse or pressing a mouse button or keyboard key). When *specifying* the action portion of the user interface, the designer typically moves a simulated input or changes the status of one of its buttons, and then performs some operation (see Figure 5-6).

The system attempts to guess (or infer) the relationship of that action to

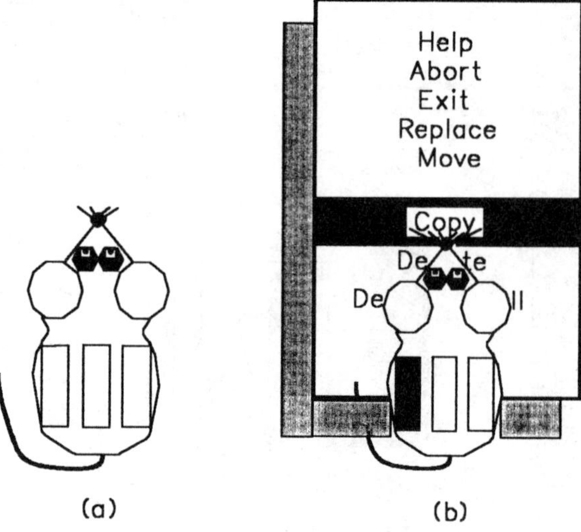

(a) A simulated "mouse" pointing device with three buttons. The device can be moved by pointing at the "nose" (using a real pointing device), and the buttons can be toggled by pressing over them. In (b), the simulated "mouse" with its left button down is being used to program a menu of strings by demonstration. The rectangle in reverse video (now over "Copy") will follow the mouse while the left button is down.

Figure 5-6. Using a simulated mouse.

existing elements of the user interface based on context, and asks the designer if the guess is correct (see Figure 5-7). If it is correct, code will be generated by the system to handle this action. If it is incorrect, other guesses are tried, or the designer can explicitly specify the relationship.

The guesses are encoded as simple condition-action rules, and the generated code is put into small, parameterized procedures which can be called from application programs or used in other user interface procedures created by demonstration.

AUTOPROGRAMMER

AutoProgrammer[7] is a classical example of an interactive computer programming system which automatically constructs computer programs from example executions given by the user. Unlike the recent work focusing on building highly interactive graphical interfaces, this work is aimed at the development of a simple, reliable, effective, and convenient *program synthesizer.*

An AutoProgrammer system for integer calculations has been implemented and tested extensively by Biermann and Krishnaswamy.[7] The implemented instructions are *add, subtract, multiply, divide, move, read, write, call subroutine,*

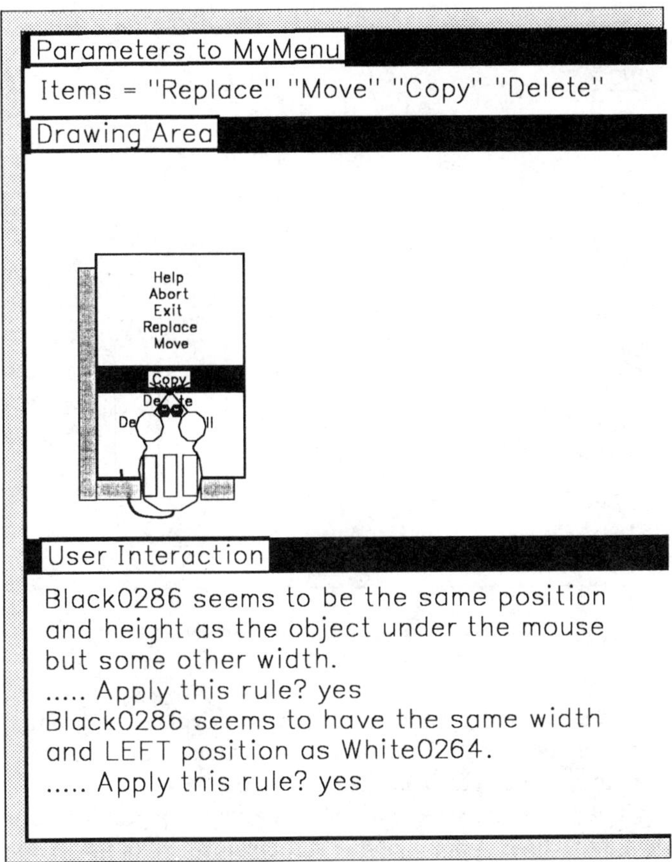

Figure 5-7. Defining an interaction, using the simulated mouse.

and *comparison operations* (greater than, equal to, or less than). The allowed data structures are individual variables, linear, and rectangular integer arrays.

The example calculation begins with a declaration of the name of the routine to be created and any parameter inputs to be included with its call. Then the data structures which are to appear on the screen are declared. The declarations include not only arrays and variables but also pointers into arrays. Thus, if *I* is declared as a pointer into linear array *A*, and *I* has the value 3, then an arrow labeled *I* will point to the third location in *A*. We can refer graphically to the location *A(I)* by touching the pointer and to location *A(3)* by touching the actual location *A(3)*. Figure 5-8 gives some examples of data structure declarations as shown on the AutoProgrammer screen.

Once the data structures have appeared on the screen, one may begin the

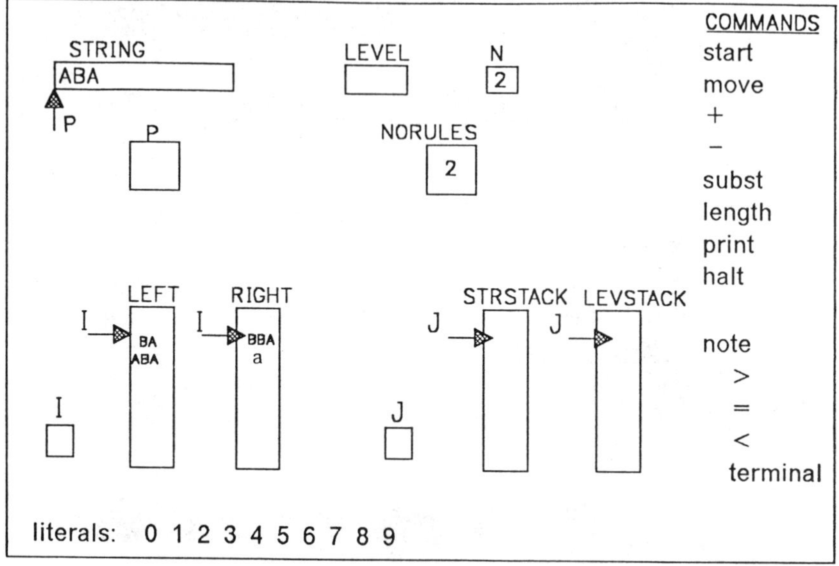

Figure 5-8. Example of Autoprogrammer screen.

sample calculation using the graphic input device (a light pen in the implemented system). In the following discussion, a graphical input, on one pair of *x,y*-coordinates, is referred to as a *touch* or *hit*.

The instructions to the system are indicated by sequential touches of the command name which appears on the screen and each of its operands. The system stores a detailed history of all the steps executed in the process, and then synthesizes the shortest possible program which is capable of executing the examples.

AutoProgrammer has been used to create a large number of programs, including a few examples as complex as a small compiler for a simple Algol-like language called *Y73*. In the following, we use simple examples to give the flavor of the AutoProgrammer approach.

First, we use an example from Biermann and Krishnaswamy[7] to show the "demonstrational" aspects of the process. Let us assume that we wish to create a program called POWER which reads an integer X, a positive integer N, and computes *X* ** *N*. First, three variables, X, N, and ANSWER, are declared and the AutoProgrammer screen appears as shown in Figure 5-9.

Next, an example computation must be done. The purpose is to demonstrate the desired behavior of the routine. Figure 5-10 shows the calculation of 3^2.

The demonstration consists of a sequence of hits. The first hit on the

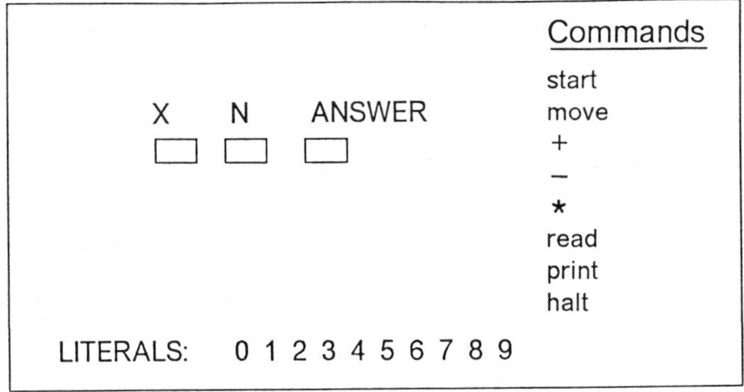

Figure 5-9. Autoprogrammer screen before hand calculation of X**N.

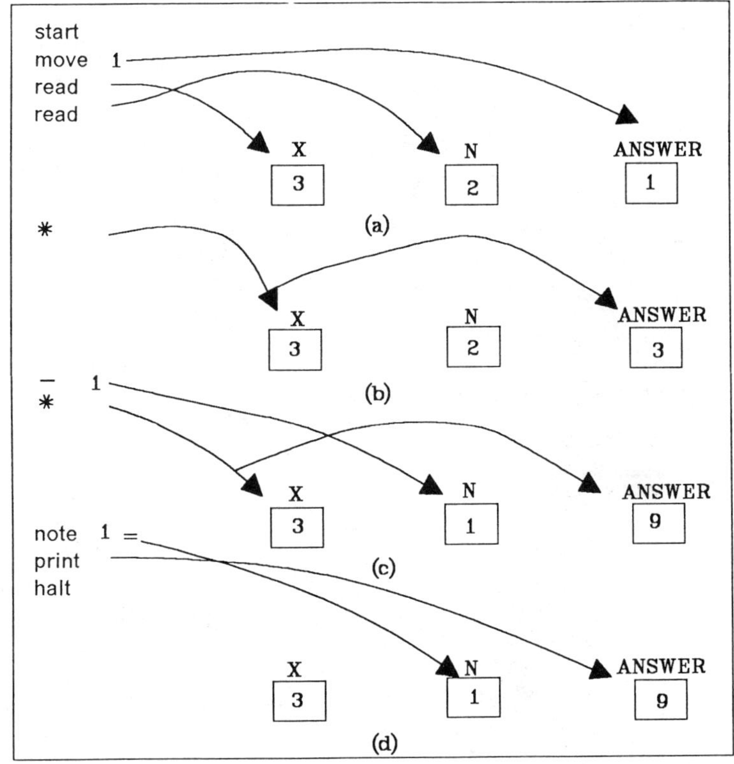

Figure 5-10. Demonstrating by hand the desired behavior of POWER.
(a) Beginning the calculation.
(b) Computing the first power of X.
(c) Computing the second power of X.
(d) Noting the termination condition and printing the result.

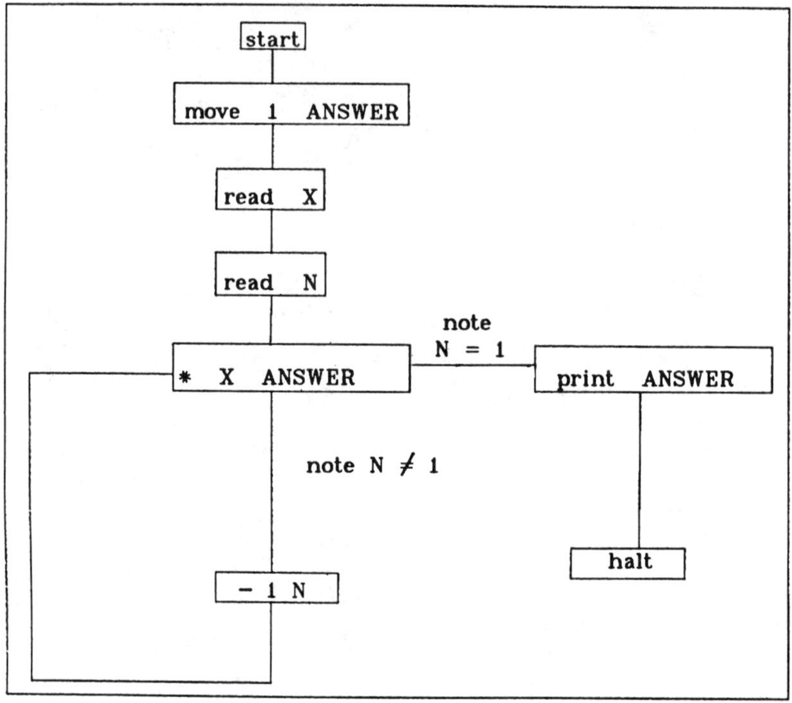

Figure 5-11. Automatically created routine POWER.

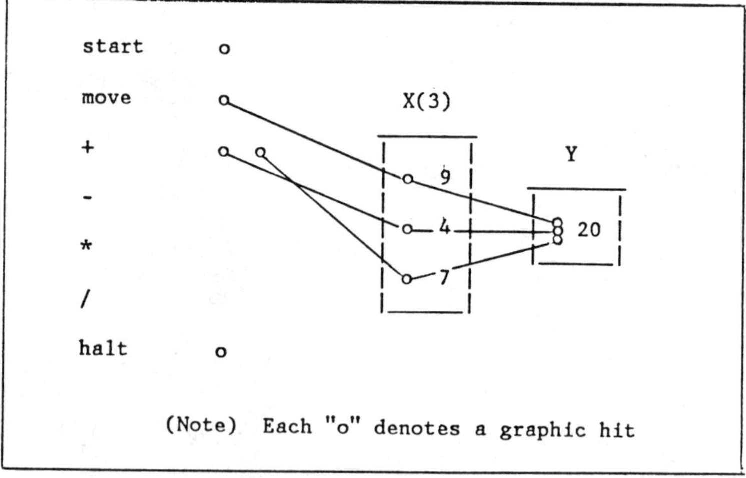

Figure 5-12. Graphic hits that demonstrate column addition.

AutoProgrammer screen is the *start* instruction, the second is *move,* the third is the literal *1* at the bottom of the screen, the fourth is *ANSWER,* and so forth. After the last instruction, *halt,* has been executed, the system creates the program shown in Figure 5-11.

Program synthesis is done from the example sequence of instructions. To give some idea of how a program might be synthesized from examples, we use materials from Biermann.[5]

Let us assume that we want to create a program that adds a column of numbers. The data structures are declared and are displayed on the screen with sample data. Then an example is executed with the light pen, using available commands which are also displayed (see Figure 5-12).

The eleven graphic hits shown in Figure 5-12 result in the computation trace of five AutoProgrammer instructions:

(1) start
(2) move X(1) Y
(3) + X(2) Y
(4) + X(3) Y
(5) halt

The task of the program synthesizer is to find the shortest program, not counting indexing instructions, that can execute this computation trace. The synthesis method is to move down the trace sequentially and for each executed instruction either (1) create an instruction in the program to do that execution or (2) find a previously created instruction in the program to do that execution and add transitions properly to guarantee that the instruction execution will be performed properly.

Beginning with the first two instructions of the trace, the program construction starts as shown in Figure 5-13(a). The third instruction in the trace is examined to see whether any program instruction could have done this task, and finds that none could. So another program instruction is added to the constructed partial program, as shown in Figure 5-13(b).

Comparison of the fourth instruction in the trace with the already created instructions in the program indicates that the instruction (+ X(2) Y) in the program might also be able to perform (+ X(3) Y). The goal is thus to merge these two instructions by inserting proper indexing instructions.

The problem of adding indexing instructions is formulated as follows:

a. Which transitions should have associated indexing instructions?
b. Which indexing form should be attached to the chosen transition?
   $I \leftarrow C$ (i.e., initialize the index I with constant C)
   or
   $I \leftarrow I + C$ (i.e., increment the index I with constant C)?
c. What should be the values of the constants?

(a)

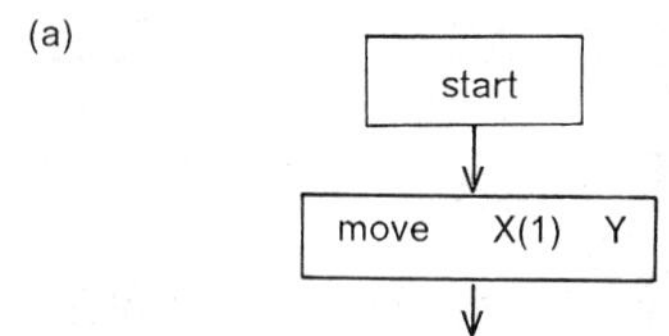

(b)

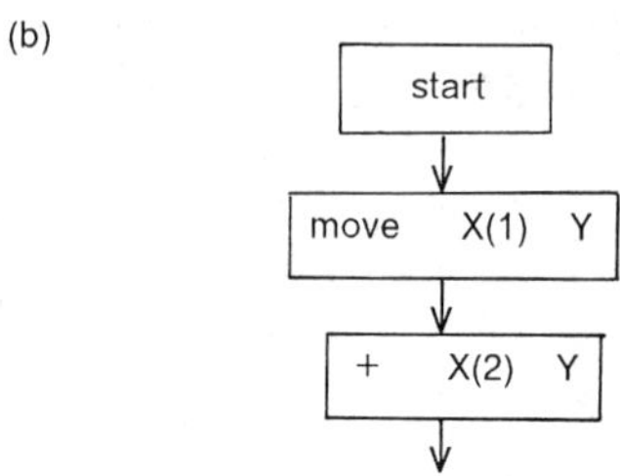

(c)

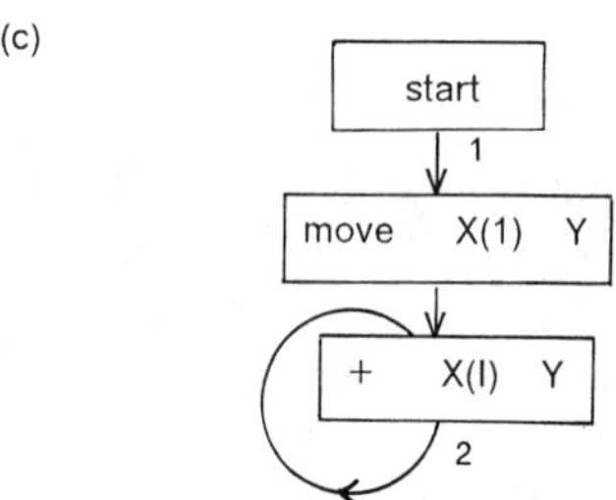

Figure 5-13. Constructing the example program.

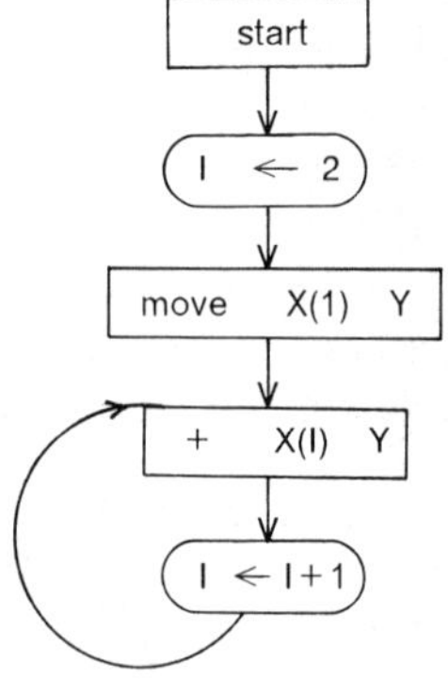

Figure 5-14. The partial program with indexing instruction inserted.

Concerning (a), it can be shown that no transition need have an associated indexing instruction unless the instruction initiating the transition has one of the following properties:

1. It has more than one transition entering it.
2. It has more than one transition leaving it.
3. It has references to an index.
4. It is the start instruction.

Suppose m transitions have been found with property 1, 2, 3, or 4; then there are 2 ** m possible ways of assigning to these transitions their associated indexing forms, I ← C or I ← I + C. Each of these possible feasible assignments is tried until one is found such that there is a solution to the problem of determining the values of the constants. Any assignment that increments I before initializing I is considered not feasible.

Because the possible indexing instructions are so simple, the set of unknown constants can be determined by linear algebra.

Returning to the above example, the program created so far has three instructions and three transitions (see Figure 5-13(c)). The two transitions marked 1 and 2 satisfy criteria 4 and 3 above, respectively, and so may have indexing instructions attached. If we attach the form I ← C1 to transition 1 and I ← I + C2 to transition 2, two equations may be derived from the original trace:

$$2 = C1 \qquad 3 = C2 + 2.$$

There exists a solution to these equations, and so the associated indexing instructions can be added to the program, as shown in Figure 5-14.

Given this program, we would expect the fifth instruction in the trace to be (+ X(4) Y), the sixth to be (+ X(5) Y), and so forth. But, in fact, the fifth instruction is *halt,* so either a way must be found to break out of the loop or it must be concluded that the partial program is incorrect and should be changed.

The system notes the contradiction and tries to find a test that will enable the addition of a new transition out of the instruction (+ X(I) Y). It checks whether the index I equals any important variable like an array dimension, sees that I = #X (where #X is the number of entries in X), and so completes the synthesis by producing the program shown in Figure 5-15.

Working examples by hand can be tiresome because of the repetitive nature of some calculations. As an illustration, the previous example of column addition would have been significantly more bothersome if the array had twenty entries instead of three. Various ways have been developed to

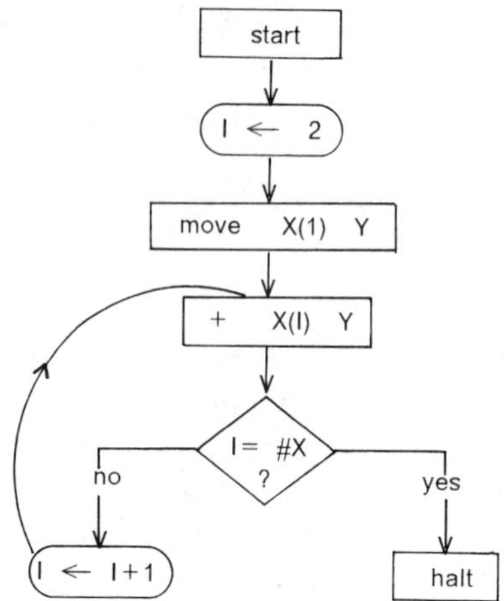

Figure 5-15. The program for adding a column. (#X stands for the number of entries in X)

add the twenty entries without having to demonstrate nineteen *add* instructions in sequence.

One technique involves the use of dynamic program synthesis and the *continue* feature. The AutoProgrammer dynamically maintains a partial program at all times during execution of the example calculation. Thus, after the third item in X is added, the partial program of Figure 5-14 exists in the machine. Interestingly enough, this partial program is capable of adding the other seventeen entries in the array without further demonstration from the user. So if at any time the system constructs a program such that the instruction just given by the user is followed by a valid transition, it flashes the word *"continue"* on the screen.

If the user wishes to allow the partial program to continue the calculation rather than doing the instructions by hand, he can simply hit the *continue* command repeatedly and watch the calculations proceed.

If the program begins some action that does not agree with the user's desire (either because the user has made an error in previous example calculations or has changed his mind about what the program should do), he can use the *backup* command to undo the undesired action. He can then insert by hand whatever instructions he prefers. Finally, if appropriate, he can return to the use of *continue* to finish the calculation. In any case, he can use *continue* to hurry through all repetitive parts of any example.

This example gives the flavor of the AutoProgrammer's approach to program synthesis without introducing the considerable complexities that arise when the process is attempted in the most general case. Biermann and

Krishnaswamy were able to prove that their program synthesis system "is both *sound* and *complete,* in the following senses: It is guaranteed that the synthesized program will correctly execute the given examples (soundness) and that every possible program (or its equivalent) can be created by the system (completeness)."[7]

PROGRAMMING BY REHEARSAL

Programming by Rehearsal[8,18] provides an interesting visual programming environment to allow curriculum designers, who may have had no previous programming experience, to design and implement educational software for their students to use. It was implemented by William Finzer and Laura Gould in Smalltalk on the Xerox 1132 Scientific Information Processor (the Dorado).

The work is based on the belief that "in the creation of educational software it is particularly important that the design decisions be made by someone who understands how students learn and what they enjoy rather than by someone whose expertise is in how computers work."[8]

Since the intended users are nonprogrammers, it is useful to introduce a metaphor in which the unfamiliar concepts of programming have familiar real-world referents. The world in which the designer works may be thought of as a *theater* where performers interact with one another on a stage by sending cues. This design environment is called the *Rehearsal World* and the process of creating a production is called "Programming by Rehearsal." Almost all of the designer's interactions with the Rehearsal World occur through the selection (with a mouse) of some performer or some cue to a performer.

The creation of a Rehearsal World production generally involves the following:

- Auditioning the available performers by selecting their cues and observing their responses to determine which are appropriate for the planned production.
- Copying the chosen performers and placing them on a stage.
- Blocking the production by resizing and moving the performers until they are the desired size and in the desired place.
- Rehearsing the production by showing each performer what actions it should take in response either to user input or to cues sent by the other performers.
- Storing the production away for later retrieval.

The following gives some background information so that one can imagine how this process can be achieved.

In the Rehearsal World, everything is concrete. Only things that can be seen can be manipulated. Selection is accomplished by pointing to the desired entity and then clicking one of the three mouse buttons. The PERFORM button is used to cause the selected entity to perform its action. The NAME button causes the name of the entity to appear at the cursor point, and the cursor becomes a text cursor. This text cursor will follow the mouse until the next click. If that click occurs in a sensitive area, the text will stick there. This is called *pasting.* If a text cursor is pasted in the help area, text describing the selected entity appears. The MENU button always produces a menu relevant to a particular entity.

The world is made visible on a large high-resolution display screen. The screen that the designer sees initially is virtually empty except for a large "help area" called the *prompter's box* in which "help text" appears and a control panel along the bottom containing six *control buttons* whose functions are specified by their labels. For example, the action of the *STAGES* button, when selected, is to produce a copy of the Stages menu and to cause it to follow the mouse until the next mouse click.

Note that the first entry on the Stages Menu (Figure 5-16) is *AnEmptyStage.* When this entry is selected, an empty stage appears on which the designer may copy performers to start a new production.

A predefined set of eighteen *performers* can be found on stages (see Figure 5-16). They are grouped into troupes: BasicTroupe, ControlTroupe, DebugTroupe, GraphicsTroupe, and TimeTroupe. Each Troupe contains a set of (primitive) performers with somewhat related functionality. For instance, the *BasicTroupe* contains a Text, a Number, and a Counter performer. The *GraphicsTroupe* consists of a Picture performer which presents a bitmap picture (selected from an existing picture dictionary) on the screen, a Traveler performer which presents a picture that can be made to move, and a Logo-type Turtle performer, as well as a Rectangle performer and a Position performer. The *TimeTroupe* consists of five performers: a digital clock, a language clock, an elapsed time clock, a wall clock, and a real-time clock. Similarly, the *ControlTroupe* consists of the Repeater, the TrueFalse, the List, and the Pointer performers. The *DebugTroupe* has only one performer, whose special functionality is obtained by selecting its STEP and RUN switches. The entire set of Troupes are referred as *Central Casting.*

Having copied some performers from Central Casting onto a stage, the designer can proceed to direct them with regard to their appearance, placement, movements, and interactions.

The Rehearsal World can also have *wings.* The wings of a stage can be thought of as an extension to the stage. Performers which are not meant to be seen by the students can be placed in the wings. Like the stage, the wings may be made any size and placed in any position the designer desires.

* PROGRAMMING BY REHEARSAL *

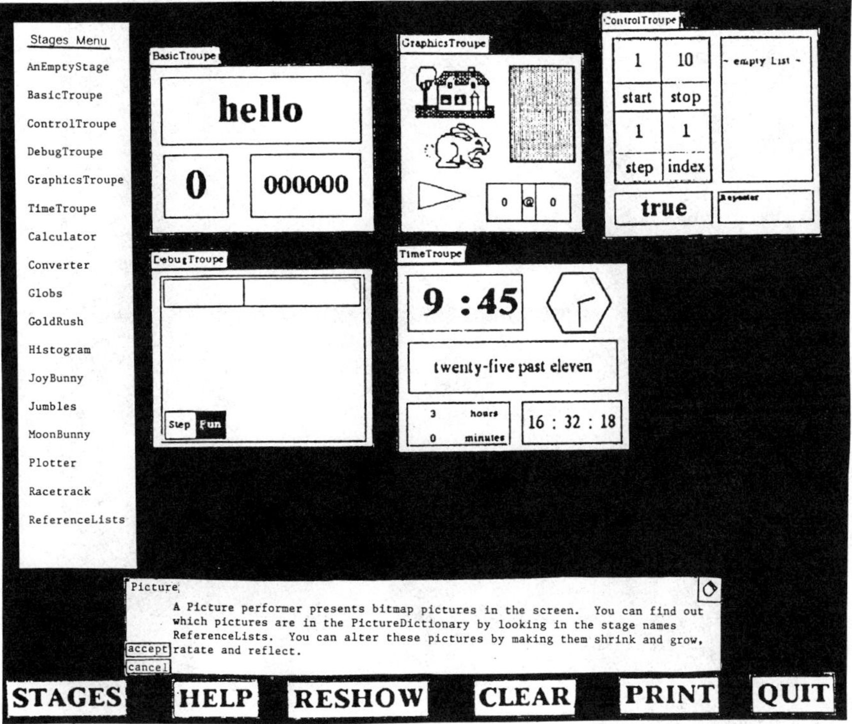

Figure 5-16. The Stages Menu and Central Casting.

The Rehearsal World theater can display any number of stages and wings at a time. Thus, for example, all of Central Casting can be made visible at the same time (see Figure 5-16).

A *cue* is a command which is sent to a performer or a stage to produce a *response.* Designers audition performers by sending them cues and observe their responses. Performers communicate with one another by sending each other cues.

In order to audition a performer to find out what it can do, a designer uses the MENU button of the mouse to elicit its *category menu* (see left panel, Figure 5-17). This menu consists of two parts. The top part always contains the most commonly used cues—*move, resize, copy, erase,* and *cleanup*—which are known to all performers. The remainder of the menu consists not of cues but of *categories of cues.* The categories near the top of this list are common to most performers (NAME & TITLE, FONTS, FORMAT, etc).

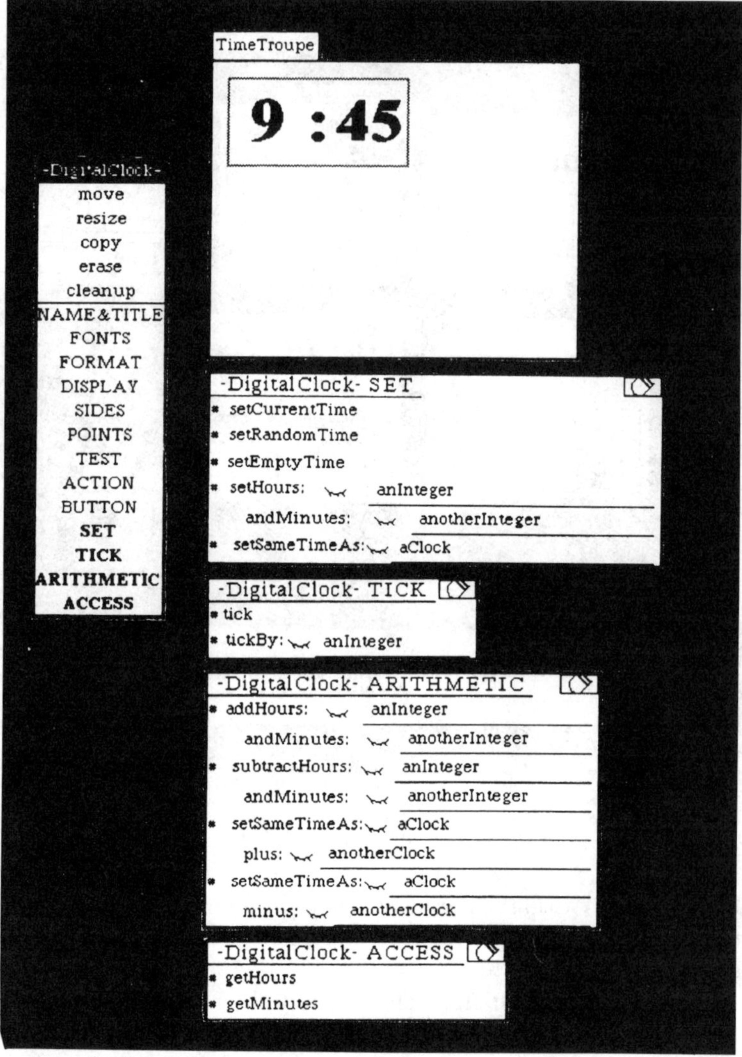

Figure 5-17. The Category menu and cues for Digital Clock performer
(© copyright 1984 Xerox Corporation. All rights reserved. Reprinted by permission.)

Those in boldface near the bottom are categories specific to the performer. For example, as shown in Figure 5-17, the categories of cue specific to the DigitalClock performer are *SET, TICK, ARITHMETIC,* and *ACCESS.* When the designer selects a category, a *cue sheet* appears for further selection (see Figure 5-17).

Figure 5-17 shows the cues for the DigitalClock performer. While some cues (like *tick*) require no further information from the designer, many others require one or more parameters to complete the specification of their function. Thus the cue *tickBy:* requires a single numeric parameter (e.g., 5) to specify how many minutes a clock should advance when this cue is selected.

Note that the presence of a parameter (in any cue) is signaled by a colon and a parameter line which is provided as a place for the designer to enter the needed information. The small icon (called the "eyecon") at the beginning of every parameter line normally has the form of a closed eye. When the eyecon is selected, the eye flies open to indicate that the parameter line is *watching*. The designer may then select a cue or do some editing or pasting. The system will generate some Smalltalk code representing what has happened and write it on the parameter line, and the eye closes again.

When a designer selects a cue from a category menu or a cue sheet, the performer *responds immediately*. Most responses produce some visible change on the screen for the designer to see. The response to a given cue will be the same for every copy of a particular performer that is made. However, different performers may respond differently to the same cue. For example, when a DigitalClock performer receives the *tick* cue, it responds by increasing its minutes value by one. When a WallClock receives the *tick* cue, it responds by moving its minute hand an appropriate number of degrees.

Some performers have been given *DefaultActions* that they perform when selected with the PERFORM button. For example, the DefaultAction of a Text performer is to make itself editable, which it indicates by showing a caret at the end of its text (see Figure 5-18); the DefaultAction of a Turtle is to follow the mouse; some performers do nothing while they are waiting for a cue.

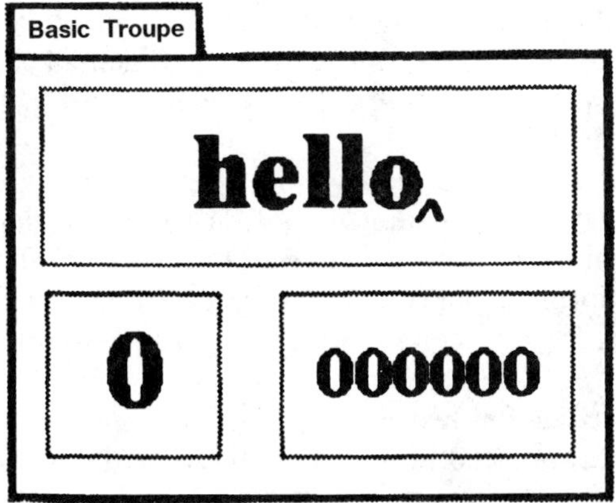

Figure 5-18. A selected Text performer showing its editing caret.

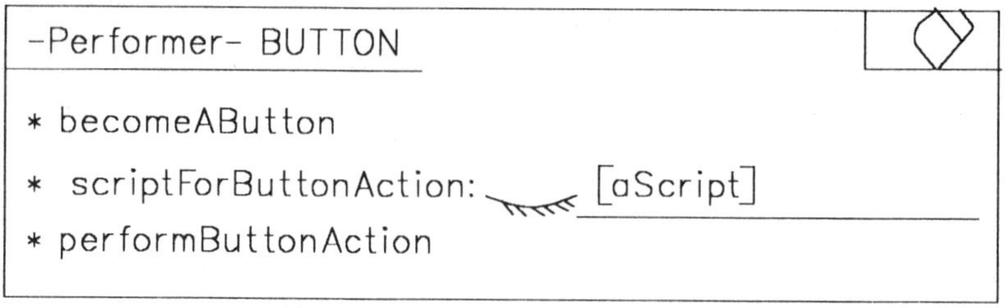

```
-Performer- BUTTON
* becomeAButton
* scriptForButtonAction:  [aScript]
* performButtonAction
```

Figure 5-19. Cue sheets with the cues *scriptForButtonAction*.

Designers cannot redefine the DefaultAction of a performer, but they can inhibit it by sending the cue *InhibitAction.* Alternatively, they can turn the performer into a *button* by using the *becomeAButton* cue, and then define its *ButtonAction* by using the *scriptForButtonAction* cue (see Figure 5-19).

In order for performers to interact as well as to act, some methods must be provided whereby the sending of a cue results in a response from some other performer besides the receiver of that cue. Declaring that a performer has become a button and defining what action it should perform is one mechanism whereby the interactions may be specified.

"The second mechanism is to define what action a performer should take when it is *changed* in some profound fashion, either by the user or by the action of some other performer. The definition of what constitutes a profound change is embedded in the description of each performer type. For example, whenever a number changes its value, or a Rectangle changes its dimensions, or a turtle changes its location or direction, its *ChangeAction* will be executed."[18] The designers may specify actions of this kind by using the *scriptForChangeAction* cue. Similar to the definition of ButtonAction, parameters to the cue for the definition of ChangeAction are scripts supplied by the designer. These scripts consists of Smalltalk statements which can often be produced by editing or pasting existing cues while the parameter line is "watching."

The stage, its wings, and all of its interacting performers constitute a production. Note that a production differs from a troupe in that the performers in a production interact with one another through their designer-specified scripts. The performers in a troupe have not been taught any interactions. (See Figure 5-20 for a screen on which a designer is constructing a new production.)

When a designer has finished copying, placing, and directing the performers regarding their actions and interactions, the production can be stored for later use by means of the *store* cue. The production may then be retrieved for further refinements or by its eventual audience, the user.

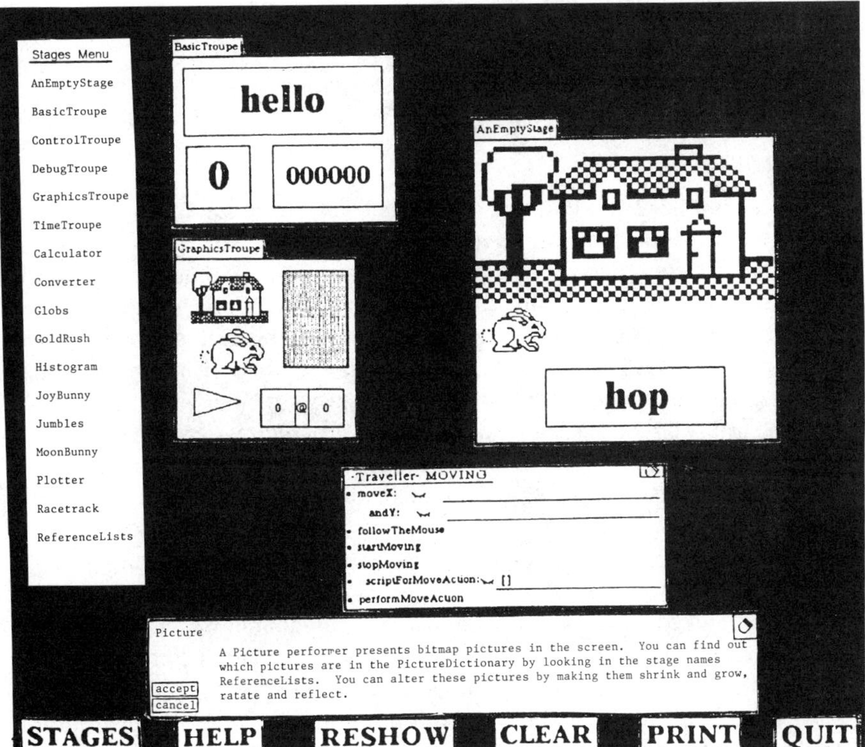

Figure 5-20. A designer is constructing a new production.

The eighteen performers in Central Casting and their predefined cues have been chosen to provide the basic functionality that every designer will need. However, no fixed set of functions will ever be adequate. In the Rehearsal World, when the designer needs a new performer, he can construct one by aggregating existing performers on a stage, teaching that stage some appropriate new cues as long as the scripts which define their actions can be constructed from existing cues.

Eventually, a designer may need a performer that *cannot* be constructed from any of the performers in Central Casting. In this case, one must work at the level of a Smalltalk-80 programmer to define new performers and new cues.

But, in many cases, the designers do not have to know the Smalltalk language, as most of the coding is done by "watching." While the eye is open, the designers rehearse a performer and the system makes a record of this rehearsal. The designers know whether or not the code is correct, not so much by reading the code but by observing whether the effect produced on the stage is the desired one.

SUMMARY

At the beginning of this chapter, we characterize the visual coaching system as one that instructs the computer to *"Do as I show you"* or *"Do according to my signal."* Depending on the center of attention, systems of the visual coaching category can further be grouped into (1) those focusing on the inductive inferencing capability so that generalized programs can be synthesized and (2) those focusing on graphical interactions in a visual environment so that program construction can be quick, easy, and enjoyable.

In the last two sections, we described AutoProgrammer and Programming by Rehearsal at some length, with the intention of showing the common characteristics as well as the distinctive differences between these two groups.

Obviously, there are many characteristics that are common to both groups. They both use examples; the user has direct visual contact with the objects of interest and can manipulate them in a natural manner with his hands; the user deals with the effects of the program rather than with the program itself; there is no need to learn a programming language.

At the same time, they both have limitations. However, other than the physical limitations imposed by the space on the screen, their limitations are not of the same nature.

The first group can produce a program from incomplete information, but it assumes that the user knows how he wants the computation to be performed. For example, column addition in AutoProgrammer requires the series of graphic hits shown in Figure 5-12. While it is reasonable to assume that the user knows that the addition is to be accomplished by (move X(1) Y) followed by (+ X(2) Y) and (+ X(3) Y), it is not reasonable to assume that, in a general case, a user (especially a nonprogrammer) will know enough about the procedural aspects of programming when he wants to have somewhat complicated computations done.

The second group, on the other hand, offers a much more intuitive environment, but the problem domain is restricted. For example, as Finzer and Gould put it, "The Rehearsal World does not provide designers with the facility to create new types of actions for new performers, and this may become a problem in the future."[18] Furthermore, there is no abstraction in the Rehearsal World and its watching facility makes no generalizations (watching merely makes a record of a performer being sent a cue, perhaps with parameters). This kind of scheme works well when the object being designed has an obvious, direct representation. But it becomes difficult when one needs to express some ideas in more abstract and general terms. Again, quoting Finzer and Gould, "As designers create increasingly large and sophisticated productions, they may find it a nuisance to have to instantiate everything (even temporary variables) in the form of a performer."[8] "Concreteness" is fine when it is used to help people understand the underlying principles, but it should not be viewed as a substitute for abstraction and generalization.

In spite of these limitations, visual coaching represents an interesting way of program construction. In the future, no doubt, we will see the merge of the techniques used by the two schools. When the two diverse disciplines (artificial intelligence and graphical interactions) are pulled together, both will benefit, and the result could be indeed exciting.

REFERENCES

1. Myers, B. A., "Visual Programming, Programming by Example, and Program Visualization: A Taxonomy," *CHI'86 Proceedings* (Apr. 1986), pp. 59-66.
2. Chang, S. K., "Visual Languages: A Tutorial and Survey," *IEEE Software,* Vol. 4, No. 1 (Jan. 1987), pp. 29-39.
3. Raeder, G., "Programming in Pictures," Ph.D. dissertation, Department of Computer Science, University of Southern California (Nov. 1984).
4. Barr, A., and Feigenbaum, E. A., *The Handbook of Artificial Intelligence,* Vol. 2, Chapter X, William Kaufmann, Inc., Los Altos, Calif. (1982).
5. Biermann, A. W., "Approaches to Automatic Programming," in *Advances in Computers,* Vol. 15, M. Rubinoff and M. C. Yovitz, editors, Academic Press, New York (1976), pp. 1-76.
6. Biermann, A. W., "Automatic Programming: A Tutorial on Formal Methodologies," *Journal of Symbolic Computation,* Vol. 1 (1985), pp. 119-142.
7. Biermann, A. W., and Krishnaswamy, R., "Constructing Programs from Example Computations," *IEEE Transactions on Software Engineering,* Vol. SE-2, No. 3 (Sept. 1976), pp. 141-153.
8. Finzer, W., and Gould, L., "Programming by Rehearsal," *Byte,* Vol. 9, No. 6 (June 1984), pp. 187-210. (Note: This is a shorter version of Gould and Finzer[18].)
9. Smith, D. C., "Pygmalion: A Creative Programming Environment," Ph.D. dissertation, Technical Report STAN-CS-75-499, Department of Computer Science, Stanford University (1975).
10. Curry, G. A., "Programming by Abstract Demonstration," Ph.D. dissertation, Technical Report No. 78-03-02, University of Washington (Mar. 1978).
11. Halbert, D. C., "Programming by Example," Ph.D. dissertation, Computer Science Division, University of California, Berkeley (1984).
12. Smith, D. C., Irby, C., and Kimball, R., "The Star User Interface: An Overview," *Proceedings of the National Computer Conference* (1982), pp. 515-528.
13. Shneiderman, B., "Direct Manipulation: A Step Beyond Programming Languages," *IEEE Computer,* Vol. 19, No. 8 (Aug. 1983), pp. 57-69.
14. Rubin, R. V., Golin, E. J., and Reiss S. P., "ThinkPad: A Graphical System for Programming by Demonstration," *IEEE Software,* Vol. 2, No. 2 (Mar. 1985), pp. 73-79.
15. Backus, J. W., "Can Programming Be Liberated from the Von Neumann Style? A Functional

Style and Its Algebra of Programs," *Communications of the ACM*, Vol. 21, No. 8 (Aug. 1978), pp. 613-641.

16. Myers, B. A., and Buxton, W., "Creating Highly-Interactive and Graphical User Interfaces by Demonstration," *SIGGRAPH'86 Proceedings* (Aug. 1986), pp. 249-258.
17. Myers, B. A., "Creating Dynamic Interaction Techniques by Demonstration," CHI + GI 1987 Conference Proceedings (Apr. 1987), pp. 271-278.
18. Gould, L., and Finzer, W., "Programming by Rehearsal," Technical Report SCL-84-1, Xerox Corp., Palo Alto Research Center (May 1984).

Chapter 6

Languages for Handling Visual Information

As we mentioned earlier, the emphasis of the visual environment is on interaction, not on languages. Visual languages, on the other hand, focus on language aspects. Depending on the objectives, visual languages can be further classified into three categories: languages for handling visual information, for supporting visual interaction, or for programming with visual expressions.

In this chapter, we discuss visual languages of the first category. These are the languages designed to process image or pictorial information.

The collection and processing of image data, based on photographs, drawings, or pictures transmitted by satellites or generated by computers, is undergoing a period of dramatic growth. When Nagy and Wagle published their survey in 1979,[1] they stated that "A recent inventory lists over 320 information systems and programs for spatial data handling." It is hard to imagine how many there are now.

The proliferation of image information systems is not surprising, since the technological advances are exciting and the potential applications are boundless. In this book, we do not attempt to cover the developments in this fast-growing field, except to bring out the differences between the languages for *processing visual information* from the visual programming languages (cf. Chapter 8) which actually facilitate *programming with visual expressions.* Readers interested in pictorial information systems may refer to a number of surveys published in the literature.[1-7]

Within the broad spectrum of pictorial processing technologies, our interest is in the languages developed for the manipulation and querying of pictorial data. To further narrow the scope without affecting the characterization of this category of languages, we omit discussion of the graphical extensions of well-known programming languages as, for example, has been done for SNOBOL,[8] FORTRAN,[9] ALGOL 60,[10] PL/I,[11] EULER,[12] ALGOL 68,[13] and Pascal.[14] Instead, we look at *languages of a higher level* and use concrete examples to elucidate their characteristics. Before we go into them, a brief note of historical interest may help to unravel a common thread.

In the early 1970s, the image processing systems designed for the handling of two-dimensional pictorial data and the database management systems designed for the storage, retrieval, and management of alphanumeric data were developed in parallel at different camps. Image processing systems were mostly designed for scientific, engineering, geographical, and medical applications. Each image processing system was tailored for a specific purpose in a special environment, which makes the sharing of pictorial data very difficult, if not impossible.

Database management systems, on the other hand, were designed for business applications. Their primary goal was to allow sharing of data while maintaining data independence and integrity and controlling data redundancy and privacy. The handling of pictorial data was not part of their domain. It was difficult, if not impossible, to use the conventional query languages to express or manipulate the spatial relationships.

By the late 1970s, technologies of pictorial data processing and database management began to merge. The growing amount of pictorial data being generated and analyzed, the expanding sphere of applications, and the ever-increasing need to share and to make pictorial data readily accessible have motivated the development of "generalized" systems. One relatively straightforward approach is to incorporate picture processing capabilities into the conventional database query languages. Consequently, a number of query languages for pictorial data are implemented as *augmented conventional query languages.*

For example, *GRAIN* (the Graphics-oriented Relational Algebraic INterpreter)[15] is an extension of *RAIN*[16], the relational algebraic interpreter developed at the University of Illinois; *GEO-QUEL*[17] is a geographical extension of *QUEL*[18], the query language developed at the University of California at Berkeley; Purdue University's *QPE* (Query-by-Pictorial-Example)[19] and Hiroshima University's *ARES*[20] are graphical extentions of *QBE* (Query-By-Example)[21], developed at the Thomas Watson Research Center of IBM; *PSQL* (Pictorial Structured Query Language)[22] of the University of Maryland is an extension of the query language, known as *SEQUEL* or *SQL*[23], developed at the IBM San Jose Research Laboratory for the relational database management System *R.* Augmented versions of SQL also serve as query languages for *ISQL* (Image-SQL)[24], *IDMS*[25], *ADM*[26], and *GADS*[27].

As another example, consider *SDMS*[28]. The usual mechanism for retrieving data from SDMS is by examining, with a joystick, a graphical data space (GDS) where pictorial representations of data are arranged (see Chapter 2). However, there are occasions when a more conventional query facility is desirable. "This can happen if the user does not know where some particular icon is spatially located, although he can describe it symbolically as, for instance, when trying to find a ship with a particular name. The symbolic query facility is also used by the database administrator to specify which tuples in a relation are to be displayed as icons in the GDS."[28] Thus, using QUEL (the query language of INGRES[18]) as the basis, additions are made for the graphical environment of SDMS. The augmented query language is called *SQUEL.*

These languages are often referred to as "pictorial query languages"—a term which may be misleading, since in most cases the query *languages* themselves are *not pictorial,* even though the data objects that they deal with are. Exceptions are QPE and ARES; they can be classified as table/form-based programming languages, since they are augmented on the two-dimensional query language QBE (see Chapter 11).

More recently, a joint effort represented by four research groups from the United States, Sweden, Italy, and Japan presented the design concepts for a generic image processing language called *IPL.*[29] The authors envision that there will be implementations of different subsets of this generic language based upon a host language such as Lisp, C, Pascal, etc.

The proposed language, IPL, is not an augmented query language. It consists of three subsets: the logical image processing language *LIPL,* the interactive image processing language *IIPL,* and the physical image processing language *PIPL.* Of these three subsets, the logical and physical image processing languages are used for processing image data; the interactive image processing language is used to support visual interactions. Again, all three subsets of IPL deal with visual objects, but the languages themselves are textual.

To give some flavor of the languages for handling pictorial information, we use GRAIN and PSQL as examples in the following discussion.

GRAIN

"Two problems can be distinguished in designing pictorial databases—the storage and retrieval of a large number of pictures, and the storage and retrieval of very large pictures, or pictures of great complexity."[15] *GRAIN* (Graphics-oriented Relational Algebraic INterpreter) was designed to address the first problem. Later, GRAIN was incorporated into *DIMAP,* a system for interactive map data retrieval and manipulation, with a zooming facility, in a distributed database environment.[30]

The primary goal of the GRAIN/DIMAP system is to investigate techniques for the efficient, flexible retrieval of pictorial data from large pictorial databases. The main idea is to represent pictorial information by both logical pictures and physical pictures. As will be seen in Chapter 11, the separation of logical pictures (or picture descriptions) from physical pictures (i.e., the original images) is also implemented in QPE.[19]

A physical picture is an image stored in an image store. A logical picture is a description (or abstraction) of the physical picture. Logical pictures are stored as relational tables in a relational database and are manipulated by means of a relational database manipulation language. Once a logical picture has been identified for retrieval, the corresponding physical picture can be generated on the output device by retrieving the bit representation from the image store.

To make the distinction among logical pictures and physical pictures conceptually clear, the following terminologies are used by Chang et al.[30]:

In Relational Database	In Image Store
d-map set	map set
d-map	map
d-frame/logical picture	frame/physical picture/image
relation	picture object set/features/overlay
tuple	picture object/feature

A *map set* is a hierarchical collection of maps, whose logical representa-

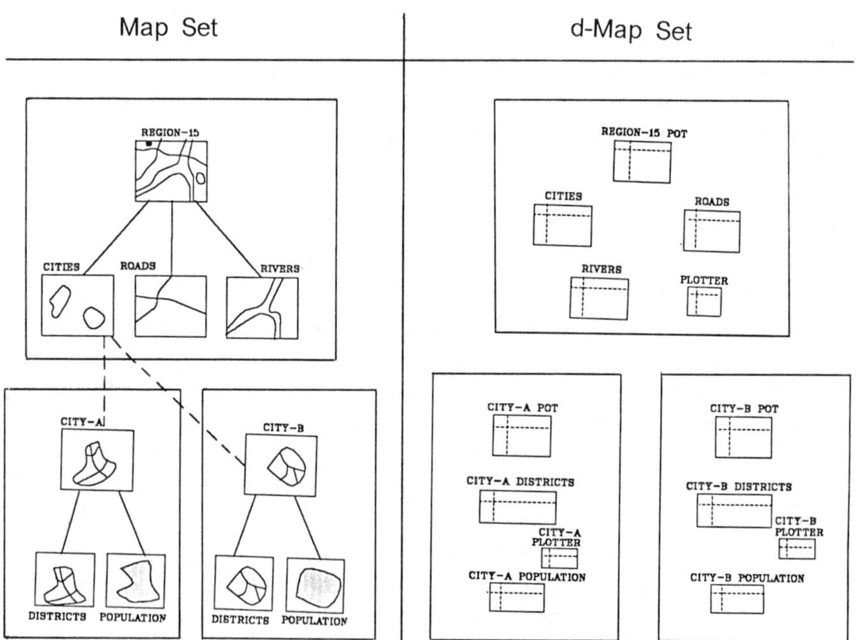

Figure 6-1. Correspondence of map set and d-map set.

tion is called a *d-map set.* The correspondence of the map set and the d-map set is illustrated in Figure 6-1.

In Figure 6-1, the map REGION-15 consists of three overlays: CITIES, ROADS, and RIVERS. In the cities overlay, there are two enlargeable picture objects, CITY-A and CITY-B, each corresponding to another map. The map CITY-A, in turn, consists of two overlays, DISTRICT and POPULATION.

A *map* is composed of one or more overlays, whose logical representation is called a *d-map.* The correspondence of the map and the d-map is illustrated in Figure 6-2. In addition to the relations CITIES, ROADS, and RIVERS, there are two additional relations, POT and PLOTTER. For each d-map, there is a special relation, POT (Picture Object Table), which contains detailed definitions of all the d-map relations. PLOTTER is a relation which associates the names of the graphics programs that can draw the picture objects corresponding to the relations in a d-frame (e.g., ./cityplot is the name of the graphics program that can draw a city).

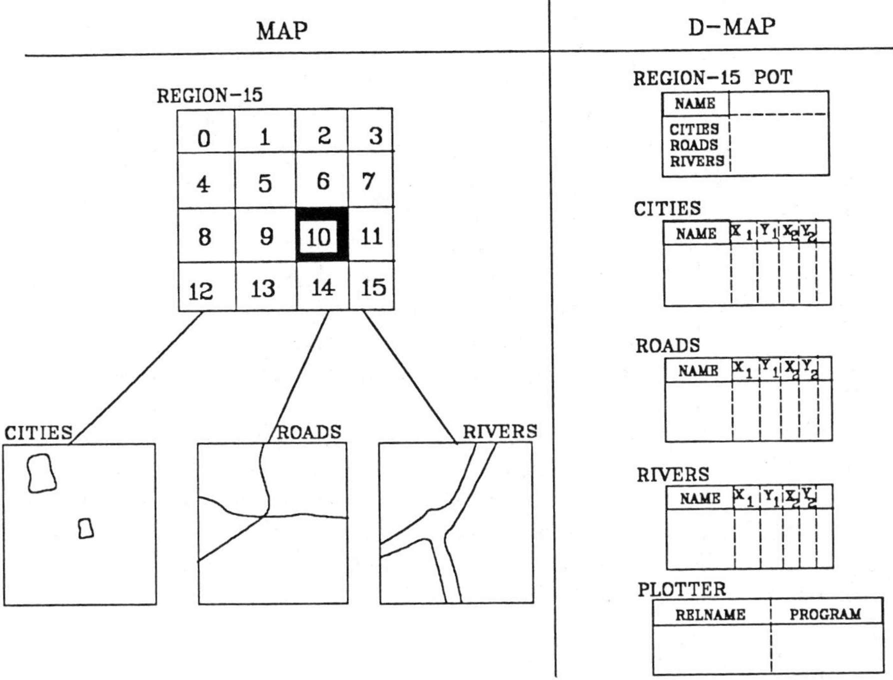

Figure 6-2. Correspondence of map and d-map.

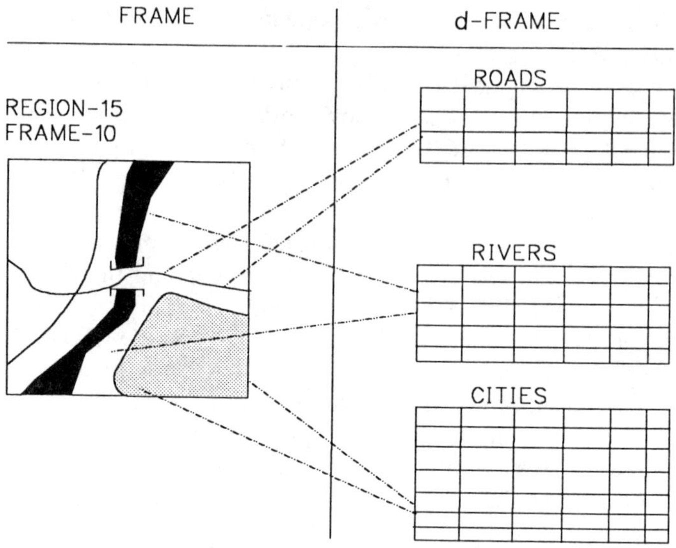

Figure 6-3. Correspondence of frame and d-frame.

A *frame* is the smallest unit for visual display, whose logical representation is called a d-frame. A *d-frame* is a set of relations from which a single frame buffer can be loaded. Figure 6-3 illustrates the correspondence of the frame and the d-frame.

Once the logical pictures are stored as relational tables, they can be retrieved and manipulated by the GRAIN language. Inquiries concerning the attributes of picture objects can also be handled by GRAIN. GRAIN language is an extension of RAIN, the Relational Algebraic INterpreter.[16] In GRAIN, a user's query is a sequence of one or more statements, where each statement is terminated by a period. Typical statement structures[31] are shown in Figure 6-4.

The command *get* is used to retrieve information associated with some or all attribute descriptors of picture objects that satisfy the condition specified. The *get* command is actually a RAIN command. The result is displayed in tabular form. No picture object's shape or geometrical description is shown in graphical form. For example, the following statement retrieves attributes of picture object named "123."

get pid, date, eye; *name equal* '123'.

The command *sketch* is used to plot a logical picture on the display screen

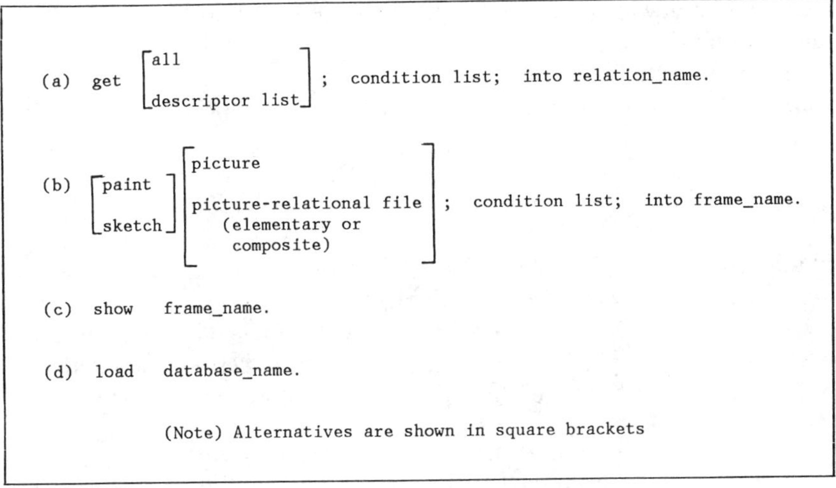

Figure 6-4. Typical statement structure in GRAIN for querying pictorial data.

as a line drawing. For example, to sketch the line drawing for the picture object "123," the following statement can be used.

sketch picture; name equal '123'.

The following are examples of using a condition list.

sketch railroad; rgage *greater than* '120'.
sketch picture; name equal 'railroad'; rgage *greater than* '120'.

If the clause "*into* frame-name" is specified with the *sketch* command, the logical picture selected will be converted into the physical picture and stored in the frame buffer named *frame-name.*

The command *paint* is used to display the physical picture on the display screen as a raster image or a line drawing, depending on the picture data type described in POT, the Picture Object Table. If the clause "*into* frame-name" is specified with the *paint* command, the physical picture will be stored in the frame buffer instead of being displayed on the screen.

The *show* or *display* command displays the physical picture stored in the named frame buffer on the screen.

The *draw* command (not shown in Figure 6-4) is used to create a line drawing for a new picture object with a given picture name. It invokes a graphics editor, which utilizes the graphic system for interactive creation of line drawings.

"Similarity retrieval" is possible. For example, to retrieve all highways which are similar to the highway named "h3," the following statement can be used:

sketch highway; *similar* (highway.name *equal* 'h3') *using* 'M1'.

In this statement, "M1" is the similarity measure routine supplied by the user for testing similarity among picture objects.

Complex retrieval can also be handled by a sequence of statements. For example, to paint a portion of a picture object with a certain color and paint other portion with a different color, the following statements can be used:

paint picture; name equal 'urban'; *with* 'red'; *into* frame-x.
paint picture; name equal 'forest'; *with* 'green'; *into* frame-x.
display frame-x.

The zooming technique introduced in DIMAP consists of vertical zoom (closeup view of a picture), horizontal zoom (display of subsets of picture objects corresponding to a selection index), and diagonal zoom (correlation capabilities among picture files based on a user-defined relation among picture objects).

PSQL

In "An introduction to PSQL: A Pictorial Structured Query Language," Roussopoulos and Leifker stressed the point that "pictorial and alphanumeric databases must be integrated but the processing of the two must be clearly distinguished. Pictures are not naturally representable in alphanumeric encodings and they should therefore be presented to the user as pictures. Alphanumeric data associated with pictures can be displayed on or beside the picture."[22]

The pictorial database maintains the associations between the spatial and the alphanumeric objects. The system supports direct spatial search (which locates the spatial objects in a given geographic area of the picture) and indirect spatial search (which locates the spatial objects based on some nonspatial attributes and uses the associations between the spatial objects on the picture to place them on it).

PSQL is an extension of SQL[23] for retrieving information from the pictorial database. PSQL supports pictorial domains whose elements are objects found in pictures—for example, points on a map, highway segments, or geographic regions.

"Each domain has its own pictorial representation and form. Pictorial domains have their own comparison operators for comparing their elements. For example, regions have operators such as *covers, overlaps,* etc. Pictorial domains also have functions defined on them which compute some simple or aggregate attribute. A simple function for a region object is *area* which computes its area. An aggregate function on a set of highway segments is *northeast* which finds the northeast coordinates of any point in a highway."[32]

Relations can be defined over alphanumeric and/or pictorial domains. The implementation of "pictorial relations" and their access is similar to that of ordinary relations, the only difference being that each pictorial relation has an extra column named "loc" for storing pointers to the picture. For example,

cities(city,state,population,loc)

states(state,population-density,loc)

time-zones(zone,hour-diff,loc)

lakes(lake,area,volume,loc)

highways(hwy-name,hwy-section,loc)

are pictorial relations.

"Although the loc column takes values of type pointer, the user can use the column name to specify spatial relationships that the tuples must satisfy. The type of a pictorial object may be of type *'point,'* as in cities, or *'line segment,'* as in highways, or *'region,'* as in time-zones and lakes."[32]

The structure of a PSQL query is of the form

select attribute-target-list

from relation list

on picture list

at area-specification

where qualification

Thus, a PSQL statement combines two types of mappings: the nonspatial mapping *"select-from-where"* of SQL and the spatial mapping *"on-at,"* which specifies the spatial qualification on the nonspatial one.

When specified, the "on-at" mapping selects one area on a picture and uses it in narrowing down the retrieval scope of the relations appearing in the "from" clause. These are then further selected by the "where" clause and used to build the nonspatial "attribute target list."

The <picture-list> for the "on" clause is simply a name list. The <area-

specification> for the "at" clause, on the other hand, is a location specification which can be either a bound variable or a location given in constant or variable coordinates. The complete syntax for the area specification, expressed in Backus-Naur form, is shown in the following:

```
<area-specification> ::=<loc-spec> [<s-rel> <loc-spec>]
<loc-spec> ::= <loc-variable>
             | {<X-axis>, <Y-axis> [, <rotation>]}
             | {<X-circle>, <Y-circle>, <radius>}
<X-axis> ::= <Y-axis> ::= <axis-begin>, <displacement>
                        | <axis-center> ± <displacement>
<rotation> ::= <integer-0-360>
<s-rel> ::= covering | covered-by
          | overlapping | disjoined
          | north | south | east | west |
          | north-east | north-west | south-east | south-west
          | nearest | furthest
          | within | outside | on-perimeter
```

Note that a location may become a single point by specifying zero displacements on the X and Y axes.

PSQL queries are preprocessed and translated into SQL statements. The only additional requirement for SQL is the capability of executing system-defined procedures from within the *where* clause. This feature is used to call the spatial operators and functions during the execution of the query.

The output of PSQL queries is directed to two output devices. The graphical output device displays the area of the picture containing the qualified spatial objects, and the standard terminal displays the alphanumeric data.

As an example, a typical simple query in PSQL is:

select city, state, population, loc
from cities
on us-map
at loc *covered-by* {4 ± 4, 11 ± 9}
where population > 450,000

This query selects all cities in the area {4 ± 4, 11 ± 9} having a population greater than 450,000. The result is a table (shown in Figure 6-5a) and a pictorial output displayed on a graphic monitor (shown in Figure 6-5b). Note that the object names are displayed on the picture to assist the user to visualize their correspondence.

(a) Tabular output

char	*char*	*real*
city	*state*	*population*
ct	*st*	*pop*
Jacksonville New Orleans St Louis Memphis Nashville	Florida Louisiana Missouri Tennessee Tennessee	540,920 557,515 453,085 646,356 455,651

(b) Pictorial output

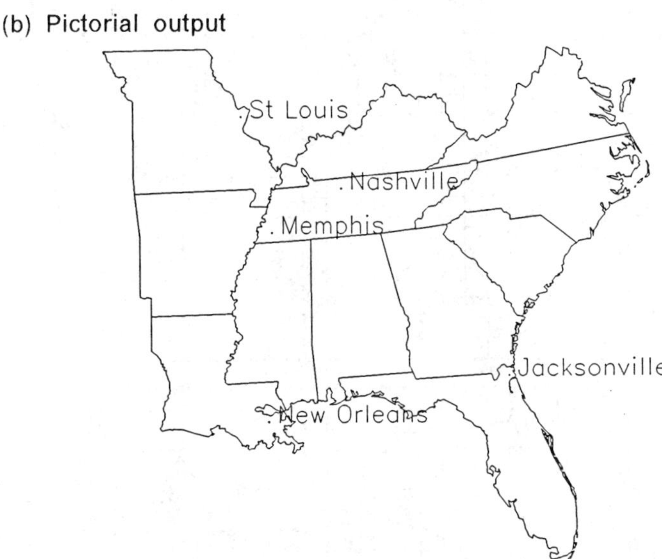

Figure 6-5. Example of PSQL Query Output.

As in SQL, PSQL mappings can have several nested levels. The query below illustrates the binding of two nested mappings by location. The state location passed from the inner level is used to direct the search in the outer level to produce the result for the query.

select lake, area, lakes.loc
from lakes
on lake-map

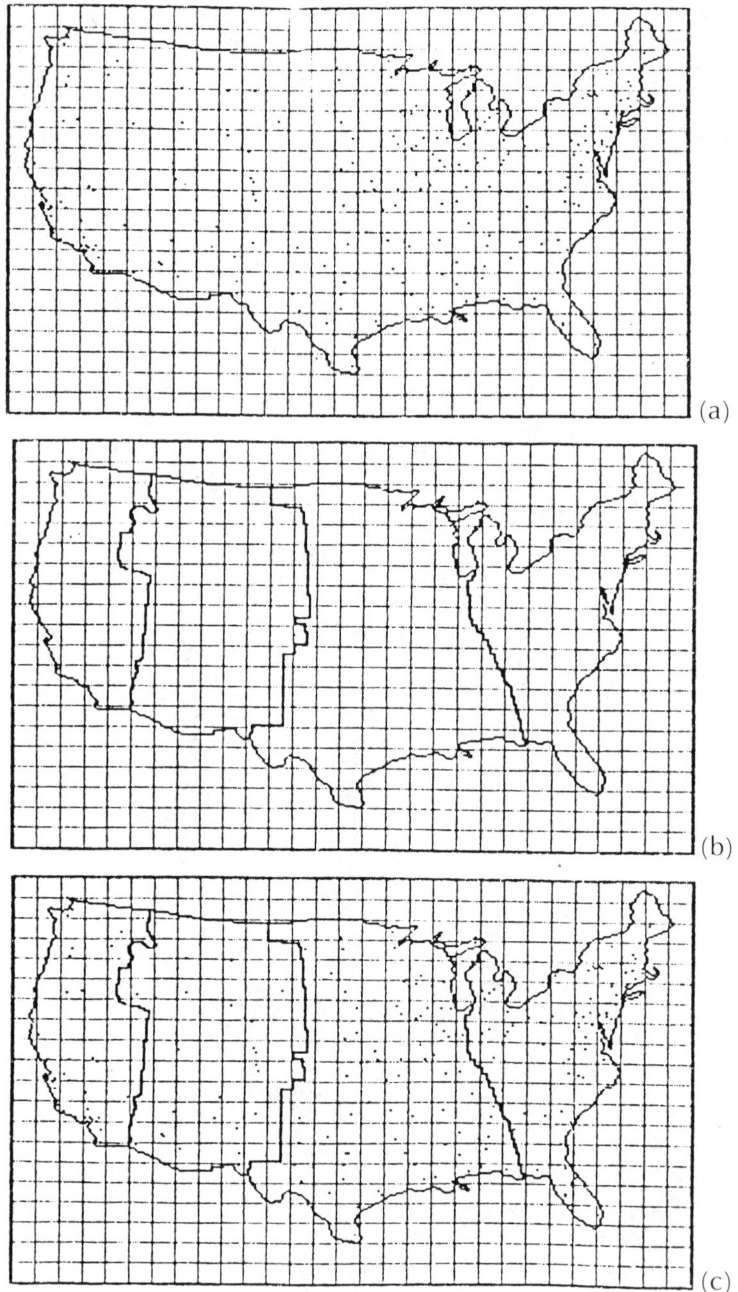

Figure 6-6. (a) US-map.
(b) Time-zone-map.
(c) Juxtaposition of the two maps.
(Roussopoulos and Leifker[22]. © 1984 IEEE.)

at lakes.loc *covered-by*
select state.loc
from states
on state-map
at states.loc *covered-by* {4 ± 4, 11 ± 9}

A very powerful operation in PSQL is the *juxtaposition* (synthesis) of dissimilar information stored in multiple pictures referring to the same geographic area.

The following example illustrates the synthesis of information found on two pictures.

select city, zone
from cities, time-zones
on us-map, time-zone-map
at cities.loc *covered-by* time-zones.loc

Figures 6-6(a) and 6-6(b) show the us-map and time-zone-map, respectively. Figure 6-6(c) shows the juxtaposition of the two. The alphanumeric data consist of the complete relations cities and time-zones displayed next to each other if the geographic area of one spatial object (city in this case) is covered by the geographic area of the other (time-zone).

Juxtaposition is performed by simultaneous search on the two (or more) maps which correspond to the same area. The entries can be juxtaposed if their associated locations satisfy the *at* clause. One may think of "juxtaposition" as a "geographic join."

REFERENCES

1. Nagy, G., and Wagle, S., "Geographic Data Processing," *Computing Surveys*, Vol. 11, No. 2 (June 1979), pp. 139-181.
2. Chang, N. S., and Fu, K. S., "Picture Query Languages for Pictorial Database Systems," *IEEE Computer*, Vol. 14, No. 11 (Nov. 1981), pp. 23-33.
3. Chang, S. K., and Kunii, T. L., "Pictorial Database Systems," *IEEE Computer*, Vol. 14, No. 11 (Nov. 1981), pp. 13-21.
4. Chock, M., Cardenas, A. F., and Klinger, A., "Manipulating Data Structures in Pictorial Information Systems," *IEEE Computer*, Vol. 14, No. 11 (Nov. 1981), pp. 43-50.
5. Preston, K., Jr., "Image Processing Software: A Survey," edited by L. N. Kanal and A. Rosenfeld in *Progress in Pattern Recognition*, North-Holland Publishing Company (1981) pp. 123-148.
6. Tamura, H., and Naokazu, Y., "Image Database Systems: A Survey," *International Journal of Pattern Recognition*, Vol. 17, No. 1 (Jan. 1984), pp. 29-43.
7. Chang, S. K., "Image Information Systems," *Proceedings of the IEEE*, Vol. 73, No. 4 (Apr. 1985), pp. 754-764.

8. Shapiro, L. G., "ESP^3: A High Level Graphics Language," *Proceedings of SIGGRAPH '75, Computer Graphics,* Vol. 9, No. 1 (Spring 1975), pp. 70-75.
9. Schrak, G., "Design, Implementation and Experiences with a High Level Graphics Language for Interactive Computer-Aided Design Purpose," *Proceedings of the ACM Symposium on Graphic Languages, Computer Graphics,* Vol. 10, No. 1 (Spring 1976), pp. 10-17.
10. Jones, B., "An Extended Algol-60 for Shaded Computer Graphics," *Proceedings of the ACM Symposium on Graphic Languages, Computer Graphics,* Vol. 10, No. 1 (Spring 1976), pp. 18-23.
11. Pfister, G. F., "A High Level Language Extension for Creating and Controlling Dynamic Pictures," *Proceedings of the ACM Symposium on Graphic Languages, Computer Graphics,* Vol. 10, No. 1 (Spring 1976), pp. 1-9.
12. Newman, W. M., "Display Procedures," *Communications of the ACM,* Vol. 14, No. 10 (Oct. 1971), pp. 651-660.
13. Denert, E., "GRAPHEX68: Graphical Language Features in Algol 68," *Computers and Graphics,* Vol. 1 (Jan. 1975), pp. 195-202.
14. Magnenat-Thalmann, N., and Thalmann, D., "Mira-3D: A Three-Dimensional Graphical Extension of Pascal," *Software Practice and Experience,* Vol. 13 (Sept. 1983), pp. 797-808.
15. Chang, S. K., Reuss, J., and McCormick, B. H., "Design Considerations of a Pictorial Database System," *International Journal on Policy Analysis and Information Systems,* Vol. 1, No. 2 (Jan. 1978), pp. 49-70.
16. Chang, S. K., O'Brien, M., Read, J., Borovec, R., Cheng, W. H., and Ke, J. S., "Design Considerations of a Database System in a Clinical Network Environment," *Proceedings of the National Computer Conference* (Jun. 1976), pp. 277-286.
17. Berman, R., and Stonebraker, M., "GEO-QUEL: A System for the Manipulation and Display of Geographic Data," *Computer Graphics,* Vol. 11, No. 2 (Summer 1977), pp. 186-191.
18. Held, G. D., Stonebraker, M. R., and Wong, E., "INGRES—A Relational Database System," *Proceedings of the National Computer Conference* (May 1975), pp. 409-416.
19. Chang, N. S., and Fu, K. S., "Query-by-Pictorial-Example," *IEEE Transactions on Software Engineering,* Vol. SE-6, No. 6 (Nov. 1980), pp. 519-524.
20. Ichikawa, T., Kikuno, T., and Hirakawa, M., "A Query Manipulation System for Image Data Retrieval by ARES," *IEEE Workshop on Picture Data Description and Management* (Aug. 1980), pp. 61-67.
21. Zloof, M. M., "Query-By-Example," *Proceedings of the National Computer Conference* (May 1975), pp. 431-438.
22. Roussopoulos, N., and Leifker, D., "An Introduction to PSQL: A Pictorial Structured Query Language," *Proceedings of the 1984 IEEE Computer Society Workshop on Visual Languages, Hiroshima, Japan* (Dec. 1984), pp. 77-87.
23. Chamberlin, D. D., Astrahan, M. M., Eswaran, K. P., Griffiths, P. P., Lorie, R. A., Mehl, J. W., Reisner, P., and Wade B. W., "SEQUEL 2: A Unified Approach to Data Definition, Manipulation, and Control," *IBM Journal of Research and Development,* Vol. 20, No. 6 (Nov. 1976), pp. 560-575.
24. Assmann, K., Venema, R., and Hohne, K. H., "The ISQL Language: A Software Tool for the Development of Pictorial Information Systems in Medicine," in *Visual Languages,* edited by S. K. Chang et al., Plenum Publishing Corp. (1986), pp. 261-284.
25. Tang, G. Y., "A Logical Data Organization for the Integrated Database of Pictures and Alphanumerical Data," *Proceedings of the IEEE Workshop on Picture Data Description and Management* (Aug. 1980), pp. 158-166.
26. Takao, Y., Itoh, S., and Lisak, J., "An Image Oriented Database System," in *Database Techniques for Pictorial Applications,* edited by A. Blaser, Springer-Verlag (1979), pp. 527-538.

27. Mantey, P. E., and Carlson, E. D., "Integrated Geographic Databases: The GADS Experience," in *Database Techniques for Pictorial Applications,* edited by A. Blaser, Springer-Verlag (1979), pp. 173-198.
28. Herot, C. F., "Spatial Management of Data," *ACM Transactions on Database Systems,* Vol. 5, No. 4 (Dec. 1980), pp. 493-514.
29. Chang, S. K., Jungert, E., Levialdi, S., Tortora, G., and Ichikawa, T., "An Image Processing Language with Icon-Assisted Navigation," *IEEE Transactions on Software Engineering,* Vol. SE-11, No. 8 (Aug. 1985), pp. 811-819.
30. Chang, S. K., Lin, B. S., and Walser, R., "A Generalized Zooming Technique for Pictorial Database System," *Proceedings of the National Computer Conference* (Jun. 1979), pp. 147-156.
31. Lin, B. S., and Chang, S. K., "GRAIN—A Pictorial Database Interface," *Proceedings of the 1980 Picture Data Description and Management Workshop* (Aug. 1980), pp. 83-88.
32. Roussopoulos, N., and Leifker, D., "Direct Spatial Search on Pictorial Databases Using Packed R-Trees," *Proceedings of SIGMOD '85* (May 1985), pp. 17-31.

Chapter 7

Languages for Supporting Visual Interactions

Recent advances in technology have made high-resolution graphics an available presentation medium on mainframes and microcomputers alike. A natural consequence of this development is the flourishing of applications employing visual interactions as a means of communication between users and their computing facilities.

Graphical displays play an important role in visual interactions. The traditional approach to creating a graphical display is to write a program which accepts parameterized input, examines a database, and then makes calls to a graphics subroutine package to create the desired display. This approach, in general, is labor intensive. The principal impediment is the use of the traditional languages, which were not designed for visual interactions.

Thus, as visual interactions are setting a trend, languages are developed to support the visual interactions. In this chapter, we describe three languages as examples of this category. They are ICDL, the icon-class description language of SDMS; HI-VISUAL, a language supporting visual interaction in programming; and Squeak, a language supporting communication with a pointing device.

ICDL, the Icon Description Language of SDMS

In Chapter 2, we describe a Spatial Database Management System (SDMS) developed at the Computer Corporation of America.[1] Underlying SDMS is the relational database system INGRES.[2] The information presented to the SDMS user, however, is expressed in graphical form in a spatial framework called the "graphical data space."

In SDMS, a user retrieves data by examining, with a joystick, the pictorial representations of the data in the graphical data space. The user can move freely through the graphical view and zoom in for a closer look at the data or back out for a more global view. In this way, a user can find the information he seeks without having to know the syntax of a query language or know exactly where in the database the information is stored.

In other words, the ability of SDMS to present graphical views of a conventional database encourages browsing by direct manipulation. However, in order to construct a graphical view, the database administrator must first describe to the system how each icon should appear and then instruct the system to create a data surface of icons for selected tuples in the database.

Class Association

The principal tool for connecting the graphical data space to the underlying database is *class association.* A class association between a relation and the graphical data space causes the creation of icons that graphically represent the tuples of the relation. Such an association has the following effects:

1. For each tuple in the relation, an icon is created and inserted into the graphical data space. If a qualification was supplied, icons are created for only those tuples which pass the qualification.
2. Each of these tuples and their corresponding icons are linked. The system maintains the correspondence between the two as the database is updated.

Icon-Class Description

When a class association is made, an icon-class description that tells exactly how to draw each icon may be specified. Certain parameters may vary each time a picture is drawn. These parameters include size, shape, color, position, and text strings.

The language for describing an icon class is called the *icon-class description language (ICDL).* It consists of a series of statements, each of which accepts some attribute value and performs some graphical operation, such as selecting a template picture, coloring some region, or inserting some text.

As an example, the ICDL statements used to generate the icons shown in the ship database in Chapter 2 are shown in Figure 7-1.

The *maximum size* of each icon is specified to prevent any one of them from becoming too large. Since relative size is a picture parameter, it is a good protection.

The *position* statement determines the placement of the icon on the graphical data space. In the example, it maps the ship's type into x coordinates and its nationality into y coordinates. The *template* statement specifies the shape of the icon by selecting among a set of pictures that have been previously drawn by the database administrator. The *scale* statement specifies the size of the icon as a function of the beam of the ship. The *color* statement specifies the color of each ship according to its readiness. Finally, the

```
icon class cluster (r)
begin
maximum size is (110,60);
position is
  (case r.type begin
        "CV":      800
        "SSN":    1600
        "SSBN":   1600
        "SSGN":   1600
        "CGN":    2500
        "CG":     2500
        "CA":     2500
        "DDG":    3200
        "FF":     3200
        "AGI":    3200
        "AO":     4000
        default:  1600
        end,  case r.nat begin
                    "US":     1200
                    "UR":     2000
                    default:  2500
                    end);
   template icon case r.type begin
        "CV":     carrier
        "SSN":    sub
        "SSBN":   sub
        "SSGN":   sub
        "CGN":    cruiser
        "CG":     cruiser
        "CA":     crusier
        "DDG":    destroyer
        "FF":     destroyer
        "AGI":    destroyer
        "AO":     oiler
        default:  cruiser
        end;
   scale is r.beam*2 percent;
   color of region 1 is case r.ready begin
        "1":      green
        "2":      yellow
        "3":      orange
        "4":      red
        default:  gray
        end;
   attribute region r.nam   from (5,16) to (70,28);
   attribute region r.ircs  from (5,28) to (70,40);
   attribute region r.conam from (5,40) to (70,52);
end;
```

Figure 7-1. Icon class description for the Ship database.

attribute region statements place the values of the ship's name, international radio call sign, and commanding officer's name into the specified location.

Not shown in Figure 7-1 is the *orientation* statement, which may be used to specify the orientation of the picture by some arbitrary angle. The default is the orientation of the original template.

Levels of Detail

An icon constructed from an icon class may have its appearance defined at several levels of detail. The bit-array description for a single level of detail is referred to as the *image plane.* The pictures for each image plane originate as templates, which are simply pictures drawn by the database administrator on a special image plane reserved for that purpose.

For example, the templates for a ship might be drawn as follows: At the least detailed image plane, the ship appears as a small rectangle. The second image plane has a rough silhouette with the ship's name and radio call sign beneath it. The most detailed image plane shows some of the ship's superstructure, and the ship's name, call sign, beam, draft, speed, etc., appear beneath the picture. These image planes at different levels allow the zooming effect by which a user sees a more detailed version of an icon by magnifying it.

The Associate Statement

After given the rules for the appearance of each icon, the database administrator creates the graphical representation by using the *associate* statement. To generate the graphical data surface of the ship database example, the database administrator would type

associate ship *using* cluster

This causes SDMS to retrieve the tuples from the relation SHIP and pass them, one at a time, to a module which interprets the ICDL for the icon class "cluster," using the values of the attributes of the tuple. For each such tuple, an icon is created on the graphical data space.

The associate statement also permits the use of a qualification to select tuples. For example, a graphical data surface containing icons for those ships having a readiness other than 1 could be created by typing

associate ship *using* cluster *where* ship.ready ! = 1.

In short, SDMS "can spatially display any data for which the database administrator can define a suitable transformation. This transformation can be accomplished within the icon-class description language without resorting to an ad hoc 'escape' to a separately compiled programming language, which is often required in other systems."[1] In this manner, ICDL serves as a language for supporting visual interactions provided by SDMS.

HI-VISUAL

HI-VISUAL[3] is a language for supporting visual interaction developed at Hiroshima University in Japan. The language is based on a "hierarchical multiple window" model, whose structure is shown in Figure 7-2.

The basic elements of the model consist of desks (virtual displays), region-frames, and viewports. They are related to each other via the successive layers of desks in the hierarchy.

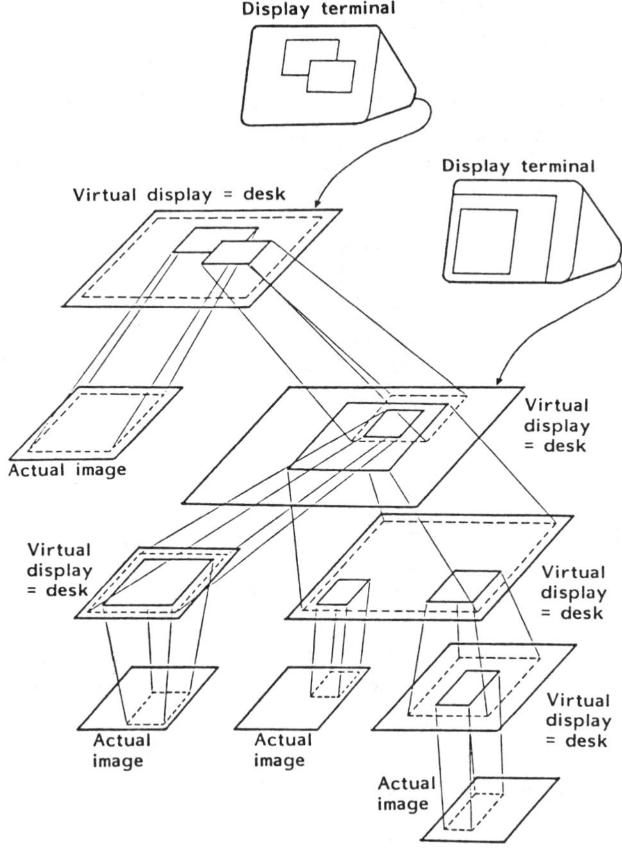

Figure 7-2. Hierarchical multiple window model.
(Hirakawa et al.[3]. Reprinted with permission from Plenum Publishing Corp.)

Figure 7-3 illustrates the relationship between a region-frame and a viewport. The part enclosed by the dotted rectangle on the lower desk is projected onto the solid-lined rectangle on the upper desk. The part enclosed by the dotted rectangle is referred to as a "region-frame," and the part enclosed by the solid-lined rectangle is referred to as a "viewport."

Among the facilities that the proposed hierarchical system can provide is the control of the display priority and the visibility of a scene or a frame. But a more interesting aspect is the control of the appearance of a scene by the selection of the basic operations ("hold," "expand," "contract," "move," "rotate") or a combination of them.

The *expand* and *contract* operations change the dimensions of a viewport or a region-frame. The *move* operation changes the location of a viewport or a region-frame. The *rotate* operation changes the rotation angle of the

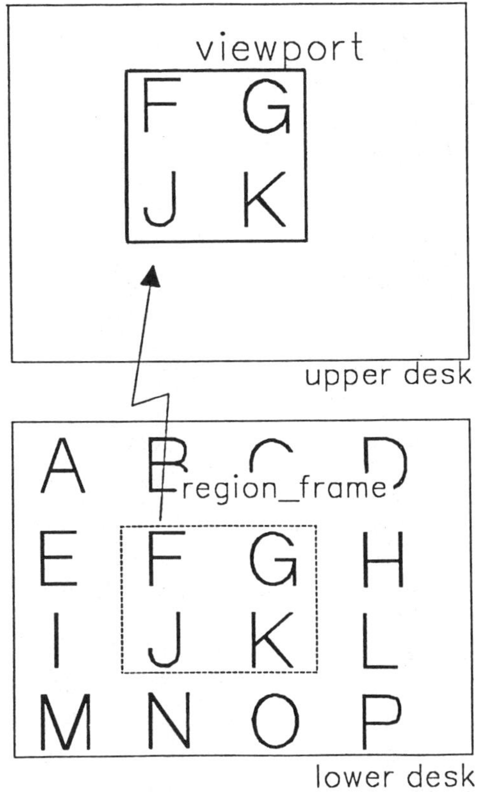

Figure 7-3. Relationship between region-frame and viewport.
(Hirakawa et al.[3]. Reprinted with permission from Plenum Publishing Corp.)

viewport/region-frame. The *hold* operation, on the other hand, means no operation. Figure 7-4 illustrates the effect of the appearance control.

Syntax for these operations in HI-VISUAL takes the following form:

operation-name (*parameter: type,* . . . , parameter:type); comments

The following are some examples of the statements that a programmer can use:

move (RF:region-frame,V:vector);	move a region-frame along a defined vector
expand (RF:region-frame,R:ratio);	exand a region-frame with the defined factor as a ratio
contract (VP:viewport,R:ratio);	contract a viewport with the defined factor as a ratio
rotate (VP:viewport,A:angle);	rotate a viewport with the defined angle

Combinations of operations can be expressed with designated key words, while the format of the statements remain the same. For example,

scroll (VP:viewport,V:vector);	combination of hold and move
zoom-out (VP:viewport,R:ratio);	combination of hold and expand
zoom-in (VP:viewport,R:ratio);	combination of hold and contract
shift (VP:viewport,V:vector);	combination of move and hold
enlarge (VP:viewport,R:ratio);	combination of expand and hold
reduce (VP:viewport,R:ratio);	combination of contract and hold
scan (VP:viewport,V:vector);	combination of move and move
expose (VP:viewport,R:ratio);	combination of expand and expand

Similarly, the connections between a viewport and a region-frame or a desk can be made or broken by statements such as:

connect (VP:viewport, RF:region-frame);	connects a viewport to a region-frame
append (D:desk,VP:viewport);	appends a viewport to a desk
remove (D:desk,VP:viewport);	removes a viewport from a desk

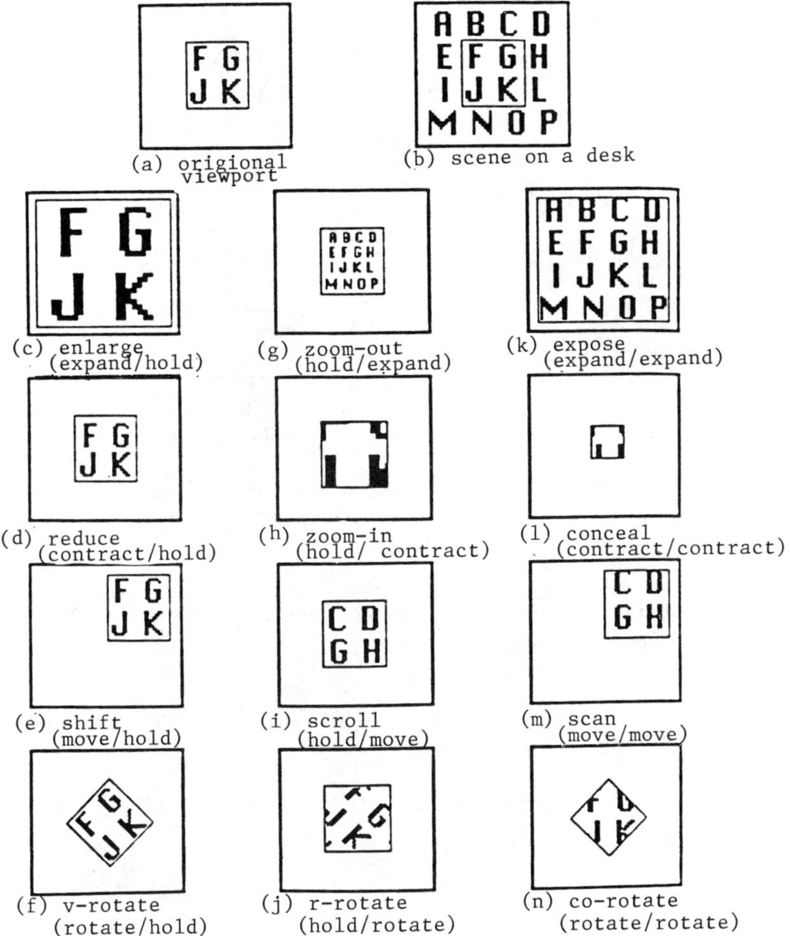

Figure 7-4. Effects of appearance control.
(Hirakawa et al.[3]. Reprinted with permission from Plenum Publishing Corp.)

Further, in HI-VISUAL, an icon is seen as a desk or an image, and is displayed as a picture through the region-frame and viewport relationship. The user can create a new icon by combining several predefined icons, as shown in Figure 7-5.

In order to manage an icon as a reference to an object, a point is provided for the association of the desk or an image with an object. This is depicted in Figure 7-6.

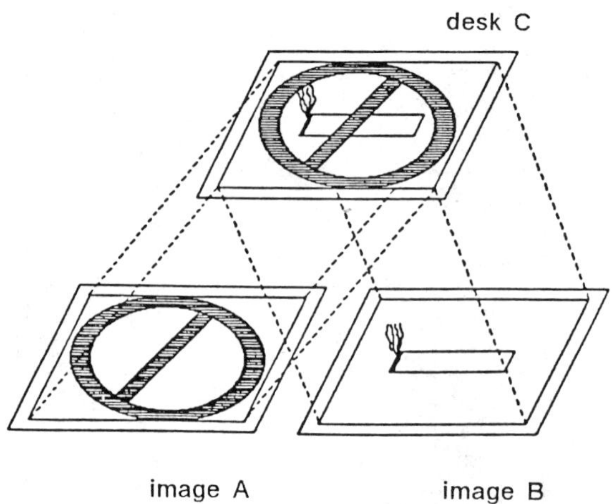

Figure 7-5. Creation of a new icon from previously defined icons. (Hirakawa et al.[3]. Reprinted with permission from Plenum Publishing Corp.)

An icon definition is thus carried out by directing a pointer to an object. The syntax of the statement is as follows:

icon-define (D:desk,O:object);
icon-define (I:image,O:object);

The association which derives from the icon definition is invoked by:

icon-associate (D:desk);
icon-associate (I:image);

At the time of this writing, HI-VISUAL is still undergoing development. Like the ICDL of SDMS discussed in the previous section, this language is a textual language designed to support visual interactions. Nevertheless, unlike ICDL, where the setting up of the graphical views requires considerable involvement of the database administrator, HI-VISUAL is designed with more user control in mind.

SQUEAK

As described in the two previous sections, both ICDL[1] and HI-VISUAL[3] are languages that support visual interaction via icons. Squeak[4], developed by Cardelli and Pike at the AT & T Bell Laboratories, also supports visual interactions but has an entirely different approach.

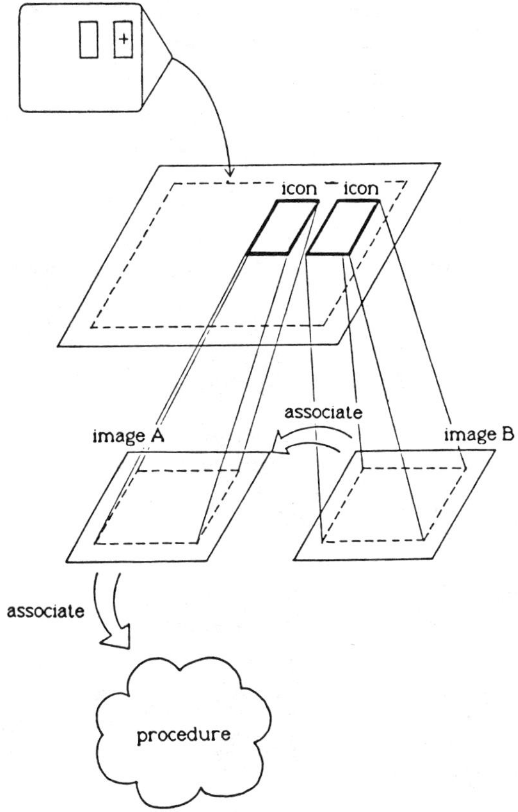

Figure 7-6. Icon association.
(Hirakawa et al.[3]. Reprinted with permission from Plenum Publishing Corp.)

According to Cardelli and Pike, "Providing a suitable graphical display is not especially difficult; what causes problems is the complicated flow of control required to deal with all the possible sequences of user actions with the input devices."[4] Squeak is a user interface implementation language that exploits the concurrency among multiple interaction devices, such as mice, buttons, and keyboards.

Squeak programs are composed of processes executing in parallel. A process, or perhaps a few processes, typically deal with a particular action or external device. The composition of processes then handles the set of actions and device events relevant to the program.

Communication between processes is achieved by sending messages via *channels.* There are two classes of channels: primitive and nonprimitive.

Primitive channels are predefined and provide access to external devices. Nonprimitive channels are for ordinary message-based communication.

The syntax *c!exp* sends the value of the expression *exp* on channel *c*. *c?var* reads the message on channel *c* into the variable *var.*

The implemented version of Squeak has defined the following primitive channels:

DN and *UP,* which report mouse button transitions
M, the mouse cursor position (*M!p* sets the cursor position; *M?p* reads it)
K, characters typed on the keyboard
T, the current absolute time
E and *L,* the mouse entering and leaving certain rectangles

The primitive channels return appropriate values. *M,* for example, returns a point data structure. *UP* and *DN* return no value. If the mouse had several buttons, they might return the mouse button number, or there could be a separate channel for each button. *E* and *L* return the appropriate rectangle. Squeak does not specify how the program announces its interest in rectangles on the display. The implemented system provides callable functions (coded in the C language) to push and pop sets of rectangles to be watched.

A process of the form *a!exp.p* is ready to output the value of *exp* on the channel *a* and then execute *p*. The value can be read by the process *a?x.p,* which binds the input value to *x,* with *x* available in (and local to) the continuation *p*. If no value is passed during a communication, one can simply write *a!* or *a?.*

The action *a!exp* cannot execute until there is a matching *a?x,* and vice versa. If more than one input is active on a channel, only one will receive the value. The others remain suspended until the next input.

Some actions can have a time-out condition. The simple process *wait [3]a?x.p* || *q* will wait for input on channel *a* for a maximum of three time units. If an *a* communication happens within that time, *p* will be executed. If communication is not achieved in time, the process will time-out and execute *q*. *wait[0]a?x.p* || *q* is equivalent to *q*.

As an example of a Squeak program using time-outs, consider the problem of detecting clicks (mouse button down and up again in a short time) and double clicks (two clicks separated by a longer but finite time) without losing any button transitions.

The following is a Squeak process that detects single clicks on a one-button mouse:

```
Click =
        DN?.wait [clickTime] (UP?.click!.Click) ||
                             (down!.UP?.up!.Click)
```

When a mouse button is depressed, Click receives a *DN* event and waits for a corresponding *UP.* When the *UP* is received, a *click* event is generated and the process restarts. If the *UP* event is not received within *clickTime, Click* emits a nonprimitive *down* event to indicate to another process that the mouse button is being held down. Then it waits for the corresponding *UP* and reemits it as an *up* signal.

The following process detects clicks and double clicks:

```
DoubleClick =
  DN?.
    wait[clickTime] UP?.
      wait[doubleClickTime] DN?.
        wait[clickTime] UP?. doubleClick!.DoubleClick
        || click!.down!.UP?.up!.DoubleClick
      || click!.DoubleClick
    || down!.UP?.up!.DoubleClick
```

If *DoubleClick* receives two clicks with the proper timing, it emits a *doubleClick* event; otherwise it emits *click, down,* and *up* events so that another process can receive them.

According to Cardelli and Pike, "Although Squeak was designed to program the lowest levels of a user interface, it can be used effectively to construct the higher levels by combining Squeak programs hierarchically, treating larger events such as menu selections in the same manner as primitive events."[4]

It should be obvious from the examples of ICDL, HI-VISUAL, and Squeak that there are many different approaches to the design of languages that support visual interactions. However, in general, languages in this category are not themselves visual.

REFERENCES

1. Herot, C. F., "Spatial Management of Data," *ACM Transactions on Database Systems,* Vol. 5, No. 4 (Dec. 1980), pp. 493-514.
2. Held, G. D., Stonebraker, M. R., and Wong, E., "INGRES—A Relational Database System," *Proceedings of National Computer Conference* (May 1975), pp. 409-416.
3. Hirakawa, M., Monden, N., Yoshimoto, I., Tanaka, M., and Ichikawa, T., "HI-VISUAL: A Language Supporting Visual Interaction in Programming," in *Visual Languages,* edited by S. K. Chang et al., Plenum Press (1986), pp. 233-259.
4. Cardelli, L., and Pike, R., "Squeak: A Language for Communicating with Mice," *Proceedings of ACM SIGGRAPH '85*(July 1985), pp. 199-204.

Chapter 8

Visual Programming Languages: A Perspective

Penguins, horses and centipedes share the concept of legs; they differ in the number of legs and details of the method of locomotion.

Lawrence Tesler[1]

Depending on one's background and sphere of interest, visual languages mean different things to different people. In order to establish a common understanding, we have classified visual languages into three categories: (1) languages for processing visual information, (2) languages for supporting visual interaction, and (3) languages for *programming* with visual expressions, i.e., the visual programming languages.

Languages in the first two categories were discussed in the two preceding chapters. Languages in the third category will be described in depth in the following three chapters. The purpose of this chapter is to put the third category (that is, the visual programming languages) in perspective. We start with a cursory review of typical examples in the first two categories to highlight the distinctions. We then narrow down to the definition of a visual programming language and present a framework for dimensional analysis so that different kinds of visual programming languages can be compared.[2]

LANGUAGES FOR PROCESSING VISUAL INFORMATION

The first category of visual languages are used for the processing of visual (or image) information. One of the earliest works in this category is the *GRAIN* (Graphics-oriented Relational Algebraic INterpreter) system reported by S. K. Chang et al.[3] In the GRAIN system, pictorial information is represented by both logical and physical pictures. Logical pictures are defined in three relational tables: the picture object table, the picture contour table, and the picture page table. The physical pictures or real images are stored in a separate image store. This distinction between logical pictures and physical pictures leads to the design of an efficient pictorial information system. At the same time, the relational database approach provides a framework for a query facility.

The user can specify the image query in the GRAIN language. In addition to the algebraic commands that are available for manipulation of relational tables, GRAIN provides many commands specifically designed for image or line drawing such as PLOT <object-name>, SKETCH <picture-name>, and PAINT <picture-name>. For example, to retrieve the image containing major highways through Tokyo, one may use the following GRAIN query:[4]

```
Sketch highway; through (cityname is 'Tokyo').
```

A more recent example of this category was described by Roussopoulos and Leifker.[5] The language, called *PSQL*, is a query language for manipulating pictorial and alphanumeric databases. It is an extension of System R's SQL language to allow direct reference to pictures and advanced processing of pictorial domains.

A typical simple query in PSQL such as

```
SELECT   city_name, state, population
FROM     cities
ON       us_map
AT       loc COVERED_BY (4 + 4, 11 + 9)
WHERE    population > 450000
```

produces a map of the area specified by the AT clause and a table containing the city_name, state, and population of all cities in that area having a population greater than 450,000. The names of the cities that met the criteria are also displayed on the map to assist the user to visualize the correspondence.

A quick observation can be made from these two examples: Although the information being handled by the languages does involve pictures, and visualization does come into play in the presentation of results, the languages themselves are textual.

LANGUAGES FOR SUPPORTING VISUAL INTERACTIONS

The second category of visual languages are designed to *support visual interactions.* For example, SDMS[6] data are stored in a conventional database but presented to the user in a graphical form. In order to construct such a display, the database administrator must first describe to the system how each icon should appear and then instruct the system to create a data surface of icons for selected tuples in the system.

To describe the appearance of each icon, one uses the icon-class description language ICDL, which consists of a series of POSITION, TEMPLATE, SCALE, COLOR, and ATTRIBUTE REGION statements. The POSITION statement determines the placement of the icon on the data surface. The TEMPLATE statement specifies the shape of the icon by selecting among a set of pictures that have previously been drawn by the database administrator. For the ship database, the SCALE statement specifies the size of the icon as a function of the beam of the ship; the COLOR statement specifies the color of each ship according to its readiness; and the ATTRIBUTE REGION statements place the values of the ship's name, international radio call sign, and commanding officer's name into the specified locations in the picture. Finally, to create a data surface of icons for selected tuples, one uses the ASSOCIATE statement. All these statements are conventional texual statements.

In the same category, but of a more general nature, is the original version of HI-VISUAL.[7] HI-VISUAL, which derives its name from "Hiroshima Visual," is based on a hierarchical multiple-window model. Users use it to define icons and to support operations on icons by statements such as icon_define (D:desk,W:window), append (D:desk,W:window), move (W:window,V:vector), rotate (W:window,A:angle), and zoom-in (W:window,R:ratio).

In short, this category of languages is designed to support visual representations and visual interactions, but the languages themselves are again textual, not visual.

VISUAL PROGRAMMING LANGUAGES

The third category of visual languages concentrates on allowing users to actually program with graphical expressions. They can be more aptly called the "visual programming languages."

Definition

A *visual programming language* can be informally defined as a language which uses some visual representations (in addition to or in place of words and numbers) to accomplish what would otherwise have to be written in a traditional one-dimensional programming language.

Note that this definition imposes no restrictions on the type of data or information. It is immaterial whether the object being operated on or being displayed to a user by a visual language is textual, numeric, pictorial, or even audio. What is important is that, in order to be considered a visual programming language, *the language itself* must employ some meaningful (i.e., not merely decorative) visual expressions as a means of programming.

Two Important Aspects of Programming Languages

When we attempt to assess a programming language, two important aspects come to mind: the level of the language and the scope of the language.

It is generally agreed that the *level of the language* is an inverse measure of the amount of detail that a user has to give to the computer in order to achieve the desired results. A language is nonprocedural (and at the highest level) if users tell the computer only what is to be accomplished, but not how to do it. A language is procedural if users need to specify the steps the computer must follow. The number and size of the required steps vary with various procedural languages. To achieve the same result, a highly procedural (low-level) language (e.g., an assembly language) requires many small, detailed steps, while a less procedural (higher-level) language (e.g., FORTRAN) requires fewer but larger steps with less detail from the user. By this measure, FORTRAN is at a higher level than an assembly language.

The *scope of the language,* ranging from the general and widely applicable to the specific and narrowly applicable, depicts how much a language is capable of doing. Using FORTRAN and an assembly language as examples again, a user might use FORTRAN to perform complicated scientific computations, but probably not use it to manage multitasking operations. An assembly language, on the other hand, can generally be used to do both. Thus, we say that the assembly language has a larger problem domain or a wider scope of applicability than FORTRAN.

Of course, there are other ways to classify or characterize a language. However, for most practical purposes, these aspects are considered two of the most fundamental dimensions in assessing programming languages. They are applicable to programming languages in general, regardless of whether the language is visual or not.

The Third Dimension of Visual Programming Languages

In order to put visual programming languages into perspective, Shu[2] introduced an additional dimension: extent of visual expression.

Visual expressions are the meaningful visual (non-textual) representations (e.g., icons, graphs, diagrams, pictures) used as language components to achieve the purpose of programming. Extent of visual expression is a relative measure of how much visual expressions are incorporated in the programming language. The more visual representations the higher the visual extent.

If there is no visual expression in the language (even though the information being processed or displayed has pictures), the third dimension simply does not apply.

Dimensional Analysis of Visual Programming Languages

In Shu[2], an analytical though qualitative approach is proposed for the comparison of visual programming languages. In essence, it involves the construction of the *profile of a language,* which characterizes the language in a three-dimensional framework. Graphically, it may be represented by the relative measures of the language on the three axes labeled "language level," "scope," and "visual extent," as shown in Figure 8-1.

Based on the principles of design, most of the visual programming languages reported in the literature fall into three broad categories:

1. At one extreme, icons are deliberately designed to play the central role in programming. Work belonging to this category is the focus of Chapter 10.
2. At the other extreme, flow charts and diagrams that are already in use on paper are either incorporated into the programming constructs, as extensions to conventional programming languages, or made into machine-interpretable units to be used in conjunction with conventional programming languages. Work in this category is discussed in Chapter 9.

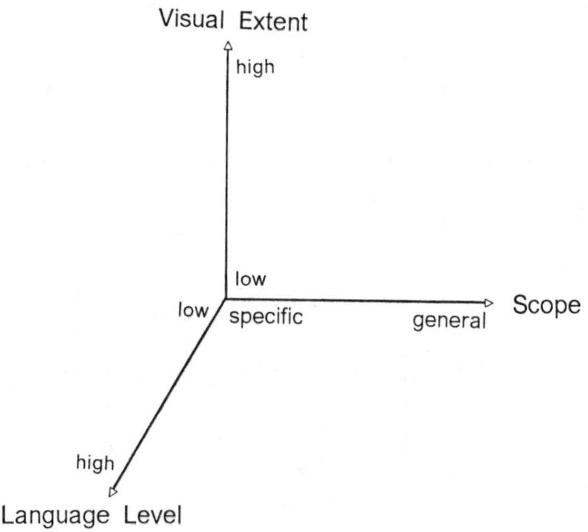

Figure 8-1. Three dimensions of visual programming languages. (Shu[2]. © 1985 IEEE.)

3. In the middle, the graphic representations are designed as an integral part of the language. However, unlike the icons in the iconic systems, they are not the "superstars" of the language; and unlike the graphical extensions, the language is not designed to be used in conjunction with some other languages and cannot function without the graphic representations. Work of this kind is the focus of Chapter 11.

Example—A Comparison of Three Languages

To illustrate how these different approaches may be compared within the framework of dimensional analysis, a brief introduction to three representative systems (Pict,[8] PIGS,[9] and FORMAL[10]) is given in the following discussion. One should keep in mind, however, that the introductions given here are very brief. Their purpose is to illustrate the merit of having some means to compare the totally different languages. To understand the languages themselves in reasonable depth, the reader should consult the chapters in which these languages are described.

The Pict System. Pict is a highly graphical system developed at the University of Washington by Glinert and Tanimoto.[8] The emphasis of Pict is to provide a programming facility in which computer graphics plays a central role. With Pict, users sit in front of a color graphics display and communicate with the system throughout all phases of their work by pointing (with a joystick) to icons in a menu tree. "With the exception of numerals and short Help messages, users rely totally on nontextual symbols. (Sub)program names and parameter passing modes, data structures, variables, and program operations are represented by icons of various sorts, while control structures such as Pascal REPEAT-UNTIL or WHILE are represented by colored, directed paths that can actually be seen."[8] User programs may be recursive and contain arbitrary chains of subroutine calls. At execution time, Pict uses simple forms of animation to make the drawing "come to life."

Its capabilities, however, are limited. "The main prototype, named Pict/D, allows the user to compose programs that do simple, numeric calculations. . . . Both the types and number of variables are quite restricted in Pict/D, with just four six-digit, nonnegative decimal integers (distinguished by red, green, blue and orange) available in each module (program or subprogram)."[8]

As a programming language, Pict is at a language level similar to that of Basic or simple Pascal. Being an iconic system, Pict has a very high extent of visual expressions. However, due to the very restricted sizes of the user program modules, the limited set of data types and language constructs, and the extremely small number of variables to which a module can refer, the scope of Pict is rather limited. Taking all three dimensions into consideration, the profile of Pict is shown in Figure 8-2.

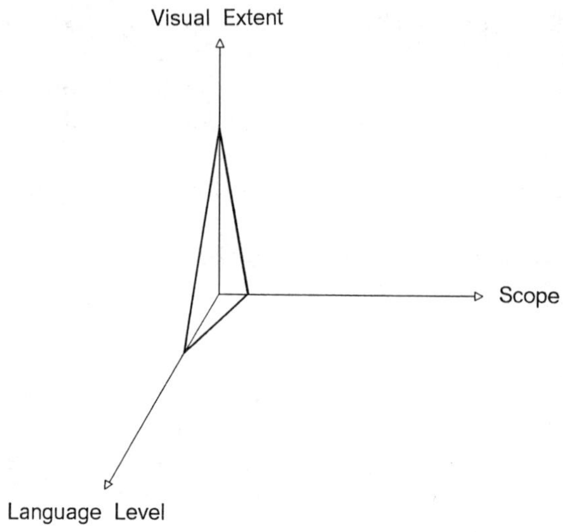

Figure 8-2. A profile of Pict.
(Shu[2]. © 1985 IEEE.)

The PIGS system. Pong and Ng[9] have implemented an experimental system for Programming with Interactive Graphical Support named *PIGS*. Like Pict, the system has been designed with the aim of supporting program development and testing in the same graphical environment. The approaches taken by the two systems, however, differ significantly.

In Pict, icons are the essential language elements and play a central role. The programming process is essentially to select and/or compose icons, to place them in proper juxtaposition on the screen, and to connect the icons by paths to indicate the desired flow of control.

PIGS, on the other hand, is a graphical extension to a conventional programming language. Nassi-Shneiderman diagrams (NSD) are incorporated into Pascal as the structured control constructs of logic flow. PIGS can interpret a program in NSD chart form, and the execution sequence of the NSD is displayed at a graphical terminal. PIGS also provides interactive debugging and testing aids to support program development. The prototype, developed at the University of Hong Kong, allows only the use of integers and one-dimensional arrays in NSD programs.

Compared with Pict, PIGS has lower extent of visual expressions but a wider scope of applicability. Since PIGS is an extension to a base language (a simple Pascal), it has the same scope and level as the base language, but now the surface of the triangle is tilted since the visual extent comes into play. The profile of the PIGS system is shown in solid lines in Figure 8-3, while its base language is shown in dashed lines.

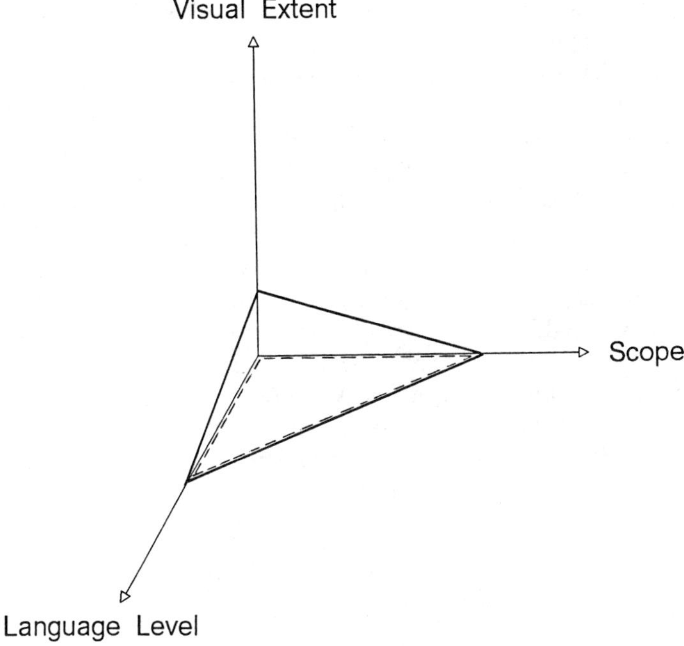

Figure 8-3. A profile of PIGS.
(Shu[2]. © 1985 IEEE.)

The FORMAL System. Note that Pict and PIGS represent two different types of visual programming languages. In Pict, icons are deliberately designed to play the central role in programming. In PIGS, NSDs are incorporated as an extension to Pascal. Yet, conceptually, they are both based on *algorithmic programming.* A user must understand the underlying concepts of variables, operations, flow of control, subprograms, recursions, etc.

In contrast, FORMAL[10] takes an *automatic programming,* rather than an algorithmic, approach. FORMAL is not designed to teach would-be programmers the concepts of traditional programming. Rather, it is designed for people to computerize many fairly complex data processing applications without having to learn or labor over the intricacies of programming.

FORMAL capitalizes on the user's familiarity with forms on two fronts: First, stylized form headings are used as visual representations of data structures (which may be quite complex, e.g., hierarchical data or nested tables). Second, the programs are also represented in forms. In using FORMAL, one starts with the visual representation of an output form and completes a program by specifying a few relevant properties within the outline of the form.

As an example, consider a Christmas party being planned for employee's children. Gifts will be given to children who are not yet eleven years old. From the information available in a PERSON form (Figure 8-4), the party organizer wishes to produce a GIFTLIST (also shown in Figure 8-4) which lists by age, for each location, the names of the eligible children (along with their parents' names). Figure 8-5 shows a FORMAL program that produces the GIFTLIST. The form heading describes the desired output structure. Under the heading, SOURCE defines the source of data, CONDITION describes the criteria for selecting instances from the input(s), and ORDER depicts the desired sequencing of instances within a form or a group.

Note that this application is not as simple as it seems. Writing the same program in COBOL or Pascal would reveal that, in addition to data extraction and selection, algorithms must be developed, written, and debugged for the necessary data restructuring shown in figure 8-6. The application only seems simple because the FORMAL program seems simple. The process of developing and coding the restructuring algorithms is undertaken by the FORMAL compiler so that the user is spared the chore.

```
|------------------------------------------------------------------|
|                             (PERSON)                             |
|------------------------------------------------------------------|
|ENO|DNO| NAME |PHONE|JC|   (KIDS)    |       (SCHOOL)       |SEX|LOC|
|   |   |      |     |  |-------------|----------------------|   |   |
|   |   |      |     |  | KNAME  |AGE| SNAME  |  (ENROLL)    |   |   |
|   |   |      |     |  |        |   |        |--------------|   |   |
|   |   |      |     |  |        |   |        |YEARIN|YEAROUT|   |   |
|==================================================================|
|05 |D1 |SMITH |5555 |05|JOHN    |02 |PRINCETON|1966  |70     |F  |SF |
|   |   |      |     |  |MARY    |04 |         |1972  |76     |   |   |
|------------------------------------------------------------------|
|05 |D1 |SMITH |5555 |05|JANE    |01 |         |      |       |F  |SF |
|------------------------------------------------------------------|
|07 |D1 |JONES |5555 |05|DICK    |07 |SJS      |1960  |65     |F  |SF |
|   |   |      |     |  |JANE    |04 |-------------------------|   |   |
|   |   |      |     |  |        |   |BERKELEY |1965  |69     |   |   |
|------------------------------------------------------------------|
|11 |D1 |ENGEL |2568 |05|RITA    |01 |UCLA     |1970  |74     |F  |LA |
|------------------------------------------------------------------|
|12 |D1 |DURAN |7610 |05|MARY    |08 |         |      |       |M  |SF |
|   |   |      |     |  |BOB     |10 |         |      |       |   |   |
|   |   |      |     |  |JOHN    |12 |         |      |       |   |   |
|------------------------------------------------------------------|
|19 |D1 |HOPE  |3150 |07|MARYLOU |10 |         |      |       |M  |SJ |
|   |   |      |     |  |MARYANN |07 |         |      |       |   |   |
|------------------------------------------------------------------|
|02 |D2 |GREEN |1111 |01|RON     |15 |         |      |       |M  |SF |
|   |   |      |     |  |DAVID   |04 |         |      |       |   |   |
|------------------------------------------------------------------|
|20 |D2 |CHU   |3348 |10|CHARLIE |06 |HONGKONG |1962  |66     |F  |LA |
|   |   |      |     |  |CHRIS   |09 |-------------------------|   |   |
|   |   |      |     |  |BONNIE  |04 |STANFORD |1967  |69     |   |   |
|   |   |      |     |  |        |   |         |1972  |75     |   |   |
|------------------------------------------------------------------|
|21 |D2 |DWAN  |3535 |12|        |   |USC      |1970  |74     |F  |SJ |
|------------------------------------------------------------------|
|43 |D2 |JACOB |4643 |09|PAULA   |07 |BERKELEY |1962  |66     |M  |SJ |
|   |   |      |     |  |PAUL    |16 |         |      |       |   |   |
|------------------------------------------------------------------|
|                   .                                              |
|                   .                                              |
|                   .                                              |
|------------------------------------------------------------------|
```

===>

```
|----------------------------|
|         (GIFTLIST)         |
|----------------------------|
|LOC|      (RECEIVER)        |
|   |------------------------|
|   |AGE|       (KID)        |
|   |   |--------------------|
|   |   | KNAME  |PARENT_NAME|
|============================|
|LA |04 |BONNIE  |CHU        |
|   |   |RITA    |ENGEL      |
|   |------------------------|
|   |06 |CHARLIE |CHU        |
|   |------------------------|
|   |09 |CHRIS   |CHU        |
|----------------------------|
|SF |01 |JANE    |SMITH      |
|   |------------------------|
|   |02 |JOHN    |SMITH      |
|   |------------------------|
|   |04 |MARY    |SMITH      |
|   |   |JANE    |JONES      |
|   |   |DAVID   |GREEN      |
|   |------------------------|
|   |07 |DICK    |JONES      |
|   |------------------------|
|   |08 |MARY    |DURAN      |
|   |------------------------|
|   |10 |BOB     |DURAN      |
|----------------------------|
|SJ |07 |PAULA   |JACOB      |
|   |   |MARYANN |HOPE       |
|   |------------------------|
|   |10 |MARYLOU |HOPE       |
|----------------------------|
```

Figure 8-4. Desired transformation from PERSON to GIFTLIST.

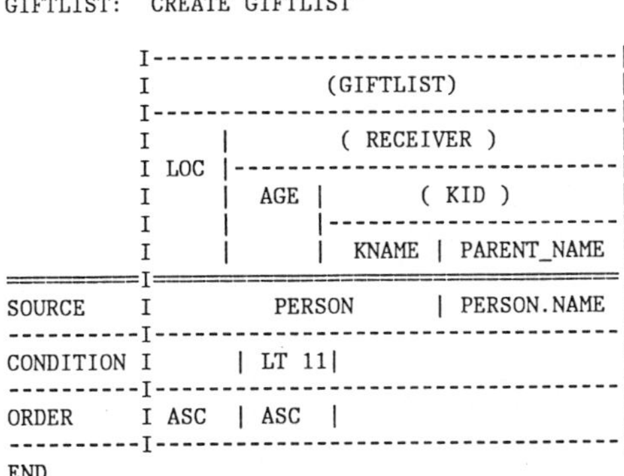

```
GIFTLIST:  CREATE GIFTLIST

           I-----------------------------------|
           I              (GIFTLIST)            |
           I-----------------------------------|
           I      |         ( RECEIVER )        |
           I LOC  |----------------------------|
           I      |  AGE  |       ( KID )       |
           I      |       |--------------------|
           I      |       | KNAME | PARENT_NAME |
==========I===================================|
SOURCE     I            PERSON     | PERSON.NAME |
----------I-----------------------------------|
CONDITION I      | LT 11|                       |
----------I-----------------------------------|
ORDER      I ASC  | ASC  |                      |
----------I-----------------------------------|
END
```

Figure 8-5. FORMAL program to create GIFTLIST.

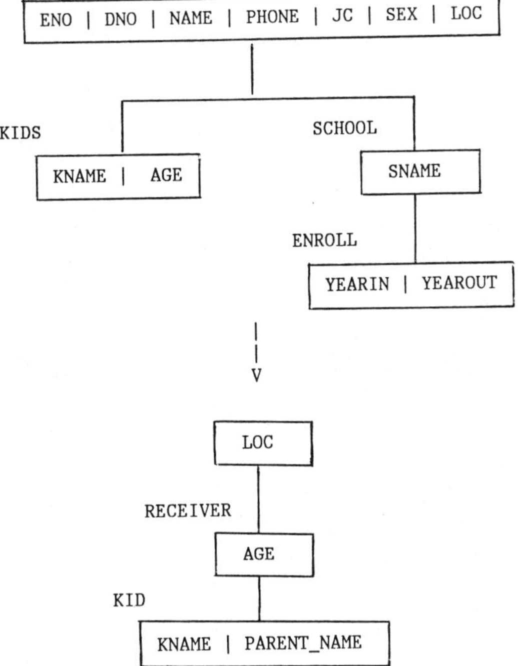

Figure 8-6. Implicit transformation of data structures when creating GIFTLIST from PERSON file.

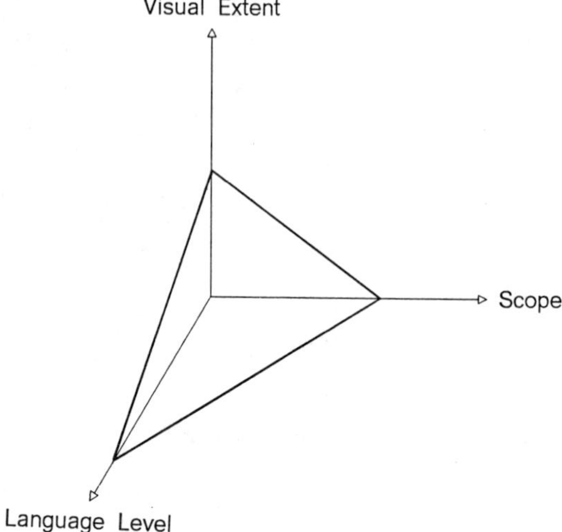

Figure 8-7. A profile of FORMAL.
(Shu[2]. © 1985 IEEE.)

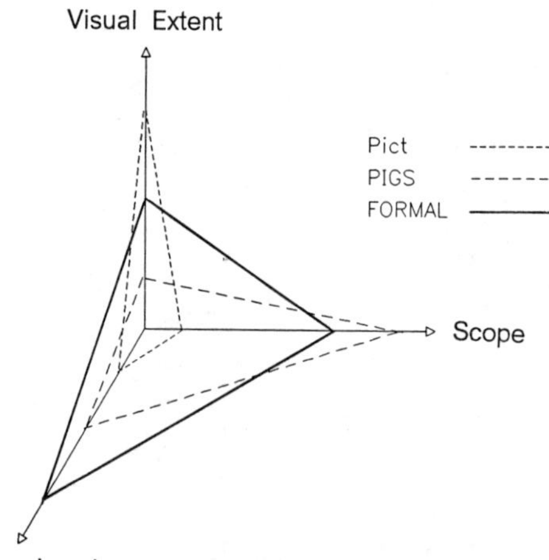

Figure 8-8. A comparison of Pict, PIGS and FORMAL.
(Shu[2]. © 1985 IEEE.)

In fact, data processing applications of a much more complicated nature can be programmed in a similar manner: *What you sketch is what you get.*

FORMAL has a wide scope of applicability. The language is nonprocedural. Users do not tell the computer what steps to follow in order to achieve the results. There are no prescriptive or control constructs. Figure 8-7 shows the profile of FORMAL.

These examples are used to illustrate an analytical approach to characterize visual programming languages in a profile expressed in terms of the level of the language, the scope of applicability, and the extent of visual expressions. This framework gives us a means to compare languages in a meaningful (although qualitative) manner. For example, by superimposing the profiles of Pict, PIGS, and FORMAL (as shown in Figure 8-8), the comparison of these three totally different languages begins to make sense.

In the following three chapters, we delve into various categories of visual programming languages in depth.

REFERENCES

1. Tesler, L. G., "Programming Languages," *Scientific American,* Vol. 251, No. 3 (Sept. 1984), pp. 70-78.
2. Shu, N. C., "Visual Programming Languages: A Dimensional Analysis," *Proceedings of the IEEE International Symposium on New Directions in Computing* (Aug. 1985), pp. 326-334.
3. Chang, S. K., Reuss, J., and McCormick, B. H., "Design Considerations of a Pictorial Database System," *International Journal on Policy Analysis and Information Systems,* Vol. 1, No. 2 (Jan. 1978), pp. 49-70.
4. Chang, S. K., "Image Information Systems," *Proceedings of the IEEE,* Vol. 73, No. 4 (Apr. 1985), pp. 754-764.
5. Roussopoulos, N., and Leifker, D., "An Introduction to PSQL: A Pictorial Structured Query Language," *Proceedings of the 1984 IEEE Computer Society Workshop on Visual Languages,* Hiroshima, Japan (Dec. 1984), pp. 77-87.
6. Herot, C. F., "Spatial Management of Data," *ACM Transactions on Database Systems,* Vol. 5, No. 4 (Dec. 1980), pp. 493-514.
7. Monden, N., Yoshino, Y., Hirakawa, M., Tanake, M. and Ichikawa, T., "HI-VISUAL: A Language Supporting Visual Interaction in Programming," *Proceedings of the 1984 IEEE Computer Society Workshop on Visual Languages,* Hiroshima, Japan (Dec. 1984), pp. 199-205.
8. Glinert, E. P., and Tanimoto, S. L., "Pict: An Interactive Graphical Programming Environment," *IEEE Computer,* Vol. 17, No. 11 (Nov. 1984), pp. 7-25.
9. Pong, M. C., and Ng, N., "PIGS—A System for Programming with Interactive Graphical Support," *Software—Practice and Experience,* Vol. 13, No. 9 (Sept. 1983), pp. 847-855.
10. Shu, N. C., "FORMAL: A Forms-Oriented and Visual-Directed Application System," *IEEE Computer,* Vol. 18, No. 8 (Aug. 1985), pp. 38-49.

Chapter 9

Diagrammatic Systems

For many years, graphs and diagrams of various sorts have been used as visual aids for the illustration or documentation of one or more aspects of the programs. But these graphical aids, by and large, did not comprise the programs themselves. They were not executable. The high cost of the graphical terminals and the large data storage needed for graphical representations have kept the graphing and diagramming techniques on paper and on blackboards.

Recently, however, due to the rapidly falling cost of the graphical displays, the availability of powerful workstations, and the desire for increased programmer productivity, efforts have been made to incorporate charts, graphs, and diagrams as graphical extensions of executable code.

Making charts, graphs, and diagrams executable has advantages, if we look at the traditional process of programming. Traditionally, programming involves several distinct phases: problem analysis, charting,* coding, translation (compiling/interpreting), and testing. And, more often than not, these processes would have to be reiterated at various points. This situation is expressed in Figure 9-1.

A serious problem with this approach has to do with the need to keep both the charts and the code (which are basically two representations of the same program) *up-to-date*. It is not surprising that somewhere in the debugging process, the chart (which is also part of the documentation) no longer

*We use the word "charting" in a broad sense. Here it means using some kinds of diagrammatic depictions (not necessarily conventional flow charts, even though flow charts are perhaps the most common forms of charting) as visual aid for program abstraction.

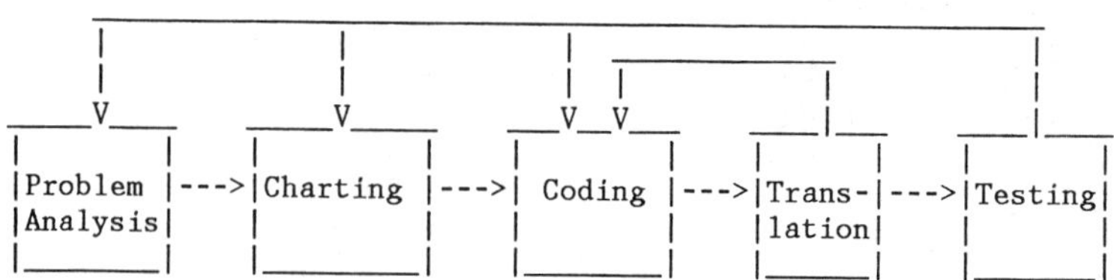

Figure 9-1. The traditional programming process.

represents the actual code that is executed, and consequently creates problems in later maintenance of the program.

Making charts executable is an attempt to collapse the two separate processes (charting and coding) into one. This not only makes programs easier to comprehend, but also easier to document and to maintain.

In this chapter, we describe several different types of graphs and diagrams, as well as the research efforts to make them executable.

VARIOUS FLOW CHARTS

Using charts and diagrams in connection with programming is a technique almost as old as programming itself. *Flow charts* were developed originally as an aid for assembly language programmers. Assembly languages have no facility to enforce structured programming. Programmers were taught to draw flow charts to make the program structures clear in their minds, so that they would not be lost in a sea of low-level details.

Figure 9-2 shows the flow chart symbols used in the early days of computing.

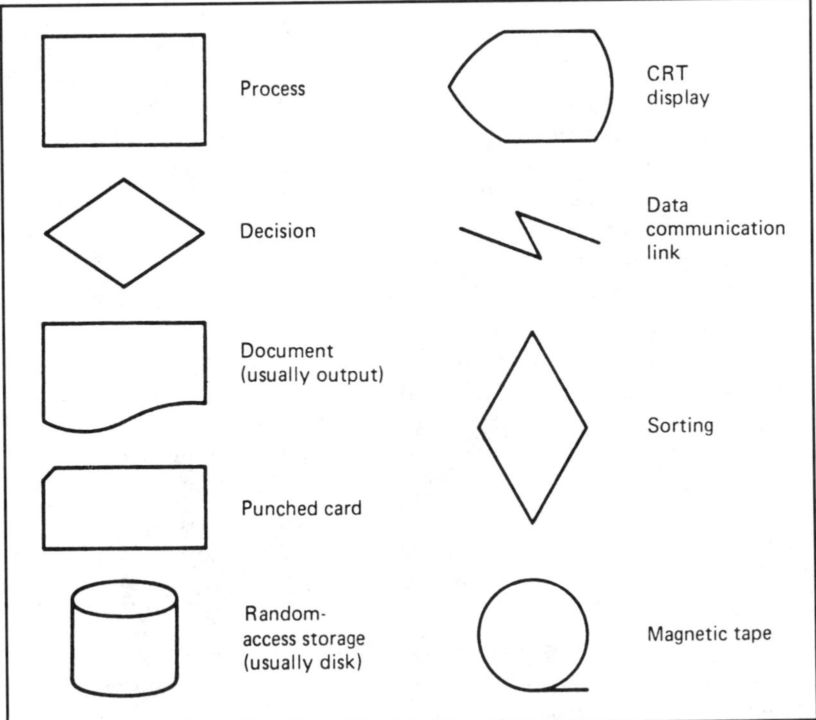

Figure 9-2. Conventional flowchart symbols. (From IBM flowcharting template X20-8020).

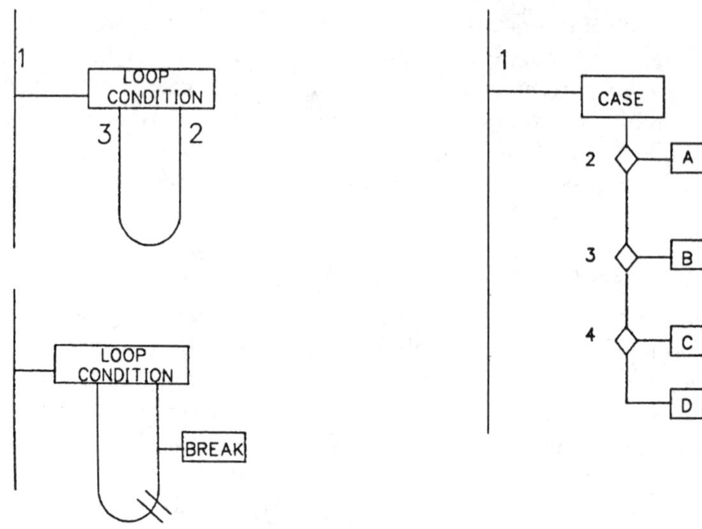

Figure 9-3. Examples of Rothon symbols.

They were few and simple. To describe the flow of control, appropriate flow chart symbols are connected by lines with arrows.

With the advent of the high-level programming languages and structured programming concepts, flow charting techniques also took on a somewhat structured approach. For example, in the method of flow charting proposed by Rothon,[1] symbols for looping and "case" constructs (Figure 9-3) were introduced, and the spatial arrangement of the symbols plays an important role in depicting the flow of control.

As a rule, the flow of control in a Rothon diagram is from left to right and from top to bottom. Nodes are visited according to this rule. When the end of a path is reached, control "falls back" to the point where the paths last split without a decision element. This point is illustrated in Figure 9-4.

The diagram is interpreted in the following manner: Follow the path via 1 and 2 to A, execute A, fall back to 2, follow path downward to B via 3, execute B, fall back to 3, no path downward so fall back to 2, both paths followed so fall back to 1, follow path downward to C via 4, execute C, fall back to 4, continue downward.

According to E. J. Brown, who has applied Rothon diagrams to data abstraction, "the method of flow charting proposed by Rothon is highly structured and has been used successfully to produce the design for real time software and operating system software. The symbols used all conform to British Standard BS4058 with the symbol for input/output omitted."[2]

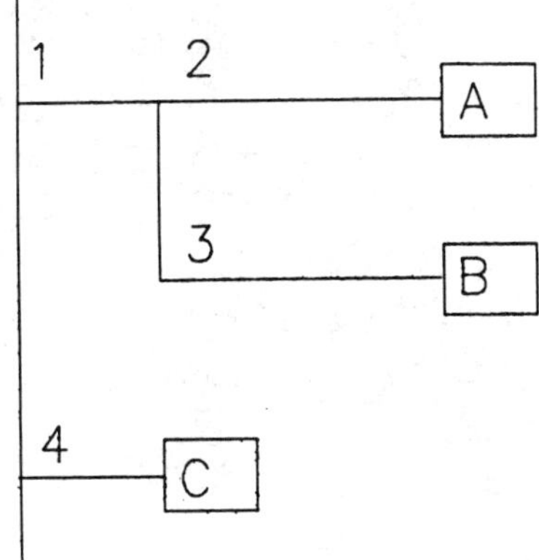

Figure 9-4. Flow of control depicted by the spatial arrangment of symbols.

Nevertheless, there was no attempt, to my knowledge, to make the Rothon diagrams *executable.* The PECAN system (see Chapter 3) has plans to support the Rothon diagram as a program view. According to Reiss, "In the short term, we are planning to do a general-purpose structured flowgraph editing view. The initial implementation of this will support Rothon diagrams and Nassi-Shneidermann diagrams."[3] That plan, as reported, is for the enhancement of program visualization, not an attempt to make diagrams part of an executable program.

FPL

FPL (First Programming Language) was developed by Robert Taylor at Columbia University's Teachers College, where it is the major instructional language used in the Computing and Education Program of that college.

Students studying FPL are encouraged to plan their programs on paper before working at the computer. Such 'paper and pencil' planning is an important aspect of FPL, and in fact, the language was originally designed with this in mind. An example of a student's sketch is shown in Figure 9-5.

FPL is based on a set of symbols shown in Figure 9-6. They are called "FPL icons" by Cunniff et al.,[4], and Taylor [5], but they resemble more closely to flow chart symbols.

The FPL symbols alone are not sufficient for successful interpretation of a program. When text (i.e., base language statements, in this case a subset of pseudo-Pascal) is added, an interpretation is possible. Thus, FPL can be characterized as incorporating executable flow chart symbols as graphical extension to a textual programming language. Figure 9-7 shows a sample FPL program and a Pascal translation.

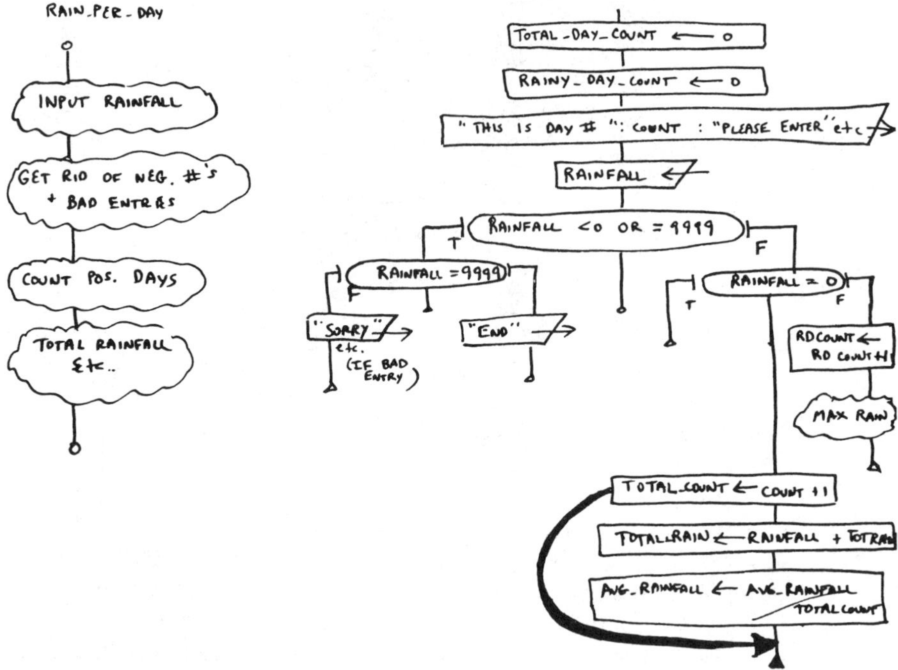

Figure 9-5. A student's sketch of a plan.
(Cunniff et al.[4] Copyright © 1986 Association for Computing Machinery, Inc., reprinted by permission.)

The system presents the user with an interactive graphical interface and allows the user to indicate what will occur next in the program flow. "The student enters a program in FPL, and upon completion, the FPL software generates a drawing of the FPL program and an executable Pascal translation."[4]

In Cunniff et al.,[4] the conceptual bugs found in the beginners' FPL programs are compared with those found in corresponding Pascal programs. "It would be impossible to make any definitive judgement on whether FPL or Pascal is a more appropriate language for beginning programmers, based on the small number analyzed for this study. However, the differences that apparently exist suggest that there may be some important advantages to the use of FPL. . . . The fact that none of the errors in the FPL program fell in the MISPLACED category indicates clearly that FPL's spatial nature affects a student's understanding of the flow of a program."[4] The most common bug was a MISSING GUARD (i.e., a failure to check for valid data), for which the spatial arrangement cannot offer much help. An example is shown in Figure 9-8.

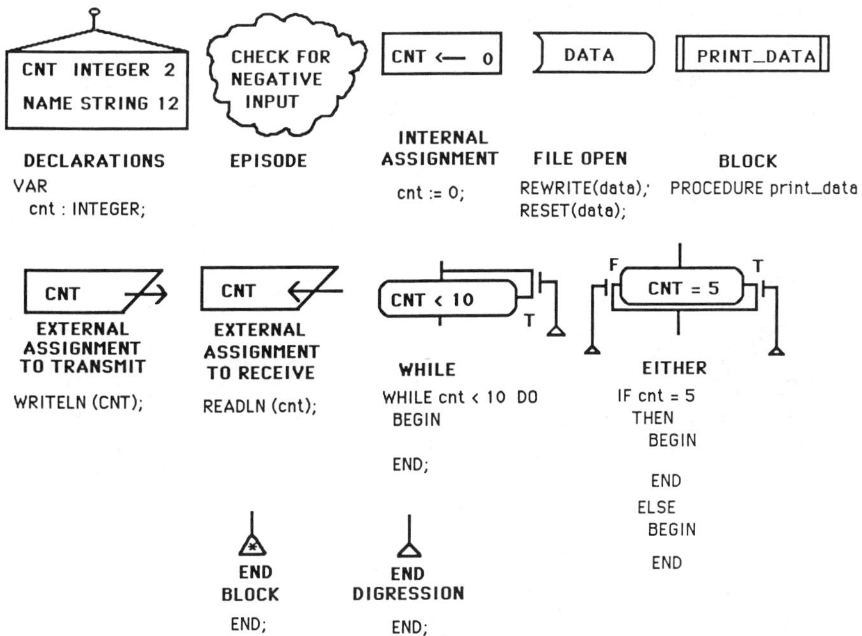

Figure 9-6. FPL symbols with corresponding Pascal constructs.
(Cunniff et al.[4] Copyright © 1986 Association for Computing Machinery, Inc., reprinted by permission.)

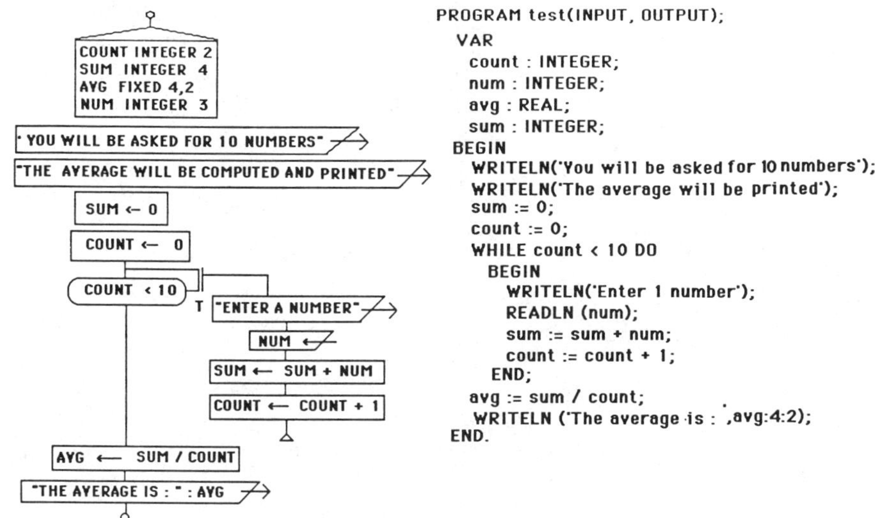

Figure 9-7. Sample FPL program with Pascal translation.
(Cunniff et al.[4] Copyright © 1986 Association for Computing Machinery, Inc., reprinted by permission.)

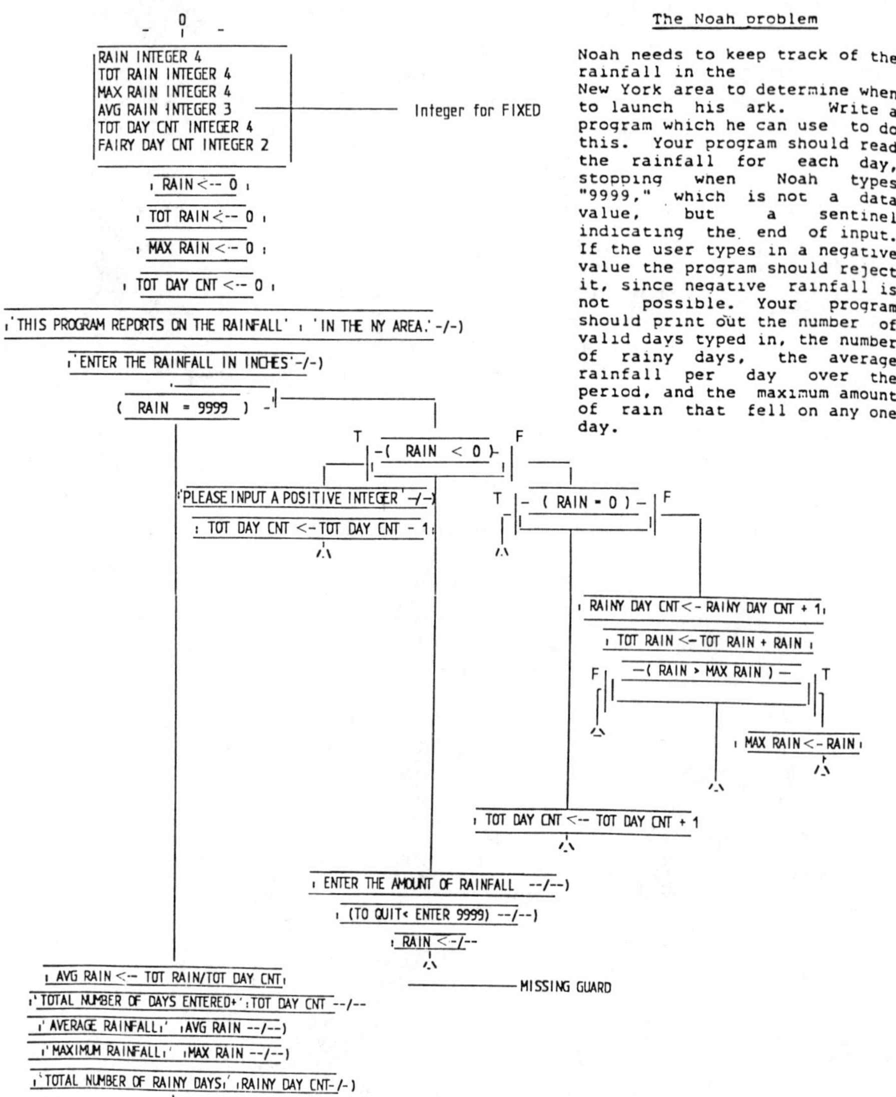

RAIN INTEGER 4
TOT RAIN INTEGER 4
MAX RAIN INTEGER 4
AVG RAIN INTEGER 3
TOT DAY CNT INTEGER 4
RAINY DAY CNT INTEGER 2
Integer for FIXED
RAIN <-- 0
TOT RAIN <-- 0
MAX RAIN <-- 0
TOT DAY CNT <-- 0
'THIS PROGRAM REPORTS ON THE RAINFALL' 'IN THE NY AREA.' -/-)
'ENTER THE RAINFALL IN INCHES'-/-)
(RAIN = 9999)
T
-(RAIN < 0)-
F
'PLEASE INPUT A POSITIVE INTEGER' -/-)
TOT DAY CNT <-TOT DAY CNT - 1
T
(RAIN = 0)
F
RAINY DAY CNT <- RAINY DAY CNT + 1
TOT RAIN <-TOT RAIN + RAIN
F
-(RAIN > MAX RAIN)-
T
MAX RAIN <- RAIN
TOT DAY CNT <-- TOT DAY CNT + 1
ENTER THE AMOUNT OF RAINFALL --/--)
(TO QUIT< ENTER 9999) --/--)
RAIN <-/--
MISSING GUARD
AVG RAIN <-- TOT RAIN/TOT DAY CNT
'TOTAL NUMBER OF DAYS ENTERED+';TOT DAY CNT --/--
'AVERAGE RAINFALL' AVG RAIN --/--)
'MAXIMUM RAINFALL' MAX RAIN --/--)
'TOTAL NUMBER OF RAINY DAYS' RAINY DAY CNT-/-)
The Noah problem
Noah needs to keep track of the rainfall in the New York area to determine when to launch his ark. Write a program which he can use to do this. Your program should read the rainfall for each day, stopping when Noah types "9999," which is not a data value, but a sentinel indicating the end of input. If the user types in a negative value the program should reject it, since negative rainfall is not possible. Your program should print out the number of valid days typed in, the number of rainy days, the average rainfall per day over the period, and the maximum amount of rain that fell on any one day.

Figure 9-8. Example of a listing of a FPL program.
(Cunniff et al.[4] Copyright © 1986 Association for Computing Machinery, Inc., reprinted by permission.)

Pascal/HSD

Notice that FPL translates structured flow charts into Pascal, thus making diagrammatic specifications executable. A similar effort, Pascal/HSD, was reported by Diaz-Herrera and Flude.[6]

Like FPL, Pascal/HSD is based on and developed from a subset of Pascal. Both FPL and Pascal/HSD choose structured flow chart symbols as graphical representations of programming concepts. Two entirely different approaches, however, are applied in using these symbols.

In the case of FPL, one can almost see the one-to-one correspondence between the FPL symbols (Figure 9-6) and their Pascal counterparts. In the case of Pascal/HSD, on the other hand, the emphasis is on providing a tool whereby the program's structured control flow and hierarchical levels of detail can be compacted and viewed as a unit.

Instead of having many different symbols, the *HSD's* (hierarchical structured diagrams) are based on two basic symbols (called "statement symbols"), which in various combinations are used to represent the language constructs.

A *statement symbol* describes a computation which can be only one of two types, namely, ACTIONs or TESTs. Any statement symbol can be recursively expanded to include an inner-level chart which serves to describe the subalgorithms. A symbol which is not refined or expanded is called a *terminal symbol.* Text in Pascal/S, a subset of Pascal, is formated to lie inside the graphic outline of these symbols.

Figure 9-9(a) shows the basic form of the *ACTION* statement symbol. The text of a terminal ACTION symbol is composed only of Pascal/S assignments and procedure calls, separated by semicolons. Figure 9-9(b) shows the basic form of the *TEST* statement symbol. The text of a terminal TEST symbol is composed of Pascal/S expressions: Boolean, CASE, and FOR.

Constructs are single-entry single-exit building blocks formed from com-

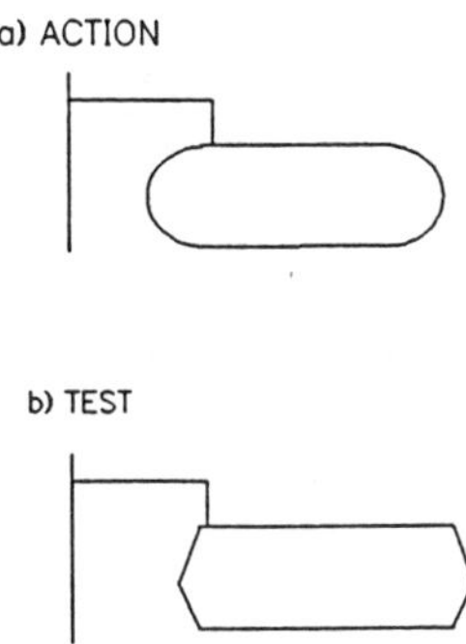

Figure 9-9. ACTION and TEST statement symbols.

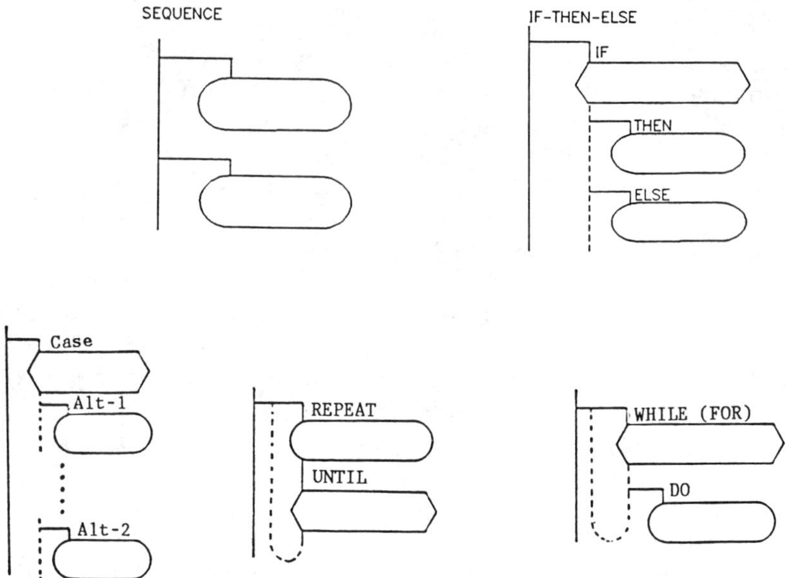

Figure 9-10. Pascal/HSD constructs.

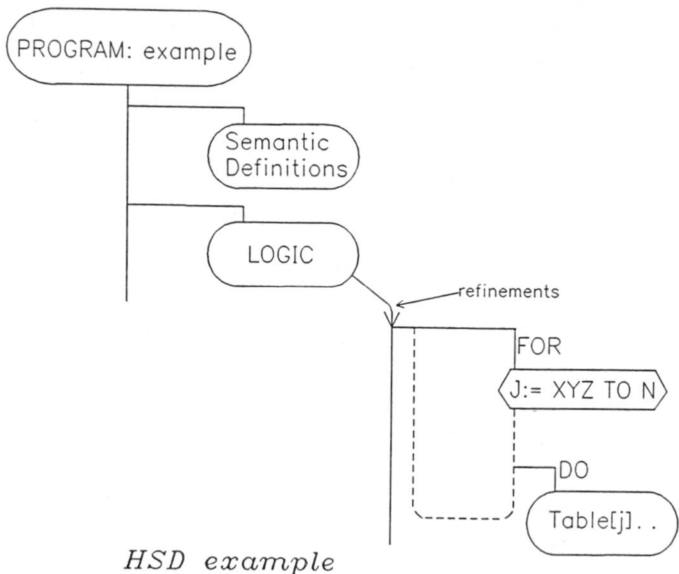

Figure 9-11. A Pascal/HSD program example.

binations of one or more statement symbols. The permitted combinations are shown in Figure 9-10. Dashed lines from the TEST symbols represent decision paths or backward jumps associated with looping constructs.

A Pascal/HSD *program* is built by connecting constructs along a vertical line (called an "execution line") to form an HSD chart. An inner-level chart is shown to the right of the construct being expanded. Thus, in the program, the flow of control is shown form top to bottom and the hierarchical levels of detail are shown from left to right. Figure 9-11 shows fragments of a Pascal/HSD program.

Program execution proceeds by traversing execution lines from the top to the bottom. If, during the course of execution, an expansion of a construct is encountered, the execution line of the inner chart is followed before the execution of the outer chart is resumed. This is repeated until the last construct of the outermost execution line has been executed.

Pascal/HSD has been designed as a program development system which includes a compiler, an interpreter, and an editor-monitor. A run-time user-interaction facility allows the progress of the compilation/interpretation to be selectively displayed at slow speed. The authors claim that "this feature provides a powerful facility for teaching both programming and compiling techniques."

VARIANTS OF NASSI-SHNEIDERMAN DIAGRAMS

Among the structured flow charts, Nassi-Shneiderman (N-S) diagrams are probably the best known.[7] The diagrams used to represent the control structures are based on the symbols shown in Figure 9-12. These symbols are combined to form an overall chart for a program. Figure 9-13, taken from Glinert and Tanimoto,[8] shows a conventional flow chart and an N-S diagram for a segment of Pascal code.

Figure 9-13 is meant to contrast the N-S diagram with the flow chart. Compared to conventional flow charts, the use of N-S diagrams not only highlights the logical structure of program components but also portrays the program in a more compact form. The scope of each construct is quite obvious from the diagram. Arbitrary transfer of control is impossible. The rectangular nature of the symbols also means that the N-S diagrams take up less space.

For these reasons, N-S diagrams (or their derivatives) have been chosen by a number of researchers as the executable charting form—which is the topic of this subsection.

A Graphics-Based Programming-Support System

A pioneering work in making N-S diagrams executable has been reported by researchers at the IBM San Jose Laboratory.[9] The primary goal of the

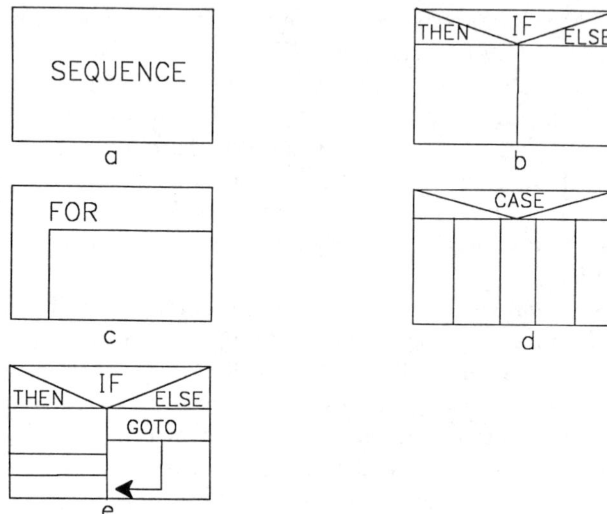

Figure 9-12. Nassi-Shneiderman symbols.

```
begin
    s1;
    if not l1
        then
          begin
              s2; s3;
          end
        else
          while L1 do
              begin
                  if l2 then
                      then s4
                      else s5;
                  s6;
              end;
     while L2 do s7;
     s8;
end
```

(a)

Figure 9-13. (a) A segment of a Pascal program.
(b) Its corresponding flow chart.
(c) An N-S structure diagram.

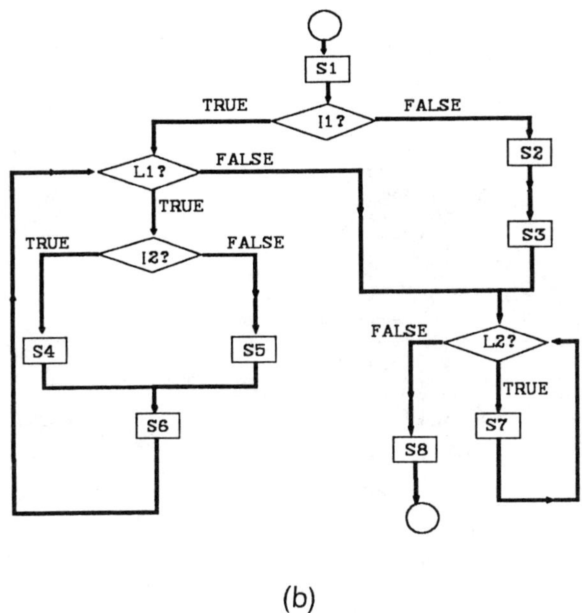

(b)

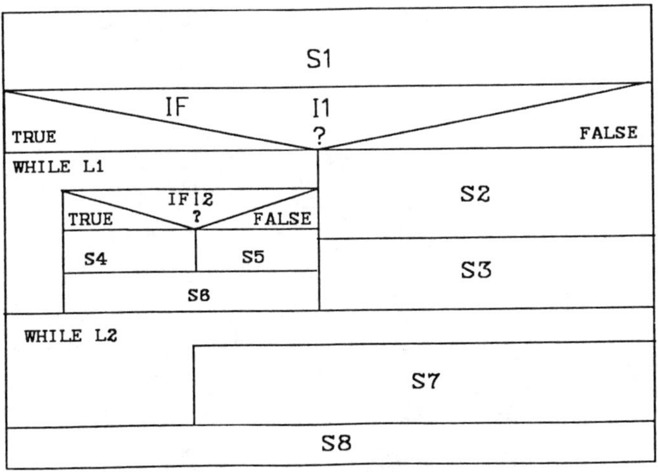

(c)

Figure 9-13. *(continued)*

NAME: dummy(nut, read, len, arrow, bee, ceed, ef3)
SPEC: a comment about the diagram goes here

PARAMETERS	NAME	EXAMPLE	DIMENSION
IN:	nut	99999	
	read	zzzz	
	len	99	
OUT:	arrow	99.99	
	bee	99999.9	
MOD:	ceed	99999	
	ef3	999999	
LOCAL VARS			
	index	999999999	
	realno	99.9999	
	table	9.99	(2,30)

Figure 9-14. An example of an NSD data definition header.

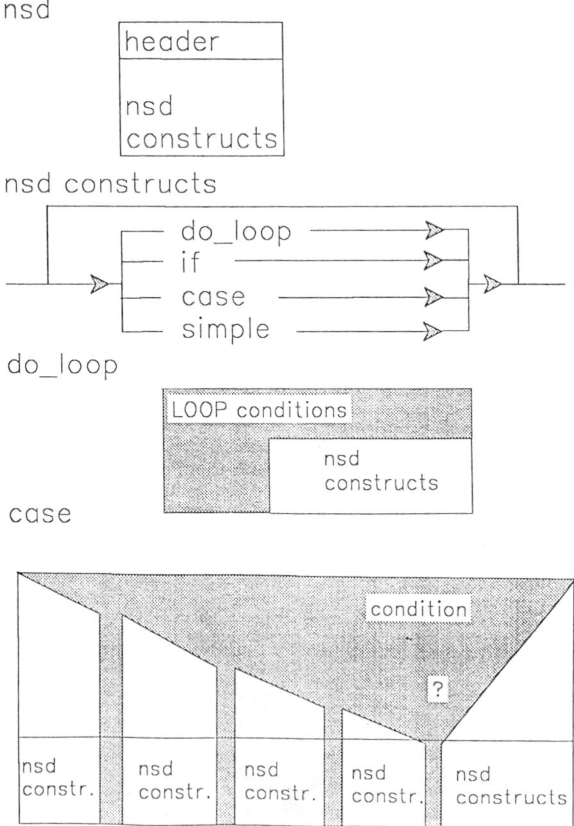

Figure 9-15. NSD syntax.

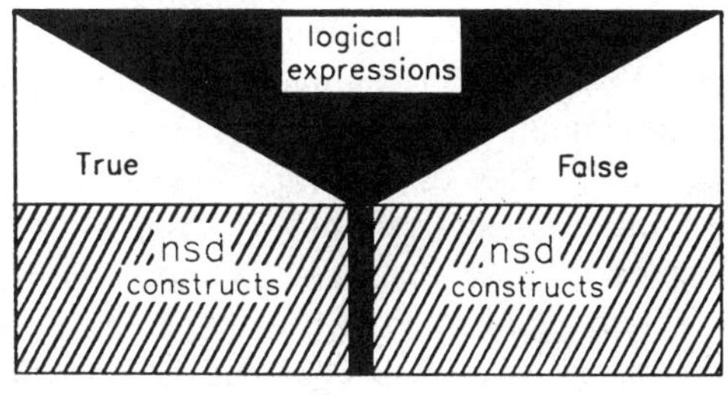

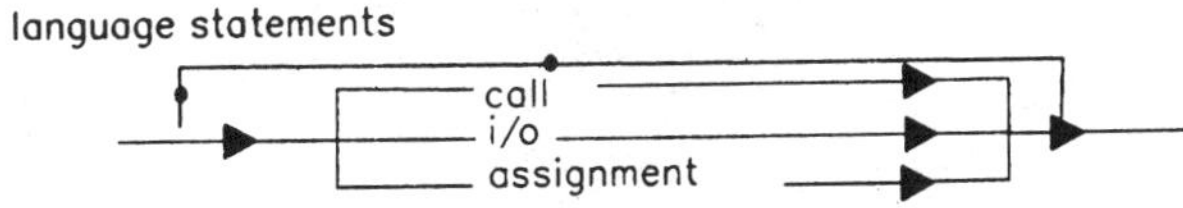

Figure 9-15. *(continued)*

Programming-Support System is the development of both a programming system and techniques for improving the quality of specifying, documenting, and producing computer programs by (1) establishing charting techniques to specify programs in a way that clearly shows their structure and logic; (2) providing an interactive graphics system for the drawing and editing of these charts; (3) providing a preprocessor/compiler mechanism to translate charts into executable code; and (4) providing self-documentation as a by-product of the program development process.

In order to carry out these goals, the diagrams proposed by Nassi and Shneiderman have been extended to include headers, and the extended forms are called *NSDs*.

Each NSD consists of two parts. The (declarative) header part includes the diagram name, a comment about its function, and definitions of its local variables and parameters. Figure 9-14 shows an example. The (imperative) body part consists of NSD constructs with embedded base language statements (in this case, PL/I). The NSD constructs specify the control flow and the base language statements specify the operations to be performed.

The allowable NSD constructs are *SIMPLE* (i.e., sequential), *IF, CASE,* and *DO-LOOP.* The allowable PL/I statements are *assignment, call,* and *imput/output.* Figure 9-15 shows the syntax.

Each NSD is a separately executable module that may contain calls to other NSDs and external subroutines. But no internal subroutines are allowed within an NSD. Figure 9-16 shows an example of an NSD with PL/I statements.

The system provides an interactive graphical interface, and displays both NSDs and messages to the user on a color graphics screen. Input is via a keyboard and a pointing device. To develop a program, the user creates an NSD diagram. First, he types in the name of the NSD, which causes the system to display either the named NSD (if it already exists) or an essentially empty diagram. The user is then ready to edit (i.e., modify or create) the NSD program.

Editing in general involves pointing to a location on the screen and typing in a single letter to indicate the desired action. For example, typing the letter "S," "I," "C," or "L" causes the system to display or embed a SIMPLE, IF, CASE, or DO-LOOP construct in an area at the pointed location. Typing the letter "T" allows text to be entered within a pointed NSD construct. Other

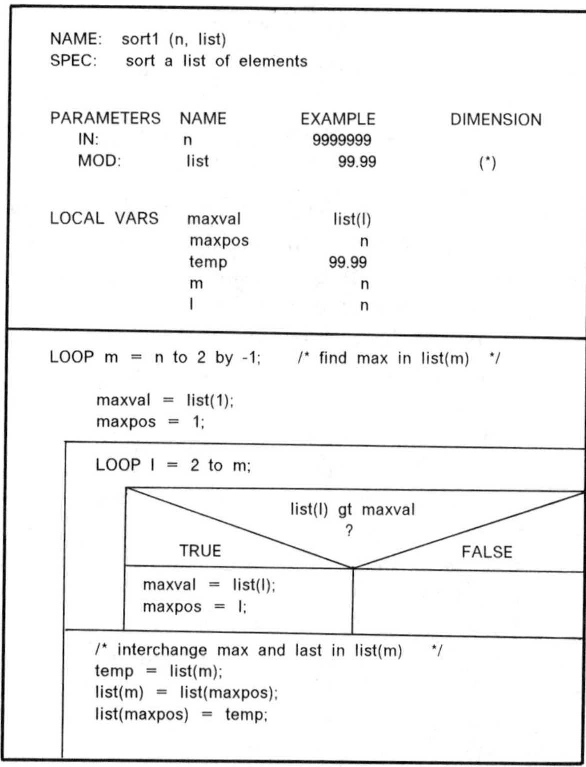

Figure 9-16. An example of an NSD program.

functions (e.g., deleting a construct or text as pointed, flipping between the header and the body) can be accomplished in the same fashion. Figures 9-17 illustrates this mode of interaction.

Figure 9-17(a) shows a display on the screen. Pointing near one of the corners between the two displayed constructs and typing "L" causes a DO loop to be inserted, as shown in Figure 9-17(b). Pointing to the existing DO loop (as shown in Figure 9-17c) and entering the command "I" causes an IF construct to be embedded (see Figure 9-17d).

To execute an NSD program, a preprocessor is invoked to translate the charts into PL/I source programs, which are then compiled by a regular PL/I

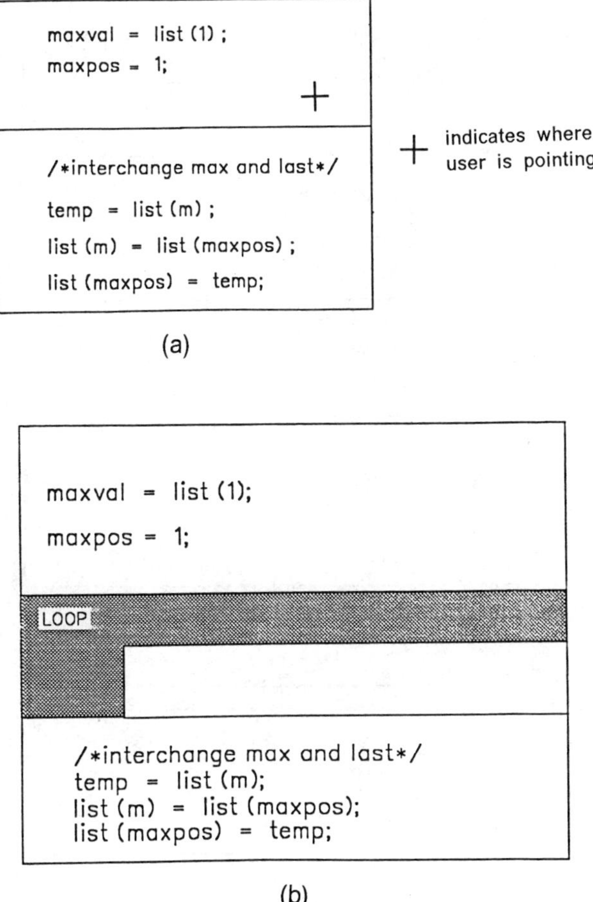

Figure 9-17. Example illustrating the mode of interaction.

compiler and executed. An example of a PL/I procedure generated for an NSD program is shown in Figure 9-18.[10]

In summary, the Programming Support System provides facilities to support most of its goals. In using the NSDs as graphical extensions to PL/I, the scope of the loops and the IF constructs is obvious, especially when they are shown in color. The common mistakes of improper closing of blocks (e.g.,

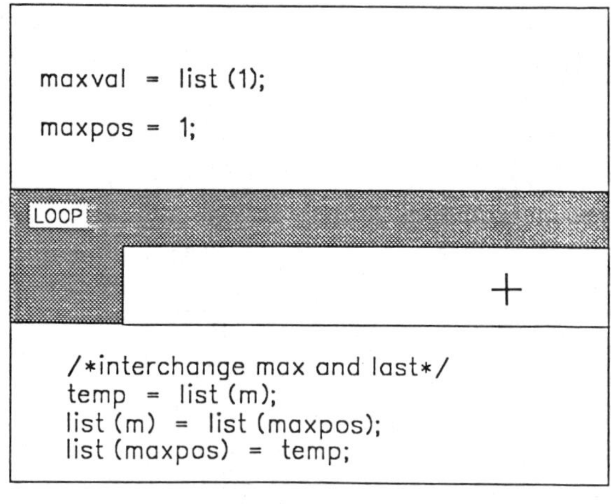

(c)

maxval = list (1);

maxpos = 1;

LOOP

TRUE ? FALSE

/*interchange max and last*/
temp = list (m);
list (m) = list (maxpos);
list (maxpos) = temp;

(d)

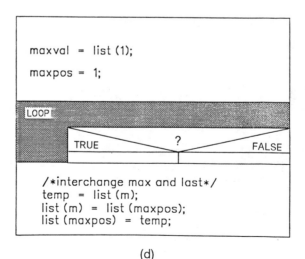

Figure 9-17. *(continued)*

missing "ENDs") and ill-formed "IF THEN ELSE" statements simply disappear.

Drawing or modifying charts is normally a cumbersome process and is often a deterrent to using charting techniques. By providing an interactive graphic editor (which serves as an automatic charting device), a dreaded task can be made more enjoyable.

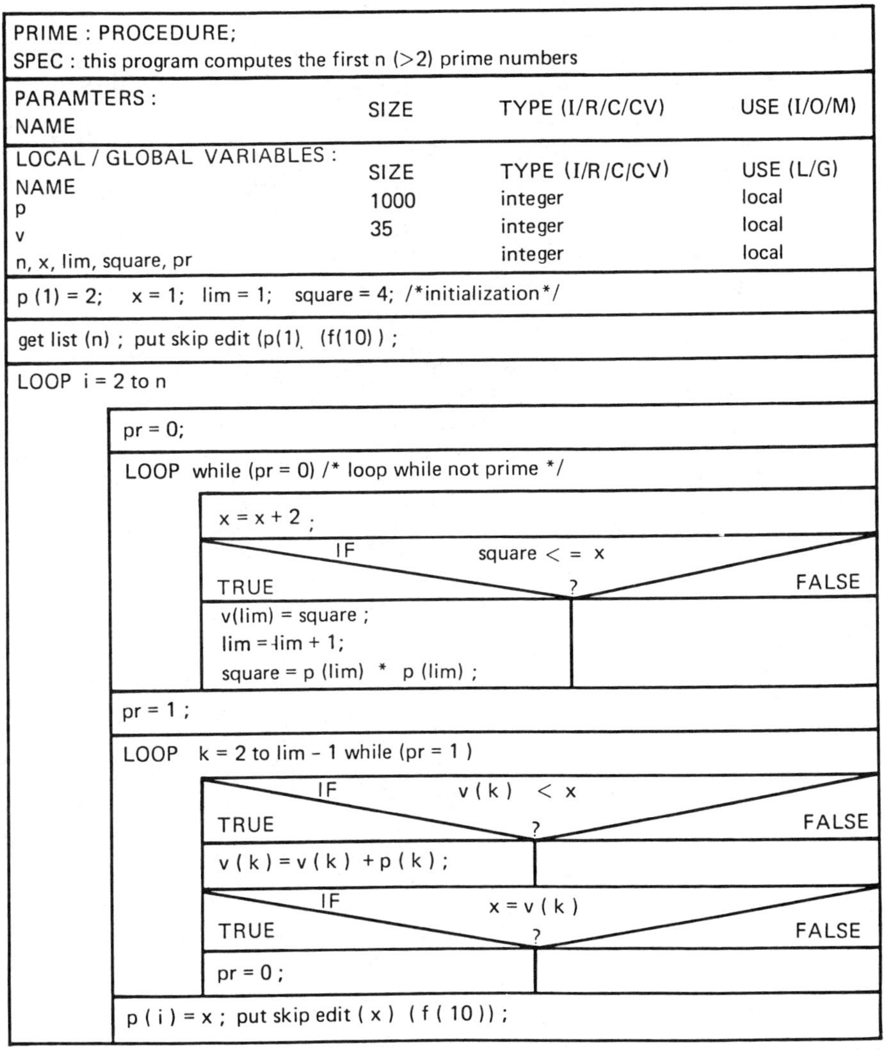

PRIME : PROCEDURE;
SPEC : this program computes the first n (>2) prime numbers

PARAMTERS : NAME	SIZE	TYPE (I/R/C/CV)	USE (I/O/M)

LOCAL / GLOBAL VARIABLES : NAME	SIZE	TYPE (I/R/C/CV)	USE (L/G)
p	1000	integer	local
v	35	integer	local
n, x, lim, square, pr		integer	local

```
p (1) = 2;   x = 1;   lim = 1;   square = 4; /*initialization*/
get list (n) ; put skip edit (p(1), (f(10) ) ;
LOOP i = 2 to n
    pr = 0;
    LOOP while (pr = 0) /* loop while not prime */
        x = x + 2 ;
        IF square < = x ?
        TRUE:
            v(lim) = square ;
            lim = lim + 1;
            square = p (lim) * p (lim) ;
        FALSE:
    pr = 1 ;
    LOOP k = 2 to lim - 1 while (pr = 1 )
        IF v ( k ) < x ?
        TRUE:
            v ( k ) = v ( k ) + p ( k ) ;
        FALSE:
        IF x = v ( k ) ?
        TRUE:
            pr = 0 ;
        FALSE:
    p ( i ) = x ; put skip edit ( x ) ( f ( 10 )) ;
```

(a)

Figure 9-18. (a) An NSD program.
(b) PL/I procedure generated for the program in (a).
(Ng[10]. © 1979 IEEE. Original art courtesy of R. Williams.)

Furthermore, with the ability to translate charts into executable codes, one does not have to be concerned with the discrepancies between the charts and the programs. The charts are the programs.

However, the system has not been evaluated in real applications. One of the unanswered questions is, how well and how conveniently can large programs be supported by this method?

PIGS

Figure 9-18 clearly demonstrates that the translation of NSDs into PL/I is quite straightforward, and it appears that preprocessors for other languages should be fairly straightforward as well.

```
PRIME: PROCEDURE;
/* THIS PROGRAM COMPUTES THE FIRST N (>2) PRIME NUMBERS
*/
DCL P                              (1000    )  FIXED(31) BIN;
DCL V                              (35      )  FIXED(31) BIN;
DCL N,X,LIM,SQUARE,PR                          FIXED(31) BIN;
P(1) = 2;  X = 1;  LIM = 1;  SQUARE = 4;  /* INITIALIZATION */
GET LIST(N);   PUT SKIP EDIT(P(1)) (F(10));
DO  I = 2 TO N;
    PR = 0;
    DO  WHILE (PR = 0) /* LOOP WHILE NOT PRIME */;
        X = X + 2;
        IF  SQUARE <= X
            THEN DO;
                 V(LIM) = SQUARE;
                 LIM = LIM + 1;
                 SQUARE = P(LIM) * P(LIM);
                 END;
            ELSE DO;
                 END;
        PR = 1;
        DO  K = 2 TO LIM - 1 WHILE (PR = 1);
            IF  V(K) < X
                THEN DO;
                     V(K) = V(K) + P(K);
                     END;
                ELSE DO;
                     END;
            IF  X = V(K)
                THEN DO;
                     PR = 0;
                     END;
                ELSE DO;
                     END;
        END;
    END;
    P(I) = X;   PUT SKIP EDIT (X) (F(10));
END;
END PRIME;
```

(b)

Figure 9-18. *(continued)*

However, the preprocessor approach has a drawback. The extra layer of software between the user and the executable code prevents interactive execution, which is useful at the debugging stage. A more dynamic environment is desirable when the program is undergoing development and testing. To allow more flexible interactions, an experimental system for Programming with Interactive Graphical Support (PIGS) has been developed at the University of Hong Kong.[11]

The PIGS system uses the extended N-S form developed by the Programming Support System,[9] i.e., the NSDs, as the directly executable chart form. The allowable NSD constructs are SIMPLE, IF, and DO-LOOP. As with the Programming Support System, the base language statements to be embedded in the NSD programs are restricted to assignments, external procedure calls, and input/output; and no nested internal procedures are allowed. The NSD modules are external to each other. Data can consist only of integers and one-dimensional arrays. The graphics editor provided in PIGS is also similar to that of the Programming Support System.

PIGS, however, differs from the Programming Support System in the following respects. First of all, a subset of Pascal (instead of PL/I) is used as the base language. Second, and more importantly, the emphasis of PIGS is on the interactive support for testing and debugging at execution, in addition to program construction.

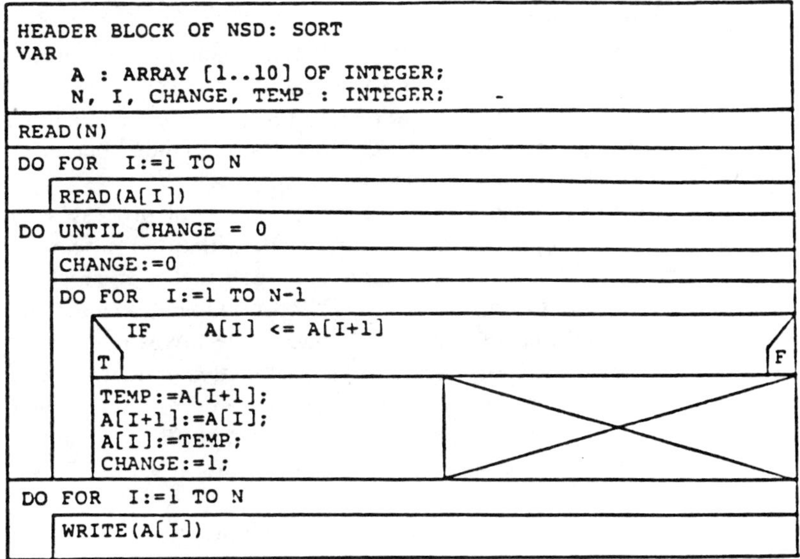

Figure 9-19. Example of a PIGS program.
(Pong and Ng[11]. Reprinted by permission of John Wiley & Sons)

An interpreter, rather than a compiler is used to allow the user to interact with the program during execution and make changes to the NSD program. If any syntax error is detected during the interpretive execution of a construct, the display will halt and allow the user to correct the error, or to interact with the program by examining or modifying the values of the variables. Immediately afterward, the execution can start again.

The user can watch and follow the logic flow of the NSD program as execution proceeds. In the course of executing each NSD construct which represents sequential, selective, or repetitive control flow, the construct outline and the embedded text are displayed and brightened up at the graphics terminal.

As an example, the NSD module for an interchange sort program is shown in Figure 9-19. Note that in the IF construct, the condition is incorrectly typed as "A[I] <= A[I + 1]" instead of "A[I] < A[I + 1]." The program loops indefinitely if some input numbers are equal. The user, on watching the never-ending display of the DO-UNTIL loop, will immediately realize that something is wrong within the loop.

Pigsty/I-PIGS

More recently, the concept of PIGS was extended to support concurrent programming.[12] Pigsty is the language based on Pascal and Communicating Sequential Processes (CSP),[13] and I-PIGS is the programming environmental designed to support Pigsty.

Like PIGS, Pigsty uses a combination of text and graphics to represent a program. The sequential part of Pigsty is based on Pascal. The control constructs are represented in structured chart form (Figure 9-20). Dijkstra's alternative *IF-FI* and repetitive *DO-OD* guarded commands[14] become the *ALT-/ALT* and the **ALT-/*ALT* constructs, respectively.

A Pigsty program consists of one or more sequential processes, each represented by a box. A process may communicate with other processes via one-directional links. The communication and synchronization mechanism between Pigsty processes is the same as the CSP communication mechanism.

I-PIGS provides editing functions to create single boxes and arrays of boxes. It can execute the chart programs via a simulated concurrent execution mechanism. The data communication between processes is animated in one of the windows on the screen. Other windows are used to show the structured chart forms of control constructs and tables of variables used in a process.

"The animations of data communication, logic flow and change of variable values allow the programmer to understand the dynamic behavior of a concurrent program more clearly and locate errors more easily."[12]

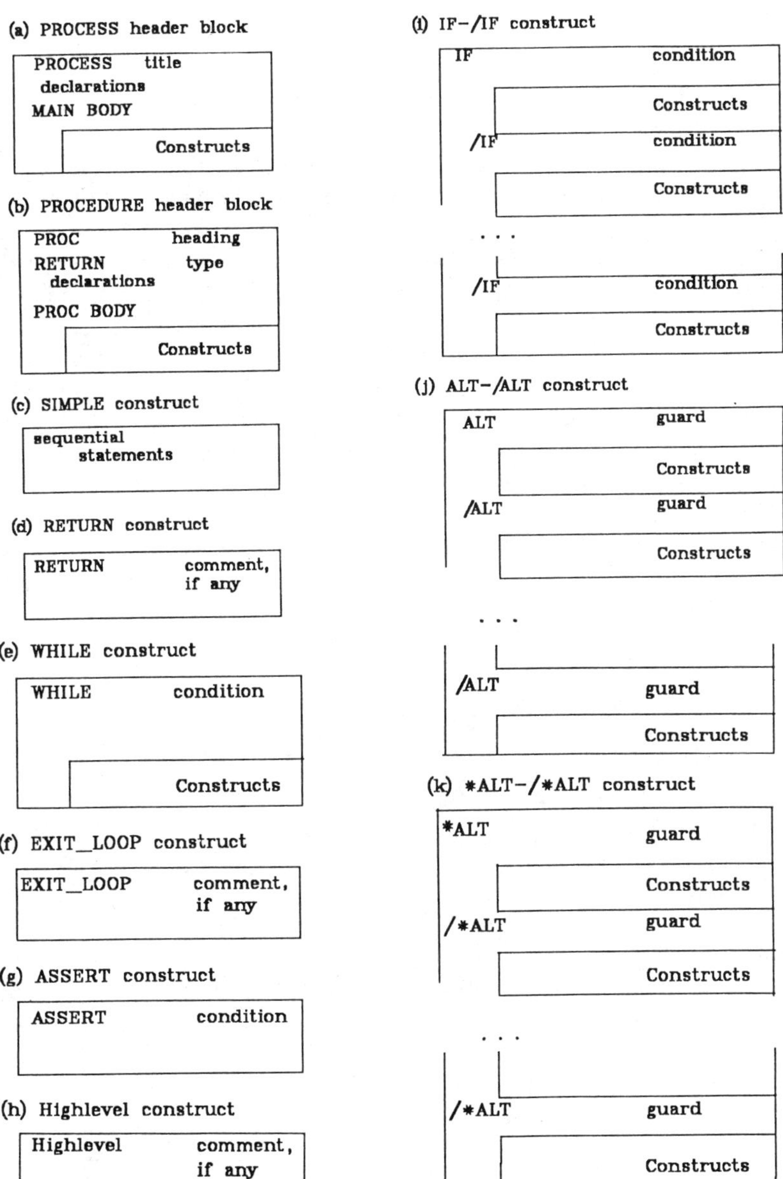

Figure 9-20. Structured charts used in Pigsty.
(Pong[12]. © 1986 IEEE.)

GRASE

GRASE (a Graphical Syntax Directed Editor for Structured Programming) was another effort aimed at providing support for structured programming based on charting techniques.[15]

The "graphical abstract language" (GAL), used in GRASE, is a variation of the Nassi-Shneiderman diagrams. The symbol set of GAL is shown in Figure 9-21.

Similar to PIGS, the base language statements to be inserted into the charting symbols are restricted to a subset of Pascal statements (see Figure 9-22 for an example), and the charts are translated into Pascal programs.

The programmer, in an interactive way, develops the program by invoking templates (which represent the different Pascal constructs) and then filling them with other templates or the text.

GRASE, however, was not designed with pointing devices in mind. The user interacts with the system via commands (e.g., $DECLAR, $IF, $WHILE, $SEC) and refers to a particular statement in the chart via a statement number. For example, given a program graph such as the one shown in Figure

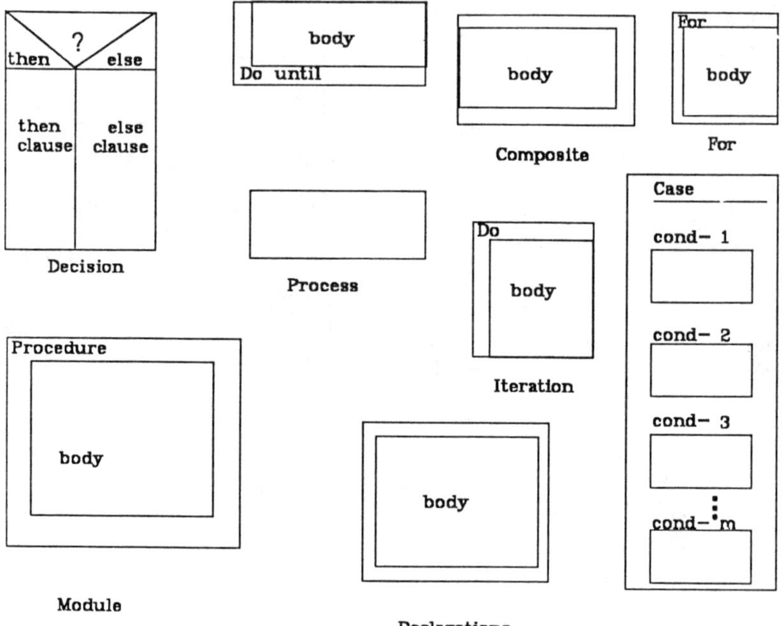

Figure 9-21. GAL symbol set.

9-23(a), the use of the 'EXP 9' command expands statement 9 into the next level of detail (as shown in Figure 9-23b). Similarly, the CONT command can be used to bring the graph to its parent level. For example, Figure 9-23(c) shows the effect of giving the command 'CONT 9' when statement 9 was in the state of Figure 9-23(b).

In summary, conceptually, GRASE does not add any novel ideas to the Programming Support System or PIGS, discussed in the previous section. But it shows how the system might be implemented without pointing devices, and how the user might control the levels of detail by using the CONTract or EXPand command on nested statements.

Note that all the languages we have discussed so far in this chapter can be characterized as *graphical extensions* to various subsets of existing programming languages (referred to as the *base languages* in our discussion). In the framework of dimensional analysis, we observe that the graphical extensions have the same application scope and the same language level as the base languages. The incorporation of the visual expressions serves mainly to make the program structure clear. Thus, as shown in Figure 9-24, if the base language is represented by the dashed lines, the profile of the extended language may be represented by the solid lines.

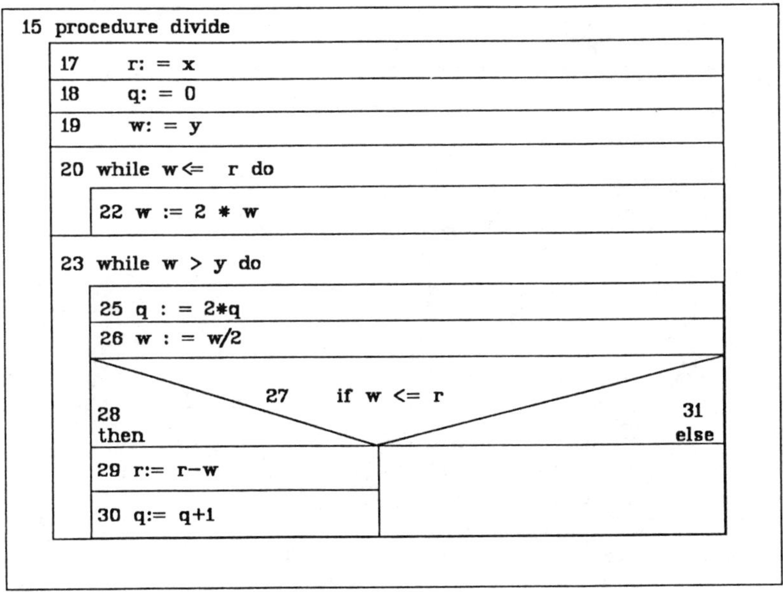

Figure 9-22. Example of a GAL program.

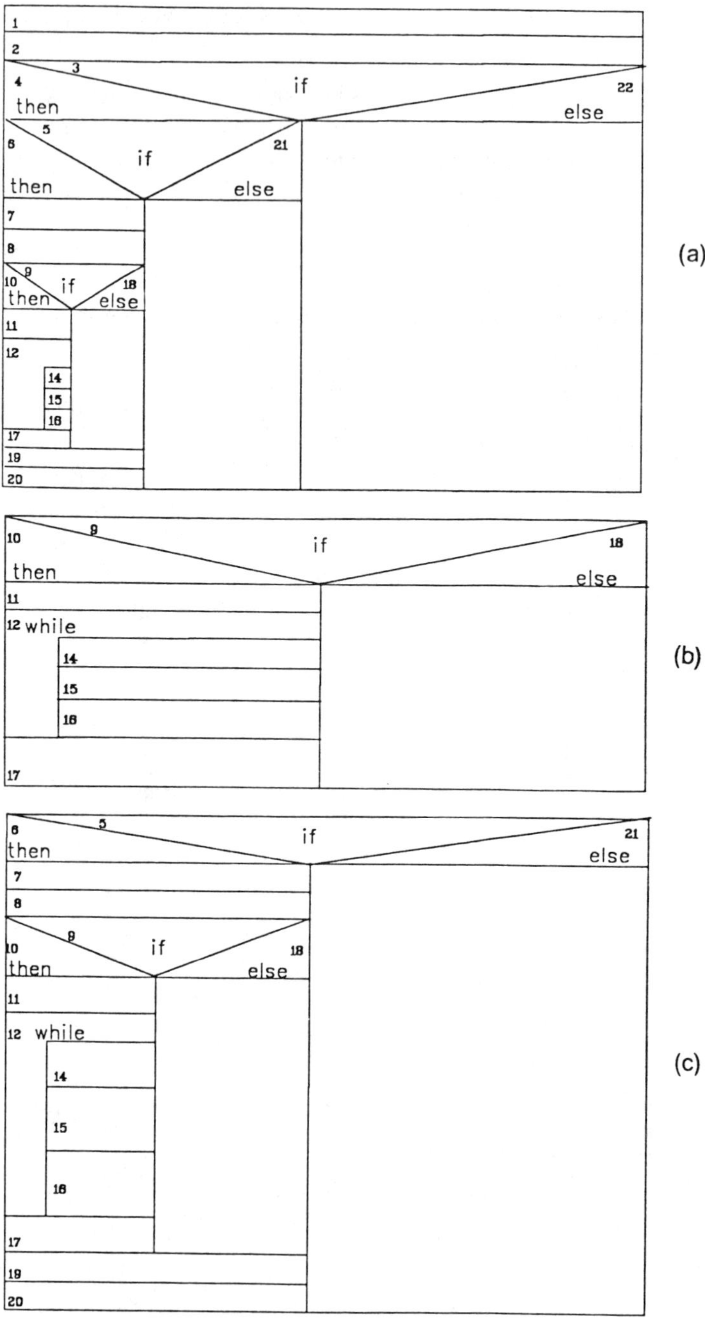

Figure 9-23. (a) A GAL program graph.
(b) Graph of statement 9 using the command 'EXP 9'.
(c) Contraction of statement 9.

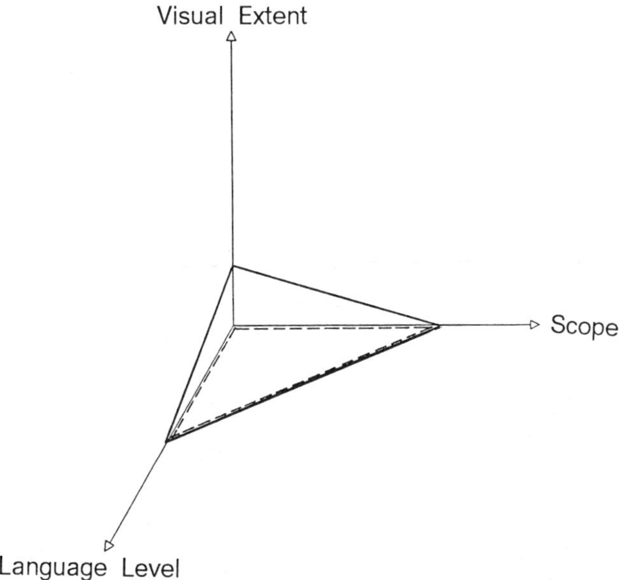

Figure 9-24. A profile of graphical extensions.

DATA FLOW DIAGRAMS

Structured charts impose structure on the flow of control but ignore the flow of data. *Data flow diagrams,* on the other hand, are used in connection with data flow languages.[16]

In contrast to the von Neumann model of computation, the data flow model has neither global updatable memory nor a single program counter. The data flow model deals only with values. An operation is enabled if and only if all the required input values have been computed. Enabled operations consume input values and produce sets of output values, which are sent to other operators that need these values. A language based on data flow concepts does not introduce sequencing constraints other than the ones imposed by data dependencies.

"A program in a high-level data flow language is directly translatable into a graph whose nodes represent functions and whose arcs represent data dependencies between functions. . . . In fact, data flow languages were originally defined as graphical languages."[17]

There are many reasons for describing data flow languages in graphical representations, Davis and Keller[16] have cited the followings:

1. Data flow languages sequence program actions by a simple data availability firing rule: When a node's arguments are available, it is said to be

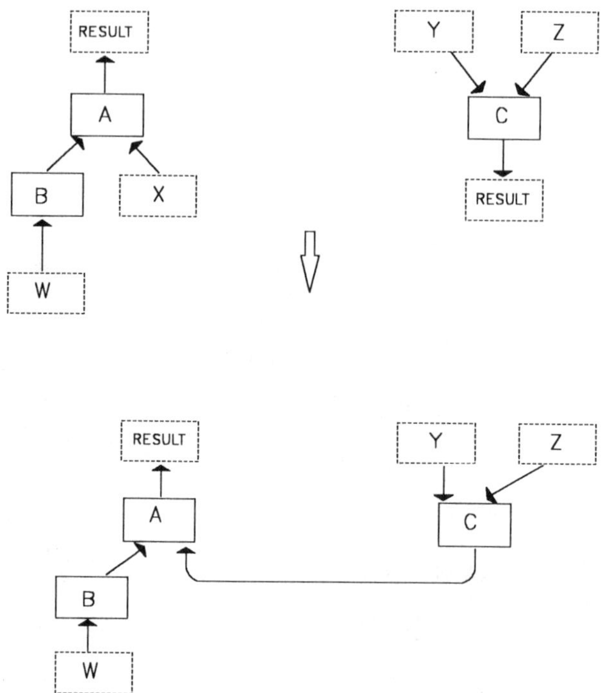

Figure 9-25. Splicing of two graphs.

"firable." After firing, the node's results are sent to other functions, which need these results as their arguments. This behavior suggests that the program can be aptly portrayed as a directed graph in which each node represents a function and each directed arc a conceptual medium over which data items flow. Phantom nodes, drawn with dashed lines, indicate points at which the program either receives data from or sends data to its environment.

2. Data flow programs are easily combinable into larger programs (see Figure 9-25).
3. Graphs can be used to present an intuitive view of the potential concurrency in the execution of the program.
4. Graphs can be used to attribute a formal meaning to a program.

The most prevailing model for data flow representation is the *token model.* In this model, data are always viewed as flowing on arcs from one node to another in a stream of discrete tokens.

When a node is labeled with a scaler function, such as + or *, it is

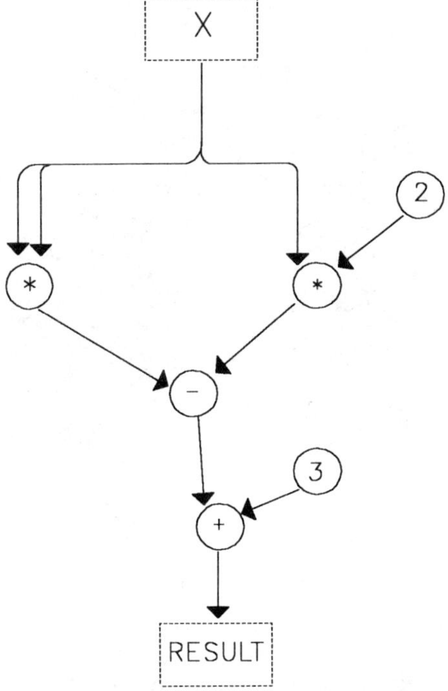

Figure 9-26. Data flow graph for $X^2 - 2*X + 3$.

understood that the function is repeated as tokens arrive at its inputs. Each repetition produces a token at its output.

For example, the graph in Figure 9-26 defines a repeated computation of polynomial function of X: $X^2 - 2 * X + 3$ for a sequence of values of X.

As another example, Figure 9-27 defines a repeated computation of:

```
IF X < 0
   THEN X = X − 1
   ELSE X = X + 1
```

Two nodes, the SELECTOR and the DISTRIBUTOR, are used as *conditional constructs.*

In the case of a SELECTOR, a token is first absorbed from the horizontal input. The value of that token, either true or false, determines from which of the two vertical inputs the next token will be absorbed. In the case of the DISTRIBUTOR, a token is absorbed from the vertical input and passed to

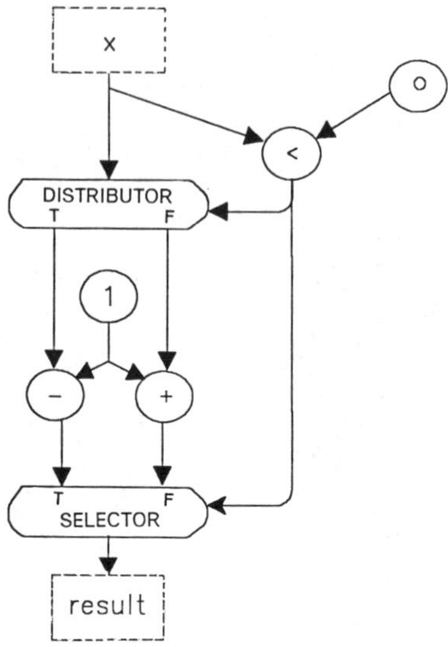

Figure 9-27. Conditional constructs.

one of the vertical outputs. Again, the choice of output depends on the true or false value of the horizontal input.

Iteration can be achieved through cyclic data flow graphs. The body of the iteration is initially activated by a token that arrives on the input of the graph. A new token, produced by the iteration subgraph, is cycled back on a feedback path until a certain condition is satisfied.

The example in Figure 9-28 illustrates Newton's method of finding the roots of a function. Node *f* could be replaced by the graph shown in Figure 9-26 (for $X^2 - 2 * X + 3$). A similar graph could replace node *f′* to compute the derivative $2 * X - 2$.

Similar to the use of subroutines in structuring conventional programs, *macrofunction* can be used to manage the complexity of data flow graphs. A macrofunction is defined by specifying a name and associating it with a graph, called the *consequent* of that name. A node in a program graph labeled with a macrofunction name is, in effect, replaced by its consequent. For example, one might wish to encapsulate the iterate subgraph in Figure 9-28 into a node called "Iterate." Macrofunctions can also be adopted for recursively specified functions. Figure 9-29 shows an example.

There are very few physical implementations of data flow diagrams as directly executable data flow programs. FGL[18] and GPL[19] are two of them.

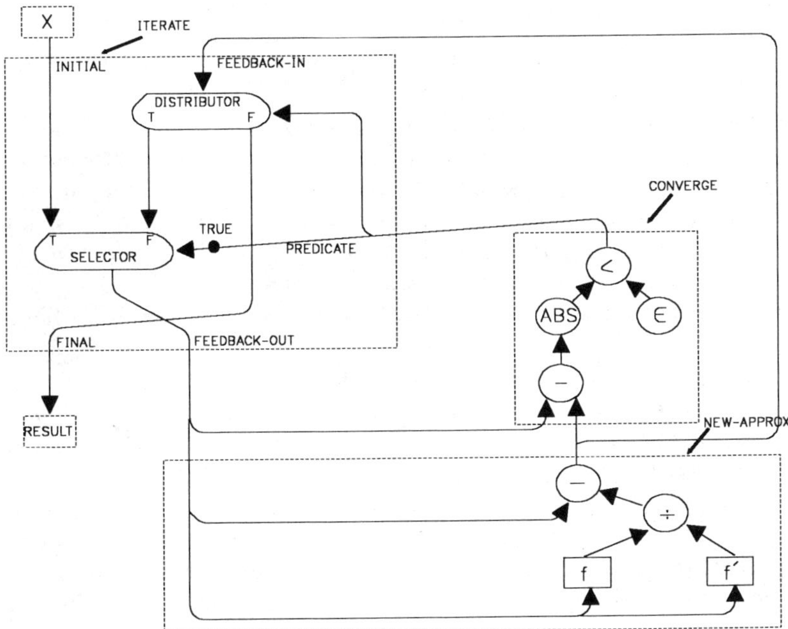

Figure 9-28. A graph of Newton's method.

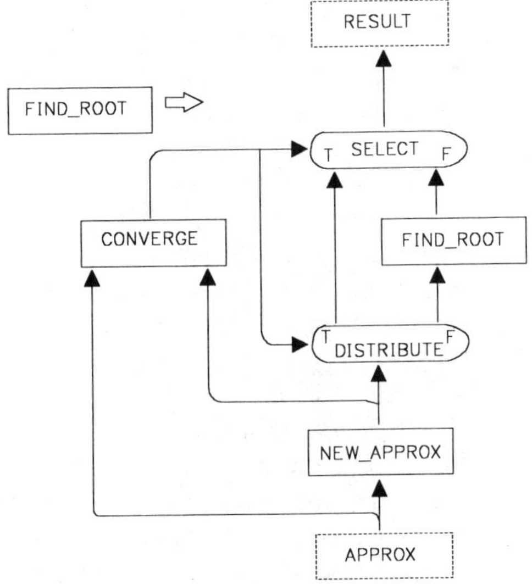

Figure 9-29. Recursive Newton graph.

STATE TRANSITION DIAGRAMS

The charts and diagrams that we have discussed so far give primary attention to the functions of the program being developed and the data upon which it operates. They are not concerned with the description of the user/computer interactions (e.g., the user/computer dialogs, the time sequence as seen by the user), the errors that may be introduced by incorrect user input, etc.

The state transition diagrams, on the other hand, are more suitable for user interface description. "One of the principal virtues of state transition diagram notations is that, by giving the transition rules for each state, they make explicit what the user can do at each point in a dialog, and what the effects with be."[20]

The basic notations for these diagrams follow fairly widely used conventions. Graphically, a state transition diagram consists of a network of nodes (representing states) and labeled, directed arcs (representing state transitions). An action or operation may be associated with any path leaving a given node. Traversal of the path causes the associated action/operation to occur.

State transition diagrams, however, do not convey information within each state (e.g., the semantic constraints on an input token, the functions to be performed on data). It is, therefore, necessary to augment the diagrams with textual descriptions of the actions to be executed. As an example, a menu selection dialog is shown in Figure 9-30.

The diagram in Figure 9-30 begins at START, where it waits for input. Based on the input, there is a transition to one of the five nodes. The input of "a"causes action 1 (shown in a small square on the path) to be performed during the transition to CASEA; the input of "?" causes a transition to HELP; etc. The text beneath Figure 9-30 shows the message displayed when a transition is made to that node.

Various extensions to the basic state transition diagrams have been proposed as specifications for the behavior of interactive systems.[21-26] Almost all of the proposals emphasize the desirability of having a precise specification of the user interface and having user involvement at the early stage of the design phase. Not many of these efforts, however, have focused on the *direct execution* of the specifications.

Having a directly executable specification provides an effective means to build user interface prototypes. A prototype not only enables the user to evaluate the planned interface in the spirit of a "test drive," but also enables the developer to evaluate user performance and user satisfaction in the early stages of the system development process. Moreover, prototyping facilitates experimentation with a number of alternatives and makes modification and revision less painful.

In the following section, we discuss two of these efforts. But before we go on, it may be worthwhile to bear in mind that there are basically two different

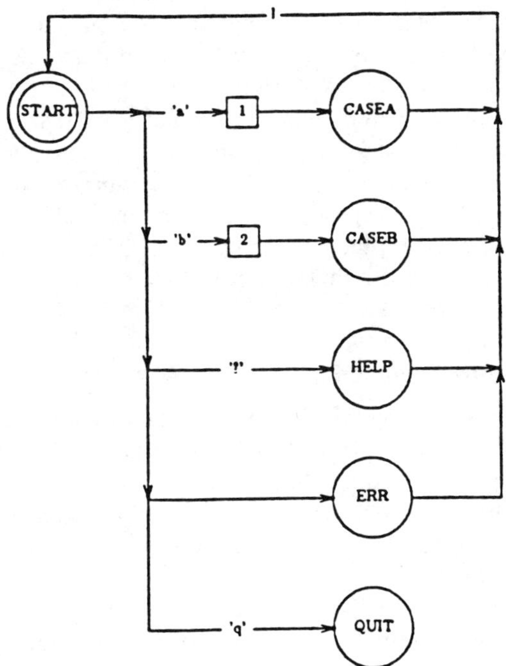


```
node START
        '               RAPID/USE Tutorial Example Program',
        '                    Please choose: ',
        '                     a - Case a',
        '                     b - Case b',
        '                     ? - Help',
        '                     q - Quit',
        '                    Your choice: '

node HELP
        'Valid commands are "a" and "b"',
        'Press any key to continue'

node CASEA
        'You are at CASEA',
        'Press any key to continue'

node CASEB
        'You are at CASEB',
        'Press any key to continue'

node ERR
        'Sorry, but you made an error – please try again.',
        'Press any key to continue'

node QUIT
        'Thank you – good bye'
```

Figure 9-30. Example of a menu selection dialog. (Wasserman[25]. © 1985 IEEE.)

groups of graphical extensions to textual programming languages. The first group (based on flow charts, Nassi-Shneiderman diagrams, and data flow graphs) concentrates on the description of program structure in terms of the flow of control/data in the program. The second group (using state transition diagrams) concentrates on the specification of interactive user interfaces.

The primary objectives in making charts/diagrams executable also differ. Generally speaking, the first group strives to eliminate discrepancies between the programs and their graphical documentations. The second group aims to produce prototypes to facilitate the experimentation with alteratives before a running system is built.

USE (User Software Engineering)

User Software Engineering (USE) is a methodology with supporting tools, developed at the University of California, San Francisco, for the specification, design, and implementation of interactive systems.[25,27-29]. With the USE approach, the user interface is formally specified with argmented state transition diagrams which may be directly executed with the application development tool RAPID/USE.

The project began (in 1977) by using a simple transition diagram model to design and build several small interactive systems. The model contained just three different symbols (see Figure 9-30):

1. *node*—shown by a circle, representing a stable state awaiting some user input. Each node has a unique name (shown within the circle). Each diagram has a single starting node (designated by two concentric circles) and a single exit node (which has no exit arcs).
2. *arc*—shown by a line with an arrow connecting nodes to one another. Each arc represents a state transition based on some input. The input is designated either by a string literal or by the name of another diagram enclosed within a pair of angle brackets. A number of arcs may emanate from each node; one of them may be left blank, in which case it becomes the default transition.
3. *operation*—shown by a small square with an associated integer. An action (represented by the operation) is to be performed whenever a specific arc is traversed. The same action may be associated with more than one arc.

As shown in Figure 9-30, a simple instance of a menu selection dialog can be specified with the basic state transition diagram.

However, it was quickly found out that even though the state transition diagrams represent a useful mechanism for modeling interactive systems, the basic form is inadequate for the range of interactions that one must model.

Worse still, the complexity of diagrams quickly became unmanageable for all but the smallest dialogs. Therefore, a number of extensions were made. They include the following:

1. For output specification, cursor and screen management symbols are included so that interactive dialog can be described on a full screen display, not just on a line-oriented basis. They are listed in Figure 9-31 and used in Figure 9-33.
2. To save an input for later processing, variables (with optional constraints on string length and value) are allowed. The appearance of a variable name on an arc emanating from a node means that the input is assigned to that variable.
3. To control situations such as immediate branching on a specific character, echo verses nonecho of user input, and branching upon expiration of time limit, transition control symbols are introduced. They are listed in Figure 9-32 and used in Figure 9-33.

To manage the complexity of the diagrams, "subconversations" are introduced. A subconversation is represented by a rectangle and works in much the same

Symbol	*Meaning*
cs	Clear screen
rxx	To row xx
cxx	To column xx
r+n	n rows up
r-n	n rows down
c+n	n columns left
c-n	n columns right
hm	row 0, column 0 (home)
rv	Reverse video
sv	Standard video
il	Insert line
cl	Clear to end of line
ce	Clear to end of screen
c_'text'	Center text
i_'text'	Insert text at current position
dc	Delete character
dl	Delete line
mark_a	Mark the place a
tomark_a	Return to the place a
t_n	Move to the column marked by tab n
display(inparam,format)	Control the formatting of a given data value

Figure 9-31. USE transition diagram screen control directives.

Symbol	*Meaning*
'text'	Branch on receipt of 'text'
name	Assign user input to variable name
!	Unbuffered single key input
+	Transition without user input
@	No echo of user input
"	Time limit in seconds
&x	Transition on receipt of specific character x
list/	Accept input until chatacter in list received
list/m	Truncate input to m characters

Figure 9-32. USE transition diagram transition control symbols.

way as a subprogram call in a conventional programming language. Transitions in the current diagram are suspended while the called diagram is executed.

Furthermore, the sequence of a dialog is often dependent on the results of actions. For example, if a user types in a name, a related action may look up that name in a table. The subsequent path is dependent on whether or not the name is found. Therefore, actions must be able to return values and it must be possible to branch in the diagram based on those returned values.

Using the extended transition diagrams, a wide range of user interfaces can be specified. A sample USE transition diagram for a library system is shown in Figure 9-33. The text associated with various nodes is shown beneath the diagram.

This diagram shows many aspects of the USE transition diagrams. The input causing state transitions is shown on the arcs. The symbol "+" indicates a transition without waiting for user input. The symbol "!" indicates a transition based on an unbuffered single character of user input.

The "programmed" *actions* are depicted in small boxes with the word "ca". The *"ca"* actions represent operations on a relational database. Another type of box, the *"do"* box (not shown in this diagram), is used to represent actions programmed in traditional programming languages such as C, Fortran 77, or Pascal.

The library system has four subconversations: inventory, lending, borrower, and status. A complete specification would consist of specifications of all of the diagrams (including the main diagram, the subconversations, and their descendants), all of the actions invoked from these diagrams, and all of the database definitions. However, even in the absence of "programmed actions," the ability to "execute" the diagrams is useful for prototyping.

"The USE methodology has evolved since the late 1970's and has been shown to be a practical method for the creation of interactive information

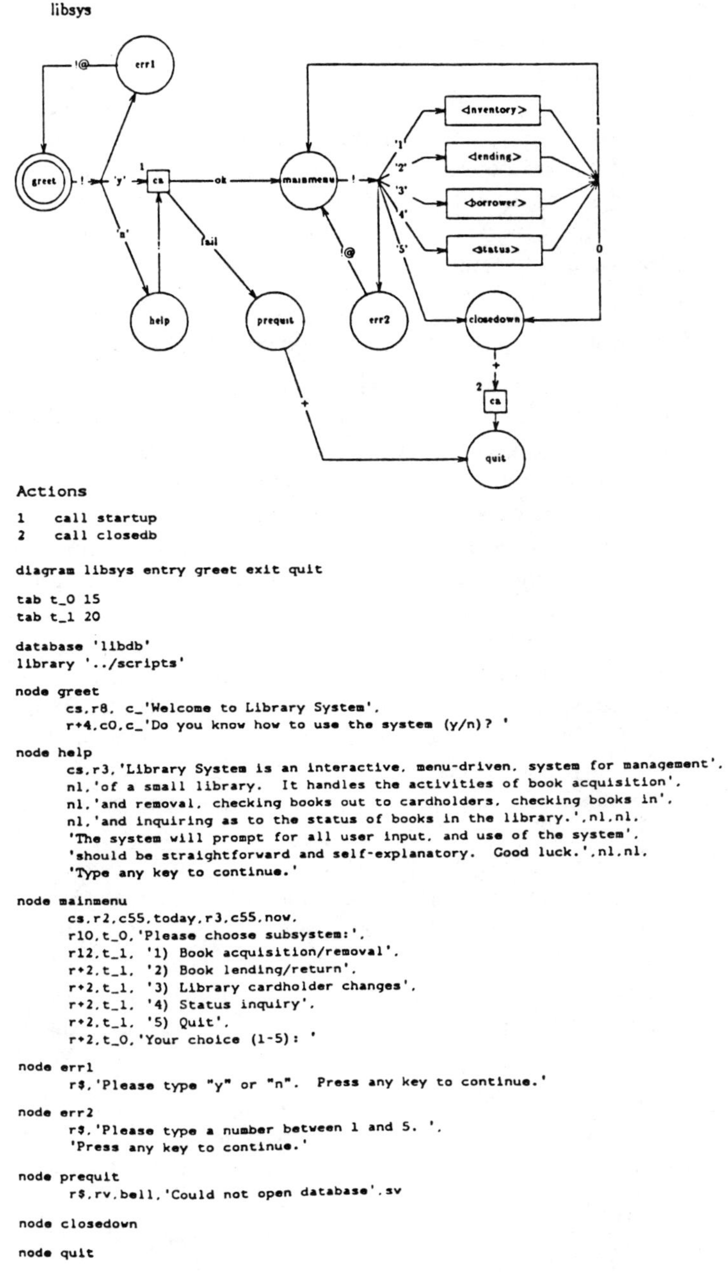

Actions

```
1    call startup
2    call closedb

diagram libsys entry greet exit quit

tab t_0 15
tab t_1 20

database 'libdb'
library '../scripts'

node greet
      cs,r8, c_'Welcome to Library System',
      r+4,c0,c_'Do you know how to use the system (y/n)? '

node help
      cs,r3,'Library System is an interactive, menu-driven, system for management',
      nl,'of a small library.  It handles the activities of book acquisition',
      nl,'and removal, checking books out to cardholders, checking books in',
      nl,'and inquiring as to the status of books in the library.',nl,nl,
      'The system will prompt for all user input, and use of the system',
      'should be straightforward and self-explanatory.  Good luck.',nl,nl,
      'Type any key to continue.'

node mainmenu
      cs,r2,c55,today,r3,c55,now,
      r10,t_0,'Please choose subsystem:',
      r12,t_1, '1) Book acquisition/removal',
      r+2,t_1, '2) Book lending/return',
      r+2,t_1, '3) Library cardholder changes',
      r+2,t_1, '4) Status inquiry',
      r+2,t_1, '5) Quit',
      r+2,t_0,'Your choice (1-5): '

node err1
      r$,'Please type "y" or "n".  Press any key to continue.'

node err2
      r$,'Please type a number between 1 and 5. ',
      'Press any key to continue.'

node prequit
      r$,rv,bell,'Could not open database',sv

node closedown

node quit
```

Figure 9-33. USE transition diagram for a library system. (Wasserman et al.[27]. © 1986 IEEE.)

systems."[29] It now has a collection of tools that support design and testing of the user interface, and the integration of the executable user interface specification with programmed actions written in programming languages and/or a data manipulation language for a relational database managed by the system. "Current research and development of the User Software Engineering methodology is focused on extending the types of media that can be supported by the specification method, on providing greater automated support for program generation, and on making Unified Support Environment available on a larger number of machines."[29]

A State Transition Diagram Language for Visual Programming

Robert Jacob of the Naval Research Laboratory has also chosen a state transition diagram as part of a methodology for designing and specifying user interfaces, but with more precise delineation on the levels of specifications. The method was described in detail by Jacob.[30] Briefly, the process of specifying user interfaces is divided into three levels:

The *semantic level* describes the functions performed by the system. It defines "meanings," rather than "forms" or "sequences." For actual execution, these functions are coded in a conventional programming language. The *syntactic level* describes the sequence of the logical input, output, and semantic operations, but not their details. State transition diagrams are used as syntactic representations. The *lexical level* identifies the devices, the display windows, the positions with which each token is associated, and the primitive hardware operations that constitute them. The lexical level is represented in the same state transition diagram notations as the syntactic specifications.

To illustrate, the syntactic level specification of a simple desk calculator simulator with the state transition diagram notations is shown in Figure 9-34.

Note that in the diagram each circle corresponds to a state. The "start" state is at the left. The "end" state is named inside its circle. There may be more than one "end" state in a diagram. Each transition between two states is shown as a directed arc and may be labeled with one of the following:

1. An input token (lowercase "i" followed by uppercase, e.g., "iNUM").
2. An output token (lowercase "o" followed by uppercase, e.g., "oREADY").
3. A nonterminal (all lowercase) defined by a separate diagram and called like a subroutine.
4. An action that invokes a semantic level function (e.g., A1), which will be executed if the transition is taken.
5. A condition, defined in the semantic level, which must be true for the transition to take place.

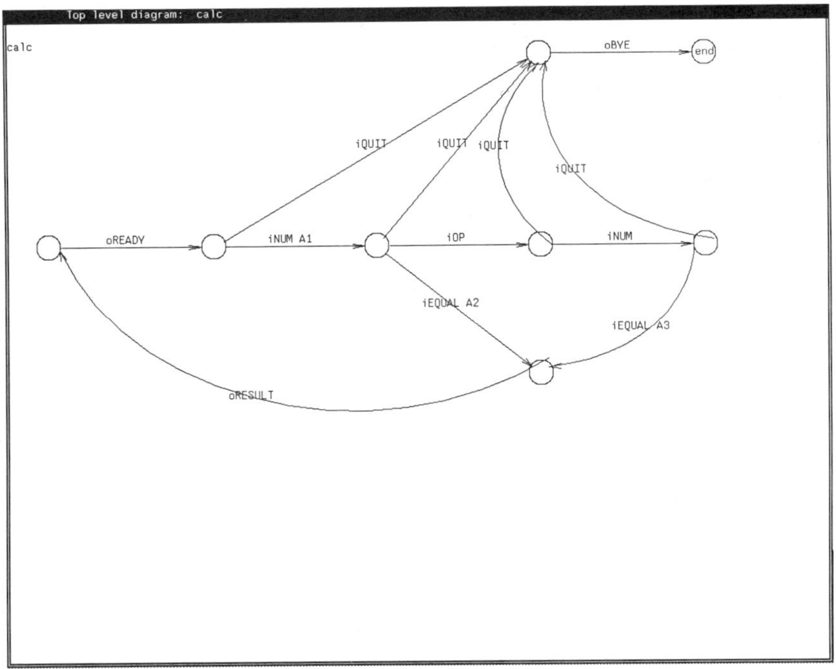

Figure 9-34. State diagram description of a desk calculator. (Jacob[20]. © 1985 IEEE. Original art courtesy of R.J.K. Jacob)

The semantic actions called by the diagram in Figure 9-34 are shown in Figure 9-35, along with their definitions, programmed in the programming language C.

A *prompt* (consisting of an output token) may also be associated with a state. Whenever that state is reached, its prompt token will be output.

The actual value received by an input token (such as the actual number obtained for the token iNUM), or put out by an output token, is available in a *variable* named *v* concatenated with the token name (e.g., "viNUM," "voRESULT").

"The language described so far is a static one that has been used to specify the behavior of a variety of user interfaces. In each case, the diagrams were designed, entered as strings of text, then executed by an interpreter."

Currently, Jacob is experimenting with the use of this language in a visual paradigm. There are at least two areas that one can investigate: a visual programming environment for the state transition language and a visual programming language for the semantic actions associated with the state transition diagrams.

```
char prevop[100] = "+", prevnum[100] = "0";

A1:  assign(*savenum1,viNUM);
     /*
      * assign is a built-in function that performs variable assignment
      */

A2:  const(*voRESULT,savenum1);
     /*
      * The function const performs a constant mode calculation
      * Repeats previous operation with new operand num,
      * and returns answer in result
      */
    const(result,num) char **result, *num; {                              const
         int ians; char strans[100];

         if (STREQ(prevop,"+")) ians=atoi(prevnum)+atoi(num);
         else if (STREQ(prevop,"-")) ians=atoi(num)-atoi(prevnum);
         else if (STREQ(prevop,"*")) ians=atoi(prevnum)*atoi(num);
         else if (STREQ(prevop,"/")) ians=atoi(num)/atoi(prevnum);

         sprintf(strans,"%d",ians); assign(result,strans);
}

A3:  calc(*voRESULT,savenum1,viOP,viNUM);
     /*
      * The function calc performs calculator operation op
      * on operands num1 and num2, and returns answer in result
      */
    calc(result,num1,op,num2) char **result, *num1, *op, *num2; {         calc
         int ians; char strans[100];

         if (STREQ(op,"+")) {
                   ians=atoi(num1)+atoi(num2);
                   strcpy(prevnum,num1);
         }
         else if (STREQ(op,"-")) {
                   ians=atoi(num1)-atoi(num2);
                   strcpy(prevnum,num2);
         }
         else if (STREQ(op,"*")) {
                   ians=atoi(num1)*atoi(num2);
                   strcpy(prevnum,num1);
         }
         else if (STREQ(op,"/")) {
                   ians=atoi(num1)/atoi(num2);
                   strcpy(prevnum,num2);
         }

         strcpy(prevop,op);
         sprintf(strans,"%d",ians); assign(result,strans);
}
```

Figure 9-35. Actions called by the diagram in Figure 9-34. (Jacob[20]. © 1985 IEEE. Original art courtesy of R.J.K.Jacob)

With regard to the first area of investigation, a visual programming environment for the state transition language is being developed. The user enters the state diagram with a graphical editor and affixes the necessary labels and actions. When execution begins, a programming window with the top-level diagram pops up. As execution progresses, the current state in the diagram is highlighted. As each subdiagram is called, a window containing the diagram pops up, with a pile of windows behind it showing the chain of diagrams that called it. As an example, Figure 9-36 shows the initial display screen during

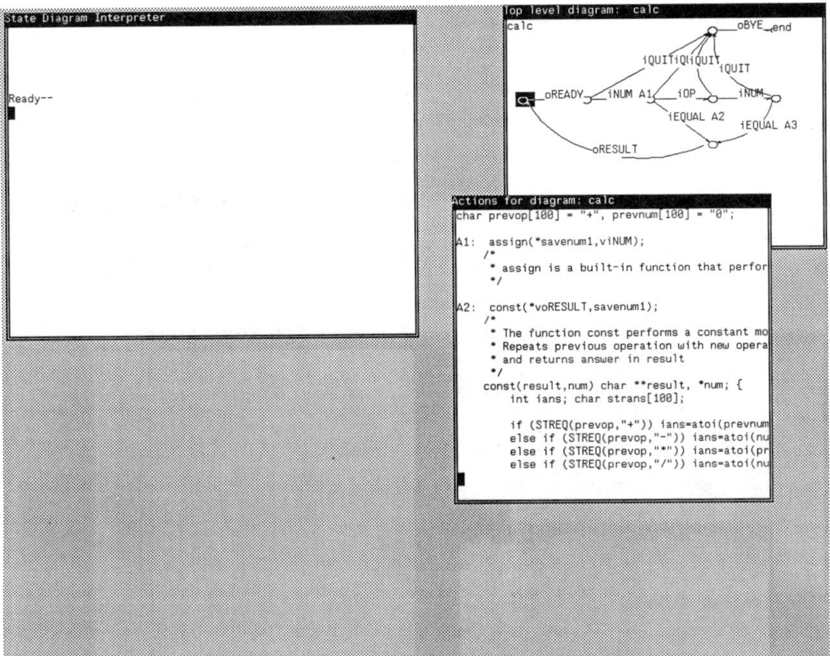

Figure 9-36. Initial display during execution of the calculator program. (Jacob[20]. © 1985 IEEE. Original art courtesy of R.J.K. Jacob)

execution of the calculator diagram, and Figure 9-37 shows the display screen after execution of the calculator diagram has progressed to the point where subdiagram calls for tokens are pending.

With regard to the second area of investigation, the problem is more difficult. One approach is to provide a (compiled) library of basic actions (add, subtract, assign, print), then allow the programmer to draw additional state transition diagrams that combine these standard actions to perform the desired functions. However, even though the state diagrams are suitable for describing the user interface behavior of a system, as a general purpose programming language, they are likely to be bulky and obscure for many actions that could be programmed clearly in other languages. Hence they are preferred for programming the syntax but not the semantics. According to Jacob, "Ideally, the present state diagrams would call the semantic actions by name, as they do now, and these actions would be programmed in a separate, more suitable *visual* programming language. This programming is possible within the present framework, but awaits the invention of a suitable visual metaphor for the action descriptors."[20]

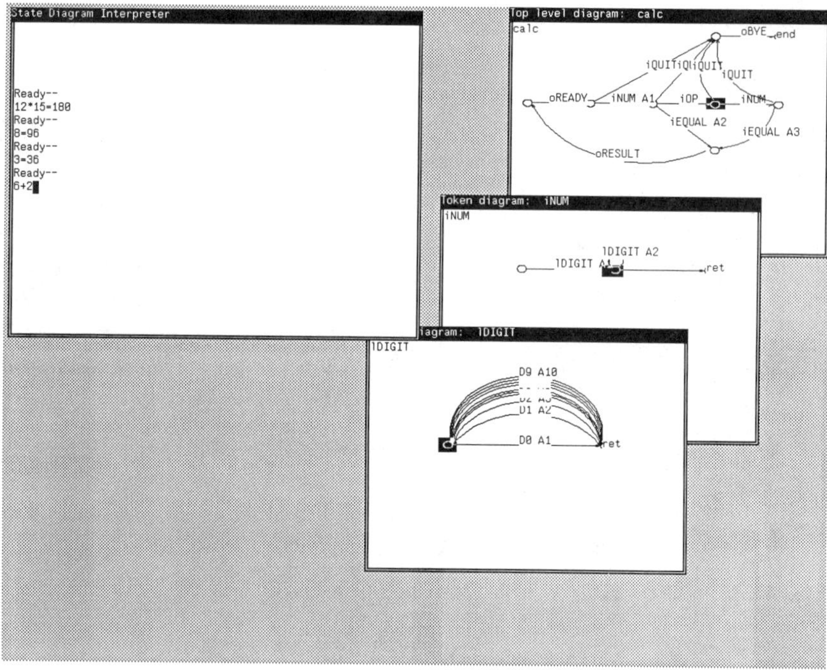

Figure 9-37. Display after execution of the calculator program has progressed to the point where subdiagram calls for tokens are pending.
(Jacob[20]. © 1985 IEEE. Original art courtesy of R.J.K. Jacob)

REFERENCES

1. Rothon, N. M., "Design Structure Diagrams: A New Standard in Flow Diagrams," *BCS Computer Bulletin Series 2,* No. 19 (Mar. 1979), pp. 4-6.
2. Brown, E. J., "On the Application of Rothon Diagrams to Data Abstraction," *SIGPLAN Notices,* Vol. 18, No. 12 (Dec. 1983), pp. 17-24.
3. Reiss, S. P., "Graphical Program Development with PECAN Program Development Systems," *ACM SIGPLAN Notices,* Vol. 19, No. 5 (May 1984), pp. 30-41.
4. Cunniff, N., Taylor, R. P., and Black, J. B., "Does Programming Language Affect the Type of Conceptual Bugs in Beginners' Programs? A Comparison of FPL and Pascal," *Proceedings of CHI'86* (Apr. 1986), pp. 175-182.
5. Taylor, R. P., *Programming Primer,* Addison-Wesley (1982).
6. Diaz-Herrera, J. L., and Flude, R. C., "Pascal/HSD: A Graphical Programming System," *Proceedings of IEEE Compsac '80* (1980), pp. 723-728.
7. Nassi, I., and Shneiderman, B., "Flowchart Techniques for Structured Programming," *ACM SIGPLAN Notices,* Vol. 8, No. 8 (Aug. 1973), pp. 12-26.
8. Glinert, E. P., and Tanimoto, S. L., "Pict: An Interactive Graphical Programming Environment," *IEEE Computer,* Vol. 17, No. 11 (Nov. 1984), pp. 7-25.
9. Frei, H. P., Weller, D. L., and Williams, R., "A Graphics-Based Programming Support System," *Proceedings of ACM Siggraph '78* (Aug. 1978), pp. 43-49.

10. Ng, N., "A Graphical Editor for Programming Using Structured Charts," *Digest of Papers, IEEE Compcon '79* (Feb. 1979), pp. 238-243.
11. Pong, M. C., and Ng, N., "PIGS—A System for Programming with Interactive Graphical Support," *Software Practice and Experience,* Vol. 13 (Sept. 1983), pp. 847-855.
12. Pong, M. C., "A Graphical Language for Concurrent Programming," *Proceedings of the 1986 IEEE Workshop on Visual Languages* (June 1986), pp. 26-33.
13. Hoare, C. A. R., "Communicating Sequential Processes," *Communications of the ACM,* Vol. 21, No. 8 (Aug. 1978), pp. 666-677.
14. Dijkstra, W. W., "Guarded Commands, Nondeterminancy, and Formal Derivation of Programs," *Communications of the ACM,* Vol. 18, No. 8 (Aug. 1975), pp. 453-457.
15. Albizuri-Romero, M. B., "GRASE—A Graphical Syntax Directed Editor for Structured Programming," *ACM SIGPLAN Notices,* Vol. 19, No. 2 (Feb. 1984), pp. 28-37.
16. Davis, A. L., and Keller, R. M., "Data Flow Program Graphs," *IEEE Computer,* Vol. 15, No. 2 (Feb. 1982), pp. 26-41.
17. Agerwala, T., and Arvind, "Data Flow Systems," *IEEE Computer,* Vol. 15, No. 2 (Feb. 1982), pp. 10-13.
18. Keller, R. M., and Yen, W-C. J., "A Graphical Approach to Software Development Using Function Graphs," *Digest of Papers, Compcon, Spring '81* (Feb. 1981), pp. 156-161.
19. Davis, A. L., and Lowder, S. A., "A Sample Management Application Program in a Graphical Data Driven Programming Language," *Digest of Papers, Compcon, Spring 81* (Feb. 1981), pp. 162-167.
20. Jacob, R. J. K., "A State Transition Diagram Language for Visual Programming," *IEEE Computer,* Vol. 18, No. 8 (Aug. 1985), pp. 51-59.
21. Newman, W. M., "A System for Interactive Graphical Programming," *Proceedings of the Spring Joint Computer Conference* (Apr. 1968), pp. 47-54.
22. Parnas, D. L., "On the Use of Transition Diagrams in the Design of a User Interface for an Interactive Computer System," *Proceedings of the 24th National ACM Conference* (1969), pp. 379-385.
23. Jacob, R. J. K., "Using Formal Specifications in the Design of a Human-Computer Interface," *Communications of the ACM,* Vol. 26, No. 4 (Apr. 1983), pp. 259-264.
24. Kieras, D., and Polson, P. G., "A Generalized Transition Network Representation for Interactive Systems," *CHI 83 Conference Proceedings* (Dec. 1983), pp. 103-106.
25. Wasserman, A. I., "Extending State Transition Diagrams for the Specification of Human-Computer Interaction," *IEEE Transactions on Software Engineering,* Vol. SE-11, No. 8 (Aug. 1985), pp. 699-713.
26. Bauer, M. A., and Ting, H. K., "Developing Application Independent Interfaces for Workstations in a Distributed Environment," *Proceedings of the ACM SIGSMALL/PC Symposium on Small Systems* (Dec. 1986), pp. 7-15.
27. Wasserman, A. I., Pircher, P. A., and Shewmake, D. T., "Building Reliable Interactive Information Systems," *IEEE Transactions on Software Engineering,* Vol. SE-12, No. 1 (Jan. 1986), pp. 147-156.
28. Wasserman, A. I., and Shewmake, D. T., "The Role of Prototypes in the User Software Engineering (USE) Methodology," in *Advances in Human-Computer Interaction,* Vol. 1, edited by H. Rex Hartson, Ablex Publishing Corp. (1985).
29. Wasserman, A. I., Pircher, P. A., Shewmake, D. T., and Kersten, M. L., "Developing Interactive Information Systems with the User Software Engineering Methodology," *IEEE Transactions on Software Engineering,* Vol. SE-12, No. 2 (Feb. 1986), pp. 326-345.
30. Jacob, R. J. K., "An Executable Specification Technique for Describing Human-Computer Interaction," in *Advances in Human-Computer Interaction,* Vol. 1, edited by H. Rex Hartson, Ablex Publishing Corp. (1985) pp. 211-242.

Chapter 10

Icons and Iconic Systems

Pictures represent the oldest form of written expression. Hieroglyph is a form of ancient writing (e.g., Egyptian, Mayan, Zapotec) in which the characters are to a substantial degree, recognizable pictures (see Figure 10-1 for an example).

Chinese, the most ancient of the living writing systems, has evolved from the pictographs that originated some four thousand years ago and have been used in their present form for more than two thousand years. Before we discuss the icons and iconic systems of today, it might be interesting to catch a glimpse of the Chinese ideograms.

REFLECTIONS ON THE CHINESE IDEOGRAPHIC SYSTEM

There are thousands of ideographic characters in the Chinese writing system. Each character represents a single spoken Chinese syllable and usually a single concept. In Figure 10-2, some of the Chinese characters in their current form are shown alongside their ancient form, known as "Jiaguwen" (甲骨文)—inscriptions on bones or tortoise shells in the Shang and Yin Dynasties (sixteenth to eleventh centuries B.C.).

Chinese characters may look strange to the Western eye. But, with some imagination, it is possible to "see" some of the concrete objects and abstract concepts in the ancient pictographic forms.

For example, as shown in Figure 10-2, a "person" is pictured as a man standing with his legs parted. The "sun" is accented with a sunspot in a circle. The "moon" is represented by a crescent, complete with the familiar dark markings. "Rain" is depicted by water droplets falling from the horizon. "Above" and "below" are symbolized by the positioning of a short stroke relative to the longer horizontal line.

To be able to read the newspapers, one would have to know several thousand Chinese characters. It would be extremely difficult to learn and remember them if not for the fact that most characters are *built* from component substructures *in an orderly fashion,* using three major character-building methods: pictographic, associative, and pictophonetic.

To illustrate the first two character-building methods, let us look at some words built from the basic characters shown in Figure 10-2. For example,

hieroglyphic
Inscription from Theban tomb of about 650 B.C.

hieroglyphics (Egyptian)

Figure 10-1. Hieroglyphic writing.

when three people are put together pictographically, you have 众, meaning a "crowd." When a person is put in an enclosed area, you have 囚, meaning "prisoner, to be imprisoned." When a person spreads out his arms, a symbol for "large" or "big" (大) is formed. Put a line over the symbol for "big" and you have 天, representing "sky." Taking a person's words (i.e., associating a person with speech or words) is an expression for "trust" (信). The sun seen through a tree (東) means "east." Combining the sun and the moon, you have an associative compound, 明, symbolizing the concept of "bright" or "brightness."

The third (and perhaps the most frequently used) character-building method (pictophonetic) involves the combination of a "pictorial" part with a "sound" part. For example, 河 and 何 are pronounced the same ("ho") but

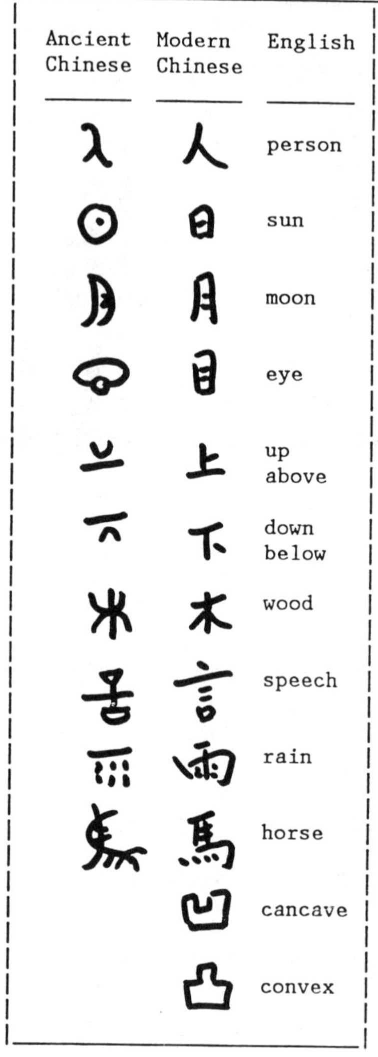

Ancient Chinese
Modern Chinese
English
人
person
日
sun
月
moon
目
eye
上
up above
下
down below
木
wood
言
speech
雨
rain
馬
horse
凹
cancave
凸
convex

Figure 10-2. Examples of Chinese characters.

have different meanings. They are pronounced the same because they have the same "sounding" part, 可. They have different meanings because they have different pictorial parts. 河 means "river"; its pictorial part, 氵, is a symbol for "water." 何 means "who"; its pictorial part, 亻 is a symbol for "person."

It is worthwhile to note that some of the lessons learned from studying the

Chinese ideograms can be useful when we engage in the development of iconic systems today. It is foreseeable that sound will become an integral part of the "audible icons." The technology is here. The reality—when the practical applications become economically feasible—is simply a matter of time. For our discussion, however, we shall concentrate on the pictographical aspects. Furthermore, we are not concerned with the Chinese language structure, which, by the way, "is remarkably simple."[1] (For instance, "Long time no see" is a word-by-word translation of a legitimate sentence.) We are only interested in the character structures.

As a literary writing system, the Chinese system is capable of expressing an infinite range of feelings, ideas, concepts, and thoughts. A vast number of words have been developed for that purpose. Programming languages do not need the same range of expressiveness as literary systems. The icons and iconic systems designed for programming purposes will never, and should never, require a vast number of ideographic characters, as the Chinese writing system does. Nevertheless, since both systems serve as a means of communication based on pictorial origins, there are some lessons that the developers of the emerging young iconic systems can learn from the oldest living one.

First, the clarity of meaning is not an automatic conseqence of using pictorial expressions. There are good pictures and there are bad pictures. Good pictures are superior in their portrayal of objects and concepts. Bad pictures are confusing and hard to remember.

Second, even though our ability in regard to pattern recognition appears to be based mainly on intuition, the roles played by the analytical capability of the human brain cannot be underestimated. As we mentioned earlier, each of the vast number of Chinese characters is different from the others. The fact that most of the characters are *built up in an orderly fashion* has greatly reduced the difficulty of trying to remember thousands of different characters.

Third, a common argument for employing graphics is that by doing so we can tap the brain's powerful pattern recognition capabilities. We must not forget, however, that the human brain is susceptible to information overload. It is important that the graphics are not so overwhelming that they can no longer be processed effectively.

Fourth but not last, it is very difficult to build an efficient dictionary for pictures. For people who understand Chinese, recognition of a character can be immediate, but looking up a word in the Chinese dictionary can be time-consuming and sometimes also difficult. Iconic systems will have to solve the same problem. When the number of icons is small, it is possible to have them presented on the screen so that the user can point to the one he wants. But this method will not work well when the number of icons is large.

In summary, all these observations point to the extreme importance of the systematic design of good representations. Ideographs that portray objects and concepts vividly are easier to learn and harder to forget. They also require less looking up in the dictionary. Ill-conceived representations, on the other hand, could end up as a mental burden. The *American Heritage Dictionary* provides two meanings for the word "hieroglyphic." One is "Written in or pertaining to a system of writing used in ancient Egypt." The other one is "Hard to read; illegible; undecipherable." It is the second meaning that we must try to avoid.

On the positive side, it is interesting to note that, in spite of the fact that not all Chinese characters are easy to learn, thousands of characters can be learned by the average person. Somehow, characters developed from pictorial representations are more interesting and exciting than unadorned alphabetic letters laid out one after another. A written Chinese character has a more direct connection with its meaning than a written word in English does. In English, the sequence of letters spelling "horse" has meaning only through the mediation of the sounds they represent. The shape of the letters has no relation to the concept. To a Chinese person, the character for "horse" looks like a horse, complete with mane and four legs (Figure 10-3). The image is so vivid that one can almost sense the animal galloping across the page.

The same could be said when we compare the iconic programming languages with the textual ones.

Figure 10-3. Horse in Chinese.

In other words, the pictorial form of expression is not a panacea for all the problems of communication, but pictures do seem to provide an incentive to learn. Challenge, fantasy, and curiosity (the three most important factors that make computer games so captivating[2]) are all there when we deal with pictorial systems.

In a whimsical manner, history repeats itself. Pictorial representations, the oldest written expressions, have entered into a new incarnation. This time around, pictograms are not devised for written communication between human beings. They are being developed as a means of communication between humans and machines.

CONTRAST WITH VISUAL COACHING

At this point, it may be worthwhile to reiterate that programming by example or programming by demonstration is another technology that attempts to make programming easier. In essence, the user writes a program by giving examples to the computer of what he wants the program to do. The system records, and hopefully also generalizes, what has been demonstrated (with or without inference) for later reuse.

One should keep in mind, however, that programming by example or demonstration is a *program development methodology,* not a programming language. Even though both the programming by example or demonstration and the programming languages are used to produce programs, there is a sharp contrast in the two approaches. In the former, the computer is instructed to *"do as I show you,"* where the "showing" relies heavily on interactions. In the latter, the computer is instructed to *"do as I tell you,"* where the "telling" is expressed in terms of language constructs.

Incorporating graphics or pictures into the programming process adds an interesting and useful dimension to the human-computer communication. Thus, when a programming language takes on visual expressions, it becomes a visual programming language. When a demonstrational system takes on visual representations, it becomes a visual coaching system (see Chapter 5). But the fundamental principles underlying these two different approaches ("Do as I show you" verses "Do as I tell you") are basically *not altered* by the inclusion of graphical symbols.

For instance, Finzer and Gould's "Programming by Rehearsal," (see Chapter 5) a system designed for nonprogrammers to create educational software, relies almost completely on interactive graphics. The system is based on a theater metaphor in which the designer creates a "production" in the Rehearsal World. The basic components of the production are predefined sets of "performers" and "cues." "Almost all of the designer's interactions with the Rehearsal World are through the selection (with a mouse) of some performer

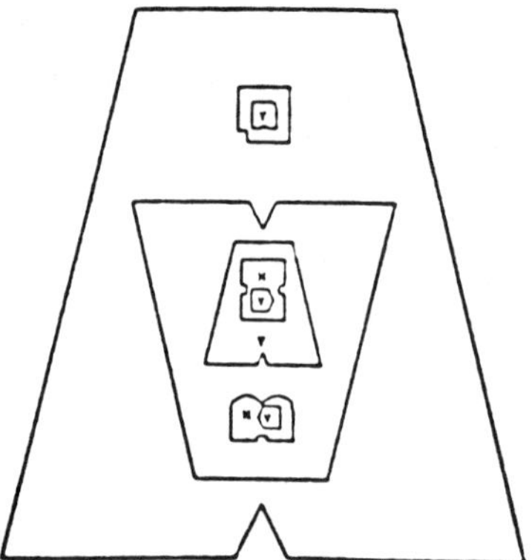

Figure 10-4. A VennLisp form.
(Lakin[13]. Reprinted by permission of Plenum Publishing Corp.)

or of some cue to a performer."[3] The design and programming process consists of moving performers around on "stages" and showing each performer what actions it should take in response either to the student (user) input or to cues sent by other performers. This process is called "rehearsing the production." The production can be stored away for later retrieval. Clearly, this is a case of programming by demonstration in a highly visual environment. Nevertheless, it is not a visual programming language system, in spite of the fact that everything in the Rehearsal World is visible.

SOME RECENT EFFORTS IN ICONIC PROGRAMMING LANGUAGES

In the last few years, a significant number of iconic languages have been reported in the literature. At the gross level, they have basically the same goal: to use icons as programming language constructs. Yet, like all human endeavors at the emerging stage, each system has a different approach to the goal. In the following sections, we first discuss briefly some of the representative systems and then focus on the Xerox *Star*,[4-8] the *Pict* system,[9] and the *Show and Tell*.[10-12]

VennLISP

VennLISP[13] is an example of having *executable graphics* based on Lisp. The language, which uses enclosures rather than parenthesies to denote the nesting of function calls, is an alternate notation for Lisp programs. Visual objects are used to direct computation, and the results of the computation are also visual objects. Figure 10-4 shows a VennLISP form for

```
(AND (NOT (NULL? Y))
     (OR (AND (EQUAL? X (FIRST Y)) Y)
         (MEMBER? X (REST Y)) ) )
```

Figure 10-5. Typical Tinkertoy icons.
(Edel[14]. © 1986 IEEE, original art courtesy of M. Edel.)

The outermost shape in Figure 10-4 is the VennLISP function AND, which has two arguments represented by the forms inside it. The functions nested within are represented in the same manner recursively down to the variables X and Y, which are evaluated by looking up their values. The program is a recursive definition of the membership test; it determines whether the visual object which is bound to X is a member of the visual objects which is bound to Y.

As a matter of interest, the long-term goal of Lakin's research is computer understanding of how humans use graphics to communicate. Spatial parsing facilitates computer understanding of visual communication by recovering syntactic structure so that a spatial arrangement of visual objects can be interpreted as a phrase in a particular visual language. VennLISP is but one of the various forms of "visual communication objects" that Fred Lakin has applied his spatial parsing techniques.[13]

Tinkertoy

Tinkertoy[14] is another example of executable graphics based on Lisp.

Tinkertoy programs are "built," rather than written, out of icons and interconnections that can be "snapped" together. Typical icons in Tinkertoy are shown in Figure 10-5. Note that the icons have input and output sites through which they can be connected to form structures. For example, a typical function icon consists of a dark rectangle containing the function name, with argument sites on the left and an output site on the right. When an icon is evaluated, the result of evaluation is returned in the output site.

An icon is evaluated by pressing the right button of the three-button mouse over it or by being called as an argument to another function. Pressing the left button over an icon picks it up. After being picked up, the icon follows the mouse until it is dropped. Dropping an icon with a site on a compatible site forms a connection between the two, i.e., the sites are snapped into position. The middle button brings up a menu of commands that can be applied to the selected icon. Pressing buttons outside of an icon accesses commands that are not associated with a specific icon.

An example of a Tinkertoy session is shown in Figure 10-6. The tall window acts as a general-purpose system interface. The smaller windows show the functions being edited.

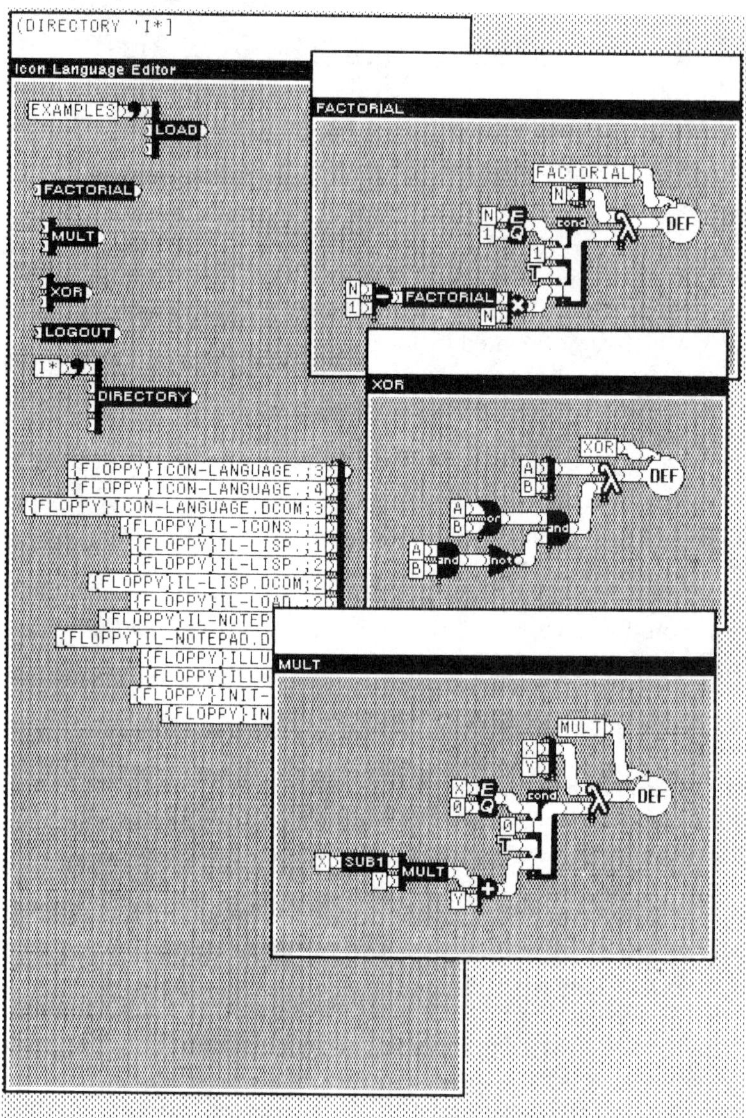

Figure 10-6. Example of Tinkertoy session.
(Edel[14]. © 1986 IEEE, original art courtesy of M. Edel.)

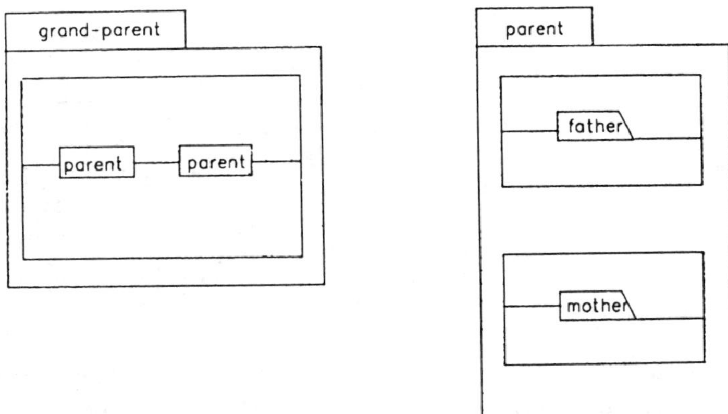

Figure 10-7. Example of procedure declarations in Dialog.I.

Dialog.I

Dialog.I[15] is an iconic programming langauge based on logic programming and its programming environment. The programmer "draws" a program as a picture which represents a set of Horn clauses. The system compiles the picture into string expressions and evaluates them. For example, Figure 10-7 shows a Dialog.I program corresponding to

grand-parent(X,Y) <− parent(X,Z), parent(Z,Y).
parent(X, father(X)).
parent(X, mother(X)).

IDEOSY

IDEOSY[16] is an experiment in the use of a formal semantics as the basis for a programming system and in the use of an ideographic language as the primary means of user-computer communication. The foralism is based on Milner's Calculus of Communicating Systems (CCS).[17] Ideographs are used to represent the various elements and operators of CCS.

As an example, Figure 10-8 defines the behavior of an agent P which can either (1) execute a sequence of two communication actions (named "a" and "b") and then terminate or (2) execute an action named "c" and then reproduce the behavior of P.

The symbol stands for an agent identifier. Juxtaposed boxes define an "exclusive or" of the alternatives enclosed in each box. The symbols and are ideographs for input and output actions. Actions arranged diagonally from upper left to lower right define a sequen-

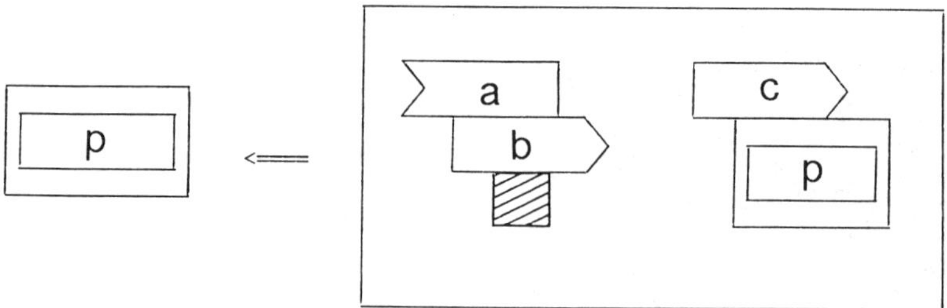

Figure 10-8. An example in IDEOSY.

tial execution of those actions. Finally, a hashed square box depicts an agent that does not perform any action but represents the termination of an agent.

The IDEOSY system has a syntax-directed editor which supports the definition of various equivalence properties and the proofs of such equivalence. It also has an interpreter that can interprete the CCS specifications.

PROGRAPH

PROGRAPH is "a functional, data flow oriented language expressed graphically."[18] PROGRAPH treats data as "signals." Signals enter or leave a "frame" through "wires" and are manipulated by "operation boxes."

The fundamental construct of PROGRAPH is the *definition frame* (or simply a *frame*). The body of a frame consists of a network of operation boxes and nodes connected by wires. An *operation box* (or simply a *box*) performs the function indicated by the name or symbol inside it. *Wires* represent the flow of information.

Executing a frame consists of firing the boxes in its body which are *armed* —that is, those boxes whose inputs have been loaded with all the data necessary to perform the operation which the box represents. *Firing* means that the box operation is applied to the input data and the results are passed, when applicable, through its output wires to the inputs of other boxes. Execution continues until there are no more armed boxes. We use three examples, taken from Mativin and Pietrzykowski,[18] to show the flavors of PROGRAPH.

The example in Figure 10-9 reverses the order of an arbitrary list of elements. For instance, if the list (a,(2,c),b,x) is input, then (x,b,(2,c),a) will be the output. The *IF_THEN* box has two compartments—the logical and the tranformational. The logical compartment is identified by the IF label in the banner portion. The oval-shaped box denotes an operation whose result is Boolean. The transformational compartment (identified by the THEN or ELSE in the banner portion) specifies the operations to be executed when the appropriate conditions are met.

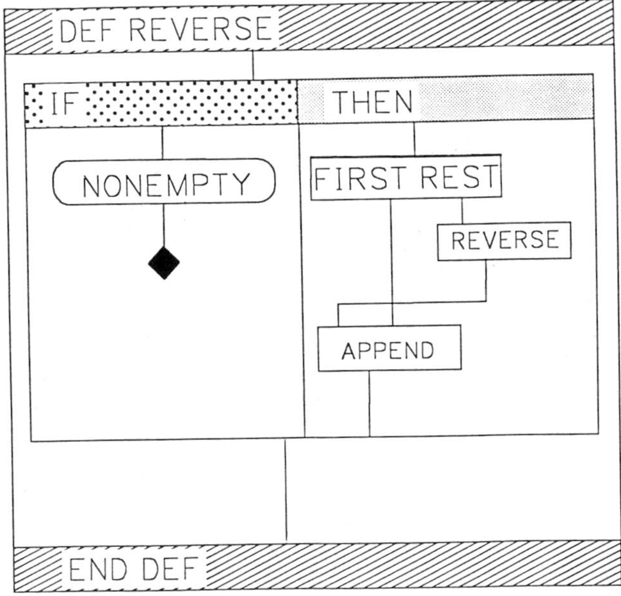

Figure 10-9. PROGRAPH example 1 (reversing order of a list).

In the *THEN* compartment of *REVERSE* are two system operations which deal specifically with lists. *FIRST REST* expects a list on its single input. It returns the first element of the list by its left output and the remainder of the list by its right output. *APPEND* has two inputs. The data from the right input are added as the last element to the list from the left input and passed to the output.

The example in Figure 10-10 defines a matrix multiplication operation. A matrix is represented as a list of lists, where inner lists correspond to the matrix rows. The *APPLY TO ALL* complex consists of a transformational compartment with a variable number of inputs and outputs. The operation within the body of the complex is applied to corresponding elements of the inputs. *TRANSPOSE* is a system operation whose function corresponds directly to the transposal of matrices. For example, given the list ((1,7,5),(2,3,3)) as input, the output list will be ((1,2),(7,3),(5,3)). The '*' box in Complex 3 multiplies corresponding elements of the rows of matrix a and the columns of matrix b. The resulting lists are summed by the '+' box in Complex 2.

The third example depicts how database operations can be handled. Figure 10-11 finds the name of a department that a student with a given student number is majoring in. In similar manner, records can be added or deleted.

PROGRAPH is being developed as a full-fledged programming language.

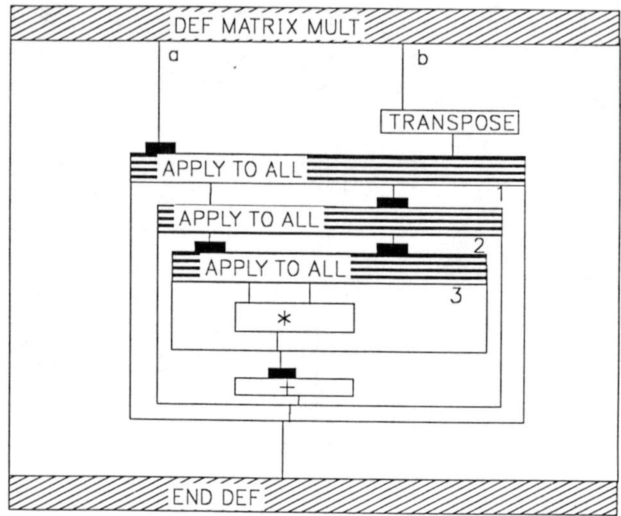

Figure 10-10. PROGRAPH example 2 (matrix multiplication).

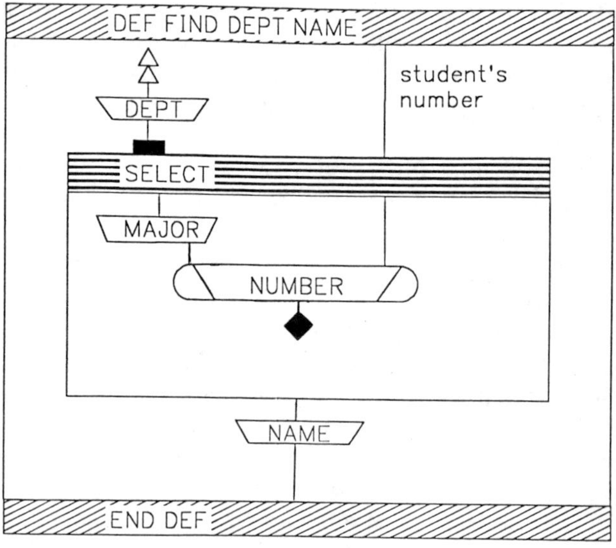

Figure 10-11. PROGRAPH example 3 (data retrieval).

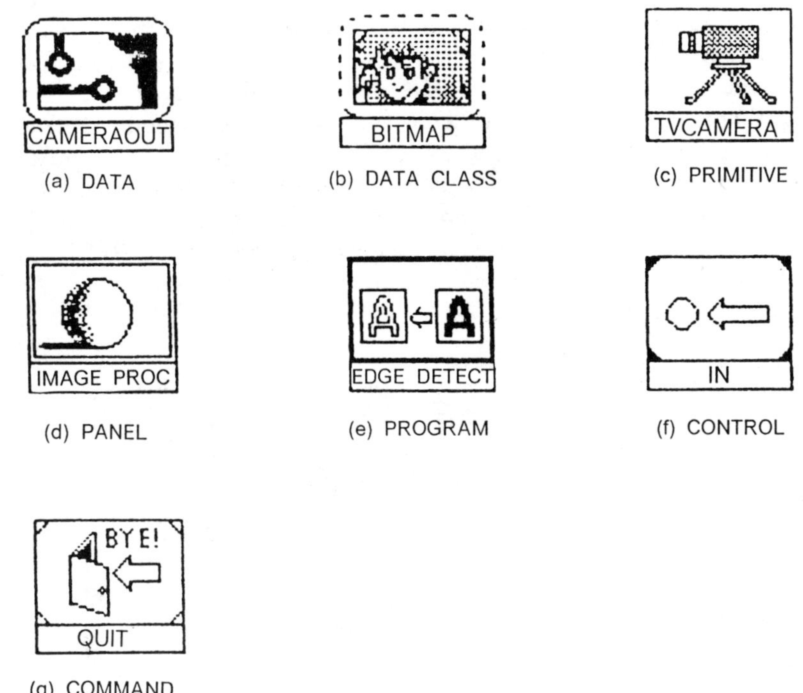

Figure 10-12. Examples of Icon types in HI-VISUAL. (Hirakawa et al.[20] Reprinted by permission of T. Ichikawa.)

It has long lists of syntactic symbols and predefined operations, and "is still undergoing changes and being expanded."[18]

Extended HI-VISUAL

HI-VISUAL was originally reported as a language supporting visual interaction in programming.[19] It is now being extended to be an iconic programming language[20] which exhibits a strong influence of the Hiroshima group's interest in image processing.

In the extended HI-VISUAL, there are seven types of icons (see examples in Figure 10-12): (1) the DATA icon representing data such as characters, numbers, and images; (2) the DATA CLASS icon representing a class of data; (3) the PRIMITIVE icon representing a built-in function supplied by the system; (4) the PANEL icon representing a display space; (5) the PROGRAM icon representing a program supplied by the user; (6) the CONTROL icon representing control flow; and (7) the COMMAND icon representing system operations such as RUN, UNDO, and EXIT.

Program development in the extended HI-VISUAL is carried out by selecting icons from a menu of icons and specifying connections between them. Figure 10-13 shows an example of a program. This program represents an image processing routine for the detection of cracks in an input image. First, the image from the TV camera is binarized by the built-in function called BINARIZE. The binarized image is then process by CRACK DETECT and EDGE DETECT. Finally, ouputs of these two processes (C.D. OUT and EDGING OUT) are combined by SYNTHESIZE to form SYNTH. OUT.

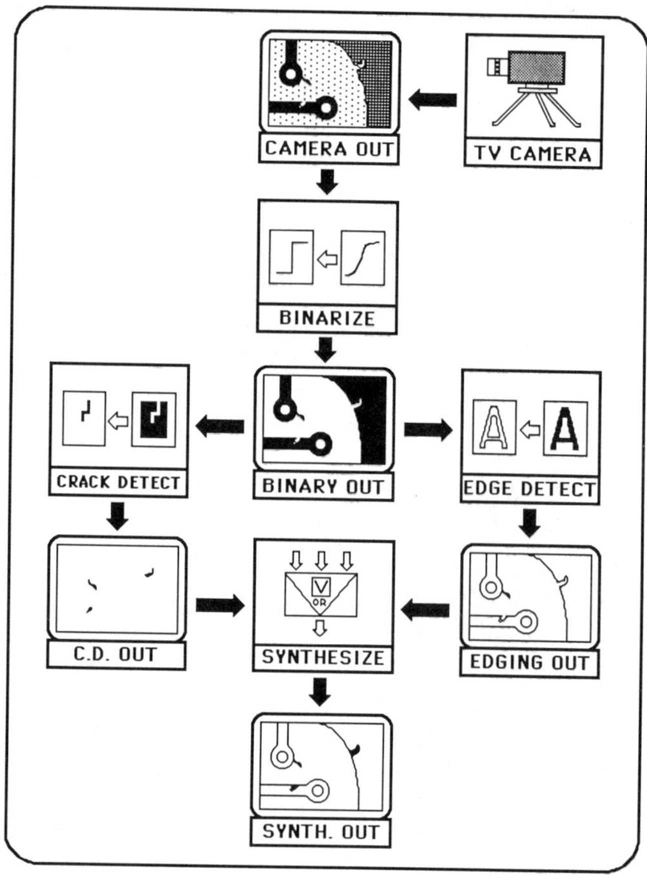

Figure 10-13. Example of a program in extended HI-VISUAL.
(Hirakawa et al.[20] Reprinted by permission of T. Ichikawa, original art courtesy of T. Ichikawa.)

Two types of iteration icons are provided. They are called "counter loop" and "condition loop" in HI-VISUAL. Examples are shown in Figures 10-14 and 10-15, respectively.

Iconic systems are being reported in the literature at an ever-quickening rate. Some of the efforts have shown well-developed results; some are still at the developing stage.

In the remaining sections of this chapter, we delve into three representative systems in detail. First, the Xerox Star system is used as an example, since it is one of the better-known systems and is often credited as being the forerunner of the iconic systems. Its underlying "desktop" metaphor has had widespread influence on many of the later commercial products. Second, the Pict system is described as a *programming facility* in which graphics plays a central role. Underlying Pict is the Pascal constructs and the concepts of control flow. The third system, Show and Tell, also aims at keyboardless programming but is based on the concepts of data flow and "completion."

Thus, the Xerox Star, Pict, and Show and Tell serve as examples of various conceptual models and design principles underlying the common goal of using icons as programming constructs. These three systems are discussed in the chronological order in which they were reported in the literature. In doing so, we hope to illuminate some of the progress made in the last few years in terms of iconic language design. Our focus will be on the *language* aspects, as opposed to the environment and the tools (e.g., windows, menus, pointing devices, editing facilities).

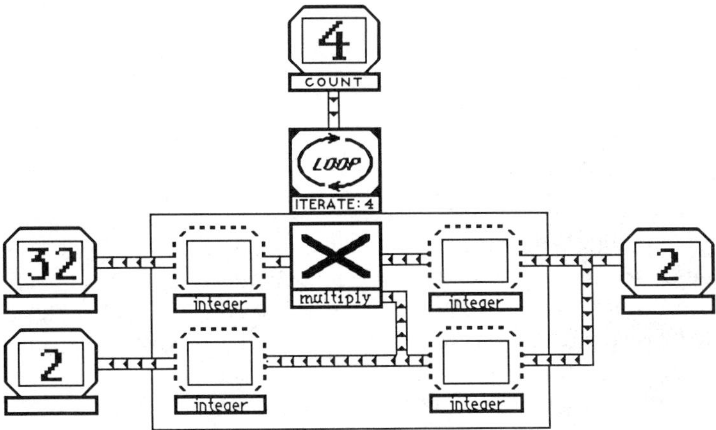

Figure 10-14. Example of a "counter loop".
(Hirakawa et al.[20] Reprinted by permission of T. Ichikawa, original art courtesy of T. Ichikawa.)

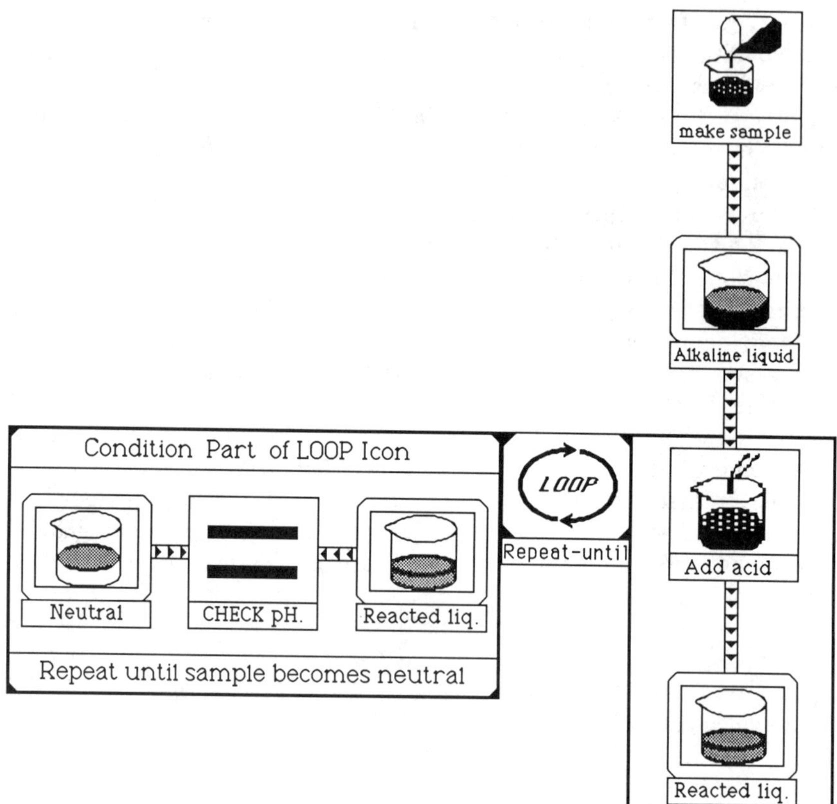

Figure 10-15. Example of a "condition loop".
(Hirakawa et al.[20] Reprinted by permission of T. Ichikawa, original art courtesy of T. Ichikawa.)

THE XEROX STAR SYSTEM

In the last few years, we have seen a flurry of guidelines for designing enjoyable user interfaces. One of the guidelines concerns the use of metaphors. "In addition to being emotionally appealing, fantasies that are analogous to things with which the users are already familiar can help make the systems easier to learn and use."[2] The user interfaces for the Xerox Star workstations is an example that makes extensive use of metaphors.

The Star system was announced by the Xerox Corporation in April 1981. One of the most important principles underlying the Star interface is to apply the user's familiarity with office objects to a new situation—the computer. Considering the charter set for the Xerox Palo Alto Research Center (PARC) when its door was opened in 1970, the orientation on business office is not surprising. C. Peter McColough, president of Xerox at that time, "called for making the Xerox Corp. 'the architect of information' for the business office."[21] The Xerox PARC had one unifying vision for nearly all of the 1970s. As George E. Pake, founder of the Xerox PARC, put it, "At PARC we thought that the systems of business relevance would be office information systems (indeed, OIS was a widely used set of initials in our work and planning)."[21]

The Star designers devoted several work-years at the outset of the project discussing and evolving what they considered an appropriate model for an office information system: the metaphor of a physical office.[4] Eventually, an electronic desktop complete with familiar office equipment (e.g., printers, file drawers) was chosen. Arranged on the electronic desktop on the user's screen are documents, folders, file drawers, printers, in-baskets and out-baskets, etc., depicted as small pictures, or icons.[5] Figure 10-16 shows a sample desktop display.

Interaction with the Star system involves a mouse and command keys. A user can select a Star object by pointing to the relevant icon with the mouse and clicking one of the mouse buttons. The selected icon is highlighted. The user then presses a command key that affects the selected icon.

For instance, a user can "open" a document by selecting a document icon (with a mouse) and pushing the OPEN key on the keyboard. When opened, an icon expands into a larger form called a "window." The contents of an icon are displayed in the window. Furthermore, once selected, objects may be moved, copied, or deleted by pushing the MOVE, COPY, or DELETE key on the keyboard. This enables a user to read documents, inspect the contents of folders and file drawers, send and receive mail, etc.

Classes of Star Icons

At the highest level, Star has two classes of icons: data icons and function icons.[5]

Data icons represent objects on which actions are performed. There are three types of data icons: document, folder, and record file.

A *document* is the fundamental object in Star. Most often a document contains text, but it may also contain illustrations, mathematical formulas, tables, footnotes, and formating information. When opened, documents are shown on the display screen. A *folder* is used to group data icons together. It can contain documents, record files, and other folders. A *record file* is a collection of information organized as a set of records.

Function icons represent objects that perform actions. There are many kinds of function icons.

A *file drawer* serves as an interface to the file server. A document is transferred to a file server by moving it to a file drawer; it is retrieved by

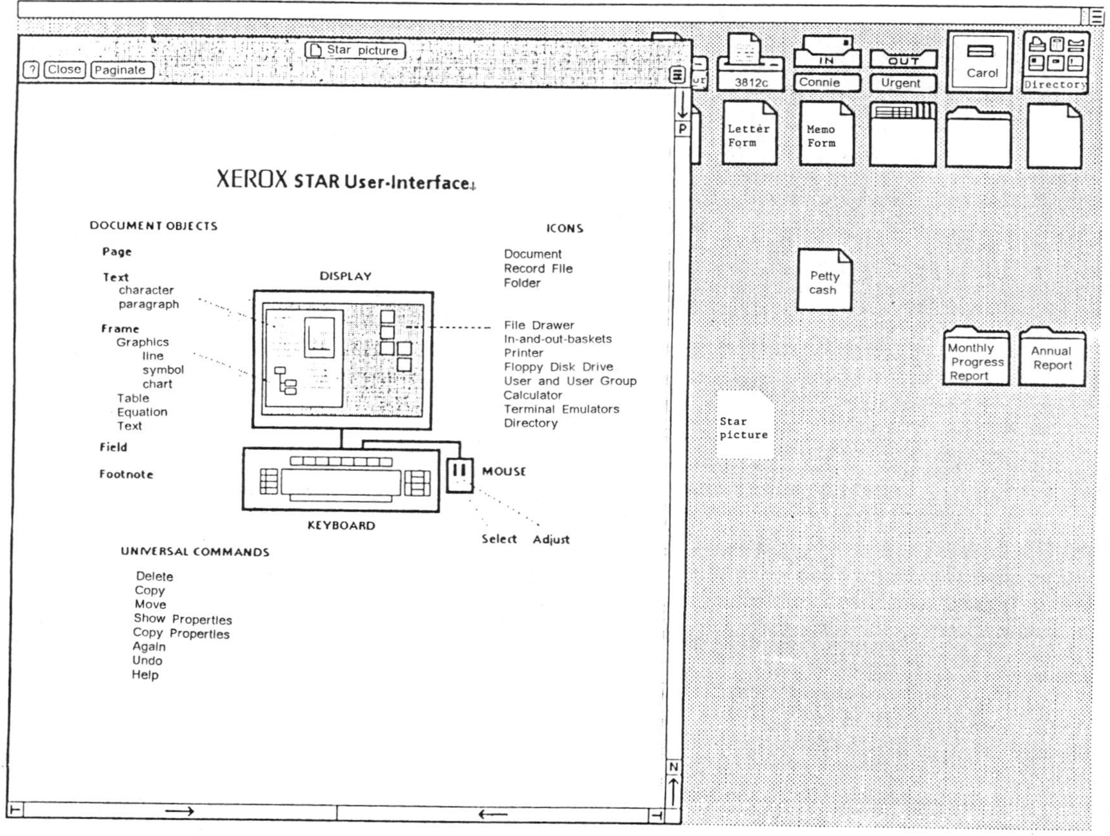

Figure 10-16. A desktop as it appears on the Star screen.
(Smith et al.[4]. Reprinted with permission of Xerox Corporation.)

opening the file drawer and moving or copying it back to the desktop. The contents of file drawers can be shared by multiple users. The ability of people to look at and/or modify file drawer contents is controlled by access rights associated with the file drawers.

The *in-basket* and *out-basket* provide the principal mechanism for the mailing system. Electronic mail is sent by moving an icon to the out-basket, and incoming mail is accessed by opening the in-basket. *Printer* icons provide access to printing services. The *floppy disk drive* icon allows a user to move data icons to and from a floppy disk inserted in the machine.

The *terminal emulation* icons permit the user to communicate with existing mainframe computers using existing protocols.

The *user* icon displays the information that the system knows about each user: name, location, aliases if any, access level, etc. *User group* icons contain individual users and/or other user groups. They serve as access control lists and distribution lists.

A *directory* icon provides access to network resources.

In addition, there are *calculators* that let users perform arithmetic operations.

Property Sheets

At a finer level of detail, the Star world is organized in terms of objects that have *properties* and upon which actions are performed. A few examples of *objects* in Star are text characters, paragraphs, pages, graphic lines, formula elements, and icons.

Properties of an object depend on the type of the object. For example, properties of text characters include type style, size, face, and posture (e.g., bold, italic). Properties of graphic lines include thickness and structure (e.g., solid, dashed, dotted). Properties of a document icon include name, size, creator, and creation date.

In order to make properties visible, Star uses the notion of property sheets. Figure 10-17 is an example of the property sheet for text characters. It appears on the screen whenever you make a text selection and push the PROPERTIES key.

Option Sheets

Similar to having property sheets to make the properties of an object "visible," Star has option sheets to make the arguments to a command visible. Figure 10-18 is the option sheet for the FIND command, showing both the Search and Substitute options. The last two lines of options appear only when CHANGE IT is turned on.

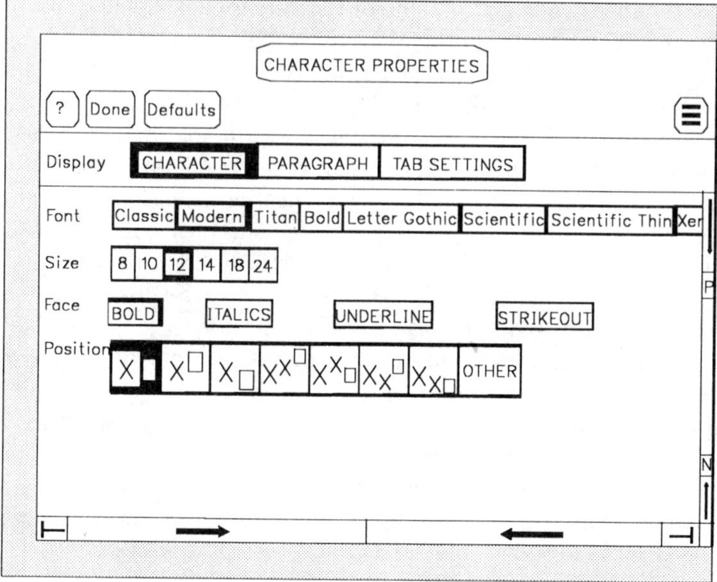

Figure 10-17. Property sheets for text characters.

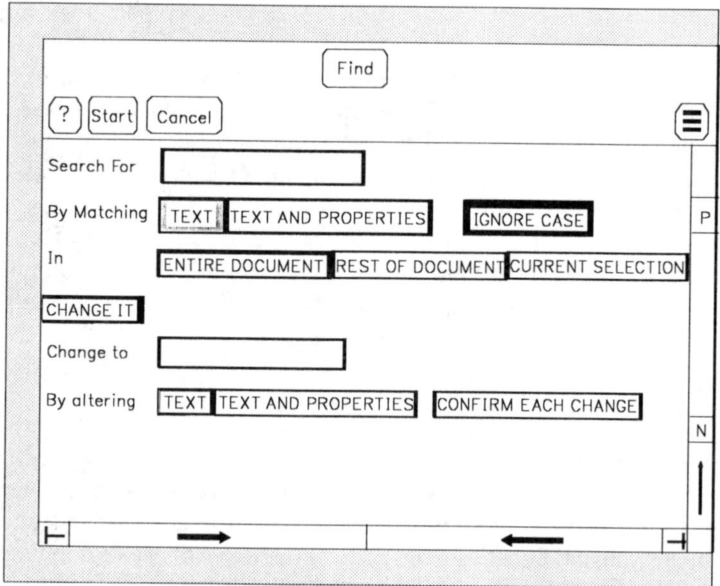

Figure 10-18. Option sheet for the FIND command.

Windows

Icons on the desktop show their names, but not their contents. To show an icon's contents, the user selects the icon and pushes the OPEN key. A window appears on the screen. For documents, the window shows a page in the document; for folders, a pictorial list of the icons in the folder. Similarly, for other kinds of icons, the window shows their contents.

Window contents, such as text in a document, may be selected, moved, copied, or deleted in the same fashion as icons on the desktop. New text can be added to the selection simply by typing it.

More than one icon may be opened at a time. Windows in Star do not overlap. Each window has a header containing the name of the icon and a menu of commands that may be selected (*CLOSE* for removing the window from the screen, *?* for help, etc).

Commands

In addition to OPEN, Star has a few universal command keys that can be used throughout the system regardless of the type of object selected. They are MOVE, COPY, DELETE, SHOW PROPERTIES, COPY PROPERTIES, AGAIN, UNDO, and HELP.

Of these commands, MOVE is probably the most powerful. In its simplest usage, the MOVE command allow the user to organize the electronic desktop. The user selects an icon and pushes the MOVE key. Then, as the user moves the mouse, the icon follows it. Clicking again releases the icon from the mouse and leaves it on the desktop.

When an icon is opened, MOVE may be used to manipulate the contents in the window in the same way as icons can be manipulated on the desktop. During text editing, MOVE may be used to rearrange letters, words, sentences, etc. During graphics editing, it may be used to move picture elements around.

If an icon is moved into an container icon, instead of onto a spot on the desktop, it is put into that container. A document is printed by moving the document icon to a printer icon. A document is put into a folder by moving the document icon into the display of an opened folder. And so on.

COPY is similar to MOVE, except that the original object is left behind untouched. Instead, a copy of the original object is moved.

In summary, the Star is a "direct manipulation" system.[22] Seeing and pointing is preferred over remembering and typing. The traditional commands are no longer necessary. You "store" or "retrieve" a file by moving an icon into or out of an opened file drawer or folder. You "send" or "receive" mail by moving an icon to an out-basket or from an in-basket. You print a document by moving an icon to the printer. You look up the properties of an object by selecting an object and pushing the PROPERTIES key. And so forth.

The famous WYSIWYG (or "What You See Is What You Get") refers to the situation in which the display screen portrays a rendition of the printed page. Star has a powerful editor for document creation on the screen.

"Xerox devoted about thirty work-years to the design of the user interface. It was designed before the functionality was fully decided. It was designed before the computer hardware was even built."[5] The paramount concern was to define a conceptual model of how the user would relate to the system. The influence of the desktop metaphor upon the computer industry has been clearly felt. Apple Computer's Lisa and Macintosh are examples of this influence.

User Programming in Star

Now let us look at Star from a visual programming language point of view.

In terms of the extent of visual expression, Star rates high. Its emphasis, however, is at the "command" language level. The main contribution of Star is making the system seem friendly by simplifying the human-machine interface for office workers who create, retrieve and distribute documents.

As far as computational capabilities are concerned, "calculators" exist to let a user perform arithmetic operations. But for more complicated computations, users have to "escape" to a *conventional language called CUSP* (for CUStomer Programming) at some bottom level.

Basically, the capability of arithmetic computations for data processing is embodied in the "fill-in rules," specified as property of fields. Figure 10-19 shows a form with an open property sheet for a field with a fill-in rule.[6] "The fill-in rule is executed either when the user moves to the field with the NEXT key, or when the user asks for all the fields in a document to be recomputed."[8]

The expressions used in the fill-in rules are part of CUSP. The syntax of CUSP is somewhat English-like but has many characteristics of conventional programming languages. The following is an example taken from Halbert.[8] The first statement puts 0 into the sum field; the second computes and stores the mean of the ages of all the Smith children listed in the Families table; and the third prints a letter if the CreditBalance field is negative.

```
STORE 0 INTO Sum;

STORE MEAN [Families[Row CALLIT Parent
    WITH Parent.LastName = "Smith"].Children.Age]
    INTO AverageSmithChild;

IF CreditBalance < 0 THEN
    MOVE THE Document WHOSE NAME IS "PleasePay"
    TO THE Printer WHOSE NAME is "Gutenberg";
```

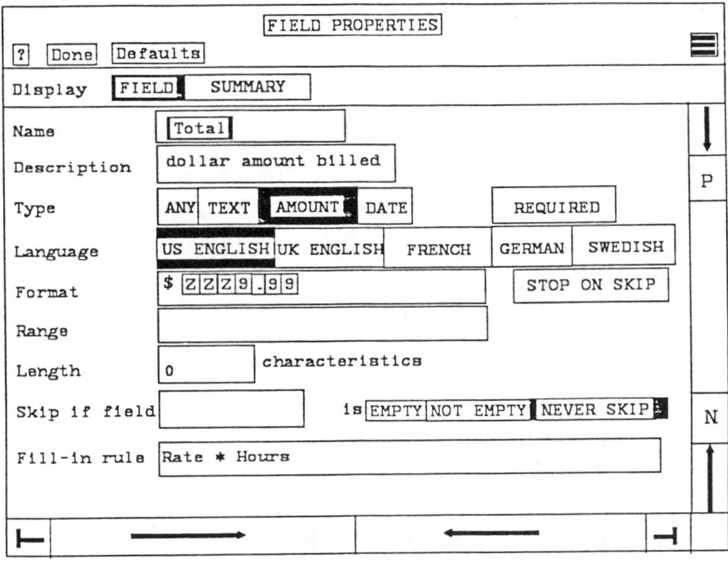

Figure 10-19. Property sheet for a field with a fill-in rule.

Cusp programs exist either in fill-in rules or in special frames called *Cusp buttons.* If the user pushes the button on the mouse for selection while over a Cusp button, the code in the button is executed.

The Star designers do recognize that "the complexity of user applications is essentially unbounded, which makes some sort of programming language virtually mandatory."[6] Unfortunately, what is envisioned is that: "Eventually, CUSP will become a full programming language, with procedures, variables, parameters, and a programming environment."[6]

Underlying this approach is the dictum: "Simple things should be simple; hard things should be possible."[6] Star was designed primarily for simple things. When Cusp is excluded from evaluation, Star rates low in terms of the scope of applicability.

As far as giving directives to the computer is concerned, Star users move the mouse and click the buttons. With some practice, a user can move the cursor to the desired icon and push the appropriate button to select the desired action faster than one can type the commands at a keyboard. However, the tasks are still performed in a step-by-step manner. For computations, "The calculators are user tailorable and extensible. Most are modeled after pocket calculators—business, scientific, four function—but one is a tabular calculator similar to the popular Visicalc program."[5] Pocket calculators require many small steps to perform computations. Rated on the language level, Star is relatively low.

Accordingly, Figure 10-20 shows a profile of Star in terms of the three-dimensional space discussed in Chapter 8.

THE PICT SYSTEM

Another highly graphical system, developed at the University of Washington, was reported by Glinert and Tanimoto.[9] Unlike Xerox's Star, which uses the office as its operational metaphor, Pict is designed to aid program implementation. Its emphasis is to provide a programming facility in which computer graphics plays a central role.

Central to the design of Pict is the following philosophy:

> If we could, we might well prefer to program in the following manner, at least for certain types of applications:
>
> - Select images that visually represent the data structures and variables needed.
> - Draw the desired algorithm as a logically structured, multi-dimensional picture.
> - Watch the program run and see the results being generated.
> - If the program isn't doing what is expected, see where and when the error(s) occur.[9]

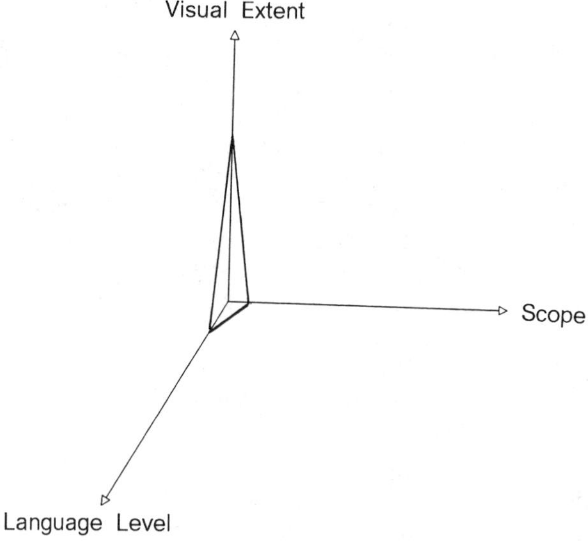

Figure 10-20. A profile of star.
(Shu[22a]. © 1985 IEEE.)

With Pict, users sit in front of a color graphics display and communicate with the system throughout all phases of their work by pointing (with a joystick) to icons in a menu tree. "With the exception of numerals and short Help messages, users rely totally on nontextual symbols. (Sub)program names and parameter passing modes, data structures, variables, and program operations are represented by icons of various sorts, while control structures such as the Pascal REPEAT-UNTIL or WHILE are represented by colored, directed paths that can actually be seen."[9]

Several prototype Pict systems have been implemented at the University of Washington. As a programming language, Pict is at a language level similar to that of Basic or simple Pascal. User programs may be recursive and contain arbitrary chains of subroutine calls. At execution time, Pict uses simple forms of animation to make the drawing come to life.

To illustrate the operations of Pict, a set of figures is shown.

Figure 10-21 shows the Pict display presented to the user at the beginning of a session. There are five distinct areas in the display (see Figure 10-22). They are used to show the program name, active subsystem, help message or data value, system menu or input keyboard, and user program itself or icon editor's easel.

In the initial screen (Figure 10-21), the system menu area displays four icons that denote Pict/D's major subsystems. These are, from top to bottom, *programming, erasing, icon editor,* and *user library* (represented, respectively, by a small flow chart, a hand holding up an eraser, a hand writing with a pen on paper, and a shelf of books).

Figure 10-23 shows the user program library. The library icon is redisplayed

Figure 10-21. An initial display in Pict.
(Glinert and Tanimoto[9]. © 1984 IEEE, original art courtesy of E. Glinert.)

(Sub) program name	(Sub) system indicator	Help bulletin board/ data structure display
System menu / input keyboard	User program / Easel	

Figure 10-22. Areas of display.

Figure 10-23. Program library.
(Glinert and Tanimoto[9]. © 1984 IEEE, original art courtesy of E. Glinert.)

in the system menu area as the first entry. Below it there are four entries showing the routines in the program library: a driver routine, a routine that calculates binomial coefficients, a factorial function, and a program for natural number multiplication by means of repeated addition. The icon for the last routine (i.e., the integer multiplication routine) is shown blown up in the user program/icon editor's easel area.

The routine itself (for integer multiplication by means of repeated addition) is shown in Figure 10-24. The Pict/D code is equivalent to the Pascal program shown in Figure 10-25.

The user can edit or run a program by selecting the icon from the user

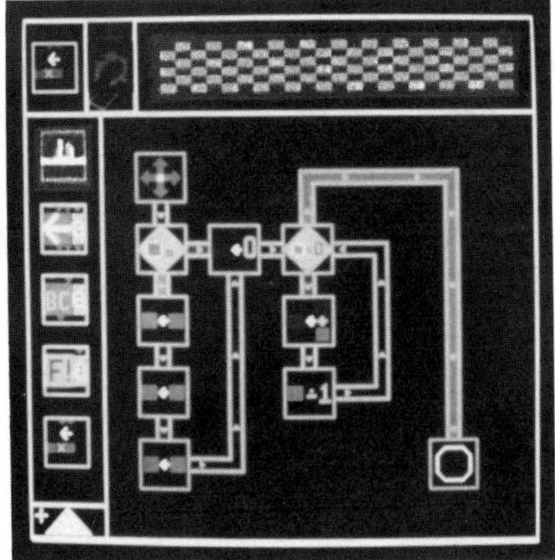

Figure 10-24. Multiplication by repeated addition.
(Glinert and Tanimoto[9]. © 1984 IEEE, original art courtesy of E. Glinert.)

```
type SixDigits = 0..999999;

function Red (Green, Blue: SixDigits) : SixDigits;

(*multiply two natural numbers by means of
  repeated addition*)

var Orange : SixDigits;

begin

   if Blue > Green then

   begin
      Orange := Blue;
      Blue := Green;
      Green := Orange;
   end;

   Red := 0;
   while Blue > 0 do

   begin
      Red := Red + Green;
      Blue := Blue -1;
   end;

end;
```

Figure 10-25. A Pascal program equivalent to Figure 10-24.

library. In Figure 10-26, the driver routine is selected. This routine is programmed to read in a value *n* and invoke the factorial program that recursively calculates *n!*.

To run this program, the user points to any spot in the routine (in the user program area). Figure 10-27 shows what happens next. A numeric soft keypad appears with red "reject" and green "accept" boxes and awaits input. When a read operation is encountered, the keypad flashes different colors to alert the user. The four numeric registers (color-coded red, blue, green, and orange) in which computations will be performed are also displayed.

Next, Figure 10-28 shows various steps in the recursive calculation of *7!*,

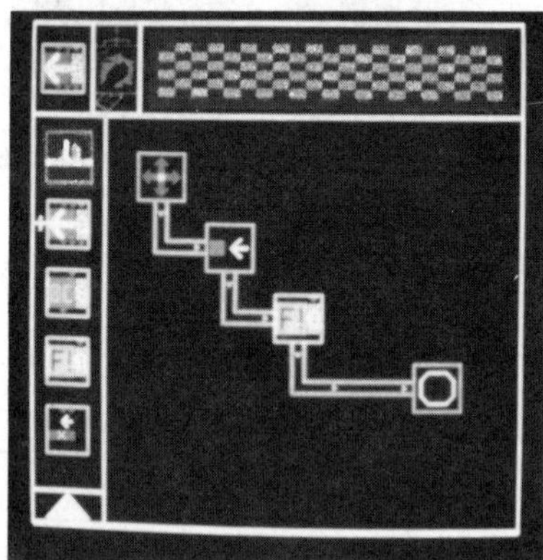

Figure 10-26. Driver routine on display.
(Glinert and Tanimoto[9]. © 1984 IEEE, original art courtesy of E. Glinert.)

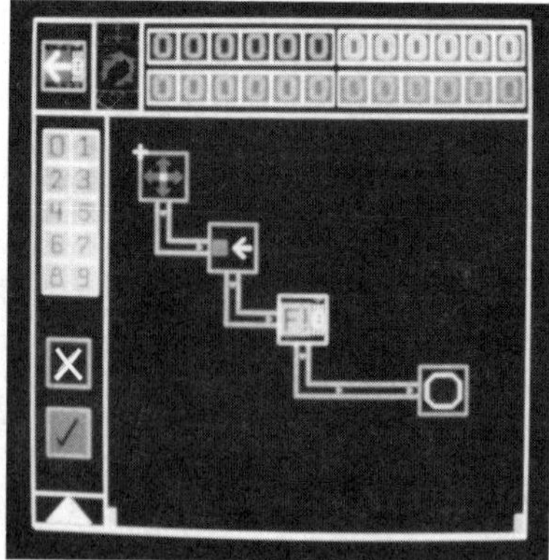

Figure 10-27. Driver routine is selected to run.
(Glinert and Tanimoto[9]. © 1984 IEEE, original art courtesy of E. Glinert.)

The run-time stack height is shown at both edges of the main area of the user program. A white box moves along a flow of control path, making explicit and visible the progress through the program as it is being run.

Eventually, program execution terminates when a *stop/return* sign is reached, and a green check mark appears in the upper left corner (the program name area) of the screen, as shown in Figure 10-29.

Of course, before a program can be selected and run, one must write a program. In writing a program, the first step is to devise an icon as the program name. Next, icons denoting the various operations needed to perform the calculations must be selected from a predefined set and placed in the program area of the screen. These must then be connected by paths to indicate the desired flow of control. To connect two icons with a flow path,

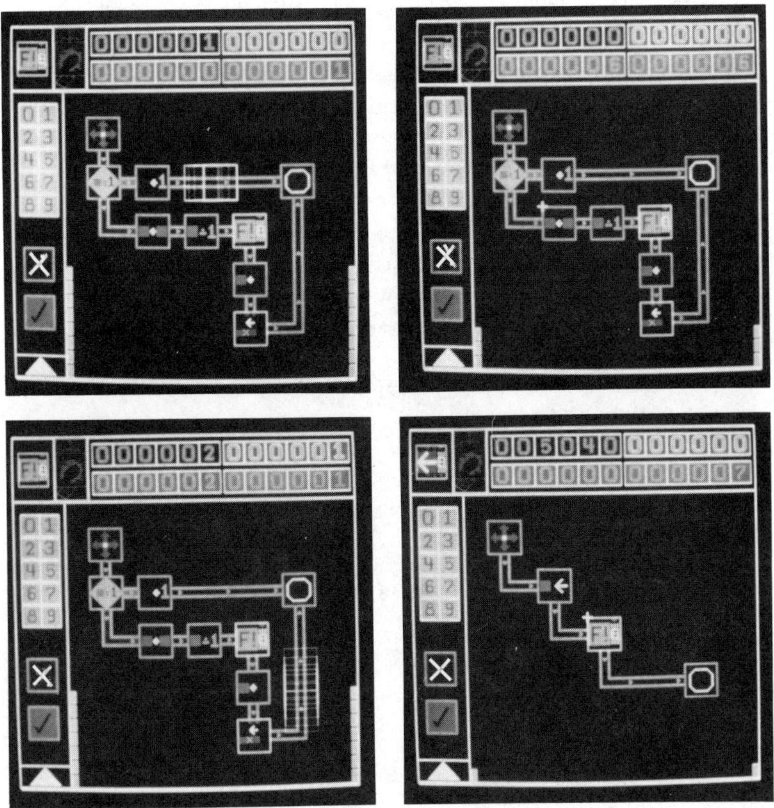

Figure 10-28. Various steps in the recursive calculation of 7!.
(Glinert and Tanimoto[9]. © 1984 IEEE, original art courtesy of E. Glinert.)

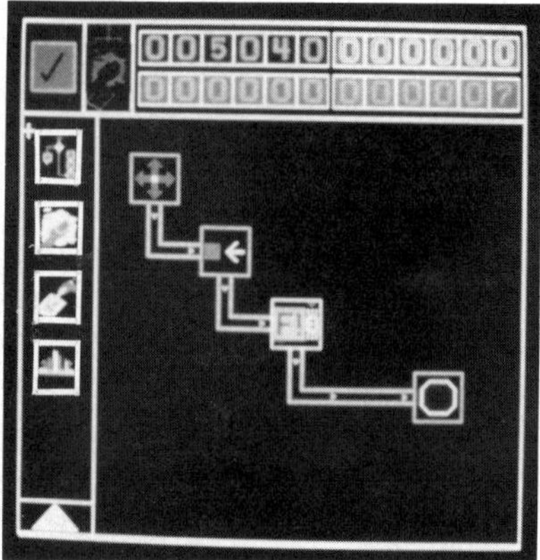

Figure 10-29. Execution terminates.
(Glinert and Tanimoto[9]. © 1984 IEEE, original art courtesy of E. Glinert.)

the user need only point to the desired end points. Pict/D will find the shortest path possible between the indicated icons.

In this way, the user "draws" a program with the joystick. "User drawings are not free-form, but rather have the flavor of one-of-a-kind jigsaw puzzles with juxtaposed, predefined components."[9]

Pict systems were intended to serve as experimental prototypes capable of supporting the implementation of programs similar to those often assigned to students in introductory programming courses.

The Pict/D language primitives are defined as follows in Backus-Naur form:[9]

<language primitive> ::=
    <system control>
    | <declarative op>
    | <boolean op>

<system control> ::=
    'start(entry point)'
    | 'stop/return'

<declarative op> ::=
    'add' | 'subtract'
    | 'increment by 1'
    | 'decrement by 1'
    | 'set to 0'
    | 'set to 1'
    | 'assign a copy'
    | 'input from joystick'
    | 'write to disk file'

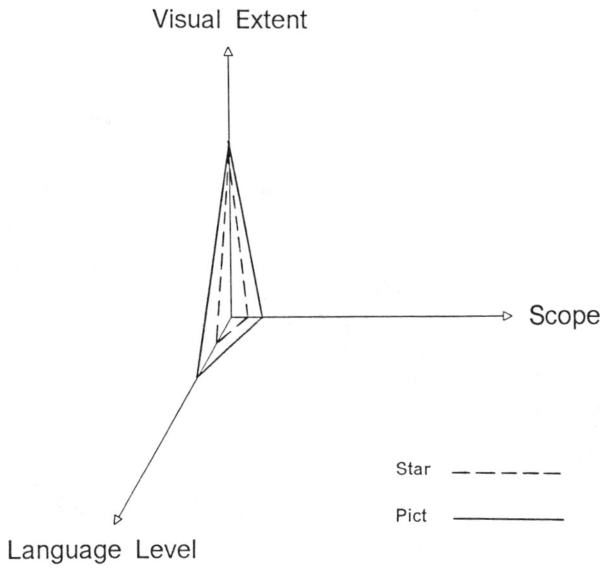

Figure 10-30. A comparison of Pict with Star.

<boolean op> ::=
'>' | '=' | '<' | '=0' | '=1'

"As it stands, Pict/D is quite suitable for initiating novices into the world of computer programming."[9]

However, beyond that, the applicability of Pict is quite limited. The limitation is due to the very restricted size of the user program modules, the limited set of data types and language constructs, and the extremely small number of variables to which a module can refer. For example, only four six-digit nonnegative decimal integers, distinguished by the colors red, green, blue, and orange, are available in each program or subprogram. The authors acknowledge that "To woo the expert user, we must significantly expand the system's capabilities."[9]

In terms of the three-dimensional framework discussed in Chapter 8, a comparison of Pict and Star is shown in Figure 10-30.

In summary, Pict provides *an easier and more natural way for novices to learn programming* than conventional, text-based programming languages. Pict users never touch a keyboard once the system has started up. A programming process consists essentially of selecting and/or composing icons, placing them in proper juxtaposition on the screen, and connecting them by paths to indicate the desired flow of control. But conceptually, this is *algorithmic programming.* When using Pict, one must understand the underlying concepts of variables, operations, flow of control, subprograms, recursions, run-time stacks, etc.

THE SHOW AND TELL SYSTEM

Another iconic system designed for keyboardless programming is the Show and Tell system. Similar to Pict, in Show and Tell program construction requires no typing, except for textual data entry. A pointing device, a mouse, is the primary mechanism for user-computer interaction. In both systems, the programming process involves essentially selecting icons and/or composing and placing them in proper juxtaposition on the screen. Icons are graphical symbols that have associated syntactic and semantic rules of language elements.

The underlying semantic models of the two systems, however, are different. Working with Pict involves working with language elements similar to that of Basic or simple Pascal, but visually. A Show and Tell program, on the other hand, is a partially ordered set of nested boxes and arrows, based on the concepts of dataflow and completion.

The Show and Tell system was developed as the first phase of a visual programming research project at Washington University by T. D. Kimura and his colleagues. The concept of keyboardless programming began forming in 1984 when Kimura was involved in a clinical data retrieval system for a large medical facility. "The technical capabilities of the system were very advanced, but the system was not as successful as he had hoped. Why? 'The doctors did not relate very well to the computer keyboarding or to highly structured commands,' explains Kimura."[23]

The Goals

The underlying premise of the project is that *programming* will be required by every user of future information systems, in spite of many would-be available application software packages. "The research problem was to investigate the possibilities and limitations of computers at home in future information oriented society."[10] This goal is divided into three phases: the long-term, short-term, and immediate goals.

The long-term goal is to construct a computer system which accomplishes integration on three fronts: integration of environments in home, work, and school; integration of applications in communication, computation, and databases; and integration of communication media (image, audio, and text).

The short-term goal is to construct a visual language for keyboardless programming which embodies traditional programming constructs such as assignment, iteration, recursion, exception, concurrency, and record structure.

The immediate goal was to design and implement a language as a case study so that the research problems of the long-term and short-term goals could be addressed. The result, funded by the Computer Services Corporation (CSK) of Japan, is a computer language for school children. The language is called "Show and Tell language (STL)" and "can be characterized by the term *Programming in MacPaint,* one of the most popular application software for Macintosh."[10]

Show and Tell is expected to play a key role in the next two phases of research activities at Washington University. In the remainder of this section we present the syntax, the semantics, and the underlying concepts of Show and Tell. The focus will be on the *language aspects.* The tools provided and the mechanics of composing or executing the programs (e.g., menus, editing facilities) will not be discussed.

Conceptual Model

When using the Show and Tell language, one can think of the computation problems as *puzzles* with one or more pieces missing. A puzzle is solved when the missing piece(s) are found and the puzzle is completed. The missing piece(s) to a puzzle is called its *solution.* The process of finding the solution is called *completion.*

In Show and Tell, completion of a puzzle can be achieved in one of two ways: completion by computation or completion by database search of existing solutions. These two ways are illustrated in Figures 10-31(a) and (b).

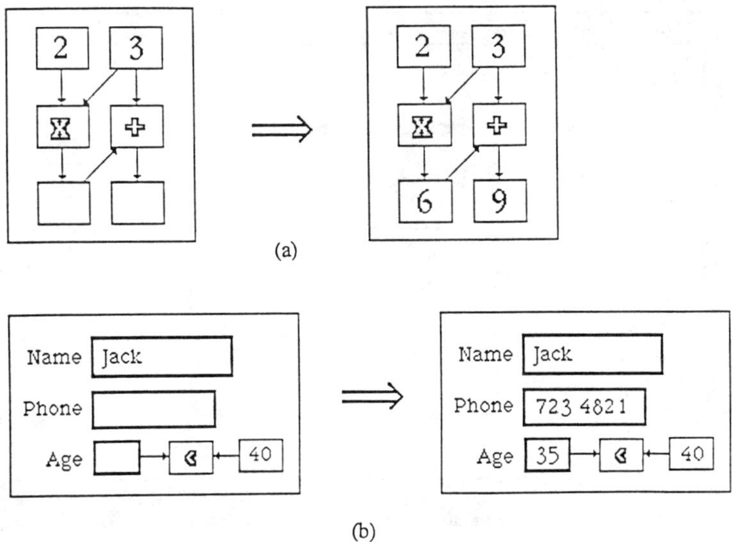

Figure 10-31. Solving a problem by completing a puzzle.
(With the permission of T.D. Kimura, Department of Computer Science, Washington University in St. Louis)

Components of a Puzzle

A Show and Tell puzzle consists of three components: name, background, and boxgraph. A *name* is a bit image (in an area at the upper left corner of a window) used to identify a puzzle. A *background* can be any text or picture used as comments about the puzzle. The *boxgraph* is the main component of a puzzle that the STL system interprets. An example is shown in Figure 10-32.

Boxgraphs

A boxgraph consists of one or more boxes connected by a set of arrows. Formally, it is a partially ordered set of nested boxes, characterized as a directed acyclic multigraph.[11]

A box may be empty or may contain a data object (e.g., a number, text, or picture), a predicate, an operation (represented by the name of a puzzle), or another boxgraph. Boxes can be nested. An arrow directs the flow of data from one box to another. Each arrow can have only one originating box and one destination box. A box, on the other hand, may be connected to several other boxes, but each relationship between boxes must be represented by a different arrow.

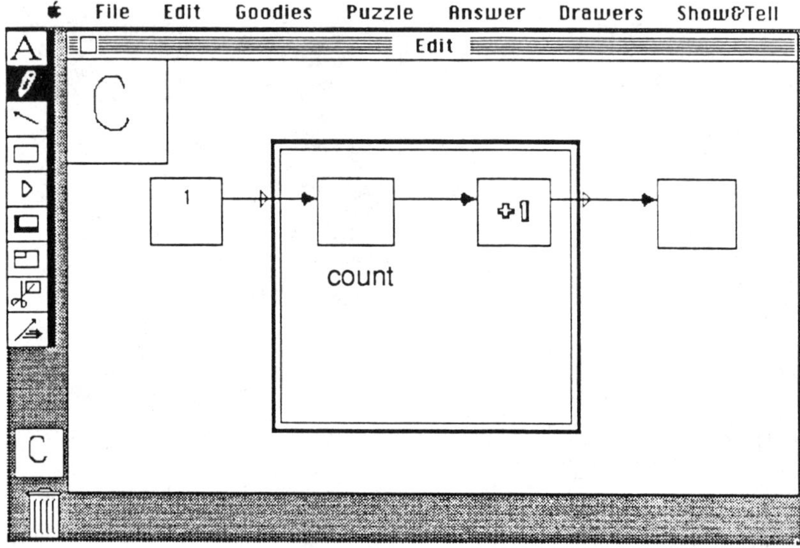

Figure 10-32. Example of a boxgraph.
(With the permission of T.D. Kimura, Department of Computer Science, Washington University in St. Louis)

Consistency

A boxgraph is *consistent* if there is no conflict, directly or indirectly, among the contents of the boxes; otherwise it is *inconsistent.* For example, a boxgraph is inconsistent when a data value is directed to another box containing a different value, or when two different values are transferred to the same destination box. The effect of inconsistency is, by definition, to

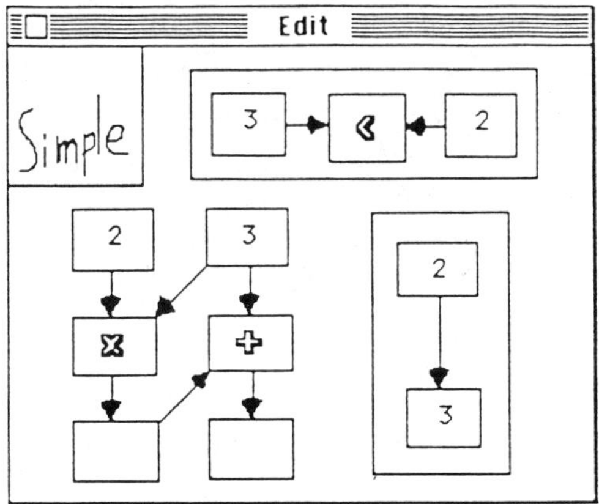

(a) Simple Box-Graph before Execution

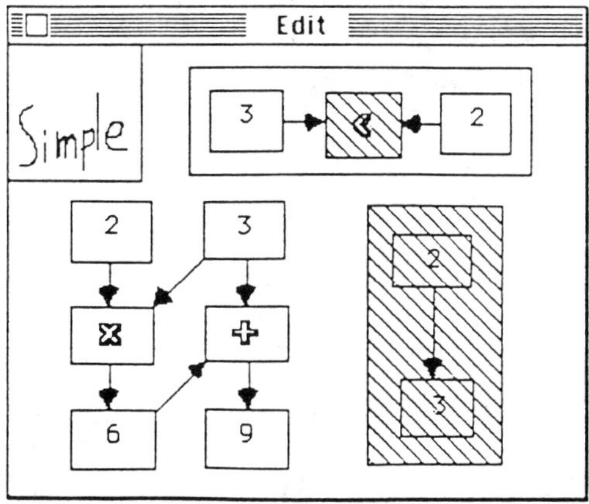

(b) Simple Box-Graph after Execution

Figure 10-33. A box graph before and after execution.
(With the permission of T.D. Kimura, Department of Computer Science, Washington University in St. Louis)

make the boxgraph noncommunicative and nonexistent when viewed from the outside. Any dataflow passing through a box containing an inconsistent boxgraph is terminated at the box.

A computation in Show and Tell involves both finding data to fill the empty boxes and testing the consistency of the boxgraph. All inconsistent boxgraphs are *shaded* by the system when solutions are derived. Figure 10-33(a) illustrates a puzzle consisting of three independent boxgraphs: one to fill in empty boxes and two for testing inconsistencies. Figure 10-33(b) displays a solution obtained by the Show and Tell system.

Different Types of Boxes

There is only one kind of arrow, a solid line with an arrowhead. There are eleven different types of box frames (Figure 10-34). Different semantic rules and programming concepts are associated with each type of box. We shall focus on the first seven types. They are the ones that have been implemented at the time of this writing.

Closed/Open Boxes

The first two types of boxes (i.e., *closed* and *open*) are used to specify the *containment of any inconsistency* that may occur within the box while a solution for the puzzle is derived. A closed box confines any inconsistency within the box. An open box, on the other hand, allows inconsistency to flow out into the surrounding environment.

Inconsistency is similar to exception in traditional programming Languages, and a closed box defines the scope of inconsistency in a similar way as the begin-end block structure defines the scope of exception. By judicious

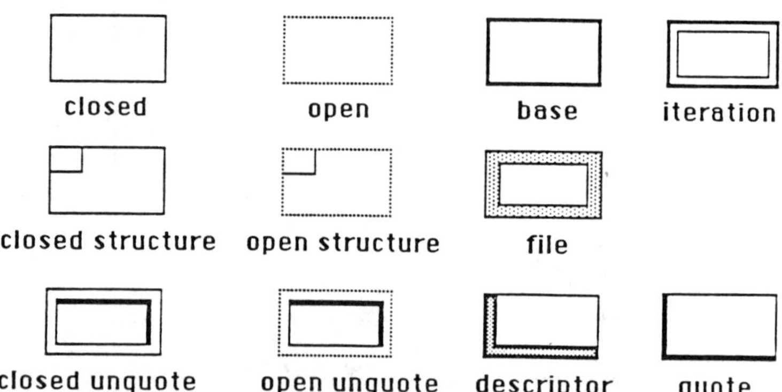

Figure 10-34. Different box frames.
(With the permission of T.D. Kimura, Department of Computer Science, Washington University in St. Louis)

control of the open/close boxes, one can make use of the effect of inconsistency as a switching mechanism. Figure 10-35 illustrates this switching capability.

Base Boxes

The set of empty boxes in a boxgraph is called the *base* of the graph. Base boxes serve two functions in Show and Tell. When used in a database schema or a database query, the base boxes represent record fields in a record structure. We will see examples of this usage later. When used in a computational puzzle, a base box that has only outgoing arrows represents an in-box, while a base box that has only incoming arrows represents an out-box. This usage is illustrated in Figure 10-36. Figure 10-36(a) implements a logical AND operation in Show and Tell. Figure 10-36(b) shows "0" (in the out-box) as the result of solving Figure 10-36(a) when the in-boxes contain "0" and "1." Note that the inconsistent box becomes nonexistent and nothing flows out of it.

Iteration Boxes

The *iterative looping* construct in a traditional programming language corresponds to the *folding abstraction* in Show and Tell. *Folding* consists of collecting a set of repetitive boxgraphs into a compact representation called the *iteration box*. For example, the boxgraph in Figure 10-37(a) can be folded

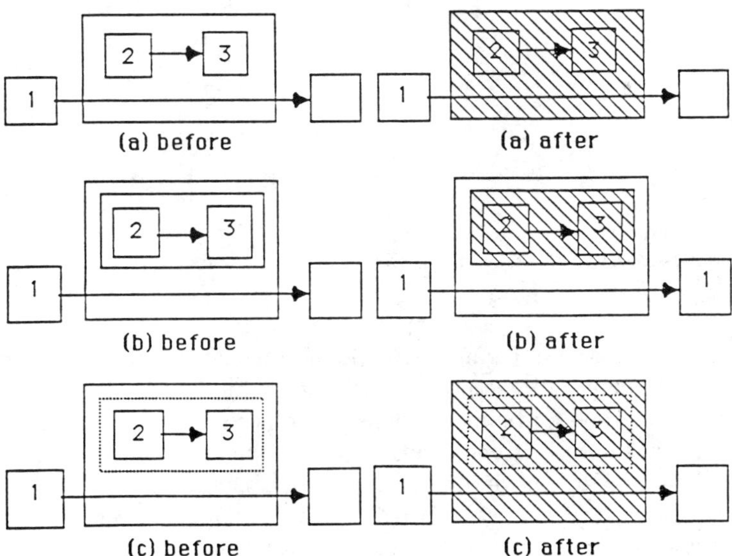

Figure 10-35. Switching with consistency.
(With the permission of T.D. Kimura, Department of Computer Science, Washington University in St. Louis)

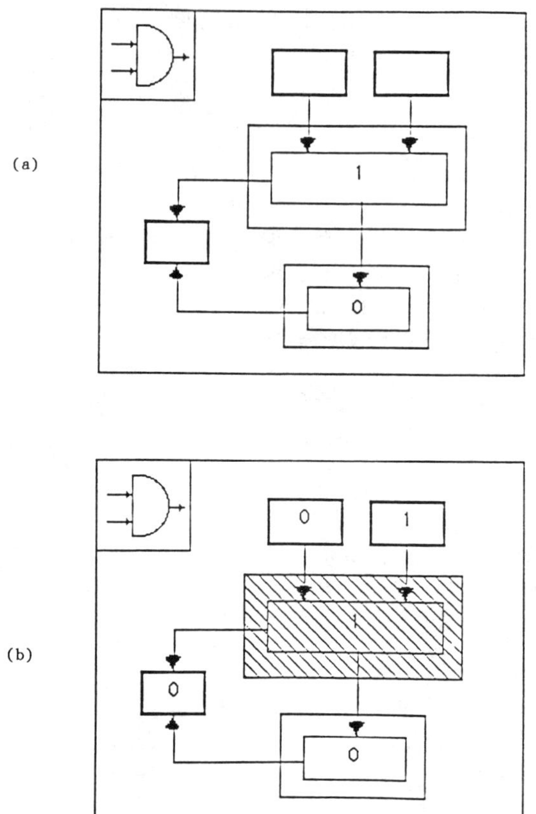

Figure 10-36. AND operation
(With the permission of T.D. Kimura, Department of Computer Science, Washington University in St. Louis)

into the form shown in Figure 10-37(b), and the specification of folding an unbounded number of components using iteration box is shown in Figure 10-37(c). A method for bounded folding is shown in Figure 10-37(d).

There are three different forms of communication among the folded components and their environment: sequential, parallel, and global. Sequential iteration is represented by a pair of sequential ports (small triangles) attached to the iteration box. Parallel iteration is represented by a parallel port (a striped rectangle) attached to the iteration box. When an incoming arrow is attached to the iteration box without passing through any communi-

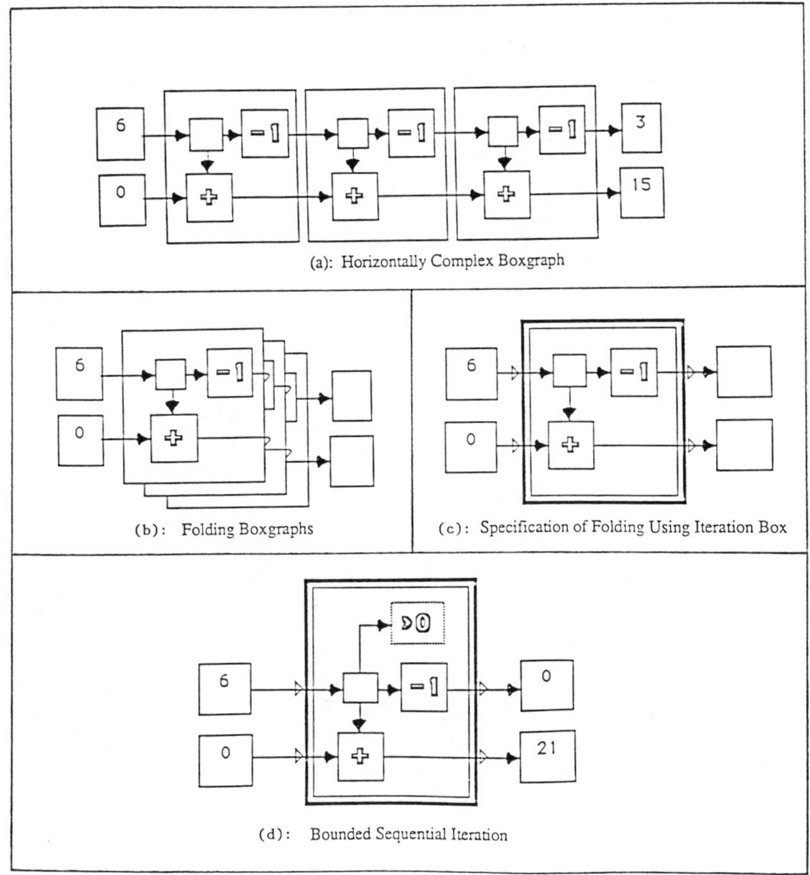

Figure 10-37. Folding abstraction
(With the permission of T.D. Kimura, Department of Computer Science, Washington University in St. Louis)

cation port, the incoming value is a global value. These three types of communication are shown in Figures 10-38, 10-39, and 10-40, respectively.

The next three boxes (Closed Structure, Open Structure, and File boxes) are used for database schema and queries. Before we deal with them, let us discuss the handling of functions and recursiveness in Show and Tell.

Functions and Recursive Procedures

As we mentioned earlier, a box may contain an operation, represented by the name of a puzzle. *Naming* is an abstraction mechanism for reducing the complexity of a boxgraph. It corresponds to the procedure concept in a traditional programming language.

For example, having defined two names as shown in Figures 10-41(a) and (b), the boxgraph shown in Figure 10-41(c) can be replaced by the simpler boxgraph shown in Figure 10-41(d).

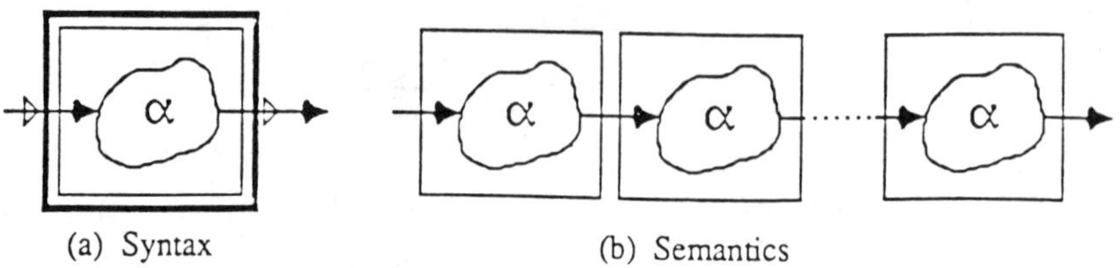

Figure 10-38. Sequential iteration.
(With the permission of T.D. Kimura, Department of Computer Science, Washington University in St. Louis)

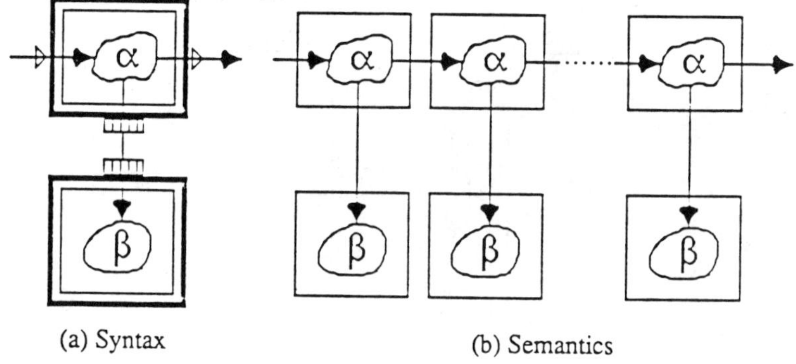

Figure 10-39. Parallel iteration.
(With the permission of T.D. Kimura, Department of Computer Science, Washington University in St. Louis)

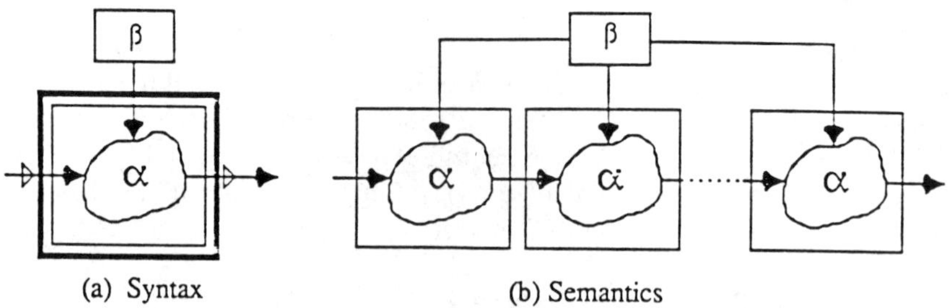

Figure 10-40. Sequential iteration with global inputs.
(With the permission of T.D. Kimura, Department of Computer Science, Washington University in St. Louis)

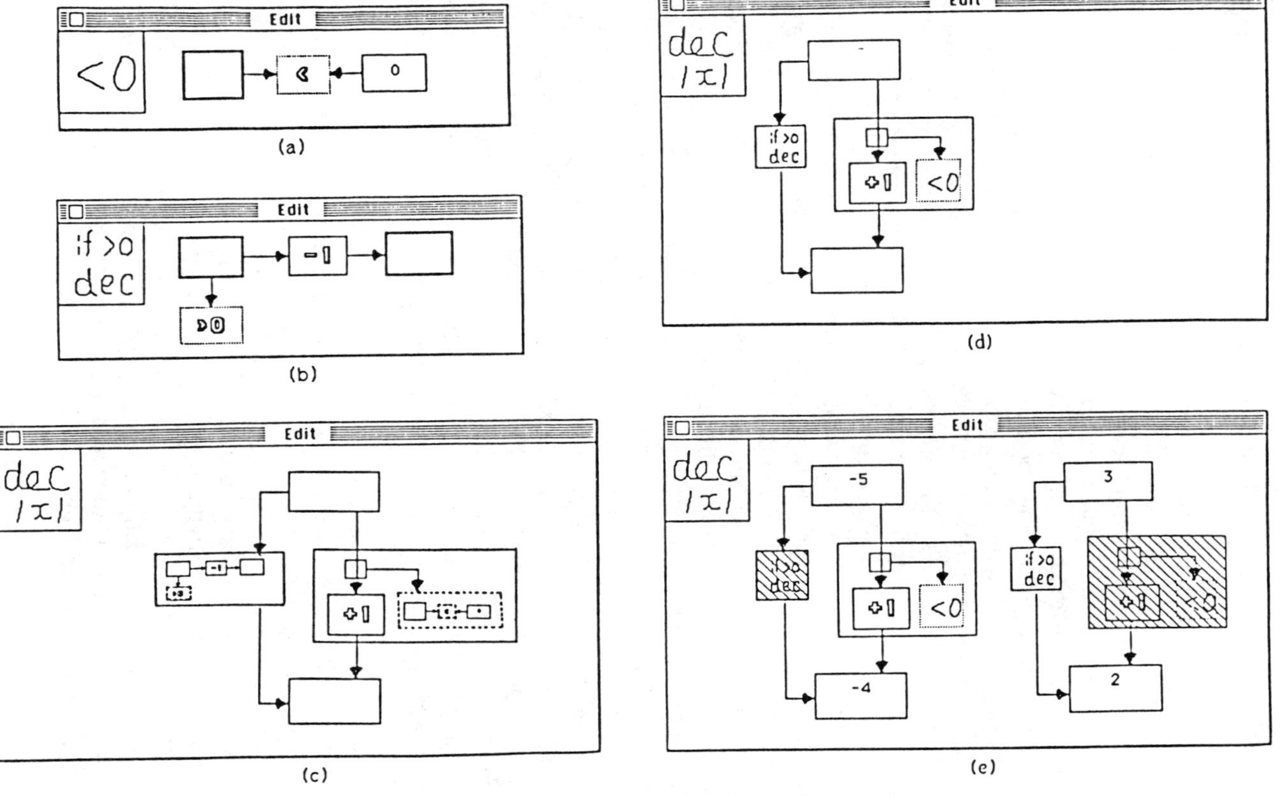

Figure 10-41. Function with exception.
(With the permission of T.D. Kimura, Department of Computer Science, Washington University in St. Louis)

Note that Figure 10-41(a) defines a predicate for testing whether a number is negative or not; and Figure 10-41(b) defines a function that returns the input value minus one if the input is positive; otherwise it returns the exception (inconsistency). Any occurrence of a puzzle name in a boxgraph can be replaced by the boxgraph associated with the name without changing the consistency of the original boxgraph. Figure 10-41(e) illustrates the result of executing a boxgraph in which the same computation is duplicated with two different input values, one positive and the other negative.

In a name definition, the base boxes specify the input and output parameters for the named boxgraph. When used as a subroutine, the arrows coming into the named box denote the actual arguments. Similar to the traditional programming languages, the association of the formal parameters with the actual arguments in STL is governed by a binding rule.

When there are two or more input parameters, the binding rule is positional in that both the base boxes in a name definition and the arrows incident with an operation box that contains the name are lexicographically covered by the *(x,y)* coordinates. On the Macintosh screen, the *x*-coordinate increases from left to right and the *y*-coordinate from top to bottom.

In a similar manner, naming abstraction can be used to reduce the complexity of a recursive puzzle. For example, Figure 10-42(a) is a recursive puzzle shown as a nested boxgraph. This boxgraph can be approximately represented by Figure 10-42(b), where the name is defined by Figure 10-42(c). The representation is approximate because Figure 10-42(b) represents an unbounded nesting, while Figure 10-42(a) has a fixed nesting depth of three. An example of naming a bounded nesting is given in Figure 10-42(d), where the nesting depth is determined by the input value. The dynamic expansion of the nested boxgraph terminates when the input value is no longer greater than 0.

In addition to the recursive computation for positive numbers, the puzzle in Figure 10-42(d) specifies the behavior of encountering nonpositive value in the in-box. If input is 0, the 0 in the left-hand box will flow into the out-box as the result. If the input is less than 0, inconsistency will be the result. Figure 10-42(a), on the other hand, provides no such provisions. Regardless of whether the value placed in the in-box is positive, negative, or 0, the behavior is the same. It should be obvious that a puzzle which is functionally equivalent to that of Figure 10-42(d), but constructed in the same fashion as Figure 10-42(a), i.e., without using the name abstraction, would be more complex than the puzzle shown in Figure 10-42(a).

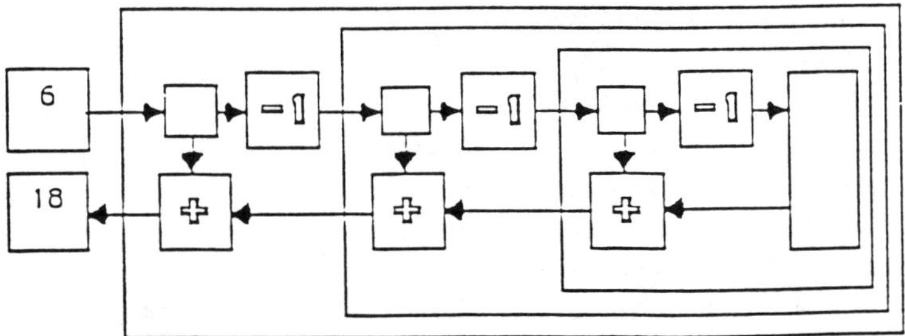

(a): Complex Boxgraph

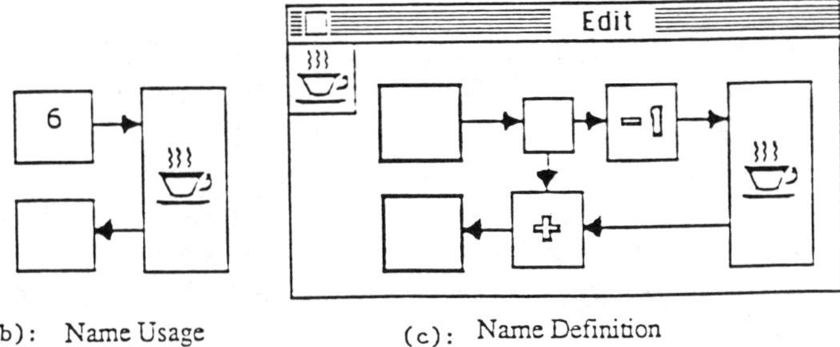

(b): Name Usage

(c): Name Definition

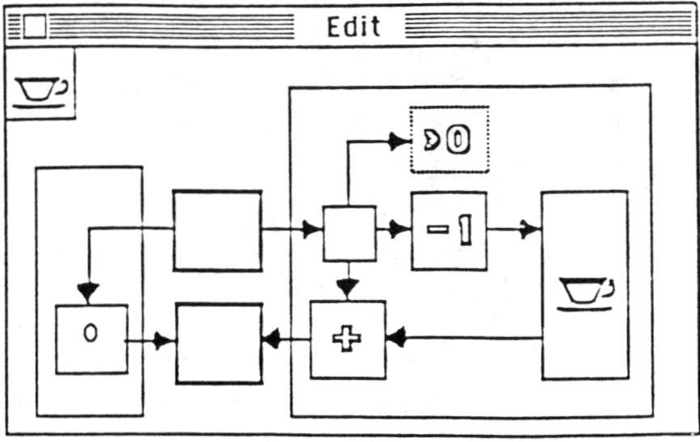

(d): Bounded Expansion of Operation Box

Figure 10-42. Reduction of complexity through naming machanism.
(With the permission of T.D. Kimura, Department of Computer Science, Washington University in St. Louis)

File Boxes and Structure Boxes

A *file* in Show and Tell is a sequence of known solutions for a puzzle that has base boxes. When the puzzle consists of base boxes only, and no arrows, it defines a record structure in a traditional programming language, where each base box represents a record field. An example of a simple file definition is given in Figure 10-43.

For data query there is a browsing mechanism to search through a small file, record by record, directly on the edit window. Figure 10-44(a) is an example of a direct query specification. After the user selects the "find" menu command, the system completes the boxgraph with the first solution in the file that makes the boxgraph consistent (as in Figure 10-44b). The "Find Next" menu command can then be used to find the next solution in the database meeting the constraints.

Another method of data query is through a file box and a structure box. A *file box* containing a name represents the solutions saved in the file of the named puzzle. In operation, it is equivalent to a parallel iteration that produces or accepts a sequence of records (see Figure 10-45).

All records in a file have the same record structure. A *structure box* allows the user to access the record fields within a record structure. A structure box has a name area. When a name is inserted in the name area of the structure box, the system displays the base boxes of the named file. The user can then make use of some of these base boxes to construct a new puzzle. The puzzle in Figure 10-46 illustrates how a structure box can be used to print the records whose score is less than or equal to 100.

Another interesting point concerns the integration of image, audio, and text. Show and Tell uses the Macintosh built-in speaker and the Smooth Talker synthesized speech driver from First Byte to generate its voice output.

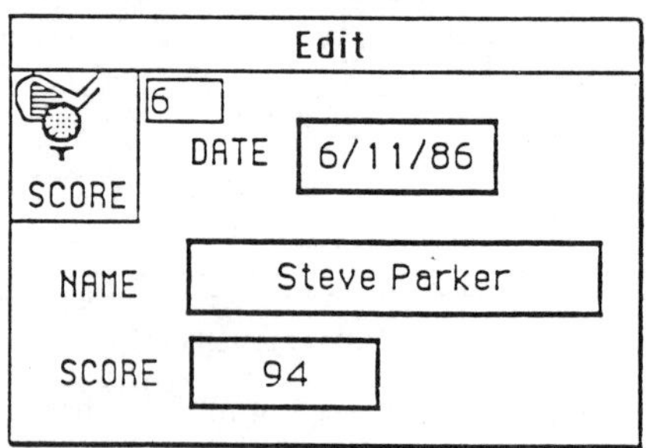

Figure 10-43. A simple file definition.
(With the permission of T.D. Kimura, Department of Computer Science, Washington University in St. Louis)

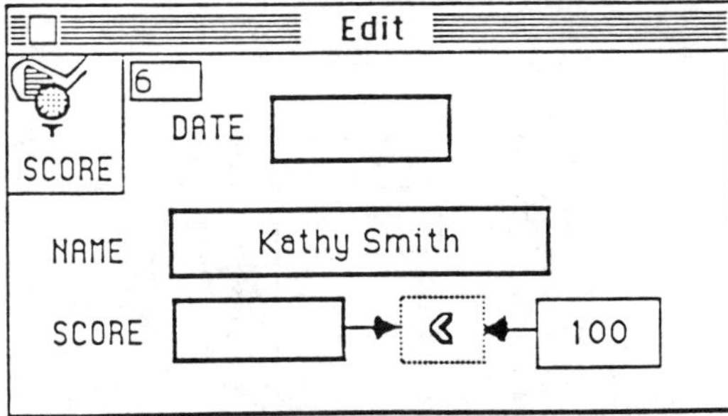

(a): Direct Database Query (Specification)

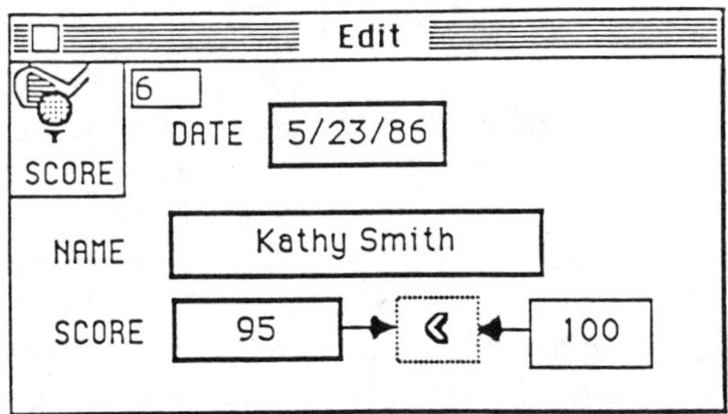

(b): Direct Database Query (Answer)

Figure 10-44. Database query.
(With the permission of T.D. Kimura, Department of Computer Science, Washington University in St. Louis)

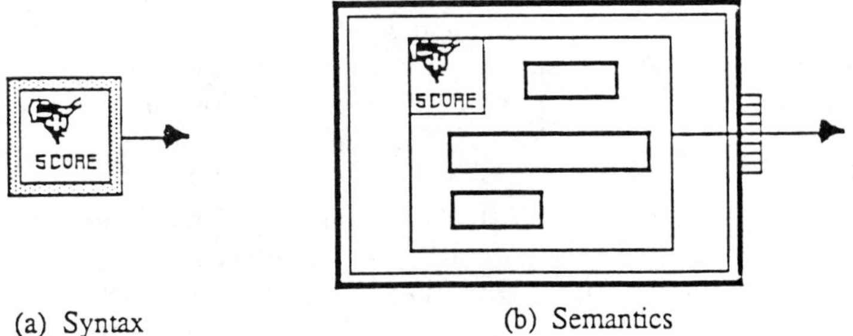

(a) Syntax (b) Semantics

Figure 10-45. Semantics of file box.
(With the permission of T.D. Kimura, Department of Computer Science, Washington University in St. Louis)

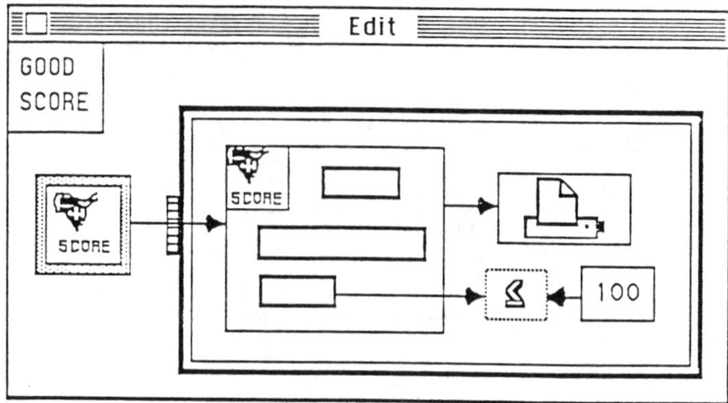

Figure 10-46. Structure box for record selection.
(With the permission of T.D. Kimura, Department of Computer Science, Washington University in St. Louis)

A database can contain pictures as well as text. But no operation on the picture data type is available, nor is the identification operation. The system cannot decide whether two pictures are identical or not. Nevertheless, it is a step toward providing the user with an integrated environment that allows uniform handling of pictorial and textual data with optional voice output.

In the concluding section of Kimura et al.,[10] the authors stated, "Visual Programming (VP) is a new research area of importance. . . . We have introduced the term *keyboardless programming* as a paraphrase of VP assuming that when we minimize the usage of a keyboard as a text generator, we maximize the visualization of programming concepts. We have designed and implemented a visual language Show and Tell for keyboardless programming to investigate how far we can achieve this goal. Our results show that it is possible to eliminate entire keyboard usage from programming (except for data entry), if it is for computation and database query. This does not show, however, that Show and Tell is a better visual programming language. Sometimes VP is tedious even for novice end users, and traditional textual programming can be simpler." We shall return to this point later on in the last chapter.

Putting the pros and cons of textual verses visual programming aside, let us summarize what has been accomplished by Show and Tell.

Many of the programming concepts have been implemented in Show and Tell in a two-dimensional "box and arrow" syntax. They include assignment, arithmetic operations, iteration, recursion, concurrency, exception, synchronization, etc. As an iconic programming language, Show and Tell is more powerful than the other iconic systems that we have discussed in this

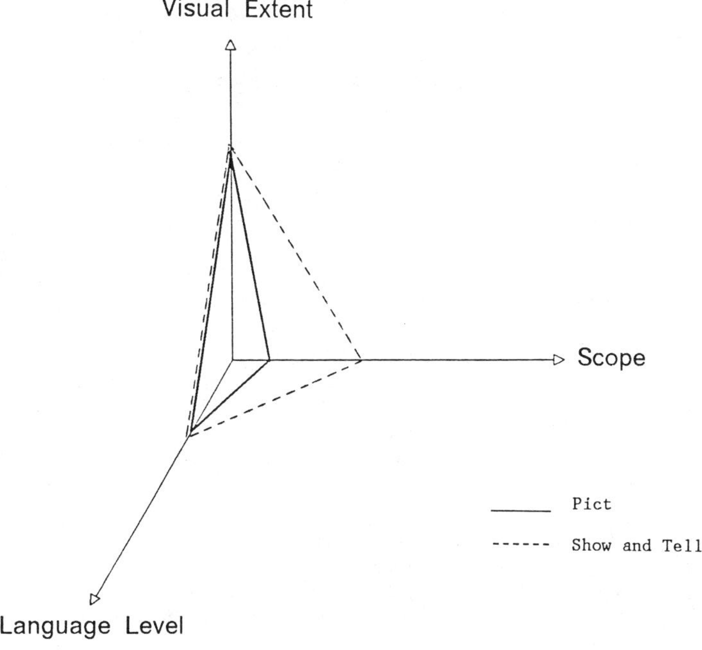

Figure 10-47. A comparison of Pict with Show and Tell.

chapter. It has widened the scope of applicability for iconic systems. In terms of the three-dimensional framework discussed in Chapter 8, we may compare the profile of Show and Tell with that of Pict, as sketched in Figure 10-47.

REFERENCES

1. Wang, W. S-Y., "The Chinese Language," *Scientific American*, Vol. 228, No. 2 (Feb. 1973), pp. 50-63.
2. Malone, T. W., "Heuristics for Designing Enjoyable User Interfaces: Lessons from Computer Games," in *Human Factors in Computing Systems*, edited by J. C. Thomas and M. L. Schneider, Ablex Publishing Corp. (1984).
3. Finzer, W., and Gould, L., "Programming by Rehearsal," *Byte*, Vol. 9, No. 6 (June 1984), pp. 187-210.
4. Smith, D. C., Irby, C., Kimball, R., Verplank, W., and Harslem, E., "Designing the Star User Interface," *Byte*, Vol. 7, No. 4 (Apr. 1982), pp. 242-282.
5. Smith, D. C., Irby, C., and Kimball, R., "The Star-User Interface: An Overview," *Proceedings of the National Computer Conference* (Jun. 1982) pp. 515-528.
6. Purvy, R., Farrell, J. and Klose, P., "The Design of Star's Records Processing: Data Processing for the Noncomputer Professional," *ACM Transactions on Office Information Systems*, Vol. 1, No. 1 (Jan. 1983), pp. 3-24.

7. Bewley, W. L., Roberts, T. L., Schroit, D., and Verplank, W. L., "Human Factors Testing in the Design of Xerox's 8010 'Star' Office Workstation," *Proceedings of CHI '83* (Dec. 1983), pp. 72-77.
8. Halbert, D. C., "Programming by Example," Ph.D. dissertation, Department of Computer Science, University of California, Berkeley (1984)
9. Glinert, E. P., and Tanimoto, S. L., "Pict: An Interactive Graphical Programming Environment," *IEEE Computer,* Vol. 17, No. 11 (Nov. 1984), pp. 7-25.
10. Kimura, T. D., Choi, J. W., and Mack, J. M., "A Visual Language for Keyboardless Programming," Washington University Technical Report WUCS-86-6 (June 1986).
11. Kimura, T. D., "Determinacy of Hierarchical Dataflow Model: A Computation Model for Visual Programming," Washington University Technical Report WUCS-86-5 (Mar. 1986).
12. McLain, P., and Kimura, T. D., "Show and Tell User's Manual," Washington University Technical Report WUCS-86-4 (Mar. 1986).
13. Lakin, F., "Spatial Parsing for Visual Languages," in *Visual Languages,* edited by S. K. Chang, T. Ichikawa and P. A. Ligomenides, Plenum Publishing Corp. (1986).
14. Edel, M., "The Tinkertoy Graphical Programming Environment," *Proceedings of IEEE 1986 Compsac* (Oct. 1986), pp. 466-471.
15. Kurita, T., and Tamura, K., "Dialog.I: An Iconic Programming System Based on Logic Programming," *Bulletin of the Electrotechnical Laboratory, Japan,* Vol. 48, No. 12 (1984), pp. 966-975.
16. Giacalone, A., Rinard, M. C., and Doeppner, T. W., Jr., "IDEOSY: An Ideographic and Interactive Program Description System," *ACM SIGPLAN Notices,* Vol. 19, No. 5 (May 1984), pp. 15-20.
17. Milner, R., *A Calculus of Communicating Systems.* Springer-Verlag (1980).
18. Matwin, S., and Pietrzykowski, T., "PROGRAPH: A Preliminary Report," *Computer Language,* Vol. 10, No. 2 (1985), pp. 91-126.
19. Mondon, N., Yoshino, Y., Hirakawa, M., Tanaka, M., and Ichikawa, T., "HI-VISUAL: A Language Supporting Visual Interaction in Programming," *Proceedings of the 1984 IEEE Workshop on Visual Languages* (Dec. 1984), pp. 199-205.
20. Hirakawa, M., Iwata, S., Yoshimoto, I., Tanaka, M., and Ichikawa, T., "HI-VISUAL Iconic Programming," *Proceedings of the 1987 Workshop on Visual Languages* (Aug. 1987) pp. 305-314.
21. Pake, G. E., "Research at Xerox PARC: A Founder's Assessment," *IEEE Spectrum,* Vol. 22, No. 10 (Oct. 1985), pp. 54-61.
22. Shneiderman, B., "Direct Manipulation: A Step Beyond Programming Languages," *IEEE Computer,* Vol. 16, No. 8, (Aug. 1983), pp. 57-69.
22a. Shu, N. C., *"Visual Programming Languages: A Dimensional Analysis," Proceedings of the IEEE International Symposium on New Directions in Computing* (Aug. 1985), pp. 326-334.
23. Brock, R. G., "High-Tech Hieroglyphics Make Programming Child's Play," *Data Management,* Vol. 24, No. 1, (Jan. 1986), pp. 34-36, 50.

Chapter 11

Table- and Form-Based Systems

In 1979, the CODASYL End-User Facilities Committee (EUFC) stated that "The forms approach was considered the most natural interface between an end-user and data because a large number of end-users employ forms (e.g., purchase order forms, expense report forms, etc.) or versions of forms (e.g., reports, memos, etc.) in their daily work activities as well as in their personal lives (e.g., tax forms, employment application forms, etc.)."[1] But the CODASYL committee was not the only group that considered forms as "the most natural interface." The success story of spread sheet programs testifies to the appeal of the table/form-oriented approach. Today, "form filling" is used in menu-driven user interfaces, in office automation systems, in data entry and display facilities, and in database query and update, as well as in applications involving interactive dialogs and/or formulated calculations.

In this chapter, instead of providing a quick sweep over many systems, we choose to view the field by looking in some depth at three representative systems that have been reported in the literature: QBE[2] and its derivatives, FORMANAGER,[3] and FORMAL.[4] QBE was recognized as one of the earliest database query languages that employ a *two-dimensional syntax.* FORMANAGER is an illustrative example of systems that enable data definition, entry, query, and update by filling in the forms. (e.g., IDEAL,[5] ADE,[6] FILLIN,[7] to name a few.) FORMAL, on the other hand, is a nonprocedural language that offers users a greater degree of flexibility for a *much wider range of applications.* It combines the power of automatic programming with visual programming in a *"What you sketch is what you get"* fashion.

Another reason for using these three systems as illustrative examples concerns the complexity levels of data structures that they can handle.

Both QBE and FORMANAGER have relational tables as the underlying data model. Yet, both of them recognize the need for supporting data structures or views more complex than those of the flat tables.

One of the reasons for the need to support hierarchical views, as stated by Zloof, concerns the fact that "It is sometimes more intuitive for the user to view part of his database as a hierarchical tree (such as an organizational chart), although the underlying model may be relational."[8] Proposals were made for QBE to support hierarchical views,[8] but the implemented version maps data only among flat tables.

FORMANAGER elaborated on this reason further. "Command-directed relational query languages (e.g., SQL, QUEL) and screen-oriented relational interfaces (e.g., QBE, ENFORM) are important steps toward bringing efficient application development closer to the system end-user. However, the basic data structure involved in these relational systems, the *table,* is inadequate to fully satisfy the application needs of most users. A tabular representation is not the most natural manner for viewing data in most applications."[3]* Therefore, FORMANAGER supports the manifestation of a one-branch hierarchical view in the *presentation form* (i.e., in the form that the user *sees* at the interface level). The underlying database is still relational.

FORMAL, on the other hand, takes on the hierarchical data structure from the outset. It is designed for a wide range of applications that deal with hierarchical data of arbitrary complexity. There are no limitations on the number of branches or the levels of depth in a hierarchy. A relational table is treated simply as a degenerate hierarchy, i.e., a one-level tree. Believing not only that "simple things should be made simple" but that hard things should also be made as simple as possible, FORMAL sets out to show that a nonprocedural language capable of manipulating complicated trees can be made as simple and natural as those that can handle only simple tables.

In short, within the framework of tables or forms, these three systems exemplify three different approaches to the general problem of simplifying programming for nonprogrammers. Their scope of applications varies considerably.

QBE

QBE (Query By Example) was developed at the IBM's Thomas J. Watson Research Center and released as a product by IBM in 1978 as a query language on relational databases.[10,11] Over the years, QBE has acquired a reputation as a user-friendly language. One of the unique features of this language is that a user needs to learn very few concepts in order to get started.

Underlying the language is the data model of the relational databases. The user sees his data in terms of tables, and the language operations mimics the manual table operations. Figure 11-1 shows a small department store database. The EMP table specifies the name, salary, manager, and department of each

---

*This observation agrees with D. Tsichritzis' discussion of form management.[9] In describing the OFS (Office Form System) developed at the University of Toronto, Tsichritzis stated that "In our prototype system forms are further restricted for ease of implementation. First, attributes are not compounded and are single valued. This restriction is to avoid difficulties with displaying arbitrary repeating groups under the display template. It appears, however, that users would like to have repeating groups and they should be provided."[9]

EMP	NAME	SALARY	MGR	DEPT
	JONES	8000	SMITH	HOUSEHOLD
	ANDERSON	6000	MURPHY	TOY
	MORGAN	10000	LEE	COSMETICS
	LEWIS	12000	LONG	STATIONERY
	NELSON	6000	MURPHY	TOY
	HOFFMAN	16000	MORGAN	COSMETICS
	LONG	7000	MORGAN	COSMETICS
	MURPHY	8000	SMITH	HOUSEHOLD
	SMITH	12000	HOFFMAN	STATIONERY
	HENRY	9000	SMITH	TOY

SALES	DEPARTMENT	ITEM
	STATIONERY	DISH
	HOUSEHOLD	PEN
	STATIONERY	PENCIL
	COSMETICS	LIPSTICK
	TOY	PEN
	TOY	PENCIL
	TOY	INK
	COSMETICS	PERFUME
	STATIONERY	INK
	HOUSEHOLD	DISH
	STATIONERY	PEN
	HARDWARE	INK

SUPPLY	ITEM	SUPPLIER
	PEN	PENCRAFT
	PENCIL	FLIC
	INK	PENCRAFT
	PERFUME	BEAUTEX
	INK	FLIC
	DISH	CHEMCO
	LIPSTICK	BEAUTEX
	DISH	FLIC
	PEN	BEAUTEX
	PENCIL	PENCRAFT

TYPE	ITEM	COLOR	SIZE
	DISH	WHITE	M
	LIPSTICK	RED	L
	PERFUME	WHITE	L
	PEN	GREEN	S
	PENCIL	BLUE	M
	INK	GREEN	L
	INK	BLUE	S
	PENCIL	RED	L
	PENCIL	BLUE	L

Figure 11-1. Tables of a department store database.
(Copyright 1977 International Business Machines. Reprinted with permission)

employee. The SALES table lists the items sold by departments. The SUPPLY table lists the items supplied by suppliers. The TYPE table describes each item by color and size.

The following basic concepts are fundamental to QBE:

1. Programming is done within two-dimensional skeleton tables.
2. User can retrieve, insert, delete, or update data by using P., I., D., or U. operators, respectively. (Note that all operators in QBE end with a period.)
3. The distinction between a *constant* and an *example element* is important. Constants are *literal* values. Example elements are *variables.* When placed in a field of a table, an example element represents an instance of possible value in that field. To distinguish an example element from a constant, an example element is either underlined (e.g., <u>S</u>) or begins with an underscore character, "_" (e.g., _S).

Query Operations

Initially, the user is presented with a table skeleton on the screen, as shown in Figure 11-2. The retrieval operator (P.) stands for "print" or "present." If the user puts P. in one of the spaces in the skeleton table, he wants QBE to fill in that space. Thus when P. is placed in the table name field, it becomes a query, asking for all the available table names (Figure 11-3). The result of this query yields the following display:

EMP
SALES
SUPPLY
TYPE

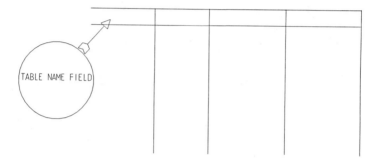

Figure 11-2. A table skeleton.
(Copyright 1977 International Business Machines. Reprinted with permission)

P.			

Figure 11-3. Retrieval of table names.
(Copyright 1977 International Business Machines. Reprinted with permission)

If the user places TYPE P. in the table name field, the system fills column headings for the table named TYPE (Figure 11-4). Similarly, Figure 11-5 presents items of green color, and Figure 11-6 presents all colors.

Retrievals can be qualified. Figure 11-7 shows a query that presents the names of employees who work in the TOY department and earn more than 10000. Note that no person qualifies in this case.

The Example Element Concept

The example element concept covers a wide variety of database operations such as cross-referencing between fields, formulating conditions, and mov-

TYPE P.			

YIELDS

TYPE	ITEM	COLOR	SIZE

Figure 11-4. Retrieval of column headings.
(Copyright 1977 International Business Machines. Reprinted with permission)

TYPE	ITEM	COLOR	SIZE
	P.	GREEN	

yields

TYPE	ITEM
	PEN
	INK

Figure 11-5. Retrieval of green colored items.
(Copyright 1977 International Business Machines. Reprinted with permission)

TYPE	ITEM	COLOR	SIZE
		P.	

yields

TYPE	COLOR
	WHITE RED GREEN BLUE

Figure 11-6. Retrieval of all colors in TYPE table.
(Copyright 1977 International Business Machines. Reprinted with permission)

EMP	NAME	SAL	MGR	DEPT
	P.	>10000		TOY

YIELDS

EMP	NAME

Figure 11-7. Find the names of employees who work in the Toy department and earn more than 10000.
(Copyright 1977 International Business Machines. Reprinted with permission)

ing data from one table to a new table. Examples of its usage include the following:

Figure 11-8: Find the names and salaries of the employees who earn more than Lewis.

Figure 11-9: Find the names of the employees who earn more than their managers.

Figure 11-10: Print out each department with its corresponding suppliers.

Figure 11-11: Print the names of the employees whose salaries are greater than the sum of those of Jones and Nelson.

Figure 11-12: Print the names of the employees whose salary is between 10000 and 15000, but not 13000. The use of the same example element JONES in all three rows implies that these three conditions are ANDed. The same result could be achieved explicitly, as shown in Figure 11-12(b).

Figure 11-13: Print the names of the employees whose salary is either 10000 or 13000 or 16000. Different example elements are used in each row, so that the three lines express independent queries. The output is the union of the three sets of answers. The same result could be achieved with a condition box.

EMP	NAME	SAL	
	P.	P.>S1	
	LEWIS	S1	

YIELDS

EMP	NAME	SAL
	HOFFMAN	16000

Figure 11-8. Example elements used as links in the same table.
(Copyright 1977 International Business Machines. Reprinted with permission)

EMP	NAME	SAL	MGR	DEPT
	P.	>S1	JONES	
	JONES	S1		

YIELDS

EMP	NAME
	LEWIS
	HOFFMAN

Figure 11-9. Two links in the same table.
(Copyright 1977 International Business Machines. Reprinted with permission)

SALES	DEPT	ITEM
	TOY	INK

SUPPLY	ITEM	SUPPLIER
	INK	IBM

YIELDS

ZZZ	THING	XXX
	STATIONERY	FLIC
	STATIONERY	CHEMCO
	HOUSEHOLD	PENCRAFT
	STATIONERY	PENCRAFT
	⋮	⋮

ZZZ	THING	XXX
	P. TOY	P. IBM

Figure 11-10. Retrieval of collected output from multiple tables.
(Copyright 1977 International Business Machines. Reprinted with permission)

EMP	NAME	SAL
	P.	S1
	JONES	S2
	NELSON	S3

YIELDS

EMP	NAME
	HOFFMAN

CONDITIONS
S1 > (S2 + S3)

Figure 11-11. Use of Condition box.
(Copyright 1977 International Business Machines. Reprinted with permission)

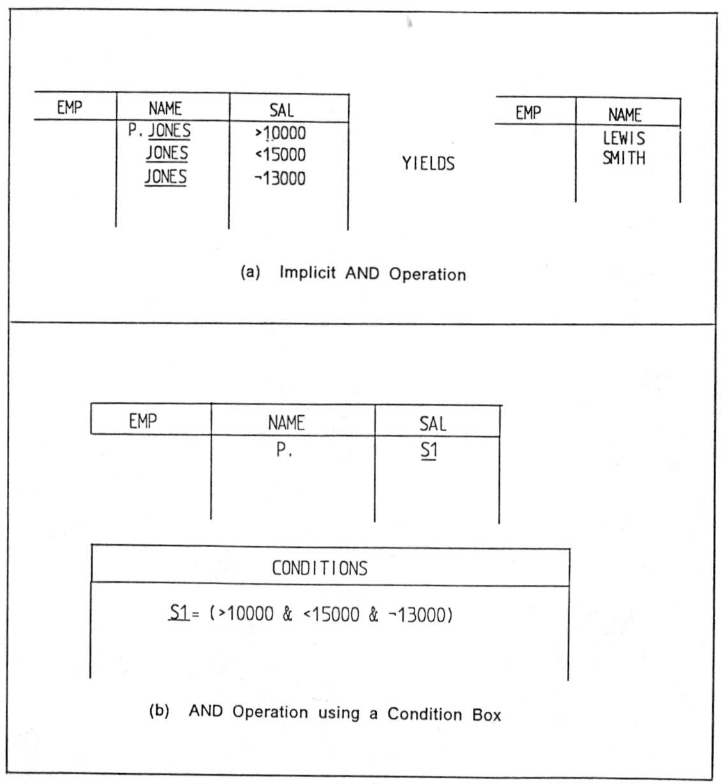

EMP
NAME
SAL
P. JONES
JONES
JONES
>10000
<15000
¬13000
YIELDS
EMP
NAME
LEWIS
SMITH
(a) Implicit AND Operation
EMP
NAME
SAL
P.
S1
CONDITIONS
S1= (>10000 & <15000 & ¬13000)
(b) AND Operation using a Condition Box

Figure 11-12. Examples of AND operations.
(Copyright 1977 International Business Machines. Reprinted with permission)

EMP	NAME	SAL
	P. JONES	10000
	P. LEWIS	13000
	P. HENRY	16000

YIELDS

EMP	NAME
	MORGAN
	HOFFMAN

Figure 11-13. Implicit OR operation.
(Copyright 1977 International Business Machines. Reprinted with permission)

Built-In Functions and the ALL. Operator

There are six built-in functions in QBE. They are CNT. (count), SUM. (sum), AVG. (average), MAX. (maximum), MIN. (minimum), and UN. (unique). These functions operate on sets of values specified by the ALL. operator. The ALL. represents a "multiset," i.e., a set that retains duplicates. Examples consist of the following:

Figure 11-14: Print the sum of the salaries of employees in the TOY department.

Figure 11-15: Print the names of departments that have more than three employees. Note that, in this example, grouping is accomplished by double underlining TOY for an explicit "group by" operator. In a later version, G. is used as the "group by" operator.

Insertions, Deletions, and Updates

Insertions (I.), deletions (D.) and updates (U.) are done in the same style as query (P.) operations. Examples consist of the following:

Figure 11-16: Insert into the EMP table a new employee of the TOY department whose name is JONES, whose salary is 10000 and whose manager is HENRY.

Figure 11-17: Delete all employees of the TOY department from the EMP table.

Figure 11-18: Update HENRY's salary to 50000.

Figure 11-19: Insert into the EMP table an employee named HENRY in the TOY department, whose manager is LEE and whose salary is the same as that of LEWIS.

Figure 11-20: Delete all employees who work in departments that sell pens.

EMP	NAME	SAL	DEPT
		P. SUM ALL. S1	TOY

YIELDS

EMP	SAL SUM
	21000

Figure 11-14. Qualified retrieval using built-in function.

EMP	NAME	DEPT
	ALL. JONES	P. TOY

YIELDS

SALES	DEPT
	STATIONERY

CONDITIONS
CNT. ALL. JONES > 3

Figure 11-15. A condition on the set of items.

EMP	NAME	SAL	MGR	DEPT
I.	JONES	10000	HENRY	TOY

Figure 11-16. Simple insertion.

EMP	NAME	SAL	MGR	DEPT
D.				TOY

Figure 11-17. Simple deletion.
(Copyright 1977 International Business Machines. Reprinted with permission)

EMP	NAME	SAL	MGR	DEPT
U.	HENRY	50000		

Figure 11-18. Simple update.
(Copyright 1977 International Business Machines. Reprinted with permission)

EMP	NAME	SAL	MGR	DEPT
I.	HENRY	S1	LEE	TOY
	LEWIS	S1		

Figure 11-19. Query dependent insertion.
(Copyright 1977 International Business Machines. Reprinted with permission)

EMP	NAME	SAL	MGR	DEPT
D.				D1

SALES	DEPT	ITEM
	D1	PEN

Figure 11-20. Query dependent deletion.
(Copyright 1977 International Business Machines. Reprinted with permission)

Table Creation

So far, we have discussed how a user can retrieve information from existing tables or modify the contents of existing tables. But before any of these operations can be done, tables used for the operations must have been created.

Creation of a table consists of two steps. First, the table must be defined. Then data must be inserted.

To define a table, one starts with a table skeleton, and then fills in the table name, column headings, and attributes of the data. For example, to create a new table with table name EMP and column headings NAME, SAL, MGR and DEPT, the user fills in the headings by inserting the field names as shown in Figure 11-21. The I. on the right of EMP refers to the whole row of column headings.

"Row attributes" are used to describe the data. The user can ask for the names of the row attributes as shown in Figure 11-22. The result is a display (Figure 11-23) showing the row attribute names for data types, length of the fields, primary keys, name of the underlying domain, and the optional null symbol (Figure 11-23). The user then defines the attributes by filling in the corresponding rows, as shown in Figure 11-24.

Having specified the table definition, the user can enter data into the table by insertion as described in the previous section. The new table is a base

I. EMP I.	NAME	SAL	MGR	DEPT

Figure 11-21. Creation of Headings.
(Copyright 1977 International Business Machines. Reprinted with permission)

I. EMP I.	NAME	SAL	MGR	DEPT
P. XX				

Figure 11-22. Retrieval of attribute names.
(Copyright 1977 International Business Machines. Reprinted with permission)

EMP	NAME	SAL	MGR	DEPT
TYPE				
LENGTH				
KEY				
DOMAIN				
SYS NULL				

Figure 11-23. Display of attribute names.
(Copyright 1977 International Business Machines. Reprinted with permission)

EMP	NAME	SAL	MGR	DEPT
TYPE I.	CHAR	FLOAT	CHAR	CHAR
LENGTH I.	20	B	20	12
KEY I.	K	NK	NK	NK
DOMAIN I.	NAMES	MONEY	NAMES	DEPARTMENTS
SYS NULL I.		—	—	—

Figure 11-24. Definition of row attributes.
(Copyright 1977 International Business Machines. Reprinted with permission)

table stored in the QBE database. Queries may then be formulated against the table.

Recall that the result of a query is displayed, but not stored. The user can create a "snapshot" table (i.e., one that contains collected data from various tables at a particular point in time) or a dynamic "view" of data collected from various tables, in a fashion similar to the creation of a new table.

Extensions to Office Activities: QBE/OBE and QBE/PC

QBE offers a convenient way for a user with little or no previous programming training to get information from existing tables. QBE/OBE[11] and QBE/PC[12] represent the more recent efforts that aim to extend the concepts of QBE to include office activities such as word processing, report writing, graphic presentations, and electronic mail.

Both QBE/OBE and QBE/PC follow the two-dimensional programming style of QBE. The object domain, however, is extended beyond that of tables. It includes menus, reports, charts, and graphs. These objects are used in a manner similar to that of the relational tables of QBE. Programming is accomplished by placing operators in selected areas within the objects, and example elements are used to link data from one object to another.

For example, suppose that manager LEE wishes to send a letter to each of his employees informing them of his pending vacation. The names and locations of LEE's employees must be extracted from the EMP table and placed in the body of the letter. This is achieved by mapping appropriate example elements in much the same way that data is mapped from one table to another. After the letter is composed, the distribution of the letters is achieved by an S. command, using an example element, N, as a destination address. The program is shown in Figure 11-25.

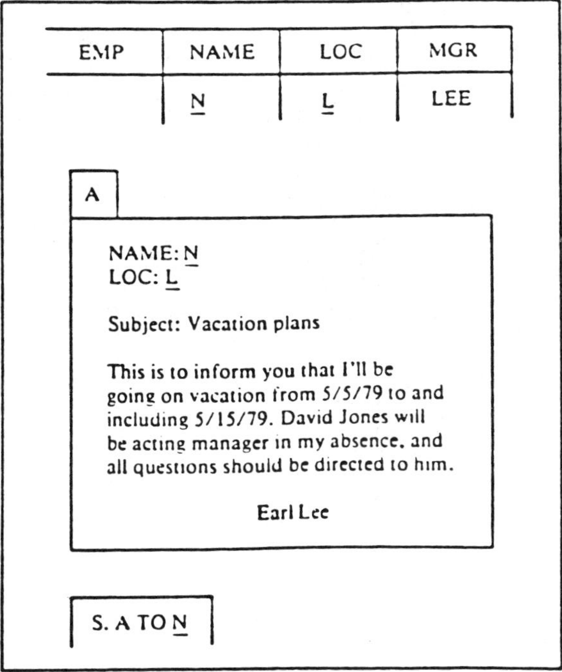

Figure 11-25. An object distribution program. (Zloof[11], © 1981 IEEE.)

As another example, suppose we want a horizontal bar graph displaying hardware and software sales for the year 1986. All required information exist in a database table named SALES. Figure 11-26 illustrates how the graph can be generated. Because the table contains the sales data for each quarter, the graph plots the sums of the hardware and software sales grouped by state over the quarters of the year 1986. The G._ST example element expression in the bar chart specifies the variable for the vertical axis, along which bars are drawn. The SUM._HW and the SUM._SW example element expressions specify the variables whose values determine the bar length. For each state there will be a hardware sales bar and a software sales bar.

Extension to Pictorial Data: Query by Pictorial Example (QPE)

The popularity of QBE has led to the design of a query language, based on QBE, for *IMAID*, an integrated image analysis and image database management system.[13]

IMAID is a relational database system interfaced with an image analysis

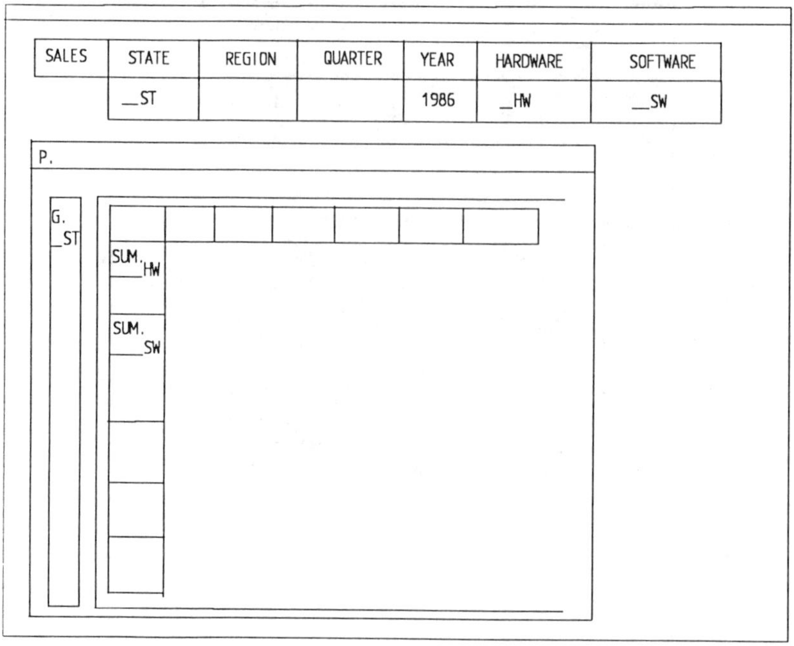

SALES	STATE	REGION	QUARTER	YEAR	HARDWARE	SOFTWARE
	_ST			1986	_HW	_SW

P.

G.
_ST

SUM.
_HW

SUM.
_SW

Figure 11-26. Using example elements to map data from a table to a bar graph.

system. By using pattern recognition and image processing *(PRIP)* functions, pictorial descriptions are extracted from earth resources satellite (Landsat) images. These pictorial descriptions (i.e., line drawings or sketches of pictures) and inherent registrations of pictures can then be converted into relations. The original images are kept in a separate picture store.

If a user's query can be satisfied by the relational database, there is no need to retrieve and process the original pictures, thus reducing the need to process vast amounts of imagery data. If, on the other hand, the extracted picture descriptions are not sufficient, images from the picture store can be retrieved and processed.

As an example, Figure 11-27 shows a picture sketch (a road map) that resulted from applying the pattern recognition and image processing functions to Landsat images.[13]

Five relations (shown in Figure 11-28) are constructed to represent the pictorial data. The *ROADS* and *CITIES* relations are defined on the same attributes that specify the frame number, the identification number, and the x-y coordinates of the two endpoints of each line segment. The ROADS relation is constructed from Landsat images, while the CITIES relation is constructed from digitized maps. The names of roads and cities are defined

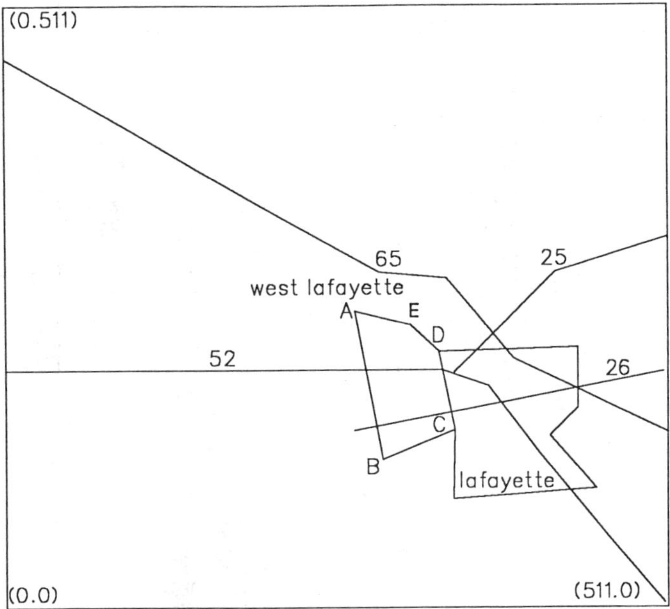

Figure 11-27. Simplified map of Lafayette and West Lafayette. (Chang and Fu[13]. © 1981 IEEE.)

interactively in the relations *RONAME* and *CINAME*, respectively. The *POS* relation stores the inherent registration information of an image. It specifies the frame number, the x-y coordinates of the center, and the location of the stored image.

On the simplified map (Figure 11-27), West Lafayette is bounded by the line segments AB, BC, CD, DE, and EA. They are represented by the first five tuples in the relation CITIES of Figure 11-28. The remaining TUPLES in CITIES describe the boundaries of Lafayette.

QPE is the query language proposed for IMAID. The tabular query formulation, introduced in QBE, is adopted in QPE. A set of pictorial operators is added to handle the spatial relationships among various picture objects.

At the time of the Chang and Fu article,[13] QPE was in its development stage. Figure 11-29 lists the pictorial operators. The letters attached to the end of the name of a pictorial operator denote the type of required operands. P, L, and R stands for point, line, and region relations, respectively. The required operands of pictorial operators are sets of segments. Their results are also sets of line segments. The operators can be used in the same manner as other relations.

The following examples, extracted from Chang and Fu,[13] illustrate the flavor of QPE.

CITIES

FRAME	CIID	X1	Y1	X2	Y2
301	1	243	261	260	163
301	1	260	163	312	180
301	1	312	180	301	232
301	1	301	232	283	256
301	1	283	256	243	261
301	2	301	231	312	183
301	2	312	183	315	120
301	2	315	120	431	119
301	2	431	119	391	160
301	2	391	160	423	185
301	2	423	185	409	238
301	2	409	238	301	231

CINAME

FRAME	CIID	NAME
301	1	WEST LAFAYETTE
301	2	LAFAYETTE

ROADS

FRAME	ROID	X1	Y1	X2	Y2
301	1	0	482	290	294
301	1	290	294	329	286
301	1	329	286	380	223
301	1	380	223	463	172
301	1	463	172	504	134
301	2	0	243	296	223
301	2	296	223	332	221
301	2	332	221	361	209
301	2	361	209	388	152
301	2	388	152	490	22
301	3	340	219	402	277
301	3	402	277	507	316
301	4	235	191	400	195
301	4	400	195	508	204

RONAME

FRAME	ROID	NAME
301	1	65
301	2	52
301	3	26
301	4	25

POS

FRAME	XSIZE	YSIZE	XCEN	YCEN	LOC
301	512	512	1792	256	/PIX/301

Figure 11-28. Relations of Figure 11-27. (Chang and Fu[13]. © 1981 IEEE.)

- Pictorial union of two given regions: UNION-RR.
- Pictorial intersection of two given regions: INT-RR.
- Pictorial intersection of a given region and a given line: INT-LR.
- Pictorial intersection of a given region and a given point: INT-PR.
- Pictorial intersection of two given lines: INT-LL.
- Pictorial union of two given lines: UNION-LL.
- Construct a line to connect a given point and its nearest point in a given region: LINE-PR.
- Construct a line with the minimum distance from a point to a given line: LINE-PL.
- Construct a line to connect the two nearest points in two given regions: LINE-RR.
- Extract a line from a given line between two given points: LINE-PPL.
- Construct a point as the center of a given line: POINT-L.
- Construct a point as the center of the boundary of a given region: POINT-R.

Figure 11-29. Pictorial operators in QPE.
(Chang and Fu[13]. © 1981 IEEE.)

Figure 11-30: Print the names of roads that appear in the same frame as the city of Lafayette.

Figure 11-31: Find the portion of Interstate Highway 65 that is enclosed within the city boundaries of Lafayette. Note that, in this example, R1 is an intermediate result table for all the boundary segments of Lafayette. L1 is an intermediate result table for all the road segments of Interstate Highway 65. The result is in the L2 relation, established through the pictorial operator INT-LR (L1, R1), which uses relations L1 and R1 to construct the intersection of a set of lines and a set of region boundaries. The resulting relation L2 is defined on the default domains X1, Y1, X2, and Y2.

These examples illustrate how a two-dimensional programming language may be used to query pictorial data. They also bring out another point. Since QPE is based on the approaches of QBE, it inherits both the strong and weak points of QBE. While the concepts underlying QBE (and other relational

CINAME	FRAME	CIID	NAME
	10		LAFAYETTE

RONAME	FRAME	ROID	NAME
	10		P.MAIN

Figure 11-30. Print the names of roads that appear in the same frame as the city of Lafayette. (Chang and Fu[13]. © 1981 IEEE.)

CINAME	FRAME	CIID	NAME
	3	5	LAFAYETTE

CITIES	FRAME	CIID	X1	Y1	X2	Y2
	3	5	X	Y	Z	W

R1	X1	Y1	X2	Y2
	X	Y	Z	W

RONAME	FRAME	ROID	NAME
	4	7	65

ROADS	FRAME	ROID	X1	Y1	X2	Y2
	4	7	S	T	U	V

L1	X1	Y1	X2	Y2
	S	T	U	V

L2 = INT-LR(L1,R1)

Figure 11-31. Find the portion of Interstate Highway 65 that is enclosed within city boundaries of Lafayette.
(Chang and Fu[13]. © 1981 IEEE.)

systems, for that matter) are simple, the queries become complicated when more than two tables must be cross-referenced.

FORMANAGER

The goal of FORMANAGER[3] is to design and develop an office information system on the basis of forms which would provide the user with:

- Interactive application design using forms (application, in FORMANAGER, means data retrieval, update, insertion, deletion, and computation based on current values in a form, e.g., totals).
- A hierarchical *view* of data presented to the user within forms.
- Access to an underlying relational database system with a relationally complete query capability.
- Multipage-screen user interface and menu-driven forms processing.

A *form,* in FORMANAGER, is different from a *table.* A table is an entity stored in the database. A form has the appearance of a paper form. The body of a form generally contains background text and blank positions called *fields.* Data for these fields may be contained in one or more tables.

Form Design

A person who interacts with FORMANAGER is either a form designer or an application user. (Of course, it is possible that a person might play different roles at different times.) Before a form is used by an application user, the appearance and processing capabilities of a form must be *specified* by a form designer. Specification consists of a form schema *and* a form template.

A *form schema* is composed of *field definitions.* Each field is defined by a name, a position on the form, a domain (which determines the type of data values, the length of the field, and whether repeating values are allowed on the form), and a field specification (which defines the relationship of the field to the data in the underlying tables and determines whether the field is a search field, a display field, or an entry field for input and update).

The remainder of the form is described by the *form template.* The template contains the fixed text, graphics, and special nondatabase fields (e.g., page number) that appear on the form.

The Specification Process

A form is specified interactively by the form designer. The specification process involves two stages:

1. Define the structural layout (form syntax), using a full screen editor.
2. Define the form semantics (discussed below) by responding to a series of questions.

Figure 11-32 illustrates the *syntax* structure of an example form. A field is delimited by a pair of brackets and can contain a search, display, or computation value. Fields for a repeating group are denoted by a field name followed by a period and a digit which indicates the occurrence of the repetition. If data retrieved have more instances than those provided in a form, the user is allowed to leaf through a multipage form display.

```
PAGE [page    ]                                              DATE: [idate ]

                              ABC INC.
                           9999 Main Street
                         Los Angeles, CA 90025


                            I N V O I C E
                                 for
                     ORDER NUMBER  [orderno   ]

        S   [custname    ]                      S   [shname      ]
        O   [custaddr    ]                      H   [shaddr      ]
        L   [custcity    ]                      I   [shcity      ]
        D                                       P

        T                                       T
        O   [custphon    ]                      O   [shphon      ]

CUSTOMER NUMBER:    [custno     ]

===========================================================================
 ITEM |  PART NO. |      QTY      | DESCRIPTION   |  UNIT $   |  AMOUNT
---------------------------------------------------------------------------
  1   | [pt.1   ] | [qt.1      ] | [it.1        ] | [pr.1   ] | [am.1        ]
  2   | [pt.2   ] | [qt.2      ] | [it.2        ] | [pr.2   ] | [am.2        ]
  3   | [pt.3   ] | [qt.3      ] | [it.3        ] | [pr.3   ] | [am.3        ]
  4   | [pt.4   ] | [qt.4      ] | [it.4        ] | [pr.4   ] | [am.4        ]
  5   | [pt.5   ] | [qt.5      ] | [it.5        ] | [pr.5   ] | [am.5        ]
  6   | [pt.6   ] | [qt.6      ] | [it.6        ] | [pr.6   ] | [am.6        ]
  7   | [pt.7   ] | [qt.7      ] | [it.7        ] | [pr.7   ] | [am.7        ]
  8   | [pt.8   ] | [qt.8      ] | [it.8        ] | [pr.8   ] | [am.8        ]
---------------------------------------------------------------------------

                                         SUB-TOTAL ====> | [sub-tot    ]
                                               TAX ====> | [tax        ]
---------------------------------------------------------------------------

                                             TOTAL ====> | [total      ]

===========================================================================
```

Figure 11-32. An INVOICE form.

The *semantics* for each field are specified through a dialog. Each field must be mapped to certain database attributes or other form fields to define its contents. The specification of a field involves defining the field types and the field actions. The *field type* defines the usage of the field in the form application. A field can be used for one or more of the following functions: search, display, or entry. A *field action* describes the ways in which a user can perform an action on the underlying database. An *input* action enables new data to be added to a database table. An *update* action causes data to be entered into a database table to replace existing data.

FORMANAGER translates all insert and update actions into the appropriate *SQL* commands[14] on the underlying database tables.

Relating data values over several database tables is done by specifying multiple table.field names for a field on a form. For example, the field orderno in the INVOICE form would be specified as

ORDER.ono, PARTLIST.ono.

Once a form specification is complete, FORMANAGER stores it in a directory for later use. Form operations are translated into relational queries in SQL. In the example, the INVOICE form specifications would be transformed into the SQL query shown in Figure 11-33.

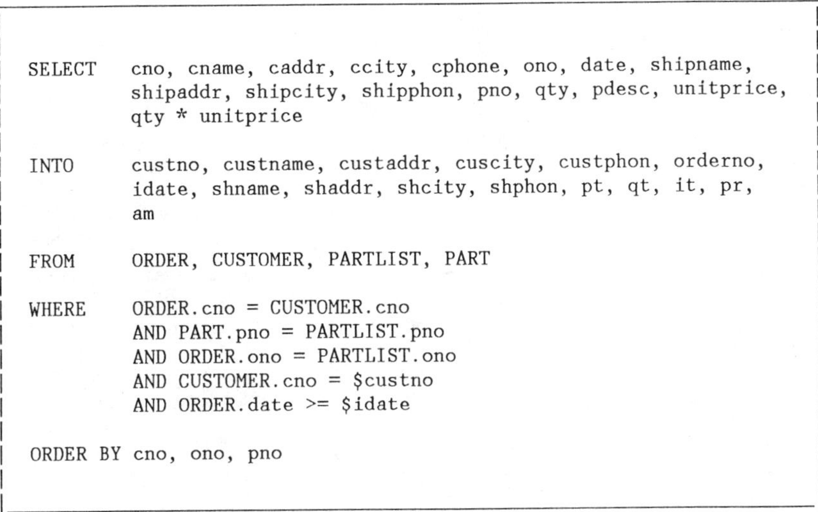

```
SELECT    cno, cname, caddr, ccity, cphone, ono, date, shipname,
          shipaddr, shipcity, shipphon, pno, qty, pdesc, unitprice,
          qty * unitprice

INTO      custno, custname, custaddr, cuscity, custphon, orderno,
          idate, shname, shaddr, shcity, shphon, pt, qt, it, pr,
          am

FROM      ORDER, CUSTOMER, PARTLIST, PART

WHERE     ORDER.cno = CUSTOMER.cno
          AND PART.pno = PARTLIST.pno
          AND ORDER.ono = PARTLIST.ono
          AND CUSTOMER.cno = $custno
          AND ORDER.date >= $idate

ORDER BY cno, ono, pno
```

Figure 11-33. SQL query transformed from INVOICE form.

```
PAGE 1                                                DATE: 1/1/84

                        ABC INC.
                    9999 Main Street
                  Los Angeles, CA 90025

                     I N V O I C E
                          for
                ORDER NUMBER  __________

    S  __________                S  __________
    O  __________                H  __________
    L  __________                I  __________
    D                            P

    T                            T
    O  __________                O  __________

CUSTOMER NUMBER:   C0103______

==========================================================================
ITEM | PART NO. |    QTY    | DESCRIPTION | UNIT $ |  AMOUNT
--------------------------------------------------------------------------
  1  | _______  | ________  | __________  | ______ | _________
  2  | _______  | ________  | __________  | ______ | _________
  3  | _______  | ________  | __________  | ______ | _________
  4  | _______  | ________  | __________  | ______ | _________
  5  | _______  | ________  | __________  | ______ | _________
  6  | _______  | ________  | __________  | ______ | _________
  7  | _______  | ________  | __________  | ______ | _________
  8  | _______  | ________  | __________  | ______ | _________
--------------------------------------------------------------------------
                                     SUB-TOTAL ====> | _________
                                           TAX ====> | _________
--------------------------------------------------------------------------
                                         TOTAL ====> | _________
==========================================================================

Enter the customer number for the order invoices that you wish to view.
(Default is all customers.)

Enter the starting date for the order invoices you wish to view.
(Default is all invoices.)
--------------------------------------------------------------------------
```

Figure 11-34. Enter search keys into application.

The Processing Phase—Query Execution and Form Display

An application user interacts with FORMANAGER through an interactive screen interface. The appropriate forms for the application are presented to the user, who enters input values into certain fields. Figure 11-34 shows the screen format for a query application. In this example, the user has entered the customer number (custno) "C0103" and the starting date (idate) "1/1/84" as search variables.

The user_supplied search data are placed into the defined SQL query structure (Figure 11-33) for the data retrieval. The variable $custno is set to the value C0103 and $idate is set to the value 1/1/84 in the SQL query. This query is then sent to the database system for execution. The result of this query is placed in a relational table (see Figure 11-35).

custno	custname	orderno	idate	shname	pt	qt	it	pr	am
C0103	C. Johnson	32094	08/01/84	S. Norris	124	1	Daisy printer	2100.00	2100.00
C0103	C. Johnson	32094	08/01/84	S. Norris	130	1	Line printer	1250.00	1250.00
C0103	C. Johnson	32094	08/01/84	S. Norris	168	2	CRT terminal	750.00	1500.00
C0103	C. Johnson	32094	08/01/84	S. Norris	123	2	Smart modem	270.00	540.00
C0103	C. Johnson	32128	10/07/84	R. Thomas	124	1	Daisy printer	2100.00	2100.00
C0103	C. Johnson	32128	10/07/84	R. Thomas	123	1	Smart modem	270.00	270.00

Figure 11-35. The result table for the INVOICE application.

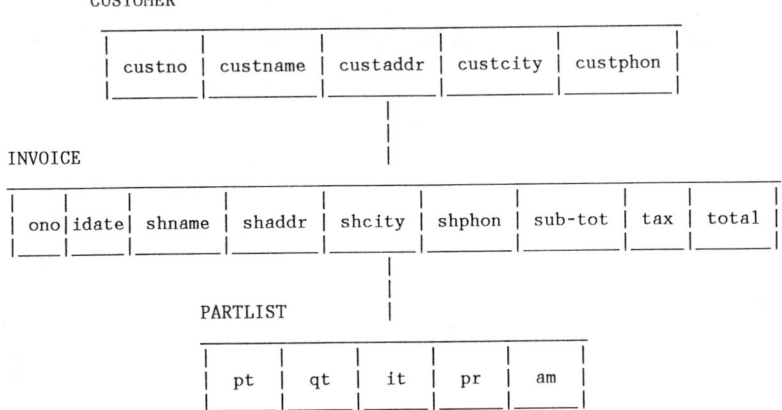

Figure 11-36. The hierarchical schema of INVOICE form.

The next step is to map the result table into the hierarchical form schema (Figure 11-36). This is easily accomplished since the tuples in the result table are ordered by the keys of a repeating group in its parent level.

The final processing step is to display the results on the user's screen. This is shown in Figure 11-37.

PAGE 1 DATE: Aug.1,1984

ABC INC.
9999 Main Street
Los Angeles, CA 90025

I N V O I C E
for
ORDER NUMBER *32094*

SOLD TO		SHIP TO	
	C. Johnson 7373 Baltimore Ave., #4 College Park, MD 20740 (301) 927-2249		S. Norris 4638 King Str. Columbus, OH 43210 (614) 384-6970

CUSTOMER NUMBER: *C0103*

ITEM	PART NO.	QTY	DESCRIPTION	UNIT $	AMOUNT
1	124	1	Daisy printer	2100.00	2100.00
2	130	1	Line printer	1250.00	1250.00
3	168	2	CRT terminal	750.00	1500.00
4	123	2	Smart modem	270.00	540.00

SUB-TOTAL ====> | 5390.00
TAX ====> | 269.50

TOTAL ====> | 5659.50

Figure 11-37. The screen display of the result INVOICE form.

FORMAL

FORMAL is an experimental application development system implemented at the IBM Los Angeles Scientific Center.[4]

Unlike QBE and FORMANAGER, whose primary interest is to simplify the means of entering, querying and maintaining data in relational database systems, FORMAL aims to provide powerful data manipulation capabilities, simply and usefully, so that a wide range of data processing applications can be programmed by people without intensive training. The emphasis on *powerful data manipulation* capabilities is motivated by the following observations.

First, while relational tables are simple and easy to comprehend, queries quickly become cumbersome and complicated when data must be retrieved from more than two tables. To support the one-to-many relationships common in the business world (e.g., a sales department has many employees and sells many items, and its physical location may be spread over a number of floors), a general hierarchical data structure would be more efficient (and less cumbersome in many cases) than the relational views.

Second, while query facilities are useful on many occasions, they are not adequate to satisfy the needs of many other applications. For example, one might want to have derived data, have arithmetic and string functions performed on the data, or have case-by-case treatment of instances, depending on the value of the instances.

Third, information processing generally involves data transformation or restructuring. When data are extracted from sources or new fields are created and placed in the output, the resulting output structure is often different (sometimes drastically different) from the structures of the sources. Systems based on relational tables are not equipped to perform data restructuring other than projection and joining of flat tables. To accommodate applications of a broader scope, it is important to have a simple yet general mechanism to support data restructuring of a more complex nature.

To address these issues, FORMAL takes a forms-oriented approach. There are several reasons for taking this approach. The most important one is the result of a close examination of the nonprogrammers' information processing needs, which reveals that much of the data manipulation can be naturally expressed or thought of as forms processing.

Like many other form-based systems, FORMAL uses the familiar task of filling in forms as a means of user-system communication. But more important, FORMAL capitalizes on the user's familiarity with forms in two significant ways: (1) Stylized forms are used as visual representations of data structures and data instances. (2) The programs themselves are also represented in forms. These points are elaborated in the following discussion.

Forms as Visual Representation of Data

FORMAL uses stylized form headings as visual representations of data structures. As an example, Figure 11-38 shows the form heading and a few instances of PERSON data.

In a *form heading,* the form name is placed on the top line. The names of the first-level components (i.e., fields or groups) are shown in columns under

```
I--------------------------------------------------------------------------|
I                               (PERSON)                                   |
I--------------------------------------------------------------------------|
IENO|DNO|  NAME   |PHONE|JC|  (KIDS)     |        (SCHOOL)          |SEX|LOC|
I   |   |         |     |  |-------------|--------------------------|   |   |
I   |   |         |     |  | KNAME  |AGE| SNAME   |   (ENROLL)     |   |   |
I   |   |         |     |  |        |   |         |----------------|   |   |
I   |   |         |     |  |        |   |         |YEARIN|YEAROUT  |   |   |
I==========================================================================|
I05 |D1 |SMITH    |5555 |05|JOHN    |02 |PRINCETON|1966  |1970     |F  |SF |
I   |   |         |     |  |MARY    |04 |         |1972  |1976     |   |   |
I--------------------------------------------------------------------------|
I05 |D1 |SMITH    |5555 |05|JANE    |01 |         |      |         |F  |SF |
I--------------------------------------------------------------------------|
I07 |D1 |JONES    |5555 |05|DICK    |07 |SJS      |1960  |1965     |F  |SF |
I   |   |         |     |  |JANE    |04 |--------------------------|   |   |
I   |   |         |     |  |        |   |BERKELEY |1965  |1969     |   |   |
I--------------------------------------------------------------------------|
I11 |D1 |ENGEL    |2568 |05|        |   |UCLA     |1970  |1974     |F  |LA |
I--------------------------------------------------------------------------|
I12 |D1 |DURAN    |7610 |05|MARY    |08 |         |      |         |M  |SF |
I   |   |         |     |  |BOB     |10 |         |      |         |   |   |
I   |   |         |     |  |JOHN    |12 |         |      |         |   |   |
I--------------------------------------------------------------------------|
I18 |D1 |LEWIS    |6673 |05|HIM     |02 |STANFORD |1940  |1944     |M  |LA |
I   |   |         |     |  |HER     |05 |         |      |         |   |   |
I--------------------------------------------------------------------------|
I19 |D1 |HOPE     |3150 |07|MARYLOU |10 |         |      |         |M  |SJ |
I   |   |         |     |  |MARYANN |07 |         |      |         |   |   |
I--------------------------------------------------------------------------|
I02 |D2 |GREEN    |1111 |01|RON     |15 |         |      |         |M  |SF |
I   |   |         |     |  |DAVID   |04 |         |      |         |   |   |
I--------------------------------------------------------------------------|
I20 |D2 |CHU      |3348 |10|CHARLIE |06 |HONGKONG |1962  |1966     |F  |LA |
I   |   |         |     |  |CHRIS   |09 |--------------------------|   |   |
I   |   |         |     |  |BONNIE  |04 |STANFORD |1967  |1969     |   |   |
I   |   |         |     |  |        |   |         |1972  |1975     |   |   |
I--------------------------------------------------------------------------|
I21 |D2 |DWAN     |3535 |12|        |   |USC      |1970  |1974     |F  |SJ |
I--------------------------------------------------------------------------|
I           .                                                              |
I           .                                                              |
I           .                                                              |
I                                                                          |
I--------------------------------------------------------------------------|
```

Figure 11-38. Form heading and a few instances of PERSON form. (Shu[4], © 1985 IEEE.)

the form name. The names of components of groups, in turn, are placed under the associated group names. Groups can be either repeating or nonrepeating. A "nonrepeating group" refers to a collection of consecutive fields (e.g., DATE as a nonrepeating group over MONTH, DAY, and YEAR). A repeating group may have multiple instances and is denoted by a pair of parentheses over the group name. Repeating groups can be nested (representing several levels of a branch) or in parallel (representing several branches of a tree). A double line signals the end of a form heading.

The form heading represents a convenient way to *precisely* describe a hierarchical structure *of arbitrary depth and width.* A relational table is simply a *flat form* of no repeating groups, i.e., a one-level hierarchy.

To view the data, values are displayed under the form heading. The compactness of the form heading enables the visualization of many instances at a time. This property is advantageous in the application development environment. Unlike the office environment, where instances of forms are sent, received, and handled one at a time, data processing applications require the handling of a collection of instances.

Form Process

In general, a data processing activity can be expressed as a form process (or a series of form processes), where each form process takes one or two forms as input and produces another form as output. As an example, Figure 11-39 shows a form process that transforms a PRODUCT form into a VENDPROD form.

A FORMAL program consists of one or more form specifications. Each *form specification* either defines a form or specifies a form process. In either case, the form heading plays an important role.

Define a Form

To define a form, the user starts with the form heading of the form being defined and completes the description by filling in datatypes of each field, and optionally also information on whether a field is a key field or an order field. As an example, see Figure 11-40(a), where a PROJECT form is defined. A few instances of PROJECT are shown in Figure 11-40(b).

DATA_TYPE describes the type of data of a field. Fixed- or variable-length character strings and numbers with or without a decimal point are acceptable data types.

KEY denotes a field (or a collection of fields) whose value uniquely identifies an instance within a form or within a group. For the PROJECT form in Figure 11-40, DNO uniquely identifies the PROJECT form instances. Within a given form instance (identified by a DNO), P JNO is the unique

```
I-----------------------------------------------------------|
I                       (PRODUCT)                           |
I-----------------------------------------------------------|
I          |        |        |(SUPPLIER)| (STORAGE)   |      |
I PROD_NO  | PNAME  | TYPE   |----------|------|-----|PRICE |
I          |        |        |  VNAME   |BIN_NO| LOC  |      |
I==========|========|========|==========|======|=====|======|
I   110    | PIPE   | PVC    | AQUA     |  B1  | SJC | 0.79 |
I          |        |        | CHEMTRON |  B2  | SJC |      |
I          |        |        |          |  B3  | SFO |      |
I-----------------------------------------------------------|
I   120    | PIPE   | STEEL| ABC       |  B4  | SFO | 4.10  |
I          |        |      | CHEMTRON  |      |     |       |
I-----------------------------------------------------------|
I   210    | VALVE  | STEEL| AQUA      |  B5  | SJC | 0.45  |
I          |        |      | ABC       |  B6  | SFO |       |
I          |        |      | CHEMTRON  |      |     |       |
I-----------------------------------------------------------|
I   221    | VALVE  |COPPER| ABC       |  B7  | SJC | 1.25  |
I          |        |      | CHEMTRON  |  B8  | SFO |       |
I          |        |      | ROBINSON  |      |     |       |
I-----------------------------------------------------------|
                             |
                             |
                             |
                             V
I-------------------------------------------------------------|
I                       (VENDPROD)                            |
I------------------|------------------------------------------|
I                  |                 (PROD)                   |
I      VNAME       |------------|------------|-------------|
I                  |  PROD_NO   |    TYPE    |    PNAME    |
I==================|============|============|=============|
I  ABC             |    120     |   STEEL    |   PIPE      |
I                  |    210     |   STEEL    |   VALVE     |
I                  |    221     |   COPPER   |   VALVE     |
I------------------|------------|------------|-------------|
I  AQUA            |    110     |   PVC      |   PIPE      |
I                  |    210     |   STEEL    |   VALVE     |
I------------------|------------|------------|-------------|
I  CHEMTRON        |    110     |   PVC      |   PIPE      |
I                  |    120     |   STEEL    |   PIPE      |
I                  |    210     |   STEEL    |   VALVE     |
I                  |    221     |   COPPER   |   VALVE     |
I------------------|------------|------------|-------------|
I  ROBINSON        |    221     |   COPPER   |   VALVE     |
I------------------|------------|------------|-------------|
```

Figure 11-39. Example of a Form process.
(Shu[4], © 1985 IEEE.)

identifier of the repeating PROJ instances; and within each PROJ instance, NAME is the unique identifier of the EQUIP instances.

ORDER specifies the ordering of instances within a form or ordering of group instances within a parent instance. Order direction is represented by ASC or DES (for ascending or descending, respectively). When there is more than one significant sort field, the order direction can be followed by

```
DEFINE PROJECT

          I--------------------------------------------|
          I                 (PROJECT)                  |
          I--------------------------------------------|
          I      |     |            (PROJ)             |
          I DNO  | MGR |-------------------------------|
          I      |     | PJNO |     (EQUIP)     | COST |
          I      |     |      |-----------------|      |
          I      |     |      |  NAME  | USAGE  |      |
==========I======|=====|======|========|========|======|
DATA_TYPE I CH(2)|CH(6)| CH(4)| CHV(8) | NUM(2) |NUM(8)|
----------I------|-----|------|--------|--------|------|
KEY       I  Y   |     |  Y   |  Y     |        |      |
----------I------|-----|------|--------|--------|------|
ORDER     I  ASC |     | ASC  |                        |
----------I------|-----|------|--------|--------|------|
END
```

(a). Example of defining a form

```
I----------------------------------------|
I                (PROJECT)               |
I----------------------------------------|
IDNO| MGR  |           (PROJ)            |
I   |      |-----------------------------|
I   |      |PJNO|    (EQUIP)     | COST  |
I   |      |    |----------------|       |
I   |      |    | NAME    |USAGE|        |
I========================================|
ID1 |112340| P11| ABCD    | 50  | 10000  |
I   |      |    | CDE     | 40  |        |
I   |      |---------------------|-------|
I   |      | P12| XXXX    | 60  |  5000  |
I----------------------------------------|
ID2 |204550| P12| XXXX    | 30  | 72500  |
I   |      |----|---------|-----|--------|
I   |      | P22| ACE     | 50  | 54560  |
I   |      |    | CDE     | 20  |        |
I   |      |    | XYZ     | 25  |        |
I----------------------------------------|
ID3 |301302| P31| XYZ     | 40  | 12450  |
I   |      |    | ABC     | 75  |        |
I   |      |    | ABCDE   | 25  |        |
I----------------------------------------|
ID5 |555555| P51| ABC     | 30  | 12345  |
I   |      |    | DUMMY   | 50  |        |
I----------------------------------------|
IDX |      | PXX|   ?     |     |        |
I----------------------------------------|
```

(b) Example of PROJECT data

Figure 11-40. Example of defining a form and sample data. (Shu[4], © 1985 IEEE.)

a digit (e.g., ASC 1) to indicate the relative significance of the associated sort fields.

A skeleton program for defining a form is shown in Figure 11-41(a).

Specify a Form Process

To specify a form process, one starts with the form heading of the desired output form and completes a program by specifying a few relevant properties within the outline of a form. Figure 11-41(b) depicts a skeleton specification presented to the user when the user indicated that he wishes to describe a form process.

```
(a).  DEFINE xxxxxxx

                I---------------------------------------------|
                I                  (xxxxxxx)                  |
                I---------------------------------------------|
                I                                             |
                I          ( complete form heading here )     |
                I                                             |
      ==========I=============================================|
      DATATYPE  I                                             |
      ----------I---------------------------------------------|
      KEY       I                                             |
      ----------I---------------------------------------------|
      ORDER     I                                             |
      ----------I---------------------------------------------|
      END

(b).  xxxxxxx: CREATE xxxxxxx

                I---------------------------------------------|
                I                  (xxxxxxx)                  |
                I---------------------------------------------|
                I                                             |
                I          ( complete form heading here )     |
                I                                             |
      ==========I=============================================|
      DATATYPE  I   (for derived fields)                      |
      ----------I---------------------------------------------|
      SOURCE    I                                             |
      ----------I---------------------------------------------|
      MATCH     I                                             |
      ----------I---------------------------------------------|
      CONDITION I                                             |
      ----------I---------------------------------------------|
      ORDER     I                                             |
      ----------I---------------------------------------------|
      END
```

Figure 11-41. (a) Skeleton program for defining a form.
(b) Skeleton program for specifying a form process.
(Shu[4], © 1985 IEEE.)

Briefly, the properties of a form process include the SOURCE of data, the fields to be MATCHed when an output instance is constructed from two input sources, the criteria or CONDITION (if any) for selecting instances from the input(s), and (if desired) the ordering of instances within a form or within a group. The description of DATA_TYPE need only be stated for the derived (new) fields or when a change in data type is desired. Normally, data type of an output field is inherited from its corresponding source field.

Note that the "END" line signifies the end of a specification. In most cases, an application can be described completely by a form specification. In some cases, however, more than one specification may be required. For instance, the implemented version limits the number of input forms to *two* for each form process. Thus, if the creation of a desired output requires data from three input forms, two specifications (representing two steps) would be necessary. One or more form specifications grouped as a unit is called a *FORMAL program.*

The following describes SOURCE, MATCH, and CONDITION in more detail.

SOURCE specifies how or where to obtain the relevant value for the operation. There are many ways to specify the sources:

1. An asterisk (i.e., "*") under one or more fields means that the value of these fields is supplied on-line at execution time.
2. A form name under one or more components specifies that the value of these components should be obtained from the corresponding components of the source form.
3. An expression involving arithmetic or string operations specifies the computation or derivation of a new value.
4. A varying assignment specifies case-by-case evaluation for a particular item.
5. Reference to a user program provides a mechanism to invoke a user function written in PL/I, COBOL, or IBM 370 assembly language. It is not expected that nonprogrammers will use this feature. Nevertheless, the "user hook" is there for those who have conventional programming skills.
6. Sequence numbers or null values.

As an example, consider the form process depicted in Figure 11-39, where the given information organized by product is transformed into an output form organized by vendor. A program (written in FORMAL) for this application is shown in Figure 11-42. Note that in this example the user has simply presented the form heading of the desired output, VENDPROD, and specified PRODUCT form as its SOURCE. From the differences in the output and

```
VENDPROD:  CREATE VENDPROD

         I--------------------------------------------------------|
         I                       ( VENDPROD )                     |
         I---------------|----------------------------------------|
         I               |                  (PROD)                |
         I     VNAME     |------------|------------|--------------|
         I               |  PROD_NO   |    TYPE    |    PNAME     |
=========I===============|============|============|==============|
 SOURCE  I   PRODUCT                                              |
---------I--------------------------------------------------------|
END
```

Figure 11-42. FORMAL program for the process shown in Figure 11-39. (Shu[4], © 1985 IEEE.)

```
PROD: CREATE PROD

        I--------------------------------------------------------|
        I                       ( PROD )                         |
        I--------------------------------------------------------|
        I          |        |      |            |    (SUPPLIER)  |
        I PROD_NO  | PNAME  | TYPE |   PRICE    |----------------|
        I          |        |      |            |     VENDOR     |
========I==========|========|======|============|================|
SOURCE  I       PRODUCT            |    <1>     | PRODUCT.VNAME  |
--------I--------------------------------------------------------|
ORDER   I   DES    |                            |      ASC       |
--------I--------------------------------------------------------|
<1>     I PRODUCT.PRICE TIMES 1.05 WHERE PRODUCT.PRICE LT 1.00   |
        I PRODUCT.PRICE TIMES 1.06 OTHERWISE                     |
--------I--------------------------------------------------------|
END
```

Figure 11-43. FORMAL program showing ORDER and case-by-case assignment. (Shu[4], © 1985 IEEE.)

input form headings, the FORMAL compiler is able to generate code to actually perform the implied data restructuring.

The example in Figure 11-43 illustrates some variations in SOURCE specifications. The values of PROD_NO, PNAME, and TYPE are extracted directly from the corresponding components in the PRODUCT form. VENDOR is obtained from VNAME of the PRODUCT form. PRICE, on the other hand, is computed according to a case-by-case varying assignment shown in note <1> of the FORMAL program.

CONDITION is a means for stating the criteria for selecting instances from input(s) for processing. In most cases, conditions can be specified under column headings, and Boolean operations are implied. As a rule, conditions specified in two or more rows under the same field (column) are "ORed." Conditions specified for different fields are then "ANDed." For

```
VPROD:    CREATE VPROD

          I---------------------------------------------------|
          I                     ( VPROD )                     |
          I---------------|-----------------------------------|
          I               |              (PROD)               |
          I     VNAME     |------------|----------|-----------|
          I               |  PROD_NO   |   TYPE   |   PNAME   |
==========I===============|============|==========|===========|
 SOURCE   I            PRODUCT                                |
----------I---------------------------------------------------|
CONDITION I  NE 'ABC'     |            | 'STEEL'  |           |
          I               |            | 'COPPER' |           |
----------I---------------------------------------------------|
END
```

Figure 11-44. FORMAL program showing CONDITIONs stated under column (field) headings. (Shu[4], © 1985 IEEE.)

```
VPROD1:    CREATE VPROD1

          I---------------------------------------------------|
          I                     ( VPROD1)                     |
          I---------------|-----------------------------------|
          I               |              (PROD)               |
          I     VNAME     |------------|----------|-----------|
          I               |  PROD_NO   |   TYPE   |   PNAME   |
==========I===============|============|==========|===========|
SOURCE    I            PRODUCT                                |
----------I---------------------------------------------------|
CONDITION I  PRODUCT.PRICE GE 1.00                            |
----------I---------------------------------------------------|
END
```

Figure 11-45. FORMAL program showing CONDITION stated "globally". (Shu[4], © 1985 IEEE.)

example, Figure 11-44 produces a form (VPROD) having the same structure as that of VENDPROD (in Figure 11-42). However, only those instances having VNAME not equal to 'ABC' and (TYPE equal to 'STEEL' or 'COPPER') will be selected from PRODUCT form, restructured according to the form heading of VPROD, and placed in the output.

There are occasions when one would like to base the selection on a field which does not appear in the output. In that case, a global condition (i.e., a condition not bounded by field separators) can be stated. Figure 11-45 shows an example.

When a global condition is specified, Boolean operations (if any) must be stated explicitly. If a user is uncomfortable with explicit Boolean expressions, he can always write a two-step program. In the first step, selections are performed to produce a temporary form which has the same structure as the source form (this enables the specification of CONDITIONs under column headings). In the second step, the temporary form is specified as source for the desired output.

The *MATCH* specification is used to tie two input forms in a meaningful way. Note that the matching is not restricted to one field from each input. But the match fields must be paired. Nor is it necessary for the match fields to appear at the top level of input form(s). Figure 11-46 is an example to create a RESDIR form from DEP and DIRECTRY forms matched on the DEP. ENO and DIRECTRY.ENO pair, where DEP.ENO is not at the top level. The form headings of the source forms are included in the example program as comments. (A comment in a FORMAL program begins with " / *" and ends with "* / ".)

It is worthwhile to note that normally an instance of output will be produced only when a *match* of input instances (e.g., DEP.ENO equals DIRECTRY.ENO) is found. However, if the user chooses to treat the *no match* situation as an error, he may do so by using an optional ELSE clause which assigns unmatched instances of a specified form to a designated error file. This option may be applied to one or both inputs. For the example in Figure 11-47, unmatched instances of PROJECT are deposited in ERPROJ, whereas unmatched instances of PERSON are deposited in ERPERSON.

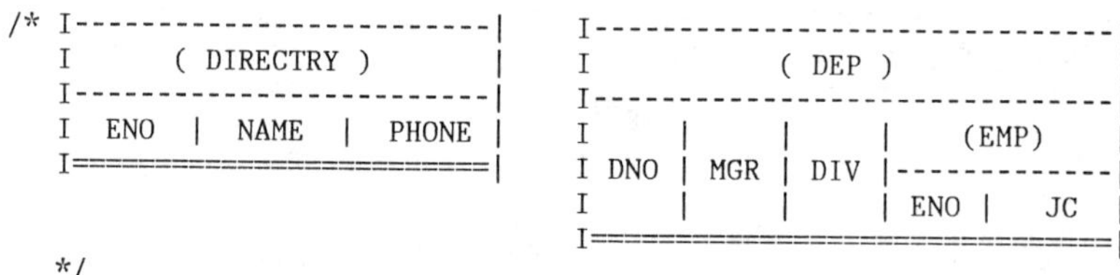

```
/* I-------------------------|     I--------------------------------|
   I       ( DIRECTRY )      |     I             ( DEP )            |
   I-------------------------|     I--------------------------------|
   I  ENO  |  NAME  |  PHONE |     I     |     |     |    (EMP)     |
   I=========================|     I DNO | MGR | DIV |--------------|
                                   I     |     |     | ENO |   JC   |
                                   I================================|
   */
```

```
RESDIR: CREATE RESDIR

          I---------------------------------------------------------|
          I                      (RESDIR )                          |
          I---------------------------------------------------------|
          I               |                 (EMP)                   |
          I               |-----------------------------------------|
          I     DNO       |    NAME      |    ENO     |    PHONE    |
==========I===============|==============|============|=============|
ORDER     I     ASC       |    ASC       |            |             |
----------I---------------|--------------|------------|-------------|
SOURCE    I     DEP       |          DIRECTRY                       |
----------I---------------------------------------------------------|
MATCH     I     DEP.ENO,         DIRECTRY.ENO                       |
----------I---------------------------------------------------------|
END
```

Figure 11-46. Example of producing an output from two inputs. (Shu[4], © 1985 IEEE.)

Another option is to create output instances based on the *prevailing* form(s). An instance of output will be produced for each instance in the prevailing form. In cases of no match, "NULL" values will be assigned to the missing values in the output instance. This option is called the "PREVAIL" option, and is used in Figure 11-48.

Figure 11-48 offers a comprehensive example, illustrating many of the features discussed above. Using data available in PERSON form (Figure 11-38) and PROJECT form (Figure 11-40b), a DEPTMENT form is created. The program looks deceptively simple. But the transformation of the source data into the target data involves very extensive data restructuring operations. This should be evident when the resulting DEPTMENT form (shown in Figure 11-49) is compared with its sources (PERSON and PROJECT forms).

Communicate with the System by "FILLING IN FORMS"

Filling in forms is used as a means of communication between the user and the system. When a user types "FORMAL," a *Reguest Form* (shown in Figure 11-50) shows up on the screen. At this time, the user may fill in a form/program name next to the chosen activity, and the system will honor his request. In case the user is not sure of the form/program name, he may enter an "*" instead, and the system will bring out a list of the names of the forms/programs available for the chosen activity.

Briefly, the Request Form shows a list of things that a person may choose to do. Entering a form name next to *"Describe a form"* causes a skeleton program for defining a form (Figure 11-41a) to appear on the screen. Similarly,

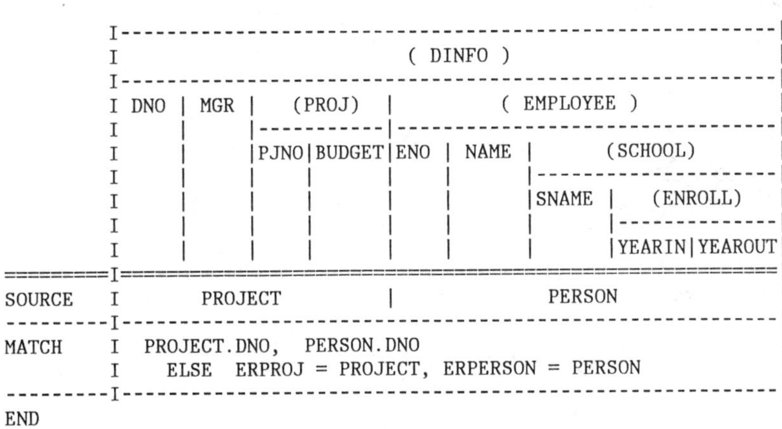

```
DINFO:   CREATE DINFO

         I--------------------------------------------------------------|
         I                            ( DINFO )                          |
         I--------------------------------------------------------------|
         I DNO | MGR |    (PROJ)    |            ( EMPLOYEE )            |
         I     |     |--------------|------------------------------------|
         I     |     |PJNO|BUDGET|ENO | NAME |          (SCHOOL)          |
         I     |     |    |      |    |      |----------------------------|
         I     |     |    |      |    |      |SNAME |     (ENROLL)        |
         I     |     |    |      |    |      |      |---------------------|
         I     |     |    |      |    |      |      |YEARIN|YEAROUT       |
=========I======================================================|
SOURCE   I         PROJECT             |          PERSON                  |
---------I--------------------------------------------------------------|
MATCH    I  PROJECT.DNO,   PERSON.DNO                                    |
         I    ELSE  ERPROJ = PROJECT,  ERPERSON = PERSON                 |
---------I--------------------------------------------------------------|
END
```

Figure 11-47. Example of creating a form from two source forms with option to deposit un-matched instances in error file.
(Shu[4], © 1985 IEEE.)

```
/****     I-----------------------------------------|
          I               (PROJECT)                 |
          I-----------------------------------------|
          I      |     |           (PROJ)           |
          I DNO  | MGR |----------------------------|
          I      |     | PJNO |   (EQUIP)     | COST |
          I      |     |      |---------------|      |
          I      |     |      | NAME  | USAGE |      |
          I======|=====|======|=======|=======|======|

I-------------------------------------------------------------------------|
I                                (PERSON)                                 |
I-------------------------------------------------------------------------|
I     |     |     |     |    | (KIDS)    |      (SCHOOL)         |    |   |
I ENO | DNO | NAME|PHONE| JC |-----------|-----------------------| SEX| LOC|
I     |     |     |     |    |KNAME |AGE|SNAME|  (ENROLL)        |    |    |
I     |     |     |     |    |      |   |     |-----------------|    |    |
I     |     |     |     |    |      |   |     |YEARIN|YEAROUT   |    |    |
I=====|=====|=====|=====|====|======|===|=====|======|==========|====|====|
****/


DEPTMENT: CREATE DEPTMENT

          I-------------------------------------------------------------|
          I                     ( DEPTMENT )                            |
          I-------------------------------------------------------------|
          I DNO|             (RESOURCE )                |    (PROJ)     |
          I    |----------------------------------------|---------------|
          I    |  JC  |          (EMPLOYEE)             | PJNO | BUDGET|
          I    |      |---------------------------------|      |       |
          I    |      |    |     |     | (SCHOOL)       |      |       |
          I    |      |NAME|PHONE| LOC |----------------|      |       |
          I    |      |    |     |     |SNAME|(ENROLL)  |      |       |
          I    |      |    |     |     |     |----------|      |       |
          I    |      |    |     |     |     | YEAROUT  |      |       |
==========I=============================================================|
SOURCE    I          PERSON                             |PROJECT| < 1 > |
----------I-------------------------------------------------------------|
<1>       I PROJECT.PROJ.COST TIMES 1.5                                 |
----------I-------------------------------------------------------------|
DATATYPE  I                                                     | NUM(9)|
----------I-------------------------------------------------------------|
MATCH     I   PERSON.DNO,   PROJECT.DNO                                 |
          I   ELSE PERSON, PROJECT PREVAIL                              |
----------I-------------------------------------------------------------|
CONDITION I     |GE '05'|          | 'LA'|                              |
          I     |       |          | 'SJ'|                              |
----------I-------------------------------------------------------------|
ORDER     I ASC|  DES   | ASC|                                          |
----------I-------------------------------------------------------------|
END
```

Figure 11-48. A comprehensive example.
(Shu[4], © 1985 IEEE.)

```
I--------------------------------------------------------------|
I                          (DEPTMENT)                          |
I--------------------------------------------------------------|
IDNO|                  (RESOURCE)                  |   (PROJ)  |
I   |----------------------------------------------|-----------|
I   |JC|              (EMPLOYEE)                   |PJNO| BUDGET|
I   |  |-------------------------------------------|    |       |
I   |  |  NAME   |PHONE|LOC|     (SCHOOL)          |    |       |
I   |  |         |     |   |-----------------------|    |       |
I   |  |         |     |   |  SNAME   |(ENROLL)    |    |       |
I   |  |         |     |   |          |--------    |    |       |
I   |  |         |     |   |          |YEAROUT     |    |       |
I==============================================================|
ID1 |07|HOPE     |3150 |SJ |SJS       |77          |P11 |  15000|
I   |------------------------------------------------|P12 |   7500|
I   |05|ENGEL    |2568 |LA |UCLA      |74          |    |       |
I   |  |LEWIS    |6673 |LA |STANFORD  |44          |    |       |
I--------------------------------------------------------------|
ID2 |18|MINOR    |2346 |SJ |UCD       |75          |P12 | 108750|
I   |------------------------------------------------|P22 |  81840|
I   |12|ANDO     |3321 |SJ |SJS       |            |    |       |
I   |  |         |     |   |BERKELEY  |77          |    |       |
I   |  |DWAN     |3535 |SJ |USC       |74          |    |       |
I   |  |GHOSH    |7649 |SJ |          |            |    |       |
I   |----------------------------------------------|    |       |
I   |10|CHU      |3348 |LA |HONGKONG  |66          |    |       |
I   |  |         |     |   |STANFORD  |69          |    |       |
I   |  |         |     |   |          |75          |    |       |
I--------------------------------------------------------------|
ID3 |08|PETER    |2046 |SJ |          |            |P31 |  18675|
I   |----------------------------------------------|    |       |
I   |07|BROOKS   |3392 |SJ |          |            |    |       |
I--------------------------------------------------------------|
ID4 |16|WADE     |1429 |SJ |          |            |    |       |
I   |----------------------------------------------|    |       |
I   |13|HUNTER   |6666 |SJ |USC       |68          |    |       |
I   |----------------------------------------------|    |       |
I   |10|KING     |6397 |SJ |UCD       |71          |    |       |
I   |  |         |     |   |          |75          |    |       |
I--------------------------------------------------------------|
ID5 |10|PARKS    |6967 |SJ |MIT       |66          |P51 |  18517|
I   |  |         |     |   |BERKELEY  |71          |    |       |
I   |----------------------------------------------|    |       |
I   |08|CHOY     |6059 |SJ |MIT       |75          |    |       |
I   |  |NEWCOMB  |7619 |SJ |          |            |    |       |
I--------------------------------------------------------------|
IDX |  |         |     |   |          |            |PXX |      0|
I--------------------------------------------------------------|
```

Figure 11-49. DEPTMENT form produced by program in Figure 11-48. (Shu[4], © 1985 IEEE.)

```
Welcome to FORMAL!

The following is a list of things that you may choose to do.

. Enter a form name or a program name next to your choice.
  (or enter a "*" to list those available for the chosen activity.)

. Issue a command directly at the bottom "====>" line
  for other activities.


|--------------------------------------------------------------|
|          Things to do                  |  Form/Program name  |
|========================================|=====================|
| Describe a form                        |                     |
|----------------------------------------|---------------------|
| Describe a form process                |                     |
|----------------------------------------|---------------------|
| Look at or modify a description        |                     |
|----------------------------------------|---------------------|
| Translate into computer program        |                     |
|----------------------------------------|---------------------|
| Run the computer program               |                     |
|----------------------------------------|---------------------|
| Enter data into a new form             |                     |
|----------------------------------------|---------------------|
| Display data of a form                 |                     |
|----------------------------------------|---------------------|
| Display data with summary              |                     |
|----------------------------------------|---------------------|
| Modify data in existing form           |                     |
|----------------------------------------|---------------------|
| Print the data                         |                     |
|--------------------------------------------------------------|



====>
```

Figure 11-50. Request Form as a means to communicate with system.

placing a name next to "*Describe a form process*" causes a skeleton program for a form process (Figure 11-41b) to appear. The user can then use the editing facility to complete the specification.

"*Translate into computer program*" causes the invocation of the FORMAL compiler. The result of translating a specification that defines a form is a set of encoded tables, representing information extracted from the FORMAL specification but in a format more suitable for machine manipulation. This set of encoded tables is entered in the catalog of form descriptions. When the defined form is needed later as a source for the creation of another form, relevant information about the defined form is extracted from the catalog. This catalogued information is also used when the user places the form name next to *"Enter data into a new form."* The system's response to this request is the presentation of a form heading on the screen in edit mode. The user may then proceed to enter data under the heading. When the entering of data is completed, the form data is transformed into "internal data" stored in the computer, ready for accessing.

Translation of a form process specification, on the other hand, causes not only an entry in the catalog of form descriptions for the target form, but also the generation of a tailored, executable program. The user may then enter the program name next to *"Run the computer program"* as a request to produce the desired output by executing the translated program.

Both the data entered via the data entry facility and the data produced by executing the translated programs are stored in a compact "internal" format. When the form name is entered next to *"Display data of a form."* the internal data are transformed into formatted data and presented under their form heading. Form data shown in previous examples (e.g., PERSON, PROJECT, DEPTMENT) are results of the requests to "Display data of a form."

"Modify data in existing form" causes the formatted data to be presented on the screen in the edit mode. Transformation from internal data is automatically performed if the formatted data do not exist or are "older" than their internal counterpart. The user may then use the editing facility to insert, update, or delete. The modified formatted data are automatically transformed and stored in the internal format.

Display Data with Summary

If, along with the data, summary information (SUM, AVG, etc.) is desired, the user may choose to *"Display data with summary."* When a form name, say DEPTMENT, is entered for this purpose, a skeleton summary program (prepared by the system for the requested form, in this case, DEPTMENT) appears on the screen.

At this time, the user may fill in "Y" (meaning Yes) for the desired summary information. No data restructuring (only presentation and aggregation) is involved in summarization. However, if a user is interested only in a subset of the data and/or wishes to have the data presented in certain order, he may specify CONDITION and/or ORDER. Example of a completed summary program is shown in Figure 11-51.

As soon as the user has filed the completed summary program, the system performs the requested selection, sorting, and summarization. If the form is not "flat," the aggregation will be performed for successive levels up the

```
          I-----------------------------------------------------|
          I                     (DEPTMENT)                      |
          I-----------------------------------------------------|
          I DNO|            (RESOURCE)             |   (PROJ)   |
          I    |-----------------------------------|------------|
          I    | JC|          (EMPLOYEE)           |PJNO| BUDGET |
          I    |   |-------------------------------|    |        |
          I    |   | NAME |PHONE|LOC|    (SCHOOL)  |    |        |
          I    |   |      |     |   |--------------|    |        |
          I    |   |      |     |   | SNAME |(ENROLL)|  |        |
          I    |   |      |     |   |       |--------|  |        |
          I    |   |      |     |   |       | YEAROUT|  |        |
==========I=============================================|
COUNT     I    |   |      |     |   |       |        |    |        |
----------I-----------------------------------------------------|
SUM       I    |   |      |     |   |       |        |    |   Y    |
----------I-----------------------------------------------------|
AVG       I    |   |      |     |   |       |        |    |   Y    |
----------I-----------------------------------------------------|
MAX       I    |   |      |     |   |       |        |    |   Y    |
----------I-----------------------------------------------------|
MIN       I    |   |      |     |   |       |        |    |   Y    |
----------I-----------------------------------------------------|
CONDITION I    |   |      |     |   |       |        |    |        |
----------I-----------------------------------------------------|
ORDER     I    |ASC|      |     |   |       |        |    |  ASC   |
----------I-----------------------------------------------------|
END

/* (NOTE) FILL IN Y FOR SUMMARY INFORMATION WHERE DESIRED
          SPECIFY ORDER/CONDITION WHERE APPROPRIATE.
          FILE IT WHEN ALL DONE.   */
```

Figure 11-51. A completed summary program.
(Shu[4], © 1985 IEEE.)

hierarchical path until the "grand" amounts are computed. The results are recorded in a summary form and presented to the user.

The internal data of the DEPTMENT form are not affected by the summarizing process. Thus, many forms of summary analysis may be requested in succession.

Figure 11-52 shows excerpts of the summary form resulting from the summary program for DEPTMENT (Figure 11-51). Note that the aggregate functions (SUM, AVG, MAX, and MIN) are computed for the PROJ.BUDGET within its parent (in this case, it is computed for each DEPTMENT instance), followed by the grand values for all instances in the DEPTMENT form.

As requested, within each DNO in the summary form, RESOURCE instances are in the ascending order of JC, and PROJ instances are in the ascending order of BUDGET. In contrast, the DEPTMENT form shown in Figure 11-49 (requested via "Display data of a form") reflects the ordering of in-

```
      I---------------------------------------------------------------|
      I                         (DEPTMENT)                            |
      I---------------------------------------------------------------|
      IDNO|              (RESOURCE)                 |     (PROJ)      |
      I   |-------------------------------------------|-----------------|
      I   |JC |             (EMPLOYEE)              |PJNO|   BUDGET   |
      I   |   |-------------------------------------|    |            |
      I   |   |  NAME    |PHONE|LOC|    (SCHOOL)     |    |            |
      I   |   |          |     |   |-----------------|    |            |
      I   |   |          |     |   |  SNAME   |(ENROLL)|    |            |
      I   |   |          |     |   |          |--------|    |            |
      I   |   |          |     |   |          |YEAROUT |    |            |
      I===============================================================|
      ID1 |05 |ENGEL     |2568 |LA |UCLA      |74      |P12 |       7500 |
      I   |   |LEWIS     |6673 |LA |STANFORD  |44      |P11 |      15000 |
      I   |   |          |     |   |          |        |    |            |
      I SUM:                                                 |      22500|
      I AVG:                                                 |   11250.00|
      I MAX:                                                 |      15000|
      I MIN:                                                 |       7500|
      I   |------------------------------------------|   |            |
      I   |07 |HOPE      |3150 |SJ |SJS       |77      |    |            |
      I---------------------------------------------------------------|
      ID2 |10 |CHU       |3348 |LA |HONGKONG  |66      |P22 |      81840 |
      I   |   |          |     |   |STANFORD  |69      |P12 |     108750 |
      I   |   |          |     |   |          |75      |    |            |
      I SUM:                                                 |     190590|
      I AVG:                                                 |   95295.00|
      I MAX:                                                 |     108750|
      I MIN:                                                 |      81840|
      I   |------------------------------------------|   |            |
      I   |12 |ANDO      |3321 |SJ |SJS       |        |    |            |
      I   |   |          |     |   |BERKELEY  |77      |    |            |
      I   |   |DWAN      |3535 |SJ |USC       |74      |    |            |
      I   |   |GHOSH     |7649 |SJ |          |        |    |            |
      I   |------------------------------------------|   |            |
      I   |18 |MINOR     |2346 |SJ |UCD       |75      |    |            |
      I---------------------------------------------------------------|
      I                            .                                  |
      I                            .                                  |
      I                            .                                  |
      I===============================================================|
SUM   I   |   |          |     |   |          |        |    |     250282|
      I   |   |          |     |   |          |        |    |           |
AVG   I   |   |          |     |   |          |        |    |   35754.57|
      I   |   |          |     |   |          |        |    |           |
MAX   I   |   |          |     |   |          |        |    |     108750|
      I   |   |          |     |   |          |        |    |           |
MIN   I   |   |          |     |   |          |        |    |       7500|
      I---------------------------------------------------------------|

DATE:   08/08/84                          TIME:   18:19:46
```

Figure 11-52. A summary form produced by the program in Figure 11-51. (Shu[4], © 1985 IEEE.)

stances in the internal data. Within each DNO, RESOURCE instances are in the descending order of JC, and PROJ instances are in the ascending order of P JNO.

Summary

In summary, FORMAL is a forms-oriented visual programming language, designed and implemented to provide *powerful capabilities* for the computerization of a *wide range* of *data processing* tasks. Data restructuring, often an integral but nontrivial part of an application, is implied in the differences in the output and input form headings. For instance, except for the process shown in Figure 11-43, all the example applications presented in this subsection involve extensive data restructuring, and all the required data restructuring is automatically performed by the compiler generated code.

Furthermore, using the visual representation of an output form as a starting point, a user can make use of powerful constructs, based on simple, familiar concepts (e.g., SOURCE, MATCH, CONDITION, and ORDER) to perform complex processing. The format and concepts of FORMAL are so simple that its power and scope of application may not be immediately obvious.

For example, the creation of DEPTMENT form from PERSON and PROJECT (Figure 11-48) involves:

1. "Projection," "restriction," and "outer-join" (to borrow the relational terminologies) of hierarchical data.
2. "Stretching" of hierarchical levels along one branch of a two-branch tree.
3. Derivation of new data.
4. Sorting of form instances within a form and sorting of group instances within parents.

All these operations are *accomplished automatically* by running the compiler-generated code. This is made attainable because the FORMAL compiler is able to (1) recognize the differences in the formalized visual representations of the input and output data structures and (2) apply its inferential capabilities to map out a strategy for comforming the input(s) to output, and use its imbeded knowledge on data restructuring to generate customized code for the situation at hand.[15] Readers who are interested in the underlying mechanism may refer to Shu[15] for detailed descriptions.

In addition, FORMAL allows the manipulation of instances by means of arithmatic and string functions, case-by-case assignments, etc.

In short, FORMAL has succeeded in automatic programming for a wide range of fairly complex data processing applications. Its success, to a certain extent, is made possible because of the visual expressions incorporated as an integral part of the language. The natural tendency of people to draw pictures of what they are attempting to accomplish in a data processing task is exploited in this approach.

The result is a new style of programming: *"what you sketch is what you get!"*

Let us now compare FORMAL with QBE and FORMANAGER in the three-dimensional framework (discussed in Chapter 8). Like QBE and FORMANAGER, FORMAL is in the middle of the scale for the extent of visual expressions. Like QBE and FORMANAGER, FORMAL is nonprocedural. Users do not tell the computer what steps to follow in order to achieve the results. The language has no prescriptive constructs.

However, because of FORMAL's ability to handle data structures much more complex than the relational tables underlying QBE and FORMANAGER, and because the functions available via FORMAL are not restricted to data entry, display, and update, FORMAL has a much larger problem domain. The scope of applicability of FORMAL is further broadened by its data restructuring and instance manipulation capabilities. The profile of FORMAL is compared with that of QBE in Figure 11-53.

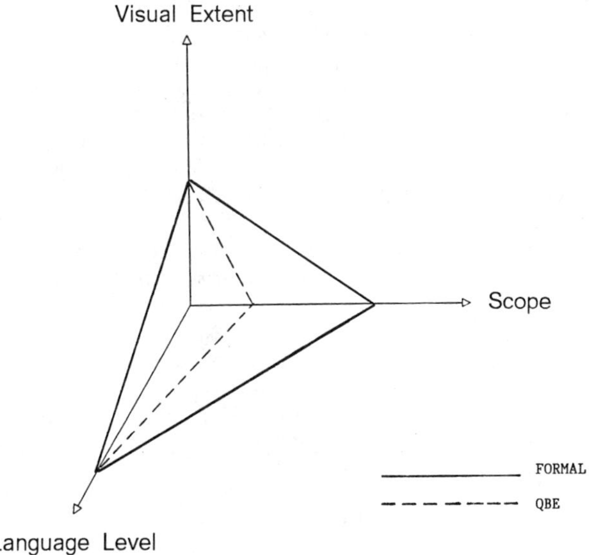

Figure 11-53. Profiles of QBE and FORMAL.

REFERENCES

1. Lefkovits, H. C., et al., "A Status Report on the Activities of the CODASYL End User Facilities Committee (EUFC), February 1979," *SIGMOD Record*, Vol. 10, Nos. 2 and 3 (Aug. 1979).
2. Zloof, M. M., "Query-by-Example," *Proceedings of the AFIPS National Computer Conference* (May 1975), pp. 431-437.
3. Yao, S. B., Hevner, A. R., Shi, Z., and Luo, D., "FORMANAGER: An Office Forms Management System," *ACM Transactions of Office Information Systems*, Vol. 2, No. 3 (July 1984), pp. 235-262.
4. Shu, N. C., "FORMAL: A Forms Oriented Visual Directed Application Development System," *IEEE Computer*, Vol. 18, No. 8 (Aug. 1985), pp. 38-49.
5. Rin, N. A., "An Interactive Applications Development System and Support Environment," in *Automated Tools for Information System Design*, edited by H. J. Schneider and A. I. Wasserman, North-Holland Publishing Company (1982), pp. 177-213.
6. Rowe, L. A., " 'Fill-in-the-Form' Programming," *Proceedings of VLDB '85*, (Aug. 1985), pp. 394-404.
7. Wartik, S. P., and Penedo, M. H., "FILLIN: A Reusable Tool for Form-Oriented Software," *IEEE Software*, Vol. 6, No. 3 (Mar. 1986), pp. 61-69.
8. Zloof, M. M., "Query-by-Example: Operations on Hierarchical Data Bases," *Proceedings of the AFIPS National Computer Conference* (Jun. 1976), pp. 845-853.
9. Tsichritzis, D., "Form Management," *Communications of the ACM*, Vol. 25, No. 7 (July 1982), pp. 453-478.
10. Zloof, M. M., "Query-by-Example: A Database Language," *IBM Systems Journal*, Vol. 16, No. 4 (1977), pp. 324-343.
11. Zloof, M. M., "QBE/OBE: A Language for Office and Business Automation," *IEEE Computer*, Vol. 14, No. 5 (May 1981), pp. 13-22.
12. Huang, K. T., Bolmarcich, A., Katz, S., and Li, R., "QBE/PC: The Design of an Integrated Software System for a Personal Computer," *Proceedings of the 1986 ACM SIGSMALL/PC Symposium on Small Systems*, (Dec. 1986), pp. 92-100.
13. Chang, N. S., and Fu, K. S., "Picture Query Languages for Pictorial Data-Base Systems," *IEEE Computer*, Vol. 14, No. 11 (Nov. 1981), pp. 23-33.
14. Chamberlin, D., Astrahan, M. M., Eswaran, K. P., Griffiths, P. P., Lorie, R. A., Mehl, J. W., Reisner, P., and Wade, B. W., "SEQUEL 2: A Unified Approach to Data Definition, Manipulation and Control," *IBM Journal of Research and Development*, Vol. 20, No. 6 (Nov. 1976), pp. 560-575.
15. Shu, N. C., "Automatic Data Transformation and Restructuring," *Proceedings of the IEEE Third International Conference on Data Engineering* (Feb. 1987), pp. 173-180.

Chapter 12

Future Prospects

Everything should be made as simple as possible. But to do that you have to master complexity.

Lammers,[1] quoting Lampson

When the renowned violinist Issac Stern was asked the difference between the great and the truly great, he replied, "The ability to communicate."

Today, one of the computer industry's most pressing concerns is the ability to communicate. After several decades of designing and modifying programming languages in an evolutionary fashion, visual programming has emerged to confront the human-computer communication problem with a revolutionary approach. Ironically, this revolutionary approach has been stimulated by the oldest form of written expression: pictures.

The programming process is a many-phased endeavor. Work on visual programming explores the use of pictures for all phases of the programming process: program design, construction, debugging, execution, understanding, and maintenance, as well as data entry, retrieval, structuring, and presentation.

The *diversity* of the activities shows one facet of the growth. Another facet is the *accelerating rate* of growth. This rapid and diversified growth is a double-edged sword. It offers new opportunities for effective human-computer communications, but it also introduces new challenges and adds more confusion to an already bewildering maze. We shall first say a few words about the nature of the confusion and then allude to some of the problems and challenges we are facing. The list of problems and challenges is not exhaustive, nor is it meant to be. Rather, the intention is to expose the *nature* of the problems and challenges.

THE NATURE OF THE CONFUSION

The most common source of confusion is perhaps due to the lack of common understanding. Looking at the pattern (Figure 12-1) introduced by the Danish psychologist Edgar Rubin in 1915, one person may see it as a picture of two men facing each other, while another may see it as a vase. Imagine the confusion that could arise when one person talks about noses

Figure 12-1. An ambiguous figure.

and chins while the other sees rim and base - a simplified but typical problem between people living in different intellectual worlds.

It is not surprising that confusion and misunderstanding often arise when people talk about visual programming. After all, the field is young, the terms have not been defined, and the examples of visual programming have come from varied backgrounds. The confusion, however, can be avoided when we establish sufficient common understanding.

THE BENEFITS OF CHARACTERIZATION

As a step toward establishing common understanding, we have examined the existing works on visual programming and classified them according to their prominent characteristics. The categorization is useful in several ways. First, it provides us with a method for untangling a multiplicity of ideas, inspirations, goals, and achievements. Second, it helps us to assimilate what we have, provides us with a guide through the labyrinth, and lays the foundation for us to proceed from breadth to depth. Third, it provides us with a framework which accommodates different points of view. Within this framework, it is easier to find a match between the tools and the goals or to evaluate the tools in terms of the goals.

A FRAMEWORK FOR ASSESSMENTS

The first two points are relatively obvious. The third point requires a little elaboration. However innovative visual programming may be, it is by no means a viable, let alone the best, solution for *all* programming problems. It has advantages in some areas and limitations in others. The framework established by the categorization enables us to look at the advantages and limitations in a more focused fashion.

For example, looking at the three categories of visualization, it is not hard to see that both visualization of data and visualization of program and execution can indeed serve useful purposes for programming in the small (see Chapters 2 and 3). The story is quite different for programming in the large. Visualization of large software design (the third category; see Chapter 4) has not received wide acclaim. The problem lies mainly in the inherent complexity of large systems. Fred Brooks, in his excellent article on "No Silver Bullet: Essence and Accidents of Software Engineering,"[2] has the following explanation:

> The reality of software is not inherently embedded in space. . . . As soon as we attempt to diagram software structure, we find it to constitute not one, but several, general directed graphs superimposed one upon another. The several graphs may represent the flow of control, the flow of data, patterns of dependency, time sequence, name-space relationships. These graphs are usually not even planar, much less hierarchical. . . . In spite of progress in restricting and simplifying the structures of software, they remain inherently unvisualizable, and thus do not permit the mind to use some of its most powerful conceptual tools. This lack not only impedes the process of design within one mind, it severely hinders communication among minds.

To understand this skepticism, one must bear in mind the context of the article, which started as follows:

> Of all the monsters that fill the nightmares of our folklore, none terrify more than werewolves, because they transform unexpectedly from the familiar into horrors. For these, one seeks bullets of silver that can magically lay them to rest.
>
> The familiar software project, at least as seen by the non-technical manager, has something of this character; it is usually innocent and straightforward, but is capable of becoming a monster of missed schedules, blown budgets, and flawed products. So we hear desperate cries for a silver bullet—something to make software costs drop as rapidly as computer hardware costs do.

Obviously, the proclamation that "software is inherently *unvisualizable*" is made from the standpoint of *building* what Brooks called "the intricately interlocked *software elephant*" (emphasis added), where the software is large and the problem derived from the "essential complexity" of software increases nonlinearly with size.

While we agree completely that a complex, interlocking software system cannot be beneficially described in a naive, unstratified manner, we must keep in mind that building large software with exponentially growing complexity is not the only essential objective of visual programming. As we have discussed in the preceding chapters, even though some efforts in visual programming do have large software design in mind, many others have different goals.

Similarly, looking at the three categories of visual programming languages, one can appreciate the strengths and weaknesses of different approaches more conspicuously in the framework established by the categorization.

The form-based language FORMAL (see Chapter 11), for example, capitalizes on people's familiarity with forms. It is designed for people who need to computerize their applications but have no desire to learn to program or no time to program in the conventional way. Automatic programming plays an important role in FORMAL. There are no pretty pictures in FORMAL, only simple, stylized form outlines. Consequently, FORMAL does not appear to be as exciting as the iconic systems. But FORMAL is practical, powerful, and concise. A user can use FORMAL to accomplish complicated real-world data processing applications on a minimal screen, without fanfare, without the need of understanding any programming concepts, and without the necessity of developing algorithms. The size of the applications also has very little effect on the complexity of the FORMAL programs. Underlying FORMAL is the dictum: Simple things should be simple; hard things should be made as simple as possible. The complexity of "hard things" is managed by the transparent automatic programming capabilities of the FORMAL system.

Iconic programming languages (see Chapter 10), on the other hand, appear to be more fun. They are good for teaching programming concepts because they provide an easier and more interesting way for novices to learn programming than conventional, text-based languages. But underneath the iconic cover are the concepts of the conventional text-based programming languages. To use the iconic languages other than play, one must understand the concepts of variables, operations, functions, loops, recursions, flow of control, data dependencies, run-time stacks, etc.

The value of introducing programming to children or novices (who would otherwise be turned off) should not be underestimated. But, beyond that, the range of applications of the iconic programming languages is generally limited. As Ellis put it, "I know of several elegant visual programming languages which are not viable beyond small toy applications because they become messy and unwieldy as the size of the application gets realistically large."[3] Ellis considered the high consumption of space on the screen as one problem encountered in these languages.

HIGH CONSUMPTION OF SCREEN SPACE

The problem of limited screen space, of course, is not unique to iconic programming systems. The development of window management is motivated by the need to have better control over the utilization of screen space. Navigation, zooming, and compression techniques provide further control over its effective use. In the case of iconic systems, the problem is more troublesome because the irregular shapes of graphical symbols and the ways to connect them consume more space than the linear notations. To deal with this problem, a number of partial solutions have been proposed. Among them are the "flexible links" in Tinkertoy[4] and the interlockable tiles in the BLOX methodology.[5]

For example, Figure 12-2 shows a screen containing some arbitrary LISP code from Tinkertoy (see Chapter 10). The two large windows show functions that consist mainly of one long PROG statement executing a sequence of functions. Figure 12-3 shows a hypothetical icon with flexible links. This type of icon might make the representation more compact by eliminating the need to fan out interconnections from functions with many inputs.[4]

The BLOX methodology is currently being developed by Glinert at the Rensselaer Polytechnic Institute. In the BLOX world, users compose programs by building structures consisting of one or more joined elements, using the usual jigsaw puzzle "lock and key" metaphor to plug protrusions into correspondingly shaped indentations so that the two juxtaposed tiles interlock. In spirit this resembles the "snapping" of Tinkertoy, but the pieces in the BLOX world appear to be more compact, and it is envisioned that the designer of a BLOX world can impose additional constraints on the joinability of the pieces. To illustrate this concept, Figure 12-4 shows possible Pascal-BLOX realizations of some conventional programming language constructs. Figure 12-5 shows a schematic fragment of a Pascal program. Figure 12-6 shows the corresponding representation in the Pascal-BLOX system.

Note that the purpose of using these examples is simply to show that the high consumption of screen space by graphical symbols is a recognized problem. Researchers are just beginning to address this problem.

SUITABLE VISUAL REPRESENTATIONS

Another key problem is to invent suitable visual representations. Although "a picture is worth a thousand words," there is no guarantee that people can interpret the meaning of a picture as intended by the designer (e.g., the warning symbols shown in Figure 12-7[6]).

This problem, again is not new. But the *new usage* of graphical representations in computer systems has spurred the surge of intensified studies. For example, Xerox has expended an enormous amount of effort on the design of the icon-oriented user interface of Star (see Chapter 10). "By the time of the initial Star release, the Functional Test Group had performed over 15 distinct human-factors tests, using over 200 experimental subjects and lasting over 400 hours. . . . The group averaged 6 people (1 manager, 3 scientists,

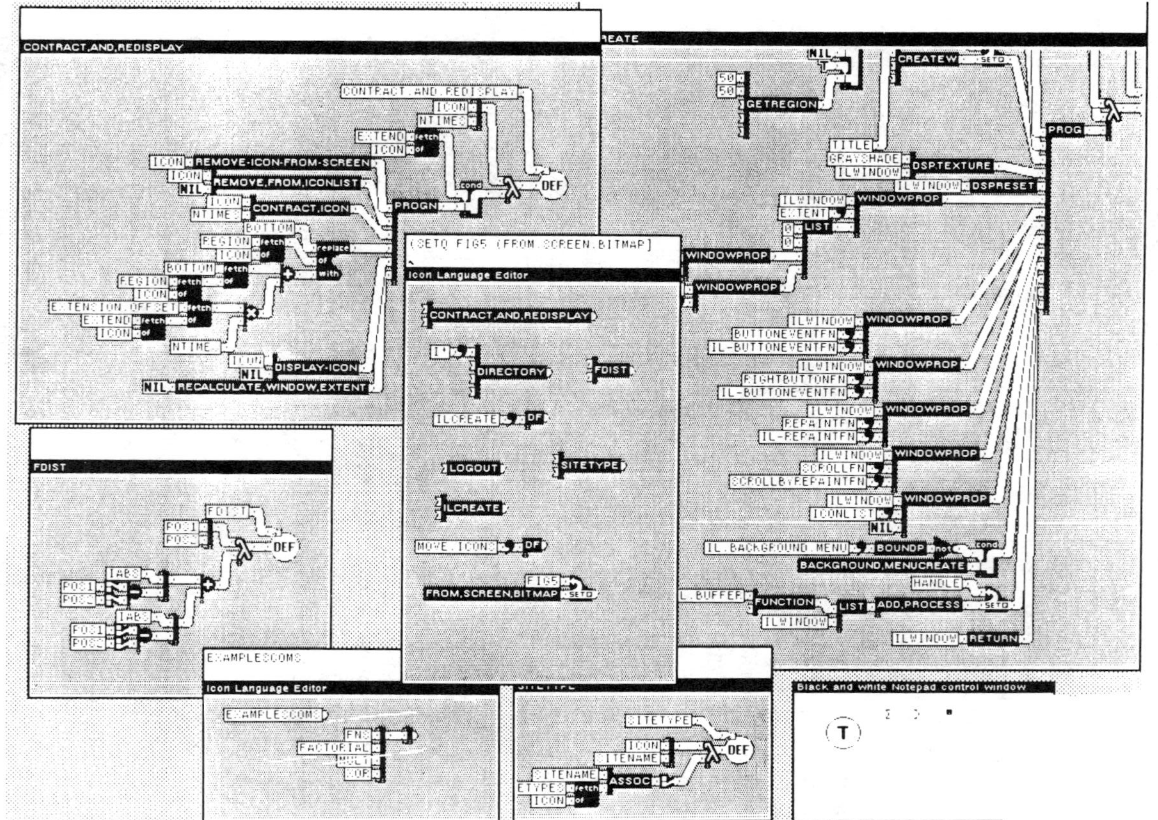

Figure 12-2. A full screen showing some code from Tinkertoy.
(Edel[4], reprinted by permission of M. Edel. Original art courtesy of M. Edel.)

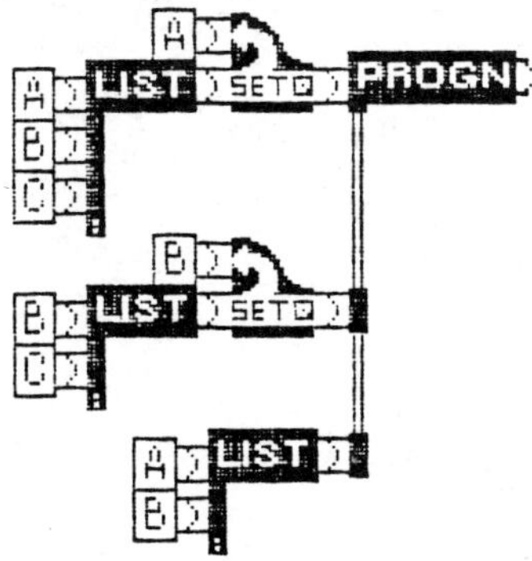

Figure 12-3. A hypothetical type of icon that extends with flexible links. (Edel[4], reprinted by permission of M. Edel. Original art courtesy of M. Edel.)

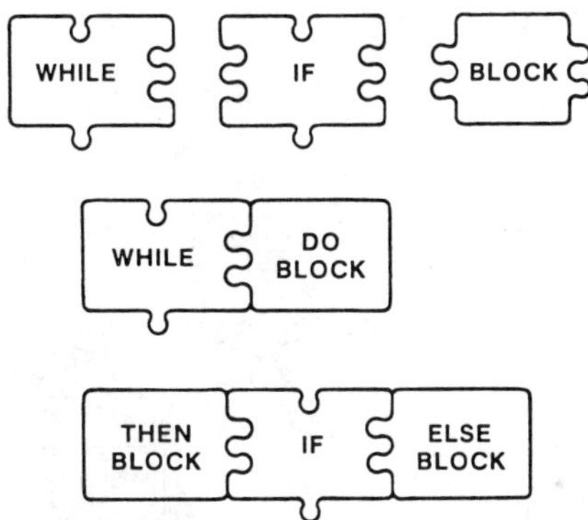

Figure 12-4. A possible Pascal-BLOX representation. (Glinert[5], © 1986 IEEE.)

and 2 assistants) for about 3 years to perform this work."[7] Included in this work was a series of tests used in helping to decide what the icons should look like. The results of this pioneering effort had a profound influence on the development of Apple Lisa, Macintosh, and many later systems.

Outside Xerox, interests in icon design and evaluation are also mounting. Aaron Marcus' "Corporate Identity for Iconic Interface Design: The Graphical Design Perspective,"[8] M.C. Maguire's "A Review of Human Factors Guidelines and techniques for the Design of Graphical Human-Computer interfaces,"[6] John Carroll and Sandra Mazur's "Lisa Learning,"[9] Kenneth Lodding's "Iconic Interfacing,"[10] Brad Myers' "The User Interface for Sappire,"[11] Gabriele Rohr's "Using Visual Concepts,"[12] Tanimoto and Glinert's "Designing Iconic Programming Systems: Representation and Learnability,"[13] and David Gittins'

```
begin
    S1;
    if not I1 then
        begin
            S2; S3;
        end;
    else
        while L1 do
            begin
                if I2 then S4 else S5;    S6;
            end;
    while L2  do  S7;
    S8;
end;
```

Figure 12-5. A schematic fragment of a Pascal program. (Glinert[5], © 1986 IEEE.)

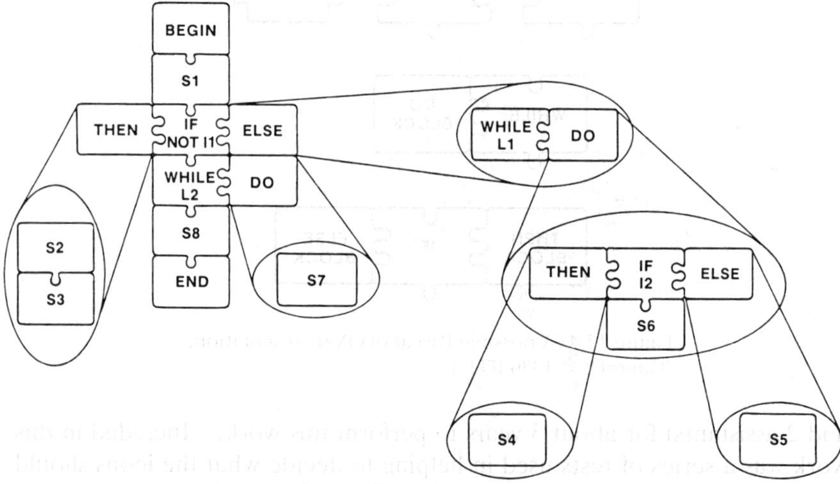

Figure 12-6. Pascal-BLOX representation of the program shown in Figure 12-5. The encircled subdiagrams are not visible at the highest display level. (Glinert[5], © 1986 IEEE.)

"Icon-Based Human-Computer Interaction"[14] represent only some of the important work in the quickly expanding field.

Their contributions are important, but most of the work in this area has focused on the use of icons or graphical representations as replacements for menus or commands. They suffer from the fixation on one particular aspect of human-computer interfacing—that is, interfacing at the command lan-

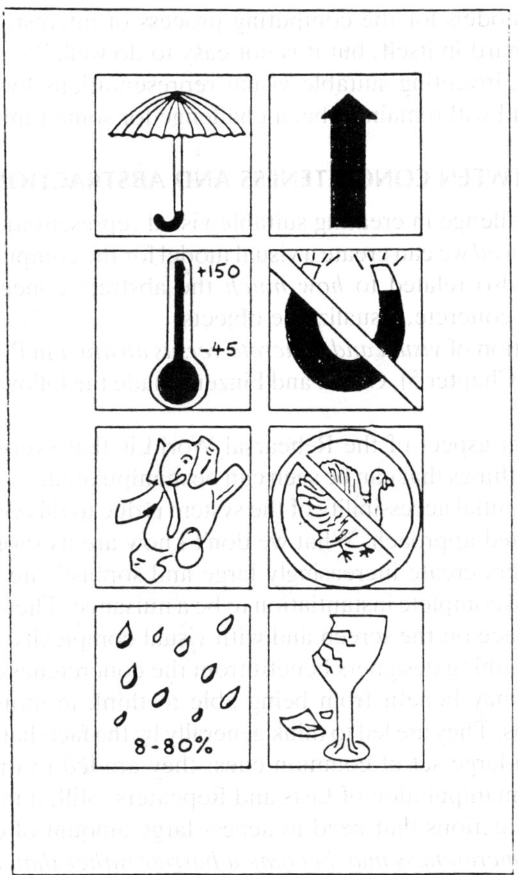

Figure 12-7. Warning symbols on packages.

guage level. At this level, icons could be designed to correspond to actual objects in the real world and carried over into the model of the system presented to the user, for instance, by using a picture of a file cabinet to represent a file stored in the system; using an eraser to represent the deletion of computer files, etc. However, in the broad scope of visual programming, one cannot always succeed in finding familiar objects to represent the more complex programming concepts.

S. K. Chang suggests that when designing visual languages, we first ask the question: How can we represent visual objects logically and logical objects visually? We then ask the question: How can we represent programming concepts visually and specify algorithms in a visual language?[15]

Tanimoto and Glinert said, "it is the job of visual language designers to create visual models for the computing process of interest. Creating such models is not hard in itself, but it is not easy to do well."[13]

In any case, inventing suitable visual representations for programming purposes is, and will remain to be, a challenge for some time to come.

BALANCE BETWEEN CONCRETENESS AND ABSTRACTION

In fact, the challenge in creating suitable visual representations is not only related to *how well* we can create a visual model for the computing process of interest. It is also related to *how much* the abstract concepts should be represented in concrete, visualizable objects.

On the question of *visual and concrete versus abstract* in Programming by Rehearsal (see Chapter 5), Gould and Finzer[16] made the following statement:

> An important aspect of the Rehearsal World is that everything is made visible; only things that can be seen can be manipulated. . . . We know that much of the initial accessibility of the system is due to this visual, concrete, object-oriented approach. What we don't know are its short-comings.
>
> As designers create increasingly large and sophisticated productions, they may find complete instantiation to be a nuisance. There are problems both with space on the screen and with visual complexity. . . .
>
> While beginning designers benefit from the concreteness, more experienced ones may benefit from being able to think in more general and abstract terms. They are led to think generally by the fact that all performers respond to a large set of common cues; they are led to think abstractly through the manipulation of Lists and Repeaters. Still, it may be difficult to build productions that need to access large amount of data. *At some point, the concreteness may become a barrier rather than an advantage.*

A delicate balance is desirable. Moreover, the desirable balance is dependent on many factors.

THE LADDERS OF LEARNING

Tanimoto and Glinert suggested that "A programming environment for novices should either incorporate or permit the incorporation of progressions of skill levels"[13] (see Figure 12-8). In the same spirit, a parallel suggestion might be: "A programming environment for novices should either incorporate or permit the incorporation of progressions of abstraction levels."

For some time now, educators have designed and applied curricula employing learning ladders. This author's first four years of schooling were under an experimental education system where the ladders of learning were incorporated for most of the subjects that we were required to learn. The same principle was adapted by many of the successful "self-studying" courses.

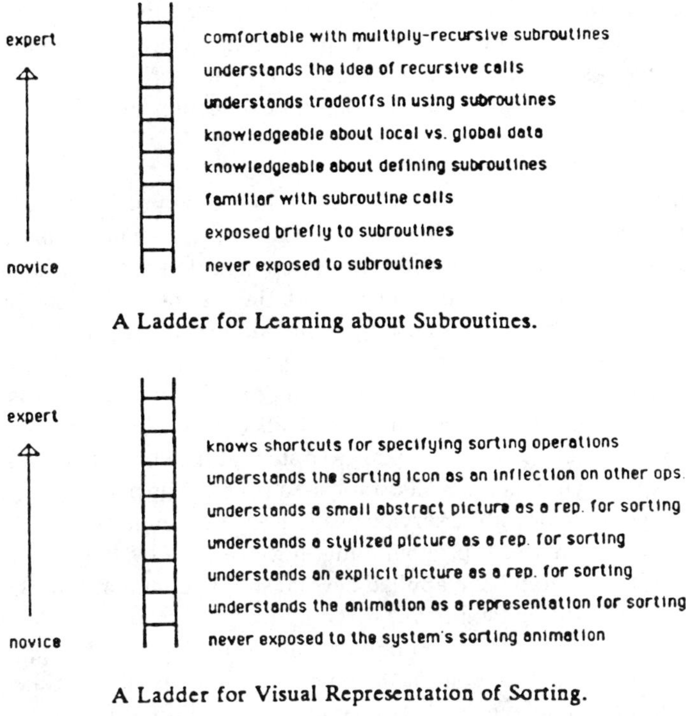

Figure 12-8. Ladders for learning.
(Tanimoto and Glinert[13], © 1986 IEEE.)

There are no *conceptual* difficulties in applying this principle to programming education. The difficulties (and thus the challenges) lie in the *actual design and implementation* of a system that supports smooth, consistent, and effective progressions in the large domain and complex environment of visual programming.

THE EFFECTIVENESS AND QUALITY OF VISUAL EXPRESSIONS

Related to the desired degree of visual abstraction is the effectiveness of visual expressions. People working in the visual programming field often express opinions with great enthusiasm—sometimes almost to the extent of religious belief. A few random quotations indicate this tendency:

> Software is a visual medium, we should resort to words as a last resort.[17]

> Interfaces which allow a user to interactively manipulate graphical objects and choose commands from menus are the wave of the future—they are easy to learn, fun to use, and effective.[18]

> The environment has to be graphical. People often think using pictures. Many of the conceptual views of programming are two-dimensional, graphical ones. The programmer must be able to work using the pictures that compose his conceptualizations and to assign meanings to these pictures.[19]

The problem is that *opinions* are too often inspired by gut feelings and too seldom backed by experimental evidence. Enthusiasm is a necessary driving force for inventions. However, while immersed in enthusiasm, one sometimes forgets that "however sophisticated and rich the graphics of a dialogue may be, it does not necessarily follow that this alone will assure that it is an effective interface to the underlying computer system."[14]

Effectiveness is a property of "quality," a complex concept that is at the same time vital, hard to define, and often difficult or almost impossible to measure. Nevertheless, it is interesting to note that the controlled evaluation of pictographic symbols is a well-established practice as part of the process of designing icons for public service use (e.g., Caron et al.[20]).

In the context of visual programming, however, the evaluation of visual expressions has seldom been applied beyond simple commands to the operating system or editing facilities. The complexity of problems to be sorted out, the heterogeneity of the user population, the diversity of the application area, the requirement to monitor over a considerable period of time, and a wide range of other factors all contribute to the difficulties of designing rigorous methods and collecting meaningful data, let along producing significant and generalizable results. But a technology can never be considered mature until it knows how to *evaluate* itself. Constant and repeated trying, evaluating, and improving are necessary parts of the maturing process.

OTHER YARDSTICKS

Aside from empirical evaluations, establishing metrics for visual programming is itself a difficult problem. Glinert[21] recently proposed a set of software metrics for assessing user friendliness which includes "characteristics of the underlying programming languages available in the environment, the variety, quality and degree of integration of the various software support tools, the choice of available I/O devices, the system's speed of performance, the type and quality of the information displayed for the user, the effectiveness of the on-line HELP system (if any), how annoying it feels to work in the environment because of its limitations and restrictions, and related matter."

Concentrating on visual programming languages, Shu[22] proposed an analytical approach to characterize programming languages in a profile expressed in terms of the level of the language, the scope of applicability, and the extent of visual expressions (see Chapter 8). This approach gives us a way to compare visual programming languages in a meaningful (although qualitative) manner. For example, by superimposing the profiles of Pict, PIGS, and FORMAL (as shown in Figure 8-8), the comparison of the three totally different languages begins to make sense.

But this is only a first step into a wide open arena. There are many challenging issues that are worthwhile exploring. For instance, can we use this approach to gauge the distance of a language from a desirable language? The answer depends, more or less, on whether we can postulate the properties of a *desired language.*

For example, we generally agree that it is desirable for a programming language to be in very high level and to have very wide scope. But we cannot agree (or have no idea), at this stage of development, on the most desirable extent of visual expressions. For example, the use of ill-conceived symbols or overly-detailed pictures may be more confusing than informative. Too many visual expressions may produce a "spaghetti" effect. It is conceivable that the program development time might be reduced when iconic representations are used for simple tasks, but there is no evidence of a similar payoff for complex tasks. Yet, intuitively, we would like to exploit the potentially powerful pictures as much as possible.

As more research is conducted and more experience is gained, we will be able to throw more light on visual programming in general and visual programming languages in particular. Hopefully, when our understanding is sharpened and deepened, the qualitative assessments can be supported by quantitative measures, and the three-dimensional framework can be meaningfully extended to a multidimensional one.

As an example, Figure 12-9 illustrates in parallel coordinates a multidimensional framework in which the fourth dimension, development time, depicts the relative length of time required to develop a program to solve a typical problem of a selected class. For example, because the FORMAL system (see Chapter 11) is able to take over, from the user, the "thinking and coding" process associated with writing algorithms for data restructuring and manipulation operations, very little effort is required from the user to solve data processing problems commonly occurring in the commercial world. Of course, there are many other possible dimensions. The key issues are what meaningful metrics to define and how to quantify them.

APPROACHES TO THE DEFINITION OF AN ICON

Another aspect of maturing is to progress steadily from intuitive to disciplined approaches. The first step toward a disciplined approach generally involves the definition of the things that we are discussing. In the world of visual programming, the definition of an icon is naturally a much discussed topic.

It is worth noting that an ISO international symbol development proce-

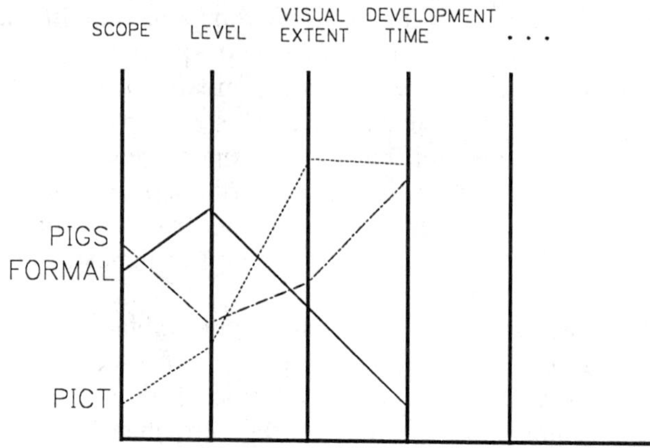

Figure 12-9. Comparison of Pict, PIGS, and FORMAL in a multidimensional framework.

dure has been designed for the development of public information symbols. The ISO approach is to create a written statement for any icon which describes (1) the graphical contents of the symbol, (2) the underlying function/object it represents, and (3) the fields to which it may be applied. In this context, techniques are available for analyzing the effectiveness of iconic signs for public service.

To illustrate that this technique can be applied to icon-based human-computer interaction, Gittins[14] defined a file deletion icon as follows:

Graphic contents	Office or domestic room waste paper receptacle.
Function/object	Deletion of computer file. Capable of reversal before regular action by system to permanently remove the file.
Application	Operating system or application program file deletion process. No security constraints. System files and programs cannot be selected.

Such an approach serves a dual purpose. Not only does it suggest an icon shape, it also allows a designer to incorporate constraints and requirements in the definition of an icon. In this example, the definition has made it clear that putting a file in the wastepaper receptacle is a reversible process, and system files and programs cannot be deleted (presumably by the unauthorized user).

S. K. Chang proposed the generalized icon concept.[15] Generalized icons are either object icons (representing objects) or process icons (representing computational processes). In either case, a generalized icon has a two-part representation, written as *(Xm, Xi)*, where *Xm* is the logical part (the meaning) and *Xi* is the physical part (the image).

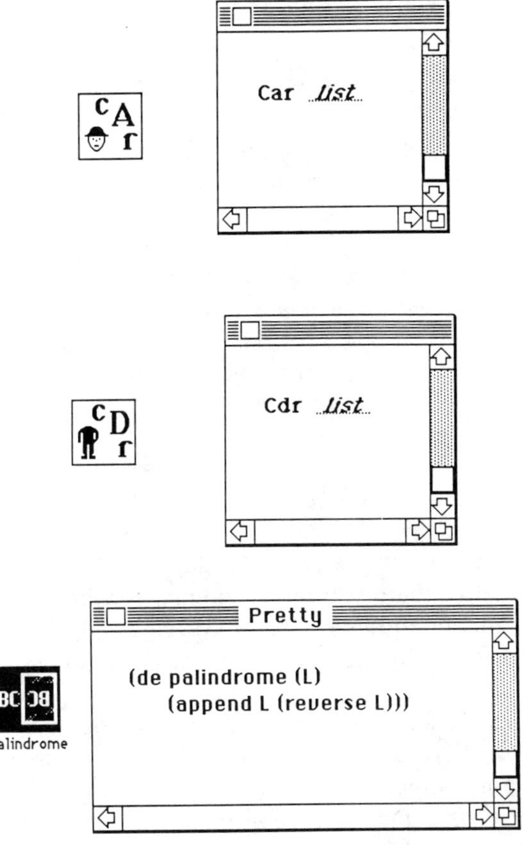

Figure 12-10. Examples of function icons in ICONLISP.
(Cattaneo et al.[3], © 1986 IEEE, original art courtesy of Genny Tortora.)

Roughly speaking, the physical and logical parts of the generalized icon representation correspond to the first two parts of the ISO symbol description, i.e., the graphical contents of the symbol and the underlying function or object it represents. But the process icon in the generalized icon concept has a much broader scope, since a computational process, by nature, has a much wider range of semantics than the public information symbols.

Similarly, Cattaneo et al., defined an icon as having a name, a physical component, and a logical component.[23] The name is an identifier which may be used for mnemonic and matching purposes. The physical component contains a graphical representation "which is a natural metaphor of the semantic value of the icon." The logical component contains the Lisp list (equivalent to the listing of a program). Figure 12-10 shows examples of primitive and user-defined Lisp functions represented in ICONLISP icons.

TOWARD A MULTIMEDIA APPROACH

Note that Figure 12-10 not only gives some flavor of icon definitions in ICONLISP but also reflects the emerging trend of having text and pictures playing complementary, rather than competing, roles. It takes very little imagination to conclude that this trend will become predominant as time goes on. For practical purposes, it does not matter whether we think of visuals as illustrating the text, or the other way around. What is important is how to utilize both, to their best respective advantages, for information understanding, communication, and processing.

It is also easy to imagine that sound (e.g., speech or music) will be used in conjunction with text and pictures. The audiovisual medium has long been established as a powerful (perhaps the most powerful) method for communication. With the advent of technology, programming in a multimedia environment is no longer out of reach.

Prototypes for multi-media human-computer interaction already exist. For example, "Put That There" is a pioneering voice-and-gesture interactive system implemented by the Architecture Machine Group at MIT.[24] It allows a user to build and modify a graphical database on a large-format video display. The goal of the research is a simple, conversational interface for sophisticated computer interaction. Natural language and gestures are used as input, while speech output allows the system to query the user on ambiguous input.

As another example, "The Intelligent Ear" is a digital dictaphone driven by an interactive graphical interface. This system experiments with the use of cross-media mapping, between audio and its visual representation, to facilitate human-machine interaction in sound editing tasks. The design emphasis is on the interface, via graphics, to audio communications. It is the beginning of an attempt to show that "a smart, and particularly a highly interactive, display has the potential to revolutionize control of otherwise non-graphical media."[25]

Programming, one might say, deals with human-computer communication at a deeper level than what we commonly think of human-computer interaction. Nevertheless, *serious programming* in a multi-media environment could become a reality in the not too distant future. Projects such as the MIT Media Laboratory's *Vivarium,* in which children simulate melodious living creatures with computers, and the VPL's *Mandala* (see Figure 1-6), both under development, are the beginning of things to come.

TOWARD FORMALISM

At present, most of the work in the field of visual programming emphasize the practical aspects of visual programming, for example, environment and tools.* But studies on the formal aspects are rapidly emerging. In the following, we discuss briefly Chang, Tortora, and Yu's "Icon purity—Toward a Formal Theory of Icons,"[26], Fred Lakin's "Visual Grammers for Visual Languages,"[27] and David Harel's "Statecharts: A Visual Formalism for Complex Systems."[28] These are three examples of the recent efforts to establish a formal foundation.

We have already mentioned S. K. Chang's proposal of a generalized icon with the dual representation of a logical part (the meaning) and a physical part (the image). Extending that concept, Chang[29] proposed a formal approach to specify icon semantics and introduced the notion of "pure icons." Only for pure icons can the logical part be completely recovered from the physical part, and vice versa.

Chang et al.[26] discussed purity-preserving conditions for iconic operators and presented a formal definition of degree of icon purity by extending an icon system to a fuzzy icon system, based on the theory of fuzzy sets. The concepts of icon purity and fuzzy icon systems can then be applied to analyze a formal specification and determine whether such icons can be used effectively in a human-machine interactive environment.

Computer understanding of informal visual communication (such as writing and drawing on a blackboard to help people think) is the broad theoretical context for Fred Lakin's work. To make the problem tractable, Lakin started with machine understanding of the visual phrases used by humans in formal, well-defined visual languages taking place in a general-purpose graphics editor.

Most of the current systems which allow creation and processing of visual objects provide some kind of special-purpose, syntax-driven graphics editor. They offer interpretive power at the expense of generality. "From a theoretical point of view, such editors never deal with the general issues of understanding diagrams: the meaning has been built into the structures and procedures of the predefined object categories."[27] In the research reported by Lakin, spatial parsing provides the flexibility to use different visual languages in the same editor, even in the same image space.

Lakin defines a visual language as "a set of spatial arrangements of text-graphic symbols with a semantic interpretation that is used in carrying out communicative actions in the world." Formal visual languages are ones which have been explicity designed to be syntactically and semantically unambiguous. For each of the formal visual languages, there is a specifiable set of spatial arrangements of elements as well-formed visual expressions in that language. Visual grammer notation is a way to describe the spatial

*Even the designers of visual programming languages often emphasize the "graphic editors" or "graphical environments" in their systems, rather than languages themselves.

criteria (or rules) which distinguish those sets of spatial arrangements and the associated underlying structures.

"Spatial parsing" is the process of recovering the underlying syntactic structure of a visual communication object from its spatial arrangement. The parser is guided by context-free grammars, expressed in the visual grammar notation, which are both visual and machine-readable. Once a visual grammar has been written for a formal visual language, parsing can be accomplished. Visual expressions can then be processed semantically, and appropriate actions can be taken. Visual grammars and semantic processing for four formal visual languages have been presented by Lakin.[27]

Orthogonal to Lakin's long-term goal of computer participation in conversational graphics is David Harel's interest in developing visual formalism for describing various kinds of complex entities, particularly those that involve many sets of objects having intricate structural interrelationships, as well as additional relations of a dynamic, causal, or other nature.

Harel[28] reported his work on managing complexity in the specification and design of large, complex reactive systems (such as multicomputer real-time systems, communication protocols, etc.) with statecharts.

A reactive system is characterized by being event driven, continuously having to react to external and internal stimuli. "The problem is rooted in the difficulty of describing reactive behavior in ways that are clear and realistic, and at the same time formal and rigorous, sufficiently so to be amenable to detailed computerized simulation."[28]

Traditional state transition diagrams describe the dynamic behavior in terms of directed graphs, with nodes denoting states and arrows (labeled with the triggering events and guarding conditions) denoting transitions. However, it is difficult to describe a complex system in this fashion because of the unmanageable, exponentially growing number of states. Harel's diagrams, which he calls *statecharts,* extend conventional state transition diagrams with essentially three elements, dealing, respectively, with the notions of hierarchy, concurrency, and communication.

In essence, statecharts constitute a *visual formalism* for describing states and transitions in a modular fashion, enabling clustering of states into superstates, orthogonality (i.e., concurrency) and refinement, and encouraging "zooming" capabilities for moving between levels of abstraction. Statecharts are thus compact and expressive. When coupled with the capabilities of computerized graphics, statecharts enable viewing of the description at different levels of detail "and make even very large specifications manageable and comprehensible." At the time of the writing, Harel reported that an implementation, called STATEMATE1, is in the final stages of construction. Evaluation of the statechart method in a number of diverse application areas is underway. "*Visual formalism* should be the name of the game," said Harel.

A NOTE OF HOPE

In summary, visual programming is an exciting young field. Historically, major new developments have come from the intersection of a multiplicity of ideas. We have revealed the diversity of visual programming. The next few years will witness a new type of quest: maturing with scientific/engineering discipline and, at the same time, striving to become a *pervasive technology.*

A pervasive technology can be characterized by being generally accessible and by offering a service perceived as usable and useful by most people. Visual programming is an approach to make programming pervasive. We have not achieved it yet, but progress has been made. Visual programming may become a fad, a toy, or a pervasive technology. Our success depends on how much we come to care about the results.

To end this book, I would like to quote a passage from *The Velveteen Rabbit or How Toys Become Real* by Margery Williams[30]:

> "What is REAL?" asked the Rabbit one day, when they were lying side by side near the nursery fender, before Nana came to tidy the room. "Does it mean having things that buzz inside you and a stick-out handle?"
>
> "Real isn't how you are made," said the Skin Horse. "It's a thing that happens to you. When a child loves you for a long, long time, not just to play with, but REALLY loves you, then you become Real."
>
> "Does it hurt?" asked the Rabbit.
>
> "Sometimes," said the Skin Horse, for he was always truthful. "When you are Real you don't mind being hurt."
>
> "Does it happen all at once, like being wound up," he asked, "or bit by bit?"
>
> "It doesn't happen all at once," said the Skin Horse. "You become. It takes a long time. That's why it doesn't often happen to people who break easily, or have sharp edges, or who have to be carefully kept. Generally, by the time you are Real, most of your hair has been loved off, and your eyes drop out and you get loose in the joints and very shabby. But these things don't matter at all, because once you are Real you can't be ugly, except to people who don't understand."
>
> "I suppose you are Real?" said the Rabbit. And then he wished he had not said it, for he thought the Skin Horse might be sensitive. But the Skin Horse only smiled.
>
> "The Boy's Uncle made me Real," he said. "That was a great many

years ago; but once you are Real you can't become unreal again. It lasts for always."

REFERENCES

1. Lammers, S. *Programmers at Work: 1st Series—Interviews*. Microsoft Press (1986).
2. Brooks, F. P., Jr., "No Silver Bullet: Essence and Accidents of Software Engineering," *IEEE Computer*, Vol. 20, No. 4 (Apr. 1987), pp. 10-19.
3. Ellis, C., "Review of the 1986 Workshop on Visual Languages," *VPLList Digest on CSNET* Vol. 1, Issue 10, (Sept 26, 1986).
4. Edel, M. W., "Tinkertoy: A Practical Iconic Programming Environment," Master's thesis, University of Illinois (June 1985).
5. Glinert, E. P., "Towards 'Second Generation' Interactive Graphical Programming Environments," *IEEE Workshop on Visual Languages* (Jun. 1986), pp. 61-70.
6. Maguire, M. C., "A Review of Human Factors Guidelines and Techniques for the Design of Graphical Human-Computer Interfaces," *Computers and Graphics*, Vol. 9, No. 3 (1985), pp. 221-235.
7. Bewley, W. L., Roberts, T. L., Schroit, D., and Verplank, W. L., "Human Factors Testing in the Design of Xerox's 8010 Star Office Workstation," *ACM Proceedings of CHI '83* (Dec. 1983), pp. 72-77.
8. Marcus, A., "Corporate Identity for Iconic Interface Design: The Graphical Design Perspective," *IEEE Computer Graphics and Applications* Vol. 4 (Apr. 1984), pp. 24-32.
9. Carroll, J. M., and Mazur, S. A., "Lisa Learning," *IEEE Computer*, Vol. 19, No. 11 (Nov. 1986), pp. 35-49.
10. Lodding, K. N., "Iconic Interfacing," *IEEE Computer Graphics and Applications*, Vol. 3 (Mar.-Apr. 1983), pp. 11-20.
11. Myers, B. A., "The User Interface for Sapphire," *IEEE Computer Graphics and Applications* Vol. 4 (Dec. 1984), pp. 13-23.
12. Rohr, G., "Using Visual Concepts," in *Visual Languages*, edited by S. K. Chang et al., Plenum Press (1986), pp. 325-348.
13. Tanimoto, S. L., and Glinert, E. P., "Designing Iconic Programming Systems: Representation and Learnability," *Proceedings of the IEEE Workshop on Visual Languages* (Jun. 1986), pp. 54-60.
14. Gittins, D., "Icon-Based Human-Computer Interaction," *International Journal of Man-Machine Studies*, Vol. 24. (1986), pp. 519-543.
15. Chang, S. K., "Visual Languages: A Tutorial and Survey," *IEEE Software*, Vol. 4, No. 1 (Jan. 1987), pp. 29-39.
16. Gould, L., and Finzer, W., "Programming by Rehearsal," Technical Report SCL-84-1 (May 1984), Xerox Corporation, Palo Alto Research Center.
17. Heckel, P., "Walt Disney and User-Oriented Software," Byte (Dec. 1983), pp. 143-150.
18. Lieberman, H., "There's More to Menu Systems Than Meets the Screen," *ACM SIGGRAPH '85*, Vol. 19, No. 3 (1985), pp. 181-189.
19. Reiss, S., "Visual Languages and the GARDEN System," Brown University Technical Report CS-86-16 (Sept. 1986).
20. Caron, J. P., et al., "Evaluating Pictograms Using Semantic Differential and Classification Techniques," *Ergonomics*, Vol. 23 (1980), pp. 137-146.
21. Glinert, E. P., "Towards Software Metrics for Visual Programming," Technical Report No. 87-16., Rensselaer Polytechnic Institute, Department of Computer Science.
22. Shu, N. C., "Visual Programming Languages: A Dimensional Analysis," Proceedings of IEEE International Symposium on New Directions in Computing (Aug. 1985), pp. 326-334.

23. Cattaneo, G., Guercio, A., Lavialdi, S., and Tortora, A., "ICONLISP: An Example of a Visual Programming Language," *Proceedings of the IEEE Workshop on Visual Languages* (June 1986), pp. 22-25.
24. Schmandt, C., and Hulteen, E. A., "The Intelligent Voice-Interactive Interface," *Proceedings of Conference on Human Factors in Computing Systems* (1982), pp. 363-366.
25. Schmandt, C., "The Intelligent Ear: A Graphical Interface to Digital Audio," *Proceedings of the IEEE International Conference on Cybernetics and Society,* " (1981), pp. 393-398.
26. Chang, S. K., Tortora, G., Yu, B., and Guercio, A., "Icon Purity—Toward a Formal Theory of Icons," *Proceedings of the 1987 Workshop on Visual Languages,* (Aug. 1987), pp. 3-16.
27. Lakin, F., "Visual Grammers for Visual Languages," *Proceedings of AAAI 87* (July 1987) pp. 683-688.
28. Harel, D., "Statecharts: A Visual Formalism for Complex Systems," *Science of Computer Programming,* Vol. 8 (1987).
29. Chang, S. K., "Icon Semantics—A Formal Approach to Icon System Design," *International Journal of Pattern Recognition and Artificial Intelligence,* Vol. 1, No. 1 (Apr. 1987), pp. 103-120.
30. Williams, M., *The Velveteen Rabbit or How Toys Become Real,* Running Press (1981).

Index